Advance Responses to
The CyberUnion Handbook:
*Transforming Labor Through Computer Technology**

"An interesting, insightful, and very important collection of essays providing the how-to that will bring labor unions into the information age. This unique work is *must reading* for unionists and for managers, academicians, and others who are concerned about how technological change will affect organized labor."
—*James T. Bennett, Editor,* Journal of Labor Research

"This book . . . is a road map for workers, providing resistance and organizing strategies for workers in the burgeoning yet largely unorganized new industries. The book documents creative methods of building and expanding workplace power."
—*Immanuel Ness, Brooklyn College, City University of New York*

"A practical, as well as visionary, survey of how unions can employ new technologies to accomplish their ongoing mission of social justice and worker empowerment. Contributors address not only the potential, but also the pitfalls of the introduction and uses of new communications and other digital technologies, and real world solutions to problems unions are likely to encounter when doing so. . . . Every local, central and state labor body, and national union should run right out (or log on) to obtain a copy."
—*Michael Eisenscher, Director of Organizational Development,*
University Council at the University of California,
American Federation of Teachers, AFL-CIO

"This handbook will be a valuable aid to others in the Labor Movement who want to seize the opportunities that the Internet offers."
—*James H. Rankin, International President, Glass, Molders, Pottery, Plastics,*
and Allied Workers International Union, AFL-CIO

"Those of us who attempt to redesign our unions, in the interest of our members, have a need for the expertise contained in this book. . . . This work can become the launching pad for the efforts of concerned members to regain control of their organizations."
—*Tom Crofton, Wisconsin Carpenters for a Democratic Union UBC LU 314*

"Upbeat, powerful, and practical. . . . This handbook provides helpful tips and tricks for labor on e-mail, computers, computing, the Web and the Internet."
—*Dan Cornfield, Editor,* Work and Occupations,
and Vanderbilt University

"*The CyberUnion Handbook* is rich with no-nonsense, concise, easy-to-process guidance for those union activists among us who are ready to 'ride the third wave' into the future."
—*Sharon R. Pinnock, Labor Futurist and*
Director of Membership and Organization,
American Federation of Government Employees, AFGE, AFL-CIO

---

*No necessary endorsement is implied by any of the organizations mentioned. They are cited for identification purposes only.

"Just as unionism is more than simply sending someone a union card, cyberunionism requires thought, effort, and heart to accommodate the tech world and the human world. [*The CyberUnion Handbook*] makes the journey less scary by providing a much-needed road map."

—Randy Perreira, Deputy Executive Director, and
Randy Kusaka, Public Information Officer,
Hawaii Government Employees Association, AFSCME Local 152, AFL-CIO

"The labor movement is positioned to play a critical role in assuring that the 'information superhighway' does not deepen the existing social inequality by creating a rich and a poor side of the highway. To play this role, we need to understand the power of the emerging new technology and determine how to make its power available to workers. This book opens the door to that understanding in a significant way."

—Gene Bruskin, Secretary Treasurer, Food and Allied Service Trades, AFL-CIO

"Shostak goes way beyond talking about the future of labor unions—to give specific tools and strategies for achieving labor's aims. This is a cyber-guidebook interwoven with compelling personal essays by people on the front lines. The book is useful [and] needed."

—Ross Koppel, University of Pennsylvania and The Social Research Corporation

"While the opportunities for labor organization are great, the political economy that has historically disenfranchised workers and opposed unions remains unchanged. . . . The challenge remains to move analysis and response to communication and Internet technology beyond The Who's adage of 'Meet the new boss, same as the old boss,' to a truly empowering use of technology for the poor, people of color, and the working class. *The CyberUnion Handbook* begins that process. The question is whether organized labor can move the process from here."

—Art Jipson, University of Dayton

"Provides the opportunity for the trade union activist to become empowered through the ability to network with brothers and sisters literally around the globe. . . . In short, here is an opportunity to take advantage of computer power for the advancement of working people."

—Alice Hoffman, Pennsylvania State University
and Past President of the Pennsylvania Labor History Society

"The question is how can we make the technology, which we will all come to use, as much like face-to-face contact as possible? . . . This book provides some practical answers that are specifically addressed to the needs of the labor community."

—Michael F. Miller, Information Systems Manager,
Hawaii Government Employees Association

THE
CYBERUNION
HANDBOOK

ISSUES IN WORK AND HUMAN RESOURCES

Daniel J.B. Mitchell, Series Editor

BEYOND UNIONS AND COLLECTIVE BARGAINING
Leo Troy

CYBERUNION
Empowering Labor Through Computer Technology
Arthur B. Shostak

WORKING IN THE TWENTY-FIRST CENTURY
Policies for Economic Growth Through Training,
Opportunity, and Education
David L. Levine

INCOME INEQUALITY IN AMERICA
An Analysis of Trends
Paul Ryscavage

HARD LABOR
Poor Women and Work in the Post-Welfare Era
Joel F. Handler and Lucie White

NONUNION EMPLOYEE REPRESENTATION
History, Contemporary Practice, and Policy
Bruce E. Kaufman and Daphne Gottlieb Taras, editors

LABOR REGULATION IN A GLOBAL ECONOMY
George Tsogas

FAMILY LEAVE POLICY
The Political Economy of Work and Family in America
Steven K. Wisensale

COLLECTIVE BARGAINING IN THE PUBLIC SECTOR
The Experience of Eight States
Joyce M. Najita and James L. Stern, editors

PAYING FOR PERFORMANCE
An International Comparison
Michelle Brown, editor

**THE FUTURE OF PRIVATE SECTOR UNIONISM IN
THE UNITED STATES**
James T. Bennett and Bruce E. Kaufman, editors

THE CYBERUNION HANDBOOK
Transforming Labor Through Computer Technology
Arthur B. Shostak, editor

THE
CYBERUNION HANDBOOK

TRANSFORMING LABOR
THROUGH COMPUTER TECHNOLOGY

Edited by
Arthur B. Shostak

Routledge
Taylor & Francis Group

LONDON AND NEW YORK

First published 2002 by M.E. Sharpe

Published 2015 by Routledge
2 Park Square, Milton Park, Abingdon, Oxon OX14 4RN
711 Third Avenue, New York, NY, 10017, USA

Routledge is an imprint of the Taylor & Francis Group, an informa business

The following permissions are acknowledged:

Chapter 4: "Cyber Drives: Organizing, Bargaining, and Mobilizing—Downloading 'E-Strategies' for 21st-century Union Action," Laureen Lazarovici. © 2001 by AFL-CIO. Reprinted with permission from the AFL-CIO leadership magazine, *America@work*, March 2001 (www.aflcio.org).

Chapter 9: "Nine Rules for Good Technology," Stephen Downes. Abridged from a much longer essay with the author's permission; reprinted here with permission from *The Technology Source*, July/August 2000 (http://horixon.unc.edu/ts).

Chapter 13: "Avoiding Shams, Scams, and Spam as You Journey the Information Super-highway," Bill Ringle. © 2001 by Bill Ringle. All rights reserved. Used with permission.

Chapter 14: "How-To's and Why Not's: A Quick Guide for Union E-Tool Use," Donna Jablonski. © 2001 by the AFL-CIO.

Chapter 18: "The Natural Life Cycle of Mailing Lists," Kat Nagel. Used with permission. Originally posted to the Early Music list, December 3, 1994 (see http://catalog.com/vivian/lifecycle.html).

Chapter 26: "Seven Guidelines from a Futures Course for Unionists," Arthur B. Shostak. An earlier and longer version of this essay appears in *Advancing Futures: Futures Studies in High Education*, edited by James A. Dator and published by Greenwood in 2001.

Chapter 39: "How the Internet Sustained a Strike," Paul Andrews. © 2001 by the *Seattle Union Record*. Reprinted with permission. From the final edition, January 10, 2001.

Chapter 41: "How a Former Union Organizer Accidentally Sparked a Nationwide Election Protest Movement, All via the Internet," Zack Exley. Reprinted with the journal's and writer's permission from *Mother Jones*, December 9, 2000.

Library of Congress Cataloging-in-Publication Data

The cyberunion handbook : transforming labor through computer technology / edited by Arthur B. Shostak.
p. cm. – (Issues in work and human resources)
Includes bibliographical references and index.
ISBN 0-7656-0802-2 (cloth: alk. paper) — ISBN 0-7656-0803-0 (pbk: alk. paper)
1. Labor unions—Computer networks. 2. Labor unions—Computer network resources.
I. Shostak, Arthur B. II. Series

HD6490.C616 C93 2002
331.88′0285—dc21   2001049501

ISBN 13: 9780765608031 (pbk)
ISBN 13: 9780765608024 (hbk)

Dedicated to the memory of two labor educator friends—Russ Allen and Hy Kornbluh—and other recently departed brothers and sisters who sought all their lives to help achieve the superior quality of trade unionism our country so urgently needs.

What does labor want?
We want more schoolhouses and less jails;
more books and less arsenals;
more learning and less vice;
more leisure and less greed;
more justice and less revenge;
in fact, more of the opportunities
to cultivate our better natures,
to make manhood more noble,
womanhood more beautiful,
and childhood more happy and bright.
    —*Samuel Gompers: 1850–1924;*
        AFL president (1886–1924)

Dedicated as well to the contributors to this handbook, union activists who have picked up the torch and demonstrated 24/7 their intention to use computer power to move labor closer to the goals that inspired Samuel Gompers, Russ Allen, Hy Kornbluh, and all the other unionists we miss and honor.

Contents

Note on URLs

Because Internet addresses are constantly changing, some of the URLs listed in this book may become out-of-date. An Internet search should help the reader find the correct URL. (Please see the "Internet Resource Guide," subhead "Searching the Net," pages 301–302, for a list of search engines.)

Series Editor's Foreword

Since the Issues in Work and Human Resources series was first conceived, a total of nine books have been published at this writing, not including the present volume. More books are in the pipeline. The series has now matured to the point where follow-up works to earlier editions are possible.

In his 1999 volume, *CyberUnion: Empowering Labor Through Computer Technology*, author Arthur B. Shostak provided a path to union organizing that simply had not been available a decade earlier. Of course, computers have been utilized by organizations of all types since the 1950s. But those early machines, and even the personal computers of the 1980s, were primarily administrative tools. They could keep records, massage numbers, and provide users with a better version of the typewriter. But they were not tools for communication.

With the advent of the Internet, however, a world of new possibilities opened. It took time to develop. As economists who have studied the computer revolution are fond of pointing out, technology standards become more and more valuable as more and more people use them. And more and more people now have access to personal computers at work, at home, or through public facilities such as libraries. So the value of using this new communications mechanism is self-enhancing. Many dot-com companies have vanished after a period of irrational exuberance in the stock market. But the underlying medium endures and expands.

Given its potential for outreach and communication, use of the Internet and other related technologies for union organizing and other union activities really is not an option. The word "option" implies something that might be rejected. But such use is a necessity. Just as no one would have seriously debated if the telephone was useful for communication and outreach during most of the twentieth century, the issue for the early twenty-first century is not "if" but "how." Undoubtedly, the art of how will evolve, but this book will provide readers with a good start.

As I noted in my foreword to Shostak's earlier book, unions face major challenges in organizing and negotiating. A new technological tool by itself cannot eliminate those challenges. But it can surely help in confronting them.

Daniel J.B. Mitchell

Preface

Why not go out on a limb?
Isn't that where the fruit is?
—Frank Scully, writer

Friends of mine who also happen to be union activists have asked me three reasonable questions since I explained my intention over a year ago to edit this publication: Why cast it as a handbook? Who am I to attempt the project? And for whom is it intended?

1. As for why I adopted a handbook format, with its focus on tips and tricks, I offer four explanations: Because readers like you asked for it. Because I need as much advice about computer uses as I can get. Because I have found that really knowledgeable types are usually willing to be very helpful. And because nothing else quite like it is available in print or on the Internet.

Ever since the publication in 1999 of my book *CyberUnion: Empowering Labor Through Computer Technology*, I have been asked for details that might enable readers to get "there" from "here." In the 1999 book ten contributors joined me in exploring "here," or how the American labor movement was then using computers, and "there," or how it might better do so. As ours was a sweeping work of analysis and advocacy, we left much of the "how to" details for a follow-up volume—this one, helped this time by forty-nine contributors (forty-five of whom are new to this volume).

I myself feel a need for this handbook because I am a late and hesitant computer user, rather than an early and enthusiastic one. I resisted for many (far too many!) years. I devalued uses made of computers by smarter and bolder colleagues. And, as a gray-haired teacher in his early sixties, I hid my growing envy of nineteen-year-olds in my classes who were "black belts" in computer use.

Having the good sense, however, to try in recent years to mend my errant ways, I am now an eager learner and a grateful reader of the handbook's instructive and reader-friendly essays. They offer tips for making better use of e-mail, list servers, Web sites, personal digital assistants (PDAs), and 101 other aides. Better still, they share insider tricks for maximizing impact, upgrading e-services, utilizing the full potential of various gadgets, and for generally working smarter rather than harder.

As if this wasn't enough, the essays also explore such controversial matters as relying on a company's computer system, censuring a chat room or list server, hiring hackers, the open source movement, cybermilitancy, boosting union democracy, and other key matters linked to computer power.

Thanks to my own background research, and especially to the wide-ranging knowledge of the handbook's contributors, I now have some idea of what certain cyberworld/labor world terms are about; for example, add-on scripts, automated buddies, CD-RW, circuit riders, cracker, cradle link, domain name, dueling videos, e-mail pager, "electronic community," "flash" messaging, Gadjet enthusiast, independent media center, Internet radio network, Linux, "meta-search" engine, modularity, online salt, open space movement, streamripper, technology committee, virtual union hall, Web tablets, and Web ring.

The handbook's essays come from as generous and cordial a group as any I have known over four decades of editing invited material. I was greatly encouraged early on by contributors eager to share hard-earned wisdom with union activists. As they believe in the "cause" of labor's steadily improving its use of computers, the essayists are selfless and tireless in their support.

While your needs, my need, and the eagerness of contributors are enough reason for this book, a fourth explanation is that there is nothing else like it available. I found a gap in our bookshelf that warranted filling, especially as tips and tricks for labor's uses of computer power may yet make a critical difference in the movement's very survival.

2. Now as for the second question—*Who am I to attempt the project?*—a few things come to mind, over and above my being fascinated by the subject and being utterly convinced labor has much at stake here—possibly everything.

Thanks to twenty-six ongoing years of teaching, and learning from union activists two weeks a year at the AFL-CIO George Meany Center for Labor Studies, I have learned a little bit about modern unionism. Thanks to forty ongoing years spent teaching college courses in industrial sociology, first at Wharton and, since 1967, at Drexel University, I know a little bit about the world of work.

And thanks to writing nineteen books since 1962 and over 140 articles, I have learned a bit about how change is resisted by social movements and by bureaucracies. About how it is championed. Assessed. And can be improved upon. Hurt by my own failures here as a consultant, though proud also of the successes along the way, I have gained several insights and lessons into how to do it better the next time around—material I share in my introductions to the handbook's forty-six chapters and fourteen parts.

Where the use of computers is concerned, I attended LaborTech conventions held in 1998 (San Francisco), 1999 (New York), 2000 (Madison, Wisconsin), and 2001 (San Francisco). These three-day events—self-sponsored by activists—highlight progress and problems in an invaluable (and unofficial) way. I have often interviewed key AFL-CIO and international union computer specialists (webmasters, etc.), and I have attended several large-scale workshops given for unionists eager to gain computer skills.

In 1999, after coining the term "CyberUnion," I wrote the first book focused on American variations on labor's use of computer power, and I urged attention to a type of computer-focused union that may soon be in the lead. In that same year I coproduced a thirty-minute VHS film, "Labor Computes: Union People, Computer Power," made up of pithy interviews with labor digerati types (copies available at a low cost on request). The only such educational film of its type, it is now being shown occasionally in this country and in other nations.

I was also invited by two business magazines, *FAST COMPANY* (Shostak 1999) and *Business 2.0* (Shostak 2000), to introduce their "new economy" readers to my ideas about CyberUnions. I wrote the first essay on the subject for *WorkingUSA* (Shostak 1999), and I authored the first such article to appear in the *Journal of Labor Research* (Shostak 2002) and another for *WorkingUSA* (Shostak 2001). Much of 2001 went into gathering material for this volume and for a Working for America Institute conference in April in San Jose, California.

Like most of you, I participate in various labor-oriented list serves and avidly "surf" both the literature and the Internet (with its estimated billion-plus pages) for relevant material. I maintain my own site (www.cyberunions.net) in an effort to centralize ideas about cyberunionism. And I regularly guide teams of students in close study of the Web sites operated by sixty-sixAFL-CIO union affiliates (along with hundreds of local union sites and several overseas sites).

3. Finally, there is the third question I have been regularly asked: *For whom is this handbook intended?* I have three audiences and sets of goals in mind. First, I have tried to provide a little something for everyone. Beginners should find many of the essays valuable in their clarity, pragmatic air, and friendliness. Those who are already comfortable online should find other essays helpful in raising their sights and pointing to more complex high-payoff advances. Even the digerati, those expert users who take excellence

for granted (their own and that of others), who live their lives as if accomplished quarterbacks, even they should find it possible to stretch some of the material to advantage.

Second, I have chosen essays specifically for readers eager to learn how unions and locals already utilizing computers well can move toward Cyber Union status. Treated explicitly in Parts V through IX, the subject is unique to this book, although it raises generic issues of keen importance to labor's effort to stay significant.

(Please note that I alone am responsible for this advocacy, and the other contributors should not be thought "guilty by association." They have no necessary allegiance at this time to my FIST prescription—its computer-based prowess at *forecasting, innovation, services,* and of honoring *traditions* for a CyberUnion, though I like to think they will all come around. With the exception of twelve of my former students among them, their essays were written entirely independent of my CyberUnion idea, and stand aside from it.)

Third, the handbook "speaks" to a type of union activist we can call "possibilists." Too worldly wise to be starry-eyed optimists, and too sage to be self-defeating pessimists, these men and women focus constructively on what might still be accomplished. They push beyond the merely difficult and boldly tackle what others prematurely think impossible.

This, then, is finally *their* handbook—done for and with "possibilists" in mind, union activists whose lives are a "worthy expression of a leaning into the light" (Lopez 1999, 413). Adroit in creatively balancing their "High Tech/High Touch" humanity with their use of "high tech" computers, these men and women just might soon tip the scales in labor's favor.

Summary

If successful, this handbook might help encourage more use by union activists of computer power. It might guide better use. It might raise consciousness about the exciting innovations already under way here and abroad. And it might raise sights about "gee whiz!" possibilities that beckon. This handbook might also spark curiosity about a model that first requires the best level of conventional achievement (Cyber Gain) before a union or local can go further (to CyberUnion stature).

One way or another, its contributors model for all of us a gutsy and inventive type of unionist on whom much of the fate of organized labor may rest. I am proud to count the thirty-five men and thirteen women as my friends, and I urge you to reach out to them for advice specific to your situation (e-mail addresses are in Notes on the Contributors).

All of the essayists join me in inviting your feedback. We are intent on updating this handbook often, especially the Web site URLs current in the spring of 2001, the better to keep it the useful tool we have intended. Please send me your constructive suggestions at shostaka@drexel.edu, and please visit my Web site—www.cyberunions.net—to keep up with developments.

References

Lopez, Barry. *Arctic Dreams: Imagination and Desire in a Northern Landscape.* London: Harvill Press, 1999.

Shostak, Arthur B. *CyberUnion: Empowering Labor Through Computer Technology.* Armonk, NY: M.E. Sharpe, 1999.

———. "Report on the Future: Futurist-CyberUnions." *FAST COMPANY*, May 1999, p. 70.

———. "CyberUnions: The Future of Labor." *WorkingUSA* 3, no. 4 (November–December 1999): 120–134.

———. "CyberUnions and Business." *Business 2.0*, September 2000, p. 32.

———. "Tomorrow's CyberUnions: A New Path to Renewal and Growth." *Working USA* 5, no. 2 (Fall 2001): 82–105.

———. "Today's Unions as Tomorrow's CyberUnions: Labor's Newest Hope." *Journal of Labor Research* xxiii, no. 3 (Spring 2002): 63–74.

Acknowledgments

Among the many union brothers and sisters who helped gather material for this volume I owe special thanks to Steve Early, Michael Eisenshauer, Stan Gordon (who got the cooperation of Nancy Shaver, Ken Phifer, and Keith Fleeman of the Montgomery County Public Libraries), Marv Hrubes, and Sally Mecklin of Ohio Civil Service Employees Association (OCSEA), American Federation of State, County, and Municipal Employees (AFSCME), who taped a key session at the LaborTech 2000 conference for me.

Several Drexel students helped out, including Mike Cloud, who referred me to a good e-commerce story; Nicole L. Whittaker, who prepared annotations of Web sites of value to unionists; Adam O'Donnell and Megan Donahue, who prepared a revealing analysis and assessment of fifty-five AFL-CIO Web sites; Patrick Ehret, Daisy Lau, and Sara Lundblad, all three of whom followed the O'Donnell and Donahue example by assessing sixty-one of the sixty-four AFL-CIO Web sites (as of June 2001); and Miguel Abrantes Antunes, who prepared a short thought-piece now nestled into the introduction to Part VI.

My brother, G. Peter Shostak, volunteered to do some Web site assessments. A daughter-in-law, Eileen Sullivan, secured some expert information about Web services. My stepson, Mathew Seng, created and now maintains the Web site I use to try to keep CyberUnionism moving forward as a subject and a movement (see www.cyberunions.net). These wonderful family members have my warm appreciation.

As always before during recent years, Drexel University librarian Ken Garson came through each and every time I posed a difficult reference question. Similarly, the cover design, as also in the case of the 1999 predecessor volume, *CyberUnion*, was ably done by another Drexel staffer, Peter Groesbeck.

My wife, Lynn Seng, went along with my crazy hours, obsessive work, and occasional fretting with her characteristic patience and humor: Without her love and support across the decades, and through the many books of mine we have "birthed" together, none of this writing would be possible or worth it.

Sharon Gehm, a Drexel staffer and friend, prepared the manuscript for the publisher with craft, sensitivity, and a "can do!" air that made it come together in a most welcome way: Every writer should be so lucky!

Without the cooperation of the thirty-five men and thirteen women who wrote for this volume, or allowed me to reprint their essays, there would be no handbook. Their cooperation and keen insights made this a labor of learning, fun, and empowerment for which I will always be grateful.

At the publishing house I had the continued support of a strong group of skilled professionals—Elizabeth T. Granda, Esther Clark, and Susan Rescigno—all of whom did a very fine job. Daphne Hougham, an external copyeditor, read and improved the manuscript in many valuable ways.

Naturally, all of these friends are hereby absolved of any blame for the handbook's various shortcomings, all of which I pledge to try and correct if you (gently) call them soon to my attention: Please e-mail me at shostaka @drexel.edu.

THE
CYBERUNION
HANDBOOK

Introduction

Imagination is more important than knowledge.
—Albert Einstein, physicist

Organized labor has at least three needs it recognizes for this sort of handbook: First, America is rushing into the information age, and labor has to keep up. Second, computerization brings with it its own set of organizational stressors, and labor needs remedies. Third, computerization tumbles over itself all the time, so chaotic are so-called advances, and labor needs to stay on top of this turmoil.

A fourth, and far more controversial "need," I believe, is that labor has to get beyond thinking that the best it can do is what I identify as the Cyber Gain model—a fairly sophisticated level of computer use. I urge consideration of another far more advanced option, one I call a CyberUnion, and in Parts V–IX, I explain why its features—computer-based futuristics, innovations, services, and traditions—appear indispensable strengths of a twenty-first–century cutting-edge labor organization.

Consider, then the case made cogently below for labor soon meeting these four needs, as this handbook's tips and tricks exist to help *you* help labor achieve that goal.

1. *Staying Up with America.* To judge from the breathless growth in the percent of the nation's computer users, America's labor movement would be wise to rapidly get online, create more and better Web sites, and employ the sort of tips and tricks highlighted in this handbook. Provided, that is, that the movement be guided by Einstein's contention above—it is far better to progress creatively than conventionally.

As for labor's motivation to act, it need only be noted that on an average day at the end of 2000, for example, some 58 million Americans logged on,

9 million over the number counted only six months earlier. Over 104 million American adults were then users of the Internet, or 56 percent of the adult population—a figure that grew to 60 percent by February 2001 (Stellin 2001). Not to be outdone, at the end of 2000 some 45 percent of youngsters under eighteen had online access (75 percent of those twelve to seventeen, and 34 percent of those under twelve) (Stellin 2001). The lead researcher gathering this data observed that "every day there are more people online, and they're doing more things" (Rainie, in Stellin 2001).

In 2000 the fastest growing segments of computer users were women, minorities, and people earning $30,000 to $50,000 (Stellin 2001). A research report in May 2001, found the biggest gain in home Web access in 2001 had been the 52 percent jump among blue-collar workers—"twice the rate that the home Web audience in the U.S. has grown . . . since March 2000." Close to 10 million "factory/laborer" types were online, as compared to 14 million "executive/management" types, a very impressive blue-collar showing (Nielson 2001).

Union households already outdistance all households in possession of at least one PC (some 60 percent in January 2000), and this gap is thought likely to persist, if not widen (Lazarovici 2001). Labor now understands the Internet is an instrument of social revolution, one that has "put power in different people's hands and connected people who have never been connected before" (Gadiesh, in Friedman 2001).

Little wonder, then, that certain academics now contend that "employee organizations will prosper in cyberspace." They believe the Internet is "the bridging technology between an increasingly heterogeneous workforce and individualistic workers, and the collective activity and solidarity that lie at the heart of trade unionism" (Freeman and Diamond, in Taylor 2001). With over 2,700 labor Web sites worldwide, and more being launched weekly, and with nearly all sixty-six American international unions online, hope grows that labor will begin to do exciting things with the new medium (Freeman and Diamond, in Taylor 2001).

Fascinating in this connection are remarks made by President Bill Clinton on January 8, 2001, in dedicating the AFL-CIO building after its multimillion high tech overhaul: "This building is a symbol of today's labor movement. It's on the same foundations you started, but you've modernized it for a new age. You've adapted to the new challenges and new opportunities. You're looking to the future. This building should be a metaphor for the future of the AFL and the future of America. You built a new building with new technology for new times on old foundations. You stayed with what was best about the past and embraced what was necessary and attractive about the future. So whenever you come in the front door of this building, think about that as a road map for your future" (Clinton 2001).

2. *Organizational Stressors.* Five sources of anxiety, however, must be addressed before labor can begin to realize the potential of its new AFL-CIO headquarters and that of the multimedia information age. The suggestions in this handbook can help, especially if employed with imagination and sensitivity.

Many in labor, for example, worry about a potential erosion in face-to-face contact, arguably labor's greatest asset in earning and holding onto members. Dues-payers like to feel recognized (and valued) by union officialdom, a feeling that impersonal e-mails may not convey. "Pressing the flesh" and "showing your face" are practices many in labor think indispensable, regardless of the time-and-energy saving alternatives championed by labor's digerati.

Many worry about loudmouths and troublemakers monopolizing dialogue in nonmoderated chat rooms and bulletin boards. They fear that "crazy talk" will drive others away and undermine the entire medium. They also worry that thin-skinned officers will be hurt by outrageous posted criticism, and they therefore insist on either strong censorship or a shutdown.

The generation gap that separates older leaders from young "hot shot" types is also a source of concern. The younger leaders are often impatient to get on with it, to rush the computerization process faster than the older (precomputer) leaders are comfortable with—a rift that exacerbates the natural divide between the generations and undermines solidarity.

Many in labor worry about loss of confidentiality. They fear that hackers and others possibly in the pay of government RICO (Racketeer Influenced and Corrupt Organizations) snoops, union busters, union-hating employers, or the "dangerous like," will break into union data banks and files.

A chill that has left its mark went through organized labor when a federal court in April of 2000 ordered seizure and search of the home computers of twenty-one flight attendants suspected of coordinating an illegal sick-out via e-mail. Never before had a court given an employer the right to tap the equivalent of a home phone, search for incriminating data on forty-three people (many more than just the twenty-one attendants), and "invade" private homes. Although fought by Ralph Nader's Public Citizen's litigation group and other like organizations, the story stays alive in labor's oral culture—and scares many computer users (Wieffering and Kennedy 2000).

Finally, many worry about the overload that e-mails entail in work lives already stretched to the limit. Union staffers complain of their inability to keep up with electronic messages rushing in, earmarked for rapid response, almost regardless of the situation of the receiver. Many staffers resent heightened expectations on them to respond almost immediately to scores of daily e-mail queries, even while their previous workload weighs heavy. As well, with blithe indifference, top officers often shift their e-mail response load to staffers.

Some staffers grumble about this unreasonable speedup, made all the less bearable by the absence of any commensurate increase in salary. Paltry compliments utterly fail to assuage the pain. Rumors of high salaries required to hire and retain computer specialists only rub salt in the wound.

All five current anxieties—possible erosion in face-to-face relations, loss of control over the medium, generation rift, loss of confidentiality, and (un-appreciated) work overload—can serve as a valuable call for overdue reforms: None need prove a paralyzing self-fulfilling prophecy. Remedies are available, and many are identified in this handbook. They include special schooling (private, discrete, and exceedingly sensitive) for older union leaders in how to use computers and password protection schemes (as used now by the AFL-CIO and various unions) (Levy 2000). Redistributed workloads, the hiring of additional aides, and overdue salary increases for those genuinely overloaded by computer inputs would go a long way toward remedying problems.

3. *Where Next?* Organized labor is challenged to stay abreast of dizzying computer changes and to advance in like fashion (Fiorito et al. 2000). On-going uses of computer power by the AFL-CIO and its affiliates may help slow, stem, and possibly even reverse labor's long-term ongoing decline—provided that, as noted at the outset, the movement keeps faith with Einstein's advice to emphasize creative rather than merely conventional thought.

Our ongoing computer revolution (better known to admirers as a Webolution) is endlessly impressive. Computer power, for example, that cost several millions dollars in 1960 sells today for less than a dollar (Gilder 2001, 8). Had you purchased an IBM PC in 1981 it would have cost the equivalent of $5,700 in constant dollars, while its counterpart in 2001 would set you back only $1,169. Your 1981 PC would have had a processor speed of 4.77 megahertz, and today it would be 356 times faster (see Chapter 12 for definitions). Your 1981 PC would have had 64 kilobytes of memory; today, 16,000 times that amount (Markoff 2001)!

Thirty-five years ago a chip factory could produce perhaps sixty transistors a day. Now, a single production line can turn out 1.6 billion in twenty-four hours (Markoff 2001). The price of a bit on a chip, once seven dollars, is now plunging close to a millionth of a cent (Gilder 2001, 7). Indeed, transistors today are nearly as cheap as the beach sand of which they are made (Gilder 2001, 8). Little wonder that the Internet has been able to double in size annually for some thirty years and increase its traffic between three and five times faster still (Gilder 2001, 152).

The computer revolution moves now beyond reliance on tethered, bulky keyboard-operated desktop PCs to the convenience of wireless, handheld, lightweight voice-activated personal digital assistants (PDAs) (see Chapter 5). We advance with smiles beyond the revolution's awkward opening act (computer-oriented lives) to a far more comfortable and productive phase (human-oriented computing).

Looking ahead to, say, 2004, information age cognoscenti expect a bright new "space," one they call Internet Two. Invigorated by profitable corporate winners (agile, global, lean, and smart), these firms will be led by entrepreneurs with fresh dreams of new info tech successes. Many, for example, "are betting they will soon rekindle the megainnovation of the Web's early days [a mere ten years ago] . . . a world of pervasive computing that lets people communicate more efficiently than ever" (Ante 2001).

Familiar options—such as wireless phones, high-definition television (HDTV), digital versatile discs (DVDs), teleconferences, Bluetooth and Linux applications—may be bolstered by "gee whiz" breakthroughs drawing on broadband and IP V.6 Internet switches, "which will enable everything with electricity to have its own Web address that will make it intelligent. So your refrigerator will be able to talk to your grocery store over the Web or your company's cash registers directly to your manufacturer's assembly line" (Friedman 2001). In short order, these Buck Rogers options should mature in application, plummet in cost, and soar in rewards.

As close as the end of 2002, for example, there may be more mobile devices than PCs accessing the Internet, so powerful appears the next "killer ap," the "teleputer" (otherwise known as an advanced wireless mobile phone). Keen competition, however, also in 2002, is expected from Microsoft's Tablet PC, a portable book-sized three-pound wireless "wonder." Proponents hail it as "a revolutionary device that actually replaces the laptop in your briefcase and the PC on your desk" (Levy 2001). By 2007 as many as 59 percent of all Americans (up from only 2 percent today) are expected to own a device that can access mobile data . . . whether a teleputer or a tablet (Gunther 2001).

Where stationary PCs are concerned, knowledgeable forecasters expect household penetration to plateau at about 73 percent by 2005, up from 57 percent in 2000, an expansion that underlines the increasing number of unionists that will be able to use labor Web sites and access labor e-mail from their living room (Baker 2001).

By 2007, then, a significant number of union influentials (officers *and* members) may carry a compact picture-phone and/or tablet computer, and dictate to it by voice and listen to it in turn (Harris 2001). They may use it to access any type of information, anywhere, at anytime; to stay in touch with significant others all the time; to send and receive messages in all languages, as if their own; and to surf the Internet and Web with the stressless help of "smart" software that provides useful information possibly even before they ask for it.

As if these hardware advances are not exciting enough, organized labor may soon have the option of group collaborative software now touted as "the next great turn of the wheel" (Ellis 2001). Known as peer-to-peer (P-to-P) programming, it circumvents centralized computer infrastructure and allows PCs to talk directly with one another.

Its creator, Ray Ozzie, believes P-to-P offers the "directness and spontaneity of a phone call, the visual immediacy of a fax, the asynchrony of e-mail, and the privacy of a closed-door meeting" (Ozzie, in Green 2001). Proponents expect it to enable users (such as far-flung union activists) to work easier and more creatively with one another than ever before possible. Skeptics agree it will be used very broadly but dismiss it as "only" another technology (Gomes 2001).

If only half of these glittering possibilities are soon realized, the rest are likely to be very close behind. Technological guru George Gilder contends, "Ready or not, the revolution will transform the landscape over the next decade" (Gilder 2000, 84). The impact is likely to continue to change reality dramatically, especially for social movements like organized labor, as it has since we entered the information age (Lee 1997). (Reflect, for a moment, on the ever-greater changes we can trace to our use of e-mail, list servers, Napster, Web sites, etc.) (Katz 2000).

Complicating matters still further, all of this is taking place in a global context: "The measure of what's happening with the Internet today is not Buy.com or the Nasdaq. It's what is happening in China, where Internet deployment is moving so fast that Chinese will be the most popular language on the Web by 2007; in India, where AOL just announced a $100 million investment; and in Europe, where the Net economy is expected to grow twentyfold by 2004" (Friedman 2001).

4. *Is There a CyberUnion in Labor's Future?* Given this turmoil, this tsunami of endless change, where might we find organized labor? Proactive, if it is to make the most of it. Reactive, if it elects to remain behind the curve— a most precarious place to be. Either labor will soon demonstrate imaginative creativity and bold risk taking, as in adopting many of the tips featured in this volume, and possibly even pursue CyberUnion stature (see Parts V–IX)), or it will run a risk of obsolescence so costly as to probably prove fatal.

Summary

The better to help us understand the challenge here, three essays follow that build on one another: The first identifies hardships often known by procomputer activists who see farther and clearer, hardships that can generally be overcome (tips are provided). The second shares a tale of steady expansion in a local's computer prowess, thanks to a cadre of persistent innovators (their tips are offered). And the third reminds us progress must go beyond high tech gains to include "high touch" advances as well. Taken together, the three essays help keep the handbook's advice—to seek really *imaginative* efforts—in perspective.

References

Ante, Spencer E. "In Search of the Net's Next Big Thing." *Business Week*, March 26, 2001, pp. 140–141.

Baker, Stephen. "A Net Not Made in America." *Business Week*, March 26, 2001, p. 124.

Clinton, William J. White House Press Release, January 8, 2001 (www. whitehouse.gov).

Ellis, John. "Grove Makes It Possible to Light Up the Edge." *FAST COMPANY*, May 2001, p. 101.

Freeman, Richard, and Wayne Diamond, as quoted in Robert Taylor, "Trade Unions: Workers Unite on the Internet." *Financial Times*, May 11, 2001, p. 6.

Fiorito, Jack, Paul Jarley, John Thomas Delaney, and Robert W. Kolodinsky. "Unions and Information Technology: From Luddites to CyberUnions?" *Labor Studies Journal* 24 (Winter 2000): 3–34.

Friedman, Thomas. "Hype and Anti-Hype." *New York Times*, February 23, 2001, p. A-17.

Gadiesh, Orit, as quoted in Thomas L. Friedman, "Hype and Anti-Hype."

Gilder, George. *Telecosm: How Infinite Bandwidth Will Revolutionize Our World.* New York: Free Press, 2000.

Gomes, Lee. "P-to-P, B-to-B—R.I.P?" *Wall Street Journal*, April 4, 2001, pp. B-1, B-4.

Green, Bill. "Jazzed About Work," *FAST COMPANY*, May 2001, p. 194.

Gunther, Marc. "Wireless E-mail." *Fortune*, March 19, 2001, p. 76.

Harris Interactive, www.harrisinteractive.com, June 10, 2001.

Katz, Jon. *Geeks.* New York: Villard, 2000.

Lazarovici, Laureen. "Cyber Drives: Organizing, Bargaining, and Mobilizing." *America@work*, March 2001, p. 9.

Lee, Eric. *The Labour Movement and the Internet: The New Internationalism.* Chicago: Pluto Press, 1996.

Levy, Steven. "Bill Gates Says, 'Take this Tablet.'" *Newsweek*, April 30, 2001, p. 67.
———. *How the Code Rebels Beat the Government—Saving Privacy in the Digital Age.* New York: Viking, 2000.

Markoff, John. "My First PC." *New York Times*, May 10, 2001, p. G-7.

Neilson/net ratings survey. "Big Blue (Collar, That Is) On-line." *Business Week*, May 14, 2001, p. EB-6.

Ozzie, Ray, as quoted in Bill Green, "Jazzed About Work."

Rainie, Lee, as quoted in Susan Stellin, "Compressed Data."

Stellin, Susan. "Compressed Data: Number of New Internet Users Is Growing." *New York Times*, February 19, 2001, p. A-19.

Taylor, Robert. "Trade Unions: Workers Unite on the Internet." *Financial Times*, May 11, 2001, p. 6.

Wieffering, Eric, and Tony Kennedy. "Search Raises Privacy Issues." Minneapolis, MN: *Star Tribune*, February 8, 2000, p. 1–A.

---

1. Cyber Birth: The Struggles of a Local Going Online

Steven J. Lelinski

With a wealth of fine essays to choose among, I have selected one that may initially surprise you. It is not the sort of upbeat material traditionally slotted at the opening of a book, not a rousing, cheerful account of a smashing victory or anything like that. Instead, it is an unsparing and challenging account of difficulties many of you will have—or already are having—in your effort to bring your union and/or local further along with computer uses.

I place it here to deliberately start the handbook on a realistic note—if also a hopeful one—as the activist below shares a tale of dedication, fortitude, and creativity, three indispensable components of the change efforts this handbook supports.

Please pay careful attention to the answers offered to these critical questions: What can I do when surrounded by doubters? What concrete demonstrations of computer-use payoff seem most useful? How might sudden-seeming "success" actually threaten your change effort, and what can you do about it?

Above all, please take careful note of the value of resolve, resiliency, and sensitive respect for those with whom you may disagree, those less enthusiastic for computer gains than the rest of us.

CyberUnion introduced the idea of using computerization to aid the labor movement. More specifically, it spelled out the various levels of cyberspace usage by unions and tried to describe the eventual optimal uses for the Internet to assist and promote labor. Within the book jargon was coined to describe the various levels of cyberspace usage that may be occurring within various unions: Cyber Naught (mouse), Cyber Drift (confused use), and Cyber Gain (conventional use). While this terminology may be new, so are the Internet and its inner workings. As people and organizations begin to find new uses for cyberspace, new verbiage will continue to join our everyday language.

It would not take a long study of my union to discover the way that it is handling computers: Cyber Naught. The union is so indifferent to the computer age that the secretaries only started using computers little more that ten years ago, solely for word processing purposes. Bookkeeping was computerized about five years ago, and the union got Internet access, in the form of an e-mail address, little over two years ago.

Only after being elected to a position on the executive board of the union did I realize how disinterested the leadership was with computerization and the Internet. I have a strong interest in these areas, but although my talents are not yet at a high level of proficiency, I attempted to spread my enthusiasm for this blooming technology to the leadership.

What I observed in the others was fear and distrust. They feared computers in general, and the Internet in particular, because they knew little about the subject. They distrusted the integrity and security of the Internet, citing any little hacking article that was printed in the local media. They would also cite cost and necessity as reasons for not investing the time or money into a "cyber investment."

To this day I truly believe that the other members on this board believed they could intimidate me into ending my quest for modernizing our union and exposing it to the Internet. Instead, I started to bring my laptop into the office and preformed work, as much as I could, with it. Slowly I noticed that they were asking questions, especially after I had typed and printed my own documents and the secretaries had not gotten to theirs yet. I felt that the union would begin to shift more dramatically toward computers and the Internet, but I did not have the background knowledge to sway them.

Then came *CyberUnion!* What excitement, combining two of my passions, unionism and computers, into one philosophy. Reading the book gave me, I believed, the edge I needed in background information to persuade the others. From the book I discovered that some of their reluctance might have to do with the age of many of them. Since they had not grown up with or had much exposure to computers, many saw computers as fancy, unnecessary technology; believing in the philosophy that, since they could run the union without the aid of computers in the past, they would not need them in the future.

As contract negotiations drew near, I assisted the president, vice president, and secretary/treasurer in obtaining comparable information on employers and other contracts, and tabulating it. Individually, I showed them how I was able to obtain much of this information directly from the Internet. Like a coffeepot percolating, I began to see their interest starting.

When it came time for surveying the membership, the board members all grumbled, complaining about who would be drafted to spend days tabulating the information. I surprised them all when I stated that I would do it alone, with only the aid of my laptop. I still recall the shock on the president's face when I handed him the survey results within seven hours. I had begun to win him over!

My next task was to get the union on the Internet. At several board meetings, I presented them with the Web pages of various unions, which I had downloaded and printed from the Web. While they did not see the practicality, I explained that we could start by just placing the most basic information out there. This information, I explained, should stop some of the trivial telephone calls that some of the members make regarding our contract or constitution. Once accepted, we could expand indefinitely.

My lobbying paid off. In July of 2000, I was allowed to start a trial Web page for the union, as long as it was not flashy and full of graphics. My euphoria disappeared and my heart sank when I realized what I had just committed myself to. While I received a great deal of information from *CyberUnion*, it did not explain how to build a Web page. Luckily, I found somebody willing to assist in this project. After several modifications and a tremendous amount of work, the site went online in August 2000.

I believe that the speed at which we went online caught the board members off guard. While they saw advantages to the site, they again started to delay the process. After excuse after excuse, they finally stated that they no longer wanted an "outside person" (the person helping me) involved. This stymied the union's sudden Internet growth.

I floundered in disbelief, until I convinced myself that I had the skills necessary to continue alone with what had been started. Not wanting to destroy the trial Web site, I taught myself, using Microsoft FrontPage, how to create a Web site by making a family Web site. By trial and error, and there was more error than trial, I slowly learned how to add photos, graphics, and animation. While my home page shows August 13, 2000, as the initial date, the site truly was not close to its present condition until late November 2000.

The union has now entered a Cyber Drift situation. While the others agree that I appear to have the proficiencies to maintain our union's Web site, they continue to bicker about its content. I hope to have these debates resolved in short order so that we can begin to approach Cyber Gain status. Unfortunately, I doubt that I will ever see my union willing to become a CyberUnion.

I truly am grateful for the insights that the book *CyberUnion* gave me. Without it I believe that my union would be somewhere in an Anti-Cyber Abyss.

2. On the Border of CyberUnionism: Lessons from Local 1613

Joseph N. Dassaro

In sharp contrast to the first essay, this second one is an account of remarkable, ongoing success. Confronting a very challenging work world, activist Joseph Dassaro responded with a very creative mix of various information technology tools, prime among which are different computer applications. The essay, strong in candor and recommendations, offers helpful answers to such questions as:

- *How can you apply a "force multiplying" approach, and why would you?*
- *What is the role here of a program coordinator? What are some good gauges of performance?*
- *How can you best handle the drawbacks of making leadership more accessible to members?*
- *What is the value of a long-range plan? Can meetings be "virtual"? Should software be standardized? What gadgets are especially promising? How can you budget for any of this?*
- *Above all, how do you steadily gain momentum and retain enthusiasm despite the inevitable "bumps in the road"?*

> *Servicing the membership is arguably the single most important thing locals and international unions accomplish.*
> —Arthur B. Shostak, *CyberUnion*

Does the following scenario sound familiar? You are an executive officer of a local union with hundreds, if not thousands of dues-paying members. There are dozens of pending arbitrations, grievances, and unfair labor practice complaints. Union members are trying to reach you twenty-four hours a day, seven days a week, fifty-two weeks a year. Your local does not have a central office or support staff, and your local leadership consists of regular member volunteers who are constantly balancing their jobs, union activities, and family time. Perhaps you sit at your desk, in your car, or on a plane reviewing an overstuffed day planner.

If any of this sounds familiar, you are not alone. My own local, for example, was very much like the troubled one above until we decided in 1995 to shuck off our Cyber Naught existence and try to achieve Cyber Gain strength—an odyssey that has us now striving to become one of America's first CyberUnions, a goal still out there ahead of us.

Guarding the Frontier

Along with six other volunteer union officers in the San Diego sector of the U.S. Border Patrol, I lead American Federation of Government Employees (AFGE) union Local 1613 of the National Border Patrol Council. We represent over 2,000 federal agents who patrol 4,255 square miles of urban, rural, and desolate terrain, twenty-four hours a day, seven days a week. Most of us are assigned to nine major stations and two substations located within San Diego County—a terrain that includes the notorious and dangerous border with Mexico. At any given time, however, one-third of our bargaining unit is assigned to Border Patrol stations located in other states. This geographic dispersion makes it logistically difficult for the local to effectively disseminate, track, and communicate information in a timely manner.

To meet these representational obstacles, we have learned to apply emerging information technologies (IT) as "force multipliers." And thanks to their impact, our local maintains a 98 percent voluntary membership rate—without our having any definitive organizing plan and in an environment that legally compels us to represent the entire bargaining unit without regard to membership status.

Many members tell us they join Local 1613 because its IT infrastructure keeps them better informed than ever before and they feel more "connected." Others join because their local is finally a handsome professional and ultramodern organization. We give our information technology program a lot of credit for all this!

Force Multiplying?

By now, you have probably asked yourself, "What is force multiplying?" Many people have asked me where I found the term. Some may recognize it from their military days, and they are correct. Force multiplying is a term used to indicate that the capabilities of a given asset may be enhanced by the introduction of another asset. For example, at a recent World Trade Organization (WTO) meeting, protestors demonstrated force multiplying: Rather than just showing up at the WTO meeting and protesting, they first conducted extensive training and organizing sessions. These were, in fact, force multipliers, as they greatly increased the eventual effectiveness of the protestors.

The theory is simple and can be employed by a local union of any size. Force multiplying is simply the leveraging of technology to maximize the effectiveness of limited union manpower, creating the appearance of almost unlimited union resources.

A simple example would be the use of an alphanumeric pager. It can be utilized by a local union president as a conduit for situational reports from union members or leaders. He can receive these reports wherever he is, avoiding the need to stop what he is doing and physically track down information. A more advanced form of leveraging technology would be the use of a handheld computer such as the Hewlett Packard Jornada 720. This device, a little larger than a standard cellular phone, would allow a union leader to keep just about every bit of union information at his fingertips, such as databases, contact information, and training manuals. The device also provides the immediate ability to send and receive e-mail from any location that has a phone, or even with a cellular phone from the back of a taxi.

Lessons Learned

Determined to modernize its operation, Local 1613 began in 1995 to employ cutting-edge advances in information technology. Our efforts since to move from Cyber Naught to CyberUnion status have taught us the value of four practical guidelines, each of which emerged through bruising trial and error. They are: (1) assign one point of contact, one individual, to oversee the entire project; (2) develop a plan; (3) talk to the members; and (4) develop and hold to very high standards.

1. Appoint one person to determine both the needs and the realistic expectations your union information technologies (UIT) program can address. That person should be responsible for research, equipment and software planning, systems design, testing, acquisition, and deployment. He or she should also develop a UIT plan to present to the membership in an effort to gain their approval and establish initial funding: Unless you gain early and decisive buy-in, you court disaster.

2. When developing the initial UIT plan, the program coordinator needs to answer some basic questions:

What Is Our IT Status Today?

Read *CyberUnion* to provide the basis for an evaluation of your local's IT infrastructure and to gain an understanding of the challenges involved. Be objective! If you already have the infrastructure but are experiencing constant chaos, throwing equipment at the problem will not solve it. There may be an underlying problem involving processes and methods.

Ask yourselves, What are our immediate and long-term UIT objectives? To improve immediate communications or simply to relay information that is not time sensitive? Are we trying to develop or improve our information storage and retrieval capabilities? Is it all of the above? Develop a series of questions, poll some key members, and ask yourself, What are we *really* trying to accomplish?

How do we address our objectives? Can we simply purchase one desktop computer and document scanner and place it in a central office? Is our workforce mobile? Will laptop computers be more suited to our situation? Should we develop a "package" (a complete IT solution) for each officer? Do we include specialized online databases such as cyberFEDS or Loislaw (www.feds.com, www.loislaw.com) in the plan or do we allow each officer to make that determination?

It is imperative that the plan author conducts proper research in this area. He or she must become very familiar with the current capabilities of specific product categories such as office suites, desktop computers, scanners, pagers, cell phones, laptop computers, and so forth. (For full product reviews, visit sites such as www.cnet.com, www.computershopper.com, and www. technolawyer.com. These same sites will provide the latest pricing information to help you establish a realistic budget.)

How Much Can We Realistically Afford to Budget for This Plan?

The union treasurer is of paramount importance when answering this question. If you find that your plan is too expensive, do not get discouraged. Request a grant from your national or international, or implement your IT plan in stages. Consider fund-raisers or other alternatives. If you have to, scale back your deployment to match your budget by prioritizing. Figure out what will have the greatest positive impact on your objectives. When preparing the budget section of your plan, be sure to include funds for annual maintenance and software upgrades.

Additionally, each local should strive for adequate asset tracking of purchased materials, particularly in instances when the equipment is deployed outside a central office (as in the case of smaller locals).

What Is Our Performance Gauge to Measure Success or Failure?

This is a critical step on the road to CyberUnionism. The program coordinator must be able to accurately assess the success or failure of his efforts. This evaluation will also provide the local an opportunity to fix problem areas. In Local 1613, we used practical, real-world tests to determine whether our plan was working or not.

In one simple test we evaluated our deployment of pagers and cell phones by paging all union officers at once with an alphanumeric message to call another officer, using their cell phone. Within minutes every officer responded. Another time we tested our document imaging and e-mail capabilities by scanning a document and circulating it via e-mail. Every officer received the document, read it, and e-mailed it back to me within twelve hours.

To be sure, there are certain drawbacks to making the union leadership more accessible to the general members. In Local 1613, our officers must routinely contend with large volumes of e-mails, voice mails, and pager messages. At one point I actually devoted four workdays just to clear my backlog of messages. The union leader must prioritize incoming messages and track his or her use of time carefully in order to avoid losing productivity.

Where Do We Want to Be in One Year, Two Years, and So On?

Developing a long-term plan will insure that resources are not squandered. Additionally, long-term plans will help your local meet the challenges of tomorrow.

3. The UIT program coordinator should address the membership, relying on his research and plan. The plan itself does not need to be a thesis. However, every member at the meeting should be provided a copy to promote a vested interest and help them feel connected. Certain key areas not only need to be addressed but must aptly demonstrate to the member that this effort is for the membership, not just for the executive officers and union representatives.

Our experience has shown that the primary area of concern by members is communications. Members want the ability to be heard on their own time and terms. This is especially pertinent in those areas where the general membership may not have the opportunity to attend union meetings. Show the members that a Web site, e-mail, cell phones, and pagers will facilitate and enhance communications.

We have also learned that members want the ability to interact with other members and officers of the local. What better way than to create a "virtual meeting" location through a Web site utilizing many of the free message board services on the Internet (like www.delphi.com). When presenting your plan to the membership, include some success stories of other locals; there are many.

Be prepared for opposition! In our particular case most of the opposition came from a sitting officer who felt that "his way" had been good enough and felt threatened by our plan. At one point our philosophical differences regarding the operation of the union almost turned physical.

Despite all the benefits information technology can and does provide now—to say nothing of what lies ahead—there will be those in the union who would rather not use these tools. We have learned it is prudent to encourage change patiently rather than try to force the matter. Often, all it takes is a little one-on-one coaching or technical support to get someone over his or her paralysis. Patience, along with persistent encouragement and unyielding expectations of eventual use seems to do the job.

4. The most effective way to maximize the use and life cycle of any computer hardware or software is through a plan of standardization. The UIT program coordinator must make every effort to purchase compatible and standardized equipment and software.

For example, in cases where the initial acquisition consists of an office software suite and several laptop computers, the coordinator should purchase several of the exact same laptops and office suite programs. Not only does this system guarantee full file compatibility for exchange and collaboration, it also provides a certain level of "built in" technical support. If someone has a technical problem with a laptop, the other users will be familiar with the same equipment and may have a solution readily available.

This same rule holds true for handheld computers, pagers, cell phones, and other items. Imagine yourself at a conference at which you forgot to pack your cell phone charger. Without standardization, there is a very good possibility you are simply out of luck. With equipment standardization, you can always borrow someone else's charger. The same especially holds true for laptop computer batteries and electrical adapters.

Mistakes of Ours That Need Not Be Yours

The guidelines presented above were the result of some minor, and some not so minor, temporary failures in implementing IT solutions within Local 1613—errors you need not repeat. For example, our initial approach in striving toward a CyberUnion model was (admittedly) not appropriately directed. Rather than identifying problems and situations in which IT resources could be used, we automatically assumed that the deployment of resources alone would be sufficient. Five years later we have learned to first identify and analyze the problem, then seek appropriate IT solutions.

The road toward a CyberUnion may at times seem circuitous and rough. For instance, in our attempts to deploy a software solution to assist our litigation efforts, we tested five software products designed for law firms. Our goal was to deploy the software to approximately forty union representatives and officers. In our headstrong attempt to force modernization, we tried three software programs, one after the other, over the course of an entire year, with each attempt being a complete failure! Eventually we determined the learning curve of the complicated legal material to be far too steep to deploy the software on a wide scale.

Simply put, without centralized offices, we could not provide sufficient training and support to ensure a successful deployment. In the end, the litigation software was provided to the president and first vice president to assist them in their litigation efforts, while the union representatives continued to rely on the time-tested and proven legal pad.

Basic Software Guidelines

As a result of our learned experience based on the convergence of problem solving and IT resource deployment, we established the following basic software standards for our local. They allow us to ensure full compatibility between our current leadership while using software as a true force multiplier. Although we find that these standards work well for us, we strongly encourage other locals to examine their particular needs to determine what works well for them. The three examples below help make our point:

1. Problem

Union officers used a variety of word processing and spreadsheet programs that were not fully compatible. Those that were, in theory, compatible, did not retain the original formatting intended by the author of the document. Additionally, officers complained about the inability to insert charts and graphics into documents.

Solution

The Microsoft Office suite (premium version: $699, premium version upgrade: $299; www.microsoft.com/office) provides the core of our software applications in one tightly integrated package that guarantees forward and backward compatibility with other versions. Additionally, Microsoft Office has the capability of opening and converting files from just about any existing program, including Macintosh versions of the Office suite.

The standard versions of MS Office contain Word, Excel, PowerPoint, and Outlook. The premium version of the program also provides MS FrontPage, a complete Web site creation and management program, and MS

Publisher, an intermediate publishing program that any user of MS Office will be able to use, and MS Access, a database creation tool.

Perhaps the most important feature of the software is the ability to instantly convert any file (including databases) into an HTML file (an Internet file type) that can be published to the Internet in a matter of minutes. Most users will probably opt for the MS Office Small Business (manufacturers suggest retail price $209.99) edition, which will provide the core components of the premium version (Word, Excel, Outlook, Publisher).

2. Problem

Local 1613 did not retain documents or case files beyond one or two years (the term of elected officers). There were no substantive records of negotiations, grievances, settlements, or correspondence. The limited files that were available were not centralized, making them inaccessible to other officers. Additionally, the union mail was picked up by the treasurer and distributed to the intended recipient at the next union meeting, which could cause a delay of up to thirty days.

Solution

Since 1996, Local 1613 has utilized Paperport, a simple document imaging program ($54.95; www.scansoft.com) for all document imaging, storage, and retrieval—effectively replacing all paper-based filing systems. The program allows the filing of document images into a familiar folder hierarchy. Users can create folders and subfolders by subject matter or any other identifier. When scanned, the software compresses the image and scans the document for key words. Documents can be instantly retrieved by conducting searches (basic or Boolean) or through manual viewing of folder contents.

In the case of union mail, the treasurer scans all incoming correspondence and disseminates the entire package via e-mail attachment to the intended recipient. The significance of this is that all union officers of Local 1613 can expect to receive their mail in a timely manner, even if they are traveling or on vacation.

3. Problem

Union officers and representatives needed a way to disseminate electronic documents to union members on a wide scale. However, many officers were fearful that the shared electronic files would be manipulated to reflect inaccurate information.

Solution

This problem was overcome using Adobe Acrobat 4.0 ($249.00 full version, $89.95 upgrade; www.adobe.com). Acrobat 4.0 allows any file to be converted to the popular portable document file (pdf) format, which is in wide-scale use. The file can then be viewed on any type of computer or operating system using the freely distributed Acrobat Reader software (available at www.adobe.com). The converted file retains its original format and fonts, which cannot be altered. Using Acrobat, conversion is as simple as selecting a different printer for printing.

The solutions provided above form the cornerstone of our standardized software approach. Of paramount importance in selecting this software was the availability of what is commonly referred to as COTS (commercially available, off-the-shelf software). Using commercial software solutions as opposed to customized software provides a guaranteed level of legacy support at a reduced expense. Whereas custom-designed software can only be changed or maintained by the original (or licensed and trained) developer, commercial software allows for a wide variety of third-party solutions and support. Customized software solutions should only be provided as an absolute last resort, and then only in situations where the data will not need to be shared.

IT Gadgets That Pay Off!

Force multiplying through information technologies has become a standard part of the operational culture of Local 1613. On a weekly basis we utilize a Listbot service (www.listbot.com), a free, Web-based service that manages a subscription e-mail service much like a Listserv (Listbot is less complicated).

Using Listbot, the union disseminates accurate and timely information to over 400 subscribers with the push of a button. The subscribers (including most union representatives) receive the information in their e-mail in-box and, when requested, print and disseminate the information to other union members.

When it is mandatory that the local communicates via traditional means, we utilize another Web-based service to decrease the workload. Using E-Letter (www.eletter.com), a fee-for-service site, local union officers have the ability to disseminate mass mailings at anytime, without time-consuming printing, folding, and stuffing. From any computer with Internet access, a local officer can log onto E-Letter, manually enter addresses, choose from a previously uploaded list, or perform a new mail merge, upload any file, and conduct a mass mailing. Similar services are available for fax broadcasting and receiving (www.jfax.com and www.efax.com).

Web-based services are not the only force multipliers. More recently, Local 1613 began using paging devices that continuously monitor existing e-mail accounts (Rim 850 through Skytel services: www.rim.net, www.skytel.com). These devices provide the ability to send and receive e-mail through a pager-like device. They also allow faxes to be sent to the pager number, from which they can be viewed on the Internet or automatically forwarded, via attachment, to an e-mail address. Additionally, they offer two-way messaging and tight integration to most PIMs (personal information managers such as Microsoft Outlook, Symantec Act, Winfax, etc.).

Recent developments in the area of handheld personal computers (HPCs) and pocket personal computers (PPCs) may lead to those computers playing a vital role in lives of unionists constantly on the move. These devices, about the size of a cellular phone, provide very tight integration (through synchronization) with the unionist's desktop computer and contain simple versions of Microsoft Word, Excel, PowerPoint, Access (in the HPC models), and Outlook.

When the unionist leaves the office (or his home), he removes the device from its cradle. The apparatus is fully synchronized with his personal information manager and contains duplicate copies of any files, e-mails, contacts, or databases that may be required. Additionally, these devices are capable of accessing the Internet either through a conventional phone line (or pay phone) or a mobile phone, providing the ability to send and receive e-mail or search the Internet from any location.

Local 1613 currently utilizes both the HPC and PPC models. Some officers even use these instruments to access special online databases such as cyberFEDS (www.cyberfeds@lrp.com) or Loislaw (www.loislaw.com). These sites provide comprehensive databases of employment and contract law (case law lookup, arbitrator biographies and decisions, Federal Labor Relations Authority [FLRA] decisions, National Labor Relations Board [NLRB] decisions, etc.). (For indepth information regarding HPC or PPC devices, see www.cewindows.net.)

Despite what many may think, these technological resources are within the reach of every local today. You do not have to be a whiz kid to use them, nor do you need to hire a professional support staff. (However, it would definitely help if you had a teenager at home!)

Summary

As recently as 1995, Local 1613 maintained no planned budget for technological resources, and there was great debate among local officers about whether or not the Internet would "really take off." In 1996 I presented an initial plan for the acquisition and deployment of IT resources. I requested only $10,000 for funding of my plan; however, by the end of the meeting's deliberations, the membership approved a motion from the floor that provided a $15,000 allocation. The members wanted to ensure enough money was available to purchase high-quality hardware and software—they wanted the job done right!

Today, information technology resources account for approximately 15 percent of our budget, and all of our executive officers routinely utilize high-speed Internet connections (if available in their area), mobile communications, and mobile computing resources. We are definitely "online," and Local 1613 cannot imagine being otherwise!

The road to CyberUnionism is a hard, and yet rewarding one. Union locals, especially sleepy "steno-pad" organizations, must become high-performance computer-aided operations. They must demonstrate custom-tailored craft in using emerging information technologies. Only then can they achieve Cyber Gain excellence, and be able to press on—as we are doing in Local 1613—to earn recognition as twenty-first–century CyberUnions.

---

3. Technology Evens the Playing Field

Lawrence R. Smoot, Jr.

Lest a costly misimpression be created that this handbook is entirely and only about hardware and software, about only "high tech" things, the nature of the essay below attests to the incomparable importance of "high touch" matters.

Computer use can and must aid the humanistic dimension of unionism, or it will never do all that it can for the movement. Indeed, unless there is a sensitive balance favoring humanism, computer inroads actually threaten to have a chilling impact. Happily, gains in having computers serve us, rather than the other way around, are already evident. The too-little-known tale below calls attention to the unique solidarity-promoting strengths of e-mail, list serves, and a dedicated Web site.

Labor's many subcultures, whether grouped by race, ethnicity, religion, gender, sexual preference, politics, craft, industry, or whatever, have much to gain from coming together in an "electronic community" of their own making and design, as illustrated by the account below. Bolstered by caring camaraderie, members can make a still-finer contribution to labor and to their own lives.

In 1977, Ken Olson, president and founder of Equipment Corporation, said, "There is no reason anyone would want a computer in their home." Today, however, almost every person in the United States has access to a computer, whether it is in his or her home, school, or public library. Just about every ad you see in print or hear on radio and TV has a Web address attached to it.

Why should organized labor be any different in the use of this technology? A Web page has become the modern "coat of arms" to represent not only companies and organizations, but families and unions as well.

I believe we have only seen the very beginnings of the full effect the Internet will have on the labor movement and the world in general. This tool has yet to be honed to a fine edge and be made a tool as common as the teaspoon—something that is there and used everyday, but not really thought of that much. We have, however, made a fine start . . . especially where smaller labor constituency groups are concerned.

I am an elected officer of the Baltimore-Washington chapter of Pride At Work, which is a relatively new constituency group of the AFL-CIO. Our basic mission is to:

- Work within the gay, lesbian, bi, and transgender (LGBT) movement to foster better understanding of the needs of LGBT union members;
- Work within the LGBT community for a better understanding of the trade union movement, its principles, and its achievements; and
- Work to organize the vast majority of unorganized LGBT workers into the trade union movement.

Just as many others have done, we too have our own Web site to tell the world what we are about, what our mission is, and just about everything else about us. It seems that in today's world you are not serious about your mission if you are without a Web site. Even smaller groups like our local chapter must produce a site that is as appealing to the eye as well as to the brain in its viewers.

Let us not forget that if you have a site, you must have an e-mail address as well; otherwise, your Web site is like a dead-end street. You need to have a way for the world to contact you, so they can give you their valuable insights, thereby keeping you abreast of what people are thinking about organizations like your own.

When you are in your beginnings as an organization, you need to be aware of every dime you spend and how it will benefit your group. Most of our members have access to the Internet, so it is a great and inexpensive way to convey information to our membership. No stamps are needed, no man/woman power hours are spent folding letters and stuffing envelopes. We simply e-mail current information, or the members can check the Web site to find out what their local chapter is doing.

This is especially effective when you need to get the word out fast about an important issue facing your membership or the labor movement entirely. What was once done via phone banking for hours, can now be done in a few minutes; just compose and send—click, click—you're done.

Our Web site (and list of e-mail addresses) is a place for people interested in helping this particular cause in other parts of the world. It is almost mind-boggling to know you can create an interactive billboard to stand alongside the world's information superhighway. Yup, just little old us here at Pride At Work, Baltimore-Washington chapter, sending our message to the world in an instant. Wielding the power of the labor movement with a few keystrokes and some HTML code.

We share many of the same workplace issues around the world; our true "union morality" is one of inclusiveness and equality for all people, period. Our Pride at Work Web site allows LGBT people elsewhere a way to keep informed of not only what we do but how we do it. They can use our activities as a model for their own if they wish to. Our own site, www.prideatwork.org, is a work in progress like any other Web site. It is in a constant state of flux, changing as the issues each take a turn on center stage.

And, oh yes, as I said in the beginning, just as with about anything else in print or other media, here's our e-mail address: prideatwork@yahoo.com. You didn't think I would forget such an important piece of information, did you?

P.S.—On a More Personal Note

At a time when I was unsure if I wanted to be alone or with other people, I turned to the Internet. There I found people like myself from all parts of the world dealing with the same issues that I was dealing with. My partner was dying from AIDS-related illnesses, and I felt helpless. This was one monster that I could not scare away, a bully that I could not stand up to. I could not protect the one I loved. My family lived over 1,000 miles away, and my phone bill was high enough already. This is where the Internet comes in. I was able to not only speak to others who could relate to my story, but I could contact my family as often as I needed.

Unlike a phone call that may come when you are not ready to deal with it, e-mail sits on the wayside patiently waiting for you. It does not mind that your eyes are blurred and you are sloppy from tears and months of ongoing pain. It just sits, and you know it will be there when *you* are ready for *it*.

There is one other wonderful thing about e-mail.

People will convey more honest thoughts and feelings, it seems, in a letter. The inhibitions of face-to-face encounters are gone for the most part. The art of letter writing seemed to disappear for a time, but the Internet and e-mail has brought that experience back to us. An experience filled with true feelings set to "paper," so to speak. I was able to relay to my family the gratefulness and pride that I felt for their support during such a difficult time in my life, and my family was able to share this simultaneously.

The Internet has given me another way to express my feelings and share the parts of my life that might help someone else.

I. Surveying the Field

*A problem adequately stated is a problem
well on its way to being solved.*
—R. Buckminster Fuller, engineer and inventor

The better to help expand our idea of what the field is *and* could be about, I want to begin with a brief review of conventional computer use: Exactly how we might soon go beyond is explained in the five brow-arching essays that follow.

While emphatically not a "magic bullet," computerization makes possible wide-scale communications of dazzling speed and enormous outreach (national and international). It enables unprecedented access by rank-and-filers to officeholders, providing a timely exchange of views among them, as well as among the members themselves via electronic bulletin boards and chat rooms (including some valuable ones run unofficially by the "loyal opposition"). Computerization bolsters mobilization for political action and strike support, and it facilitates corporate campaigns by labor that would otherwise be overwhelmed with complexity and data.

Where local unions are concerned, computerization enables international representatives and business agents to download reams of relevant material (grievance and arbitration records, previous contracts, etc.). This enables them to use their laptop on the spot to do a high-quality job directly on the shop or office floor. As well, locals can create electronic list servers to link together an entire membership. They can appeal to prospective members and can address subcultures differently. In other overdue ways, they can build a new form of "electronic community," a twenty-first–century adaptation of solidarity.

Communications in labor has historically involved a staid house organ,

27

poorly attended meetings, and many (commonly ignored) mailings. The "message" generally came from the top down and was commonly innocuous or deafening (and was just as commonly undervalued by many recipients, staff and rank and filers alike).

Today, millions of members of AFL-CIO's affiliates with a Web site can at a click of a mouse have access to facts, figures, documents, archives, rules, regulations, photos, videos, and more. They can sort this material to suit their own purposes, and they can request additional material—including streaming video subject matter and other fascinating forms of communications they are coming to expect from their locals and international unions.

Shop stewards, for example, can access revealing profiles of active mediators and arbitrators (their biases, idiosyncrasies, standards, etc.). They can access data on labor law cases and precedents. And they can secure field-proven clues as to how to best handle a grievance, arbitration, and so forth in light of yesterday's major decisions, clues the computer can format as an electronic tutorial or rule book.

Members can be briefed immediately about fast-breaking developments, and kept abreast almost in a real-time mode. E-mails can now go out in a 24/7 format as part of a remarkable new web of timely communications never possible before with mail, phone, or fax.

Especially novel is the opportunity that computer-based communication has made possible for a vast upgrade in a very old effort to forge strong bonds among unions around the world (an effort aided by Marx and Gompers alike). Although not well known by most unionists here, various federations overseas have tried to promote international solidarity for decades, such as the International Federation of Chemical, Energy, Mine, and General Workers Union (ICEM), with its 403 union affiliates in 113 countries. But making phone connections and/or airmail use has always been a hindrance. Today, e-mails flash back and forth almost in real time, aiding the conduct of far-flung port boycotts, intricate corporate campaigns, and other coordinated international activities.

Perhaps *the* most far-reaching change in labor's communications involves the newfound ability of members to reach one another—independent of officialdom. Until recently, a member could to do so only through the union's newspaper or magazine, and then only if the editors agreed. Today, grass-roots activists are busy on a 24/7 basis exchanging uncensored advice, views, and visions. Caucuses of like-minded members can link together in an e-mail list server or through a shared Web site. Solidarity is built, and the cause of union democracy can receive a very strong boost.

Where labor militancy is concerned, intriguing new tools are under consideration: Unions might encourage members to shut down or in other ways impede the use of their computers at work. Or they could create "picket lines" in cyberspace. Or urge boycotts of the products or services of targeted employers, and do this faster and with far wider coverage via the Internet than was ever possible relying on old-fashioned mailings.

Contrarily, concerning a rare, if desirable possibility, a local's effort to cocreate a high-performance workplace in partnership with a cooperative employer, a labor computer system could facilitate employee dialogue about overdue workplace boosts to productivity—complete with a union imprimatur.

Accordingly, although unable alone to "rescue" labor, gains from computer use in efficiency and effectiveness might help attract many new members. Computer use could also help bolster support of existing members (always labor's best organizers). And, in 101 other significant ways, it could rapidly aid labor's urgent efforts at recovery (see, in this connection, http://workingfamilies.com/ and http://afscme.org/publications/puttc.htm).

The five essays that follow will help us get further along, that is, begin to expand our "mind map" of labor's actual and potential use of computer power: The first offers a sweeping overview of what is happening. The second urges attention to what some think could be the next "killer ap," PDAs. The third warns against spying by power-hungry employers. The fourth demonstrates why we should go outside the world of labor in search of applicable tips and tricks. And the last essay teaches that labor worldwide has tips and tricks to share across borders.

Taken together, the essays, rich with a bevy of valuable advice, demonstrate how much we can learn from ongoing efforts to make imaginative use of computer power. They also tantalizingly suggest (as made clear in Parts V–IX) how much further we can still go.

---

4. Cyber Drives: Organizing, Bargaining, and Mobilizing—Downloading "E-Strategies" for 21st-century Union Action

Laureen Lazarovici

Thanks to an AFL-CIO publication of outstanding merit, America@work, *the wide-ranging report below draws attention to several major rewards of smart computer uses. Answers are offered to such questions as:*

- *What sort of creative moves are locals taking in their organizing campaigns?*
- *How did a pioneering use of palm pilots help improve the involvement of the Nevada labor movement in the year 2000 elections?*
- *How have labor's e-mail campaigns changed the Texas political scene?*
- *What part did celebrities play on an AFL-CIO Web site during the August–October 2000 strike of actors and actresses?*
- *How does a cyber-picket line work?*

Lessons abound, including these three: (1) E-mail and a dedicated Web site can overcome the old problem of having widely scattered sites during an organizing campaign. (2) The infoglut can be "tamed" in part by using palm organizers to keep scattered activists in touch and on top of otherwise overwhelming amounts of incoming information. (3) Video clips and digitized photos can weld together otherwise isolated members.

Downloading "E-strategies"

Linda Church works as an assistant district counsel for the U.S. Immigration and Naturalization Service [INS] amid the neon lights and Latin-jazz beat of Miami. Her other INS colleagues toil in cities as diverse as edgy downtown Manhattan and near the graceful Spanish-style arches of San Antonio, and amid the balmy tropical air of Hawaii.

Although dispersed across the country, the professional staff of the INS general counsel office—attorneys, accountants, statisticians, and engineers—became aware that some managers applied vacation and attendance policies differently than others. "We wanted equity for everyone," says Church, who spearheaded a union organizing drive with AFGE [American Federation of Government Employees]. Because the 500 workers all reported to the same general counsel, they decided to organize as a national unit. "Organizing each office individually would not have given us the clout we wanted," says Church.

The far-flung workforce posed a challenge to organizers. They could not leaflet at a plant gate or hold a membership meeting at a nearby diner. So Church turned to a technology that enabled her to spread the union message instantaneously to hundreds of people across the country: e-mail. "Over five time zones, there's really no other way to communicate effectively," she says. "E-mail was our lifeblood." Church wrote organizing updates on her home computer and set up an interactive Web site. The effort culminated in a September 1999 vote to join AFGE.

Electronic communications remained a crucial tool during contract negotiations as the new AFGE Local 511 members received and filled out contract surveys via e-mail. They now are negotiating a contract that will include clauses allowing the local to use e-mail for union representation and to post its own virtual bulletin board on the INS Web site. "Now I have a relationship with people all over the country whom I've never met," says Church, interim president of Local 511.

More and more workers are buying ever-more-affordable computers, getting online, surfing the World Wide Web, and communicating through sophisticated electronic gadgets. And unions are utilizing the power of these technologies to step up organizing, political activism, and solidarity during strikes. For many unions, technology is proving to be a crucial complement to the core strategy of building union strength: worker-to-worker contact.

Union Privilege is working to ensure that union leaders have the technology they need to help them bring a voice to working families. It is providing state federations and central labor councils that are part of the New Alliance, the union movement's restructuring and revitalizing initiative, with computers and Internet access. The union groups will have their own list servers and other specially tailored electronic communications systems to help them share information.

"CyberUnions" will allow "unprecedented access of everyone in labor to everyone else," says Art Shostak, a sociology professor at Drexel University in Philadelphia and author of *CyberUnion: Empowering Labor Through Computer Technology*. "America's new CyberUnions will show the world that unionism does 'compute' in our age of information."

New technologies "are the most accessible ways to reach employees," says Charles Craver, a labor law professor at George Washington University Law School in Washington, DC. "If unions are going to survive, they are going to have to organize healthcare, high-tech, and service workers," he says, "and unions are going to have to reach these sectors and these workers with e-mail and new technologies."

Some 60 percent of union members have computers, according to a poll by Peter D. Hart Research, Inc. conducted in January 2000. The survey also found that 74 percent of union members with computers have Internet access.

Organizing by e-mail is one of many "e-strategies" union members are employing in their efforts to strengthen the union movement and enable workers to have a voice at work. Here are examples of other union "e-action."

The Internet Plays in Peoria

The 150 workers who install and repair alarms at SecurityLink from Ameritech in suburban Chicago work out of company trucks in which they drive to different job sites directly from their homes each day. As with the organizing effort of INS lawyers, forming a union took a leap into cyberspace.

"This was a very difficult group to organize, because they were not all in one place," says Tom Hopper, business agent for Electrical Workers Local 21. Although they lost elections in 1996 and 1997, the workers were undaunted. They published a Web page with an online newsletter written by workers, with submissions coming in via e-mail.

Electronic communications helped the workers build enough cyber-solidarity that in October 1998, they won their efforts to get a voice on the job—even after the company fired organizing committee members days before the election—and today have a strong contract.

Eager to ensure their struggle would help other workers, union leaders set up "meta-tags" on their Web site, an index entry for a Web site that makes it easier for Internet surfers to find what they want and for Web sites to publicize their contents.

The foresight paid off when workers at an Ameritech subsidiary in central Illinois found Local 21's Web site and subsequently organized workers throughout the state via e-mail: "No big phone bills," says Al Morrison, who galvanized his coworkers at the Peoria subsidiary.

Other organizing campaigns are using e-mail and Web sites to mobilize far-flung workers, such as the ongoing effort among 20,000 flight attendants at Delta Air Lines to form a union with the Flight Attendants. But plenty of centralized or concentrated workplaces have benefited as well, such as the 163 high-tech workers at Tektronix, outside Portland, Oregon, who make color printers and sought to organize with UNITE.

Because the Tektronix workers have access to computers with Internet service for personal use in their break room, union organizers could visit workers during their breaks, point the computer browser to www.uniteatxerox.org and enable workers to get information about UNITE and read words of encouragement from already-unionized workers at other Xerox-owned companies. Last May the workers won their bid to join a union, and in November, another unit of 107 temporary workers also joined UNITE Local 14–Z.

Year-round Political Action

During the 1998 election season, the Nevada State AFL-CIO was using what at the time was state-of-the-art technology. Activists had contacted voters through phone banks and precinct walks, and identified pro-union voters on paper printouts with supermarket-style bar codes next to the voters' names. They scanned the bar codes and responses into a database.

But Danny Thompson, the state federation's executive secretary-treasurer, was frustrated with the process. It took hundreds of volunteer-hours to do the tedious scanning—hours that could be spent talking with voters—while producing piles of lists that quickly became obsolete. A self-described "technophile," Thompson vowed to find a better way.

He arrived at a solution after he bought palm pilots for his staff, who used the compact, hand-held computers for office management. Thompson knew the devices had the potential to do much more and hired a computer expert to develop a program to track voter contacts, creating a virtually paperless means of getting out the vote.

During the 2000 election, volunteers looked up voters' addresses on their palm pilots and recorded responses directly into the computer with a penlike stylus. They walked to the next house on their list with the help of directions generated by the computer program.

At the end of a precinct walk, the valuable data describing which voters planned to vote for proworker candidates was directly downloaded—"hot-synced" in palm pilot parlance—into a database spreadsheet. No maps, no bar codes, no waiting for printouts. "It frees the volunteers to do the worker-to-worker contact," he says. "We talked to more voters because we weren't spending time making up packets of maps and lists and scanning bar codes."

One candidate who benefited from the unions' newfound techno-savvy is John Oceguera, a member of Fire Fighters Local 1607, who won his bid for a state assembly seat: "The Palm Pilot allowed us to send people into the field with the whole district in their hands." Oceguera won by a slim margin, a victory he credits to unions' get-out-the-vote campaign. "The technology will change the face of politics in Nevada—and it was neat to be part of it."

Unions are harnessing the power of technology to advance a working family agenda not only during elections, but in off-election years as well. Texas AFL-CIO communications director Ed Sills sends out a daily e-mail newsletter with alerts for rallies and news from unions. But the newsletter's biggest impact comes during the Lone Star State's legislative session. "When there is a fast-developing action in the legislature, our activists know about it," says Sills.

Two years ago, after a legislator filed a paycheck deception bill to limit unions' ability to raise money to get their message out, the state federation e-mailed information about the author, the text of the bill, and the arguments against it. Within days, the legislator who sponsored it had received so many opposition e-mails he decided not to proceed. "Instead of just lobbyists, there were rank-and-file members contacting legislators," Sills says. "When we get everyone involved, it has a real impact."

Cyber-Solidarity

Julianna Margulies played the spirited nurse "Carol Hathaway" onscreen on the television hospital drama *ER*. But after members of the Screen Actors and Television and Radio Artists union went on strike against advertisers from August to October, in 2000, Margulies began appearing in a video portraying a union member—and this time she wasn't acting.

A video clip of Margulies was among several on the AFL-CIO Web site in support of the actors' strike. Activists logging on could view their favorite celebrities talking about the importance of joining together in a union and such key issues in the strike as demands for wage cuts by corporate advertisers, and they could e-mail the video clips to friends.

The actors encouraged supporters to boycott products made by Procter & Gamble Co., an influential advertiser involved in the strike. Visitors to the site could e-mail P&G's CEO, Alan G. Lafley, telling him they were part of the boycott. To draw union members to the site, union webmasters sent e-mails to activists who, in turn, generated 40,000 e-mails to advertisers in three weeks. The strategy was so effective that P&G board Chairman John Pepper wrote a letter to union leaders when the boycott ended, making a special request to them to take the link off their Web pages.

In October, Screen Actors Guild (SAG) and American Federation of Television and Radio Artists (AFTRA) won improved compensation for actors on TV and radio commercials. And, keeping their eyes on future technological advances, they won jurisdiction over commercials made specifically for the Internet.

Similarly, the Teamsters send regular, tailored e-mail campaign updates to Bed, Bath & Beyond and Wal-Mart customers of Overnite Inc., a company that flagrantly violates workers' right to a voice on the job.

The Web and e-mail boycott campaign was one technological component of SAG's strike technology strategy. Another was posting photos and reports from picket lines and demonstrations across the country on the union's Web site. "Part of the reason actors stuck together was because people didn't feel isolated," says Greg Krizman, SAG spokesman. "The advertisers checked out the Web site daily, too, and they realized they couldn't run from New York, Los Angeles, and Chicago to tape commercials and expect to be in for an easy ride."

Visually linking workers together in a cyber-picket line also contributed to the success of the Society of Professional Engineering Employees in Aerospace/ International Federation of Professional and Technical Engineers Local 2001. During the six-week strike at Boeing Co., Wayne Schwisow, the union's webmaster, published a daily summary of members picketing throughout the country at the Seattle-based aircraft maker's many locations. "Workers could see an immense list, and it let them know they were having an effect," he says. Union members also could register on the site with their home e-mail addresses to receive notices of rallies and news. The resulting e-solidarity helped the workers win a strong contract in January 2000.

At Boeing, as with all successful campaigns involving e-strategies, the Internet is just one part of a larger effort to communicate the desires of workers to come together into unions to improve their lives, strengthen their families, and build their communities. The core of building union strength has been workers always talking to each other, one on one. Such technologies as e-mail and Palm Pilots help amplify workers' voices "to be successful in organizing and to save money," says International Brotherhood of Electrical Workers' (IBEW) Hopper. "But you have to balance it with face-to-face contact, which is the best way to communicate with workers."

Low-Cost Computers for Union Members. Union members can get special low prices on IBM desktop and laptop computers, loaded with a choice of software. They come with one year of free Internet access. Check out www.workingfamilies.com for more information.

---

5. Info Zap! PDAs in the Hands of a Union Activist

Karin Hart

No consideration of labor's use of computer power would be complete without attention to a leading away-from-the-office technology, a contender for the title—tomorrow's "killer ap"—the personal digital assistant (PDA). Already hailed in labor circles for making a major contribution to recent political campaigns in Nevada, PDAs are of increasing interest to union activists on the go.

The essay below helps answer such questions as:

- *Just what can a union activist really do with these gadgets?*
- *How can you finesse the limit PDAs set on the size of a memo or note?*
- *Of what value are accessories like a folding keyboard and/or a digital camera?*
- *Can a map really be read on a PDA, and, so what?*
- *How vital is it to backup data on a PDA?*

• *Above all, what features possibly undervalued by current PDA users among union activists might make a valuable difference?*

Although they seem like the next new thing, personal digital assistants (PDAs), with their pastel colors and fancy attachments, have been around for more than ten years. Almost from that first generation of Apple's Newtons and Casios, some trade unionist has been trying to use one as a keeper of contacts and to manage his or her calendar appointments as an alternative to the hard copy datebook.

Earlier this year my aging car was ripped off in the dead of night right in front of my house. With this theft I lost my cellular phone, pager, a briefcase with all my lecture notes for a class I was teaching on labor economics, and an early model of the palm pilot, a PDA, that I was struggling to teach to recognize my handwriting.

With minimal inconvenience I immediately replaced the cell phone and rewrote my lecture notes. My insurance company promptly replaced the car, but I was stumped on how to replace my PDA. So I consulted with several of my Bay Area colleagues who use PDAs to discover how they used theirs and what they liked and didn't like about them.

Louise, past president of a southern California Communication Workers of America (CWA) local and current lead activist in a northern California local, is not a stranger to using the latest technology. She's had several PCs, cell and Personal Communications Services (PCS) phones, and various gizmos. She is, however, the only person I know who unfolds her keyboard at every meeting with employers and plugs it into her PDA (a Palm Pilot V) so she can input comprehensive notes at important discussions. Like any good union rep, she knows the value of keeping notes as a way to follow-up with managers on whether or not they have lived up to their end of an agreement.

Her method is really a work-around for the current generation of PDAs that limit the size of a memo or note. Louise will type the meeting notes into memos in her Palm and label them so she can connect/link them together later on after she has synchronized up the PDA for the day. On the PC she archives and prints them out to take to the next meeting.

Jeff, a vice president of the CWA local in Hayward, works with high tech every day. In his traditional job he is a systems technician installing and repairing Digital Subscriber Line (DSL) circuits and equipment for customers in the East Bay. He has been one of the strong voices inside his local union favoring increased use of new technology.

Sure, the union's office secretary has a computer for writing correspondence and typing out the final versions of newly negotiated contracts. And the treasurer has the union's membership records and accounting on another

PC. But Jeff would like to see all the officers and reps have access to PCs networked together in the office and linked to the membership via the Web.

Like many members of his local, he has a PC at home (even a laptop PC) and uses the Internet. However, like others interviewed for this essay, Jeff doesn't like how bulky or heavy laptop computers are, or their short battery life, so he got a PDA made by Sony that uses the Palm operating system. Currently, he uses it to schedule his time and to jot quick notes, but he confesses to not being very quick in writing notes by hand on his PDA. His number one use is to read e-mails he downloaded earlier in the day while linked to his PC at home.

One setback he has had in using his PDA to the fullest is that despite lots of promises, Sony has been slow to bring accessories to market. He's seen Louise in action typing in her notes at meetings they both have attended with a major employer, and he knows accessories like a folding keyboard will improve his Sony's productivity. One accessory he'd like to get in the future would convert his PDA into a digital camera. He said this would make it easier to put pictures on the Web with articles of interest to the members.

How Do I Get to Your Office?

Bill, a union officer from Oakland, is about to step out of a meeting near Second and Howard Streets in San Francisco. He pauses to think how he will get to the location of his next meeting on Pine Street, having never been there before. He draws his PDA from his pocket, an aqua-green Handspring Visor Deluxe, pulls up the map section, and taps in the address where he is and the address of his next appointment. A moment later directions appear in both text and on a map showing the best route to reach his destination. Then he puts his Handspring in his shirt pocket for easy reference later on during his walk to the Pine Street location. When he finishes there, he knows the same map feature will help him determine how to get back to BART, the subway that goes under San Francisco Bay, for his return to the union hall in Oakland. Bill told me he has already downloaded a map of London from the software's Web page for a trip he'll take later this year. He hopes that other nontourist destination cities to which he travels will soon become available.

There Are Those Who Save and Those Who Learn to Save

Backing up your data is the number one piece of advice I heard among union PDA users. A colleague, who since has passed away, had a first or second generation Casio that she had stuffed full of critical contact data, notes to herself, and a detailed calendar. Because no one ever talked about the need to save the data inside her little black box, she never considered the need to back it up. At some point disaster struck, and she couldn't get the Casio to operate, which forced her to pay serious money to get a technician to extract the data for her.

Today, most union users will employ the cradle linkup to their personal computer as a method to save their data. One told me he uses this as a way to synchronize his calendar and contacts between home and office PCs. Others use expanded memory cards that are slightly bigger then a postage stamp.

PDAs in the Future of Labor-to-Labor and
Labor-to-Neighbor Contacts

It is rumored that in the November 2000 election, a Central Valley central labor council (CLC) came up with the most innovative union uses for PDAs—data management for "get out the vote" precinct walking activities. The CLC took all of their union household voter information, computerized it, and broke it down into precincts and walking routes. Then they downloaded the info for every route into PDAs and distributed one to each pair of walkers.

After a brief training, each pair took a collection of literature to leave at households outlined in the PDA, which told them information like the name of the union member, union affiliation, and party that they were registered to vote under, the names of any other registered voters in the household, and a survey of their opinions on various labor-endorsed candidates.

Then when walkers returned, their data was uploaded via the sync cradle into the PC database. The potential for this is great as it reduces the time for data input immensely. It won't be PDAs that win an election for labor, but it may be a key tool to give us the edge in a close race.

What I did not find among the union activists I talked with was anyone using the IR, or infrared, features of their PDAs, nor was anyone using the wireless e-mail or phone options. No one was zapping their business cards around at meetings or sending private messages during bargaining sessions. It will be interesting to see if use of this picks up as more unions discover the flexibility of PDAs.

One of my technician friends from outside the union movement pointed out that unions just haven't discovered that it's easier to swap meeting notes with each other using IR. Nor have they discovered the cheaper combination of using a two-way pager enhanced with IR and their PDA instead of the wireless PDA option.

This technician suggested that zapping a text page message from the pager to the PDA makes the message easier to read and allows you a method to store it. She also noted that in addition to e-mail, she likes to read technical articles and e-books on the job during the down time of waiting for a machine to reboot or do a test routine.

For her, the biggest advantage of convertingto a full-feature PDA is the ability to eliminate the two pagers and cellular phone she is required to carry for her job. Now she carries one communications tool, instead of feeling like she is wearing Batman's tool belt.

---

6. Corporate Surveillance: Monitoring Your Monitor

Nancy Bupp

No consideration of labor's use of computer power would be complete without sounding at least one note of alarm, for as a timeless adage reminds us—every technology can be used for either good or bad reasons. Computer uses can be to the gain or loss of unionists, depending on the motives of those at the keyboard and monitor.

For example, the computer's speed, memory capacity, and maneuverability of data substantially aids the processing of fringe benefit increases won in hard bargaining. On the dark side, however, these same computer features make possible Orwellian forms of mean-spirited electronic surveillance—including e-mail and Internet monitoring—worse than any known before.

Employer monitoring of employees has taken an especially insidious form in that detection is now harder than ever. With millions of workers sitting in front of computer screens, and 70 percent of Net surfing done at work, the hazard of employer harassment is considerable (Prasso 2001). One authoritative survey in Business Week *found that from June 2000 to 2001, terminations for so-called "Net abuse" were up 10 percent, and "monitoring by employers is on the rise" (Prasso 2001).*

Union activists must understand that surveillance "may be challengeable under the NLRA as interference with concerted activity. It may also run afoul of federal and state laws prohibiting unconsented electronic interceptions" (Schwartz 2001).

All the more reason to heed the no-nonsense call for vigilance, outrage, and counterattack in the essay below. Answers are offered to such questions as:

• *Do federal laws currently protect workers from an invasion of their Internet privacy?*

- *What is the danger posed by employer offers of home computers?*
- *How varied are "high tech" tools for spying on employees?*
- *Does the National Labor Relations Board (NLRB) provide any protection against video surveillance?*
- *Above all, what is the soundest possible stance of union activists confronting the computer's part in employer malevolence?*

References

Prasso, Sheridan. "Workers, Surf at Your own Risk." Business Week, *June 11, 2001,* p. 14.
Schwartz, Robert M. "Company E-Mail Rules: Are They Illegal?" Labor Notes, *June 2001, p. 2.*

Computer technology is a great tool for unionists to use to further their causes, but we must also be aware of how computer technology is used by corporations to further *their* causes. Computers and computerized machinery are set up to regurgitate every single input and output. If the right command is given, the computer will spill its guts. Managers are quickly learning how easy it is to use these commands to keep track of the activities of employees.

Since 1998, surveys done by the American Management Association show a drastic increase in the number of companies that use technology to monitor and spy on employees. Nearly three-quarters of major U.S. companies record and review employee communications and activities on the job, including their phone calls, e-mail, Internet connections, and computer files.

New generations of software make it much easier to track every employee's activity. Some of the surveillance techniques currently marketed and available to companies include keystroke loggers (that monitor *every* keystroke and mouse click), software that takes snapshots of the computer screen, and software that keeps track of everything viewed or accessed on the Internet.

Even if the company has no written policy on personal use of the computer, it still has the legal right to discipline the workers. The basic rule is this: What a worker does on company time on company equipment is the company's business. Workers that use the computer for their own personal use can be disciplined and fired for "stealing" time from the company. Standing around the water cooler too long is child's play compared to the company monitoring exactly how fast we type and how much idle time there is between keystrokes.

Workers tend to think, in many cases, that there are privacy laws that will protect them at work, especially when it relates to e-mail. There are, however, no federal laws in place to protect employees from the employer's reading their e-mail or accessing their computer files. Anything that is on a company's computer is available for managers and bosses to read. E-mail is easily accessible to an employer, even if an employee just uses the computer at work to check personal e-mail through Web-based systems such as a Hotmail or Yahoo.

Some companies are buying their employees computers for use at their homes and providing low-cost Internet access. It is a great perk, but be aware that the company *could* monitor the use of that computer—including details of Internet usage together with e-mail.

Technology has made it easier for companies to have tighter security systems and new timekeeping systems in place. Scanning your badge to allow access into and out of buildings allows managers to track more closely the whereabouts of the employees. Most of this kind of technology is dubbed as being "for the workers' safety and security," but when does security end and spying begin? For example, cameras in the parking lot are almost always framed as trying to protect employees' cars from break-ins and vandalism. Workers usually know if there are cameras in the parking lots, but do they know about cameras hidden in the workplace? Top-quality, wireless, pinhole video cameras are currently on the market and are relatively inexpensive. These cameras, requiring only a 1/16th–inch viewing hole, can be easily hidden in everyday objects such clocks, radios, smoke detectors, exit signs, and other items that are functioning in their regular capacity.

Unionized workers have some protection from video surveillance. The NLRB has held that installation and use of such surveillance is a mandatory subject of bargaining. The cameras are so small and undetectable, though, that employers could install them and spy on employees without their ever knowing about it.

We, as unionists, must first be alert and aware that the technology exists and can be used in ways that make it very easy for employers to spy on and monitor workers. We must read, research, and educate ourselves and our brothers and sisters about computer technology and how it may be used against us. We must stay abreast of new technologies and understand the implications new technologies can have for the workforce.

Sometimes the implications are obvious, and sometimes they are not so obvious. The more we study and think about the long-range and short-range implications, the more we will be able to protect ourselves. Simply put—our goal is to take advantage of the benefits of new technologies and work around the disadvantages.

Companies whose employees do not have the advantage of a collective bargaining agreement with a grievance and arbitration procedure may very well be successful in monitoring employees and disciplining or firing them. Most unionized employees can only be fired for "just cause" and have better protections in place than does the nonunion workforce. Union representation is a major advantage to the worker subject to surveillance: Unionized workers are more likely to be able to negotiate contract language to help keep surveillance and monitoring at bay.

Our political system has evolved in a way that favors employers over employees. We must get involved in politics and try to change the slant. Computer technology has developed virtually at the speed of light, and laws have not kept pace with changes fashioned by such technology. We need to lobby for laws that keep workplaces from turning into Orwellian nightmares.

Resources

Surveillance Software

www.computermonitoring.com/
www.littlebrother.com/
www.snapshotspy.com/index.html
www.spectorsoft.com/
www.winwhatwhere.com/

Cameras

http://amanet.org (American Management Association)
www.hiddencamera.com/
www.nlrb.gov/slip323.html (National Labor Relations Board, 1997, Decisions and Orders of the NLRB 323, Slip Opinion, case no. 9–CA-32158)
www.pimall.com/nais/vid-w.html

---

7. What Unions Can Learn from Nonprofits About Using the Internet

Mark Friedman

No introduction to labor's many choices where computer power is concerned would be complete without attention being paid to organizations other than unions that are engaged in a similar exercise, especially those whose values are akin to labor's.

The essay below highlights four "gifts" in the way of field-proven guidelines from the world of nonprofit organizations. While this is a world labor knows somewhat from community service projects, it is not one commonly looked to by union activists for tips and tricks in the use of computers. Each "gift" is dealt with in sufficient detail to make likely rapid and substantial payoff for adoption. Taken along with the many URLs at the essay's close, this unusual exercise in borrowed insights offers much to the careful reader.

Use by blue-collar workers of the Internet increased 52 percent during the period 2000 to 2001. This whopping growth rate provides vast new opportunities for union organizing and constituency building (*Business Week* 2001).

Over the last few years, nonprofit organizations and their allies have found many innovative ways to make better use of computer technology. They have had to overcome a lack of funds to pay for technology, an inability to find the necessary technical help, and their own slow-moving organizational cultures. What nonprofits have learned can readily be transferred to the union environment.

Four Keys to More Successful Use of Technology

Significant elements in the successful implementation of computer technology include:

1. *Transform the way you do business:* Don't simply bring old methods to a new medium.
2. *Change the organizational digital divide:* Build up-to-date organizational computer capacities.
3. *Involve others through technology planning*: Draw from different parts of the organization.
4. *Future changes:* Recognize this will continue for the foreseeable future.

Transform the Way You Do Business

ONE/Northwest is a technology assistance center supporting environmental groups operating in the Pacific Northwest. They have published an excellent activist toolkit on their Web site at www.onenw.org. ONE/Northwest specifically suggests an online networking strategy consisting of four key elements:

Gather e-mail addresses: Ask all your current contacts for addresses; add an e-mail field to your database; publicize your organization's e-mail address widely on all your business cards, brochures, fact sheets, newsletters, and any other publications.

Establish broadcast e-mail lists (list servers) for general communication with your membership about your issues and activities. They recommend sending a brief e-mail newsletter on a monthly basis as a general update about your activities. This should be brief and consistent. Get your members used to receiving good e-mail from you on a regular basis. Send an announcement to your membership and ask them to subscribe to your online newsletter.

Some key elements to include in your e-mail newsletter are: (1) Use the subject line to catch your audiences' attention; (2) Make your key points or call to action very clear and prominent; (3) Use a table of contents at the beginning to help the reader know what follows and where, so they can skip to a desired topic and don't have to read the entire newsletter; (4) Put a message at the end of the newsletter informing the reader how to subscribe and unsubscribe; (5) Solicit feedback on the usefulness of the newsletter. You can send out surveys to provide you with real-time feedback or simply ask selected subscribers what they find more helpful and in what ways they are using it.

Establish a list for key activists who will most often respond to action alerts and other requests to attend meetings, to send letters/faxes, and to make phone calls when asked to do so.

Establish a discussion e-mail list for staff, board, and key volunteers to facilitate communication.

Create a Web site that initially focuses on providing information to your existing membership and key activists. Build a strong base for online activism among the people most interested in your work and expand it to the general public as your expertise increases.

Another example of an effective use of a discussion list server is Speaking For Ourselves, a disability rights organization. The leaders used a list server very effectively while planning a 1,000-person conference for eleven states. Each state had a planner, whom they had never met. They first held a telephone conference call to bring everyone up to speed on the details and then put everyone on the planning list server so that they could talk to each other as the conference developed. By the time of the conference, more than eighty people had joined the list server, receiving regular updates, requests for more information, and reminders on a weekly basis.

Most helpful, the state planners later reported, was hearing the different approaches states were taking on designing their presentations, including people with disabilities on their panels, and as a general reminder to get their tasks done. The planning list server enabled significantly increased collaboration between groups separated by geography and time.

The elements that led to the success of the list server were: (1) Being focused on one task (the list server was used only for conference planning); (2) Being timely and time-limited (it was closed down after the conference ended); and (3) Generating short and actionable messages.

There are currently three companies that provide free list servers being used by the majority of Internet activists. These are Topica (www.topica.com), YahooGroups (http://groups.yahoo.com), and Listbot (www.listbot.com).

And finally, a word about Web sites. You need both items of interest to draw people to the site and action items to motivate your membership and supporters to take action and support the organization. Items of interest can include pictures of people involved in activities, updates from events, birthday announcements, and training available to people. Action items help people see that they can make a difference, and include legislative issues, rallies, marches, writing letters, and educational content.

An interesting concept that unions could easily copy is Lutherans Online. They have created a way for all of their members and member organizations to create free Web sites that can include greeting cards, recipe exchanges, genealogy, classified ads, chat rooms, message boards, and free e-mail. They also provide a reduced fee Internet service to encourage their members to get online (see www.lutheransonline.com).

You can learn a lot about how to present items of interest from the major Web portals. Yahoo.com has excelled with weather, stock quotes, and individualized news clippings. Amazon.com knows who you are when you return to their Web site and gives you suggestions for books you might like based on your past purchases. You would have difficulty providing this level of individualization, but you can do the equivalent with information on companies you work for, news from the chapters, newspapers, and events occurring.

Colleges have done some of the best work in this area in setting up specialized areas on their Web sites for their alumni. They include job postings, searchable address directories for locating former classmates, alumni news, and reunion information. An excellent example of these possibilities is provided by the Sandglass Systems company (www.sandglasssystmes.com/port folio.html), which offers these services directly to colleges and universities.

Many nonprofits have found an upcoming events calendar to be one of their most interesting items on their Web site. There are many free and low cost Web-based calendars that integrate and can be provided easily on your local site. One of our favorites is provided by the nonprofit Policy Initiatives Group (www.calendars.net). Chat rooms and message/bulletin boards can be added to your site through free or low-cost Web-based servers that integrate seamlessly into your site. Examples of these free or inexpensive services are Infopop (www.infopop.com) and Multicity (www.multicity.com).

Change the Organizational Digital Divide

The wide difference in the availability and use of information technology (IT) between the world of business and nonprofits has been named the "organizational digital divide." Businesses have invested 20–40 percent of their revenues into IT. Most nonprofits, however, still see technology as an add-on and are constantly in a catch-up mode.

In response to this problem, the nonprofit world has developed "circuit riders" as a new model of providing training and strategic planning assistance. Circuit riders are ordinary people with extraordinary computer technical skill and organizational skills who work with nonprofit organizations, helping them find ways to use computer technology in their workplace.

Circuit riders are evolving into a movement of people evangelizing and promoting the benefits of technology and how it can be utilized to help small, grass-roots community organizations. Most small nonprofits don't have the funds, are unwilling, or lack the knowledge to use, purchase, and acquire technology. Circuit riders work with their existing funded projects to help them make better use of technology.

The circuit rider model is an effective way of overcoming the hesitancy of nonprofits to utilize technology. They help an organization think about its mission, where and how technology can support and promote the group's mission, and then determine what types of technology will be useful in fulfilling the mission and goals. The circuit rider can also help with equipment set up—that is, creating a local office network, getting people hooked up to the Internet and e-mail, and providing training assistance.

Unions could copy this model and set up national circuit rider teams who would work with locals in different sectors and geographical settings. Alternatively, unions could contract with existing circuit riders technical assistance efforts that have been established around the country.

Some excellent e-mail newsletters on circuit riders and technical assistance can be found at:

1. ONE/Northwest's informative monthly e-mail newsletter covering nonprofit technology assistance to conservation activists and organizations in the Pacific Northwest. You can sign up for this at their Web site (www.onenw.org).
2. By the Cup is an excellent e-mail newsletter about nonprofit technology assistance (www.techsoup.org).

3. DOT ORG is a new e-mail newsletter with practical how-to tips, tools, techniques, and case studies to help nonprofits make effective use of the Internet. It is published by two long-term Internet non-profit consultants, Michael Stein and Marc Osten. Look at back issues at www.summitcollaborative.com/dot_org.html, or to subscribe, send a blank e-mail to dotorg-subscribe@topica.com.

Involve Others through Technology Planning

Planning for adoption of new communications technologies has been found by nonprofits to be one of the most important and critical components in successful technology projects. Nonprofits have come to see that while adequate hardware and software are in short supply, far more serious and difficult to overcome is the shortage of planning for wise implementation of technology and of trained staff to use the new tools. A technology planning process helps people understand the potential applications of information and communications technology. This in turn helps nonprofits develop strategies to match appropriate technology with their organization's goals and mission. The planning process helps to bring everybody on board and to proceed while working from the same game book and set of rules.

A technology plan can be developed in a one- to two-day planning process with as many diverse parties as possible. The plan helps to build people's commitment to the future. It is often stated by futurists that the best way to cope with the future is to make it yourself. A technology plan will help bring buy-in from the diverse parties of the organization, thereby greatly increasing the chances of success. It lets everyone have an opportunity for input and for knowing where the organization is heading in the future.

Future Changes

Unions need to stay apprised of what's coming down the pike. One of the most revolutionary products will be Internet video e-mail. By the time you read this chapter, you should be able to send short video e-mail inexpensively and frequently to your entire membership. Logitech (www.logitech.com) just released an Internet video camera that will sell for around $150. It will allow you to send short five-minute videos to anyone with a Pentium computer. This could provide a very compelling method of connecting more frequently and more richly with the membership.

For example, a union president could send out a monthly video e-mail with a message about chapter activities or updates on contract negotiations. Video e-mails could also be used for training, advocacy, and issue mobilization.

Activists and organizers can use the Web to send out regular surveys to discover what the membership thinks about important issues. Then they can use the Web to organize the membership toward political action. An excellent example of this is the Justice for Janitors Web site at www.justicefor janitors.org.

Unions can help their organizers by giving them modern technology tools. The latest Palm Pilot devices (PDAs) allow activists and organizers to have the entire membership databases in their palms with weekly or monthly updates done whenever they return to the office.

Summary

In closing, please note that workers for social justice in nonprofits and unions alike have to address positive and negative aspects of computer technology. We need to find ways to mitigate and reduce related limitations: People and groups are still being left out of the computer revolution. There is a loss of privacy. There are increased work hours. And there is the challenge of a disappearance of personal time and space. We can only learn how to deal with these issues if we are actively engaged in using the technologies ourselves.

I am not just speaking to you directly, readers of this handbook, when I say this. You would not be reading my essay if you didn't believe in the potential of, and were alert to the problems posed by computer technology. I am trying to provide you with compelling arguments to convince others. Without them, we won't be able to do the job that nonprofits and labor must do if working men and women are to live the high-quality lives they dream of.

Reference

Business Week, May 14, 2001, Data: Neilson/Net ratings survey.

Resources

Technical Assistance

CompuMentor—Free software distribution to nonprofits and technical assistance and training to organizations in California: www.compumentor.org

Ebase—Database program development project by Technology Project to support environmental groups' advocacy efforts: www.ebase.org

Helping.org—New project of the Benton and AOL foundations to support nonprofits' technology needs. Allows online giving to any IRS registered nonprofit: www.helping.org

National Technology Enterprise Network (N-Ten)—A national organization devoted to the promotion of nonprofit technology usage. List server: www.nten.org

N-power—Major nonprofit technical assistance organization recently funded by Microsoft to expand its West Coast services to sites across the country: www.npower.org

OMB Watch: Nonprofits' Policy and Technology Project—Office of Management and Budget policy think tank promoting public citizenship. Excellent list server: www.ombwatch.org/npt

Organizer's collaborative—New organization to promote technology uses for community organizing. List server: www.organizenow.net

Progressive Technology Project—New organization providing funding for progressive technology needs and technical assistance: www.progressivetech.org

Project Linc—Has excellent toolkit with tutorial for first-time Internet access: www.lincproject.org

Technology Foundation—Working to revolutionize the way nonprofits achieve their mission through the use of technology: www.techfoundation.org

Technology Project—National promoter of circuit riders. Also works to promote Web-based public policy advocacy through e-mediacy: www.techrocks.org

Techsoup—New organization with newsletter and list server to support technology for nonprofits: www.techsoup.org

United Way's Gifts-in-Kind—Distributes free software to nonprofit organizations: www.giftsinkind.org

Digital Divide

Community Technology Centers Network: www.ctcnet.org

Digital Divide Network—Joint governmental, nonprofit, and foundation project to address digital divide issue. List server operated by the Benton Foundation: www.digitaldividenetwork.org

PowerUp—Nonprofit helping to overcome the digital divide for youth: www.powerup.org

Other Resources

Bobby—Web based disability check for accessibility for people with disabilities: www.bobby.org

Civic.com—A magazine devoted to governmental use of the Internet for citizen services. Has excellent examples of serving citizens in innovative and new ways: www.civic.com

GuideStar—Can accept donations on behalf of any nonprofit that files a 990 federal tax return: www.guidestar.org

Idealist—Web-based signing up of volunteers for nonprofit organizations: www.idealist.org

Nonprofit and technology publication: www.pj.org/tech/tech.htm

Nonprofit software index: www.npinfotech.org

One Economy—A national nonprofit organization whose mission is to maximize the potential of technology to help low-income people improve their standard of living and build assets: www.one-economy.com

Project Alchemy—A partnership among social justice activists, technology volunteers, innovative foundations, and the community-based groups fighting for change in communities across the Pacific Northwest: www. projectalchemy.org

Project Connect—Empowering nonprofits through technology and connectivity: www.infolineinc.org/connect.htm

---

8. Five Lessons from Union Computer Use in Sweden

Gunnar Zetterström

No attention to possible upgrades in labor's use of computer power would be complete without recognition of the global character of the matter. Having had the privilege recently of studying union uses of computers first hand in Britain, Canada, Israel, Norway, and Sweden, I am very impressed with the efforts being made to make the most of this opportunity.

The essay below is a fine example, sharing as it does transferable lessons from the ongoing computer projects of a Swedish union of workers in the finance industry. Among the many questions tackled are these:

- *Dare a union rely on the computer system of management?*
- *Can the costs of a Web site pose a hazard?*
- *What use can labor make of a popular portal?*
- *How strategic is a well-crafted, computerized membership directory?*
- *How vital is interactivity?*
- *And, above all, what could possibly be more important to union members than finding other union people making good use of union computers?*

My union, the Financial Sector Union of Sweden (FSU-S), is a white-collar union with about 34,000 members out of approximately 60,000. Some 2,500 members are computer professionals, while the rest use computers daily (PCs, handheld computers, and/or mainframes).

Now, as for advice from the FSU-U scene, I have five matters to briefly discuss. First, you should know that in my country, where about 83 percent of all employees are members of a trade union, company computer equipment can be used for union activities. Actually, it is more likely that union activities are handled through these computers than through home computers.

This is due to several reasons: (1) Most union activities are related to the workplace; (2) Most Swedish companies allow unions to use company facilities for union work. In fact, if I use my own company as an example, I am webmaster for both the concern's union's branch home page and also the home page for the IT department, and I use working time to administer both; (3) Much union work has to be carried out during office hours to be efficient. Besides, the law states that you are allowed to do this work at the office during working hours.

Here lies some good advice: Create the possibilities (negotiate!) to use the company facilities for union work. This might be a difficult task, but is also a crucial one.

A second bit of advice concerns setting priorities. All unions in Sweden have costly and well-developed Web sites. Many such sites are too costly, which is to say, they give too little back. This is something that has to be considered before Web sites grow to be *the* cost problem of unions.

Third, unions have limited monetary resources, and these need to be used for pressing problems, one of which is recruiting. This is an enormous field that covers most aspects of union work—information, policy building, marketing, networking, and so forth. But the potential of Web sites to help here has not been drawn on to the fullest extent possible. No members, no money, no resources, no union. It's quite simple.

One marketing strategy we use is to rent "space" at one of Sweden's most visited portals. Each visitor was checked to see from which company he or she was coming. If the visitor was from one of the financial institutions our union organizes, a special window appeared with a personal questionnaire intended to inform about uses the person could be making of our union. It ended with a membership application that could be sent directly to us. We got a number of members this way, all young people, of course.

As for a fourth bit of advice, to me a properly managed, computerized, and integrated member directory is *the* essence of union work. We often talk about the difficulties with information: How should we be able to recruit new members if we do not tell them what they miss if they are outside the union? And at the same time, we must take care of our members and give them value for their monthly dues. They must have valuable union information that is not accessible for people outside the union.

We are currently building this system at the FSU-S. We have integrated the member directory into all our Web systems in such a way that we can give everybody (board members, "ordinary" members, and nonmembers) exactly the information that is meant for each. We have all the discriminating data about each member available to create an information profile that gives correct information.

We are also building a future information pathway by building a list of the e-mail addresses of all members, whether it is a work e-mail address or for home e-mail. This will result in two advantages: First, we will be able to selectively send notification of new things on our Web pages or other messages by e-mail very fast. We could activate the whole organization in practically no time at all.

Second, when this e-mail-address bank contains a satisfactory number of addresses (which it does already), it will mean dramatically reduced costs for distributing information. One of our biggest expenses is postage to reach our 34,000 members. Today we are already distributing a number of paper publications as PDF files over e-mail. For members for whom we have no e-mail address, we will have a postal address label printed automatically to send an ordinary paper publication by snail mail. But still, this means greatly reduced costs.

Finally, a fifth bit of advice concerns interactivity, I think many are talking about this as "electronic communities." We want more people to participate more often. So the FSU-S is currently working with a completely new Web strategy. We are using a tool capable of creating the environments that we need to get an attractive and interactive Web site. We plan to create discussion groups for members only (using the member directory to check membership and a sign-on to secure this). We will use online surveys to get member opinions.

In closing, please remember—union work is working with people. Do not turn your union into some distant and unreachable tower, where the only contact inward is e-mail, and the only contact outward is a home page. People with questions and concerns want to find other people. When they contact their union, they want to first find people with compassion, understanding, good advice, and assistance . . . and only next, people making good use of computers.

II. How to Get Started

Even the highest towers begin from the ground.
—Chinese proverb

Neither hardware nor even software is the major challenge in getting started on the road to cyberunionism: As elsewhere in human affairs, "thoughtware" is *the* frontier. Success hinges far more on attitude and information than on things and/or computer code. Indeed, had you come online in the mid-1990s when the Internet first captured attention, you could today replace your PC of that era with one ten times as powerful and 50 percent less expensive (Edwards 2001). Much the same is true where software is concerned. Accordingly, attention belongs instead to thoughtware.

Thanks to the chapters in this section, each one rich in ideas and start-up advice, you are likely to find establishing computer options far easier than you fear. The results are also likely to prove more rewarding than you dare hope. Between here and there, however, I want to briefly share some four notions of my own, four pieces of thoughtware about getting off to the best possible footing—notions about envisioning, restraining, listening, and copying.

Guideline 1: Try Backcasting in a De Novo Way

Imagine your union or local out three or even five years from now. What would you want it to look like, at its very best? Accordingly, what decisions vis-à-vis the use of computer power do you suspect would have to be made to get it there?

Write these questions down and discuss them with key decision makers, other activists, and labor digerati types. For as consultant Seth Gordon explains, "That's what you should spend your time on. Getting these decisions right is far more important than answering your 103rd e-mail message" (Gordon 2001). Helpful here is a deliberate mental suspension of the constraints that otherwise inhibit imaginative thinking: For the moment forget about the customary shortage of funds, time, resources, and political will. Instead, imagine that they are finally ample in supply and assured over time. What then would your union or local resemble?

Free now to imagine from the beginning a finer organization out there over the horizon, you may glimpse some reforms bearing on computer use you would have immediately dismissed when in the mind frame of harsh current reality. You can later modify your "eureka" reform notions to accommodate present-day constraints, but as these empowering notions are likely to "fill the sails," you have come out ahead.

Guideline 2: Don't Oversell Computer Rewards

Resist the temptation, especially when goaded by cynics, to exaggerate what computer uses can help labor accomplish. Better to understate, and have dues-payers surprised and pleased, than overstate, and have many shrug and devalue a genuine gain.

Guideline 3: Listen to Users

Years ago, at the outset, when a very young Internet in the mid-1990s had "wannabe" users eager for advice, many consultants dictated rules and formats. At best they imitated organizations they thought were further along. At worst, they served smooth-talking self-serving vendors who had promised the moon, the stars, and just about everything else if only the decision maker would adopt their product line—regardless of issues of compatibility. This sort of overreliance on top-down plans actually masked a certain lack of courage, too strong a preference for "expert" devising, and a lack of faith in the good judgment of rank-and-file users.

The best of the consultants have long since learned to respond, rather than dictate. They now highlight field-proven possibilities, carefully keeping options open among the choices. They do so without blowing a trumpet or employing promotional Technicolor hype. They do so only after weighing feedback from knowledgeable assessors pledged to "tell the whole truth, and nothing but the truth."

The emphasis is on getting lessons from early adopters, rather than thinking for them, or worse yet, ordering them about. Computer hardware and software is changed on a 24/7 basis as recommended by user feedback. Guidance is had from a time-honored principle borrowed from engineering:

Always follow the path of least resistance. That is, always be guided by actual users.

Guideline 4: Emulate, but with a Difference

Far too many unions and locals pay far too high a price for their childish refusal to be second: "If it was not invented here, we have no interest." Pique of this costly sort has no place in matters as serious as starting and upgrading computer uses.

Far wiser is a policy of endlessly scanning the field for good ideas you can adopt and adapt—scanning the computer programs and processes of unions and locals best known to you, the relevant literature (such as the invaluable AFL-CIO magazine, *America@work*), and relevant Web sites (see those cited at the close of this volume). As well, you can profitably scan the voluminous business literature, especially rich sources of programmatic ideas like *Business 2.0*, *FAST COMPANY*, and *Wired*.

Naturally, it is vital to try and get behind the scene, beneath the hype, and beyond the "smoke and mirrors" of innovation sponsors. We have to seek the unvarnished truth, especially about masked, veiled, or otherwise hard-to-uncover weaknesses—remembering that we just might be able to remedy some of them.

Above all, custom-tailor whatever it is you are drawn to adapt. You cannot and should not attempt to clone another computer-based program as it is intimately involved with the culture of its own union or local, and that is not your culture. Focus instead on grasping the essence of the effort, its center of gravity. To paraphrase a thought of the artist Georgia O'Keefe ("It is only by selection, by elimination, by emphasis, that we get at the real meaning of things"*), do not merely reproduce, as that assures less merit than in the original.

Computer programs borrowed and then employed lock, stock, and barrel are commonly a mistake, for as a highly regarded corporate consultant advises, "Of the many things that haven't changed in the new economy, here's one more: Sameness still sucks." (Hamel 2001) Put an information age spin on a time-honored principle from systems analysis: Brilliant adaptation can reward as fully as can brilliant innovation.

To help you build brass-tack specifics on the foundation of these four general guidelines, five essays follow that underline how much is usefully known about getting going: The first sets out crisp rules for assessing any

---

*Taken in June 2001 from a wall decoration at the museum in Santa Fe, New Mexico, devoted to Georgia O'Keefe's work.

technology. The second spotlights problems union users have had, problems foreknowledge may help you avoid. The third specifies computer-taming contract language union activists can champion. The fourth defines key jargon terms. And the fifth offers tips and tricks for avoiding getting taken on the information highway. Taken all in all, the essays offer a sound boost to rewarding computer uses—and point the way to more advanced progress yet.

References

Edwards, Will. "Computer Prices Decline as Few See Reasons to Upgrade." *Philadelphia Inquirer*, May 24, 2001, p. F-5.
Gordon, Seth. "There is No Correlation at All Between Success and Hours Worked." *FAST COMPANY*, June 2001, p. 81.
Hamel, Gary. "Edison's Curse." *Fortune*, March 5, 2001, p. 178.

---

9. Nine Rules for Good Technology

Stephen Downes

Let's start with some good news, always a welcome opening. If the essay below proves as sound in forecasting as it is sage in its counsel, we have much to look forward to. Nine characteristics of a good technology are briefly discussed, the better to help guide our choices among the contradictory claims of competitive vendors. We leave the review armed with pragmatic standards for choosing among alternative hardware, software, service contracts, and similar components of our computer infrastructure—standards with decades of staying power.

Better still, we also take away a glimmer of a bright possibility—the possibility that we are moving toward simpler, reliable, and friendlier tools. If we earnestly employ the guidelines set out below, we hasten the day.

As technologies mature, they tend to become easier to use. Consider the elevator, for example. Once so finicky it needed operators to take riders from floor to floor, today's elevator functions flawlessly with little intervention on the part of users.

I believe that we currently are in a transition phase; we are moving away from complicated technologies toward simpler innovations.

What distinguishes a good technology from a bad technology? The following nine characteristics define the former. Think of them as a checklist; a technology that has more of these features is, in general, better than a technology that has fewer of them.

Good Technology Is Always Available

This distinction is what makes buses, in spite of all of their advantages, bad technology. People cannot count on catching the bus at absolutely any time of day; thus most people prefer cars. Imagine what life would be like if we had to schedule our use of the elevator. Or to make reservations to use the telephone. Good technology does not require scheduling, relocation, or set-up.

The availability requirement raises cost considerations. Equipment that costs less is more likely to be available. But cost is not the sole or even primary determinant. If a technology meets the other criteria described below, it will be made widely available despite the cost. Think of ATMs, electrical lights, and highways.

Good Technology Is Always On

Or can be turned on with a one-stroke command or, better yet, starts automatically when the need for it arises. One thing that makes the telephone useful is that we do not need to boot up the operating system before we make a call.

Devices with low-energy consumption, however, can always be on. Think of watches, telephones, and elevators.

Good Technology Is Always Connected

Good technology can send information when and where it is needed without human intervention. Again, telephones are useful because no procedure is required to connect to the telephone system.

As recently as last month, I spent fifteen minutes in a room with a dozen or so highly paid professionals waiting for an Interactive Television (ITV) system to be connected to a remote location. I have spent much time listening to my modem dial up a local provider (and luxuriate today in the convenience of an always-on digital subscriber line connection).

Good Technology Is Standardized

One telephone connects to any other telephone in the world. Standardization promotes interoperability. Interoperability means that you have choices, that you are not locked into one supplier or vendor. It means that you can adapt easily to improved versions of the same technology.

A video that is designed to be played only on a specific computer platform and e-mail that may be read only via a specific Internet service provider are examples of bad technology. Video should be viewable on all platforms and e-mail should be accessible through any Internet service provider.

Good Technology Is Simple

Simplicity is a slippery concept, but the best technologies can be learned by looking at the input device, not by studying a manual.

Here's how I distinguish between good computer programs and bad computer programs: I try to install and run the program without the use of any manual. Installation is much easier today, thanks to a good computer program called "Setup."

Running the program is a different matter. When I have to stop and think (and read very small print) about how to get rid of a paperclip icon so that I can type a letter, I know I am dealing with bad technology. Good technology, by contrast, is intuitive. Simple. To make a phone call, I dial the number. Easy.

Simplicity goes hand-in-hand with range of function. Features that you never use get in the way, and they make the product complicated and cumbersome. Look for technology that does exactly what you want: no more, no less.

Good Technology Does Not Require Parts

The bottom line is this: Do you have to purchase something on a regular basis in order to use your technology? Do you have to replace something that becomes worn out or depleted or that can be lost or stolen? The fewer times you have to purchase or replace, the better your technology; the best technology requires no ongoing purchases or replacements at all.

If parts are absolutely necessary, they should be widely available, standardized, and simple to install. DVD players, for example, will not qualify as good technologies until DVDs become as widely available as videotapes.

Good Technology Is Personalized

Some of the simplest technologies succeed because they are personalized. One of the things that makes a telephone useful is that you have your own telephone number. In a similar manner, e-mail is useful because you have your own e-mail address.

Bad technology forces you to fit its requirements. I live in Canada, so I purchased my copy of Microsoft Word there, but the default dictionary was for American English. I could install a British dictionary, but Canadian English is distinct from both British and American English. Like many users, I am forced to add each distinctly Canadian word to a custom dictionary. This is bad technology. Why can't I simply tell Word that I am Canadian (or an architect, or a member of some other specialized group) and have it retrieve the appropriate spellings for me?

Good Technology Is Modular

By "modular" I mean composed of distinct entities, each of which can work independently of the others and may be arranged or rearranged into a desired configuration with a minimum of fuss and effort. To a degree this requirement is a combination of the requirements that good technology be standardized and personalized, but modularity takes technology a step beyond either of those features.

Today's universal serial bus (USB) represents good technology because it allows computer systems to be assembled like the stereos of old.

Good Technology Does What You Want It to Do

And it doesn't do something else. "Doing what you want it to do" means the same thing as "idiot proof." Good technology minimizes the potential for operator error and thus the possibility of unexpected consequences. Good technology is also robust—less prone to breakdowns and malfunctions—and reliable. Software that crashes instead of running is obviously bad technology.

Telephone systems that connect you to India instead of Indiana are not useful.

Conclusion

It is important to remember that no technology is perfect. No technology will satisfy all nine rules. However, some technologies will satisfy more rules than others, and some technologies will even break a rule or two and still be very good technologies (if only because no better alternative is available).

That said, purchasers should insist on—and vendors should be pressed for—good technology as defined above. We spend too much time and money on new technology to be satisfied with anything less.

10. Getting On and Getting Off: Roadblocks on the Information Superhighway

Edward Hertenstein

The sooner we learn what we are up against, the stronger we are, for we gain more time to prepare a winning response. Thanks to the rare report below of current survey research, we have an early alert, a wake-up call concerning the problems unionists are encountering in the effort to become efficient and effective users of computers.

Among the other questions answered are these: What are the rankings of the most common problems in this matter? Does the type of computer service provider make a difference? How valuable is computer training? Are there differences in skills by gender? And if so, so what? Taken together, answers here can guide the focus of computer training courses a union or local might soon offer, along with the selection of enrollees.

Above all, the essay underlines the high payoff possible from the sort of survey research unionists themselves might tackle–alone, or preferably in close collaboration with supportive academics. Where the actual experience of union users is concerned, we cannot learn more from field research soon enough—and act on it ably enough.

I have been involved in teaching union members about the Internet for several years. More than 200 unionists from a variety of international unions have passed through my classes over the past six years. While most people expressed excitement about using the Internet for union purposes, a common theme that the technology is not simple to use has resonated among all the classes.

If your car stopped running once a week, froze up in the middle of traffic, and the engine needed fixing every three to four months, you would not stand for it. However, we accept that kind of performance from our computers and the Internet. CONTROL-ALT-DELETE is one of the most important keystrokes to learn. Fatal Error has become a part of the vernacular. I became interested in just how pervasive problems are, and how they affect the use of the Internet by union members.

The Survey

As a part of a survey examining the information needs and sources of union leaders in Illinois, I gave union leaders a detailed questionnaire. The first part focused on the use of the Internet. The survey asked whether respondents used the Internet, and if so, whether the access was at work, home, the public library, or the union office. It also addressed the type of Internet provider used, such as local service provider, national service provider, union network, or cable company. Additionally, the union leaders were asked how satisfied they were with the Internet; they were then asked to indicate which of thirteen different problems they may have encountered.

The problems listed were: Too much information; information too theoretical; information not useful; information not in order of relevance; information out of date; information source hard to use; I would have to pay to get the information I needed; I did not find all the information I needed; too costly; connection too difficult; hardware problems; software problems; and hard to get computer time. The union leaders were also asked to list any other problems they may have had which were not listed. An opportunity was given for individuals to list other forms and locations of access to the Internet.

The next section asked the respondents to give information about themselves and their local unions. The questions in this section included those asking what type of union official the respondent was, what sector of the economy the union represents, the size of the local and bargaining unit, and the size of the city/town where the bargaining unit is located. The final section inquired about characteristics of the individual respondent. Included in this section were gender, size of residence city/town, and amount of formal education.

The Responses

The group surveyed included union leaders throughout Illinois. The names were drawn from a list of those who filed annual union financial reports with the Department of Labor. These were either LM-2 or LM-3 reports Depending on the size of the union organization involved. Since only private-sector unions are required to file those reports, additional names were collected from directories of public-sector unions, including American Federation of State, County, and Municipal Employees (AFSCME), American Federation of Teachers (AFT), National Education Association (NEA), and Fraternal Order of Police (FOP).

The respondents were union leaders from throughout the state. The sample of 18 percent of the original mailing list was 87 percent male. Over 97 percent of the 239 respondents had at least a high school education, including 69 percent who had at least some college education. They served in a number of different positions in their unions, including elected officer (94 percent), staff representative/business agent (44 percent), shop steward (25 percent), community relations representative (13 percent), organizer, (35 percent), apprenticeship/training officer (13 percent), and political action officer (26 percent). Many reported serving in more than one capacity, so the figures add up to more than 100 percent. The average number of members in each local was 239. Bargaining units were only slightly smaller at 234.

Bureau of Labor Statistics (BLS) figures report the percentage of organized workers in each industry sector as: government, 49 percent; manufacturing, 21 percent; construction, 9 percent; transportation, 13 percent; trade, 9 percent; and agriculture, less than 1 percent. The leaders returning the survey represented workers in different sectors as follows: government, 52 percent; manufacturing, 19 percent; construction, 7 percent; transportation, 7 percent; trade, 1 percent; and agriculture, less than 1 percent. Another 12 percent of respondents listed the industry sector as "other."

Survey Results

Out of those who returned the survey, 72 percent (190) indicated that they use the Internet to get information related to union matters. On a five-point scale ranging from Very Dissatisfied to Very Satisfied, 76 percent of those (138) indicated they were either very or somewhat satisfied.

Internet access was mostly from work, although many had more than one place from which they accessed the Internet. The numbers from each location are as follows: home, 110, 58 percent; work, forty-three, 23 percent; union office, seventy-seven, 41 percent; public library, three, 2 percent; and "other," four, 2 percent. These do not add up to 100 percent due to multiple responses.

Unionists mostly used a local Internet service provider (ISP) or national service provider (such as AOL or MSN). Those two categories totaled 87.5 percent of all responses (local, seventy-five, 40.8 percent; national, eighty-six, 46.7 percent), while the use of a union network was reported by nine (4.9 percent) and cable company by seven (3.8 percent). Another seven individuals reported that they did not know what type of provider they used.

Problems

The biggest problem reported by respondents was that they did not find all the information they needed. Nearly 100 respondents (56.6 percent) indicated that this was a problem. The second most reported problem was that the information was not in the order of relevance. Over seventy union leaders (40.6 percent) felt this was a problem.

The other problems in order of response frequency were: information source hard to use, fifty-six, 32 percent; too much information, fifty-four, 30.9 percent; information out of date, forty-five, 25.7 percent; would have to pay, forty-one, 23.4 percent; information not useful, thirty-eight, 21.7 percent; information too theoretical, thirty-two, 18.3 percent; hard to get computer time, twenty-five, 14.3 percent; too costly, eighteen, 10.3 percent; connection too difficult, eighteen, 10.3 percent; software problems, fifteen, 8.6 percent; and hardware problems, ten, 4.2 percent. Some of the other problems reported included: time consuming; local too small; don't know where to look; need personal help; too slow; difficulty finding information; and access not available to all employees.

An examination across categories reveals some explanation of differences in problems encountered. One area that makes a difference in some of the problems is the type of Internet provider. Another area is the type and amount of training received by the union leader. Additionally, men and women showed some surprising differences in the rate of reporting problems.

Type of Provider

The type of provider makes a difference in a number of the problems listed. Among those who use a national service provider, 36 percent said they found too much information. Only 22 percent of those using the union network reported the same problem. On the other hand, a large number of those using the union network (44 percent) found the information too theoretical, compared to 17 percent using a local provider and 14 percent using a national provider.

A similar pattern is found among those reporting that the information is not useful. Thirty-three percent of union network users indicated that the information was not useful, while only 20 percent of those using local service providers found the same problem.

The information not being in order of relevance was a significant problem for those using union networks. Two-thirds (67 percent) of those users said they had a problem with the sorting of the information they found. This was also a problem with those using a national service provider (49 percent), while those using a local service provider were less likely to report this problem (30 percent).

Union leaders also reported more often that information on the union network was out of date (33 percent) than that on the national provider (27 percent) or local provider (24 percent). The union network received high marks on ease of use. Only 11 percent of those using union networks said they had a problem with the information being hard to use. In contrast, those using the national service provider reported this problem 35 percent of the time.

The cost of the information is a greater concern among those who use union networks. Forty-four percent of them indicated that a problem they face is having to pay for the information they need. Because the cost of local and national providers is less than that for union networks, only 27 percent of those using a local provider and 21 percent of those using a national provider reported that having to pay for the information was a problem.

Union leaders using either national service providers or union networks indicated problems with getting computer time, as well as having a difficult connection. In both categories, those using local service providers reported the problem less frequently. For problems getting computer time, 22 percent of those using a national service provider reported this problem, while 21 percent of union network users and 8.5 percent of local network users reported the same problem.

In the category of connection too difficult, 22 percent of those in the union networks reported the problem, while only 13 percent of the national provider users and 7.1 percent of the local service users indicated that they had the same problem.

Training

Training made an appreciable difference in four of the problems reported by union leaders. In two cases the training was associated with a decrease in the number of problems reported, but in two other cases it was associated with an increase in the number of people reporting problems. Fewer of those who had Internet training had a problem with the information being out of date, 27.8 percent compared to 17.4 percent. Another area in which training seemed to make a positive difference was in ability to get computer time. In that category, 15.7 percent of those without training reported a problem, as compared to 8.7 percent of those with training.

Training had a negative effect on two categories of problems. Thirty-nine percent of those with training reported problems with finding too much information, while 16.7 percent of those without training reported that problem. Additionally, 50 percent of those with training had problems with information not being in order of relevance, while only 33.3 percent of those without training had the problem.

Gender

One of the areas that surprised me was the difference shown by gender. The common view that men are better with computers was challenged in nine of the potential problems listed.

Fewer women indicated that they had problems with: information out of the order of relevance (female 26 percent, male 42 percent); information out of date (female 5.25 percent, male 28 percent); information source hard to use (female 11 percent, male 34 percent); having to pay for information (female 5.25 percent, male 25 percent); inability to find all information needed (female 26 percent, male 59 percent); too costly (female 5.25 percent, male 10 percent); connection too difficult (female 5.25 percent, male 11 percent); hardware problems (female 0 percent, male 6.5 percent); and software problems (female 0 percent, male 9.8 percent). Only in the category of difficulty getting computer time did fewer males report a problem than did females (female 21 percent, male 14 percent).

Observations

A few things come to mind as I look at the results of this survey. The first is that it does make a difference which type of ISP one uses. Next is that training does make a difference. Finally, there are some interesting results involving the gender of the computer user.

When I have taught my class in the past, I have avoided endorsing one ISP over another. When asked, I have told my students that it really does not matter. However, this survey seems to show that it does indeed make a difference. For those who answered this survey, a local ISP is easier to use, less costly, and more accessible for the union leaders who participated in this survey. Union networks have some good features, such as ease of use and relevance of information, while ease of connection, organization, and cost need to be improved to equal the overall satisfaction union leaders found with local ISPs.

As a labor educator, and especially as one who provides training in how to use the Internet, I looked with interest at the results involving training. My first thought was that maybe the training did not improve the use of the Internet; however, a close perusal offers some explanation.

The problems that persons with training reported with greater frequency were finding too much information and the information not being in order of relevance. Perhaps these problems may be a result of the fact that these individuals have acquired skills in searching for information to the point that they may be inundated with information. It also suggests to me that we could better focus training on how to filter information.

It is somewhat problematic to ascribe differences across gender lines. As with the gender pay gap, there are probably a number of factors at work here. Perhaps the women in the survey deal with computers in their work more frequently than do the men. I will not speculate on the possibility of "Mars and Venus" differences in the ability to clearly sort the information found on the Internet.

Summary

For unions to use the Internet as an important tool as outlined in the CyberUnion model, barriers to use must be surmounted. This survey identifies some of the problems encountered in the use of the Internet. I hope that it also directs us to finding solutions. The improvement of training, the improvement of union networks as ISPs, and the identification of differences in use patterns should all contribute to a better, more efficient use of the Internet in the future.

---

11. Taking More Control of Technology Issues

Nancy Bupp

Unlike the hapless unorganized 84 percent of the workforce dependent on management's goodwill, the 16 percent in union membership have in their written contract a powerful tool for retaining the security, making the gains, and enjoying the respect owed to all.

Far too few unions and locals, however, incorporate timely clauses in their contracts defining labor's part in making workplace technology decisions. Ten valuable pieces of advice are shared below, leading to the writer's closing insistence that alternatives and choices could not be more important.

A careful reading will help you answer such questions as: How important is it to create a technology committee? Write scenarios? Craft a guiding vision? And develop technology language with which to update your contract?

Above all, the essay underlines labor's responsibility for fighting anew to share power where an ancient challenge is concerned: Workplace technology, especially concerning the twenty-first–century computer, is far too consequential to be left to management alone.

If we do not define our futures, someone else will do it for us. In the past, management defined technologies that reshape our world of work and our everyday lives. Unions have traditionally allowed management to do so. But now we must move technology, and especially computer technology, to the workers' agenda.

Contract language is the place to start. If there is no language in your contract dealing with technology from the union's viewpoint, then most likely there is a management's rights clause giving all the power to management to decide about technology being developed and implemented.

There are many ways we as union members can be proactive here and help define our futures. Here are some of them:

Read, Do Research, Get Educated

We have to "educate [ourselves] for the coming conflicts" (from Mother Jones, as quoted in Bollen 2000). Read the books that management is reading. Read and study the trade magazines associated with the industry in which we do our work. Find and study the Web sites preferred by management. Systematically evaluate the social, technical, and business trends. Evaluate the consequences these trends, forecasts, and new developments have for unions and working people. These will help give us the heads-up on what is probably coming to our workplaces.

The Internet has an abundance of industry news and industry-related links. What would normally take days and weeks to research is now at our fingertips. Financial information on companies is also available (for publicly traded companies). We don't need to take our employers' word on their financial status anymore. We can do the in-depth research on the Internet ourselves.

Ask Questions

What we consider impossible today may very well be possible tomorrow. That's the pace of change. When we start thinking there is only one way to do something is when we need to break out of our box and consider other ways.

Question everything; assume nothing. For every current business practice, continually ask, How does this build the union? How does this help to mobilize the membership? Are we asking the right questions? What will technology do? What will it undo? What is the problem for which this technology is the solution? How can the union do things differently? Is there another approach? How can our use of computers help us stay on top of this or that business practice?

Ask questions no one else has the courage to ask. Ask questions instead of rushing to give answers. If we don't ask questions, we'll get no answers. Don't forget to request information from the company that will aid at the bargaining table. And surf the Internet continuously in search of still better questions—and possibly even some answers.

Anticipate

Get out ahead of what may be happening and what repercussions may follow. The key to ensuring the continued success of unions is *anticipation—* the ability to detect the need for change well ahead of the curve and create a strategy for a quick, effective, and safe way to negotiate that curve, thereby preserving jobs and protecting working people.

In order for that to happen, union members themselves must change. They can begin the change process by getting and maintaining a heightened awareness of new developments in labor and product markets, and by giving thought to the dynamics that are driving those developments. By carefully scanning the external environment and analyzing what is going on, union members can begin to make plans that take into consideration both the threats and the opportunities that are out there.

We need to use computer power to continuously scan the horizon. We must not rely on a one-time analysis. We must build computer-aided scanning of the future into regular practice, always looking forward to what is at the horizon. The fact is, many times we hear about a new technology, but we fail to realize that the technology is important. We must develop the sensitivity and skill to see challenges long before they become crises.

Form and Train Technology Committees

Technology committees should bird-dog technology issues, as safety and health committees do. The more eyes, ears, and brains we have out there to anticipate, ask questions, read, surf the Internet, and monitor key Web sites, the better off we'll be.

What would happen if we said to our members, "We're going to strike over not getting the technology clause in our contract"? They would probably say, "What? Are you kidding?" That's because technology is not an issue most understand—yet. There is a lot of training and education that needs to be done to make all our members understand the implications of technology and how it is changing our lives and workplaces.

We have many computer-literate people in our unions who would be pleased to be asked to help the union in such an important role. Assign them to use the Internet to research new technologies, industry news, and so forth.

Envision Scenarios

The purpose of scenarios is to illuminate uncertainty. Scenarios help determine the ramifications of an issue's development—along several alternative
paths—which enables the union to examine an issue's implications over time.
As opposed to trend analysis, working with scenarios is a way to build alternative futures, and spot the scenarios that could be particularly lethal—or
particularly attractive.

Plan

Have a means to take corrective action. Companies know what they are going to be doing five, ten, fifteen years down the road, because they routinely
engage in strategic planning. Why can't unions plan strategically? Don't forget about contingency plans. "What if [this] happens? Then we will do [this]."

Try to balance the short term with the long term. People tend to overesti-
mate change in the short run and underestimate it in the long run.

Become Active, Engage in Politics, Organize!

Mobilize the members around the issues of technology and get them to help
fight for the union's demands on technology. Create a list server of a cadre of
especially concerned members, each an influential person, and send out frequent e-mails and encourage interactive dialogue among them, the better to
promote bonding of key change agents. We can also use this cadre to frequently e-mail our politicians and keep them informed about the issues that
are important to working people.

Problem solving and crisis resolving leave little time for innovation. The
tendency to race headlong into the future while looking in the rear-view
mirror (to see how something was done in the past) and out the side windows
(to see how the competition is doing it) has proved to be unproductive over
the long haul. With foresight and anticipation a list server of mobilized members can do a better job for all.

Encourage Solidarity

Unions can only count on their own strength. A union has to rely first and
foremost on its own membership, its strengths, and its solidarity. Communicate via the Internet with other unions and systematically build solidarity
across trade and industry lines—all of which are being radically redefined
by information age dynamics.

The closer we stay in touch with other brothers and sisters in the labor movement and keep each other informed on new developments in our respective workplaces and industries, the better we can prepare for when these new developments reach our own workplaces. We can exchange information on problems encountered and solutions to these problems.

Develop Vision

Victory does not always go to the largest armies, the best deployment, and the most firepower. It goes as often to the smaller force with the greatest imagination, flexibility, and boldness, with the vision to make something happen.

Every vision of the future sets off its own feedback loop. One prepares for what one believes will happen. At the same time, that preparation makes it more likely that this particular future will happen. Ask ourselves what future does the union really prefer? Ask ourselves what is our union preparing for? It is not enough to do our best at figuring out what is likely to happen and then only react to it.

Develop Contract Language

Whenever a new problem emerges at the workplace, the first line of defense is the contract. Collective bargaining is the most important avenue for coping with technological change.

As the rate of technological change in the workplace increases, many bargaining units are finding that traditional contract language is not providing the necessary protection for members. It is important for all union members to analyze their contracts to see if there is technology language present, and if not, to develop a technology bargaining strategy to insert such language or improve existing language.

More and more unions are placing their contracts online on the union's home page. It is a valuable resource to be able to analyze other contracts and get ideas on contract language that may be pertinent to our own situation.

If we pay attention to all of the above, then we can better negotiate contract language that will help protect us. Remember the words "alternatives" and "choices."

Reference

Bollen, Peter. *Great Labor Quotations: Sourcebook and Reader.* Los Angeles, CA: Red Eye Press, 2000, p. 201.

12. "But the Computer Salesman Said . . ." —What All That Stuff Means

Brandon Weber

As always, there is so much more to learn. For example, my university has just advised the faculty that recommended RAM for new machines is now 256 MB, with 20 GB disk space for a laptop, 30 GB for a desktop. I was hesitant about upgrading a university computer lent to me, one I have gotten somewhat comfortable with (after three shop stays and a motherboard replacement), but I will now have to take this prod to upgrading carefully into account.

Similarly, as always, Murphy's Law chimes in when least welcomed. My DSL provider of three years good standing has just signaled, ironically via snail mail, its unexpected intention to cut off service in four weeks. This has thrown me on the mercies of a vendors' market for DSL service I did not expect or want again to negotiate.

Fortunately, with the sort of calm counsel and timely help provided by the essay below—and related others in the handbook—I can take a deep breath, hitch up my pants, and get on with it.

You, too, are likely to find in the piece reassurance and tips of value—as terms once mysterious take on clear meaning, numbers once only puzzling gain significance, and the "buzz and din" of the esoteric world of computers begins to actually make sense ("compute").

If the essay is read carefully enough, and if its tips on what to look for in hardware, software, and support systems are taken to heart, you too may come, like the advice giver, to soon calmly regard your computer as just another "wonderful tool."

Because computer technology has a myriad of uses and comes in a wide variety of flavors, it is often unclear just what a local union or activist needs to get started. That question raises another one: "Just what do you want to accomplish?"

Some of the most common goals include publishing newsletters, flyers, and leaflets; creating a presence on the World Wide Web with a Web site or Web page; networking with other locals and union activists via the Web, e-mail, and discussion groups; information and news gathering on the Internet;

Word processing (writing letters, reports, articles); and tracking dues/membership/grievances. All of these can be achieved easily within a very reasonable budget.

First, though, we need to clarify some terms that are often used in the industry. Please keep in mind that while the date this book was published is frozen, technology is not; if you are reading this a year or two from the date of publication, then note that the numbers, speeds, and sizes of everything below will change. Consult an expert if you're lost.

Technology Primer

When you go looking for a computer, you'll see something like this: "P-III 866, 256 Megs RAM, 40 Gig HD, CD-RW, DVD, 19" .28 dot pitch monitor." Don't let all those terms rattle you.

"866MHz"—The Processor

This is the basic "engine" of the computer, much like the engine of a vehicle. Where it says "Intel Celeron 600MHz" or "Intel Pentium III 866MHz," that number is telling you how fast the processor is. "MHz" is short for "Megahertz," and is a measurement of the processor speed or "cycles." The newest generation (Pentium IV) takes the speed beyond 1000MHz, which is termed "Gigahertz," or GHz.

"256 Meg"—Memory

Memory (also known as RAM) is the part of the computer that is being used while the computer is thinking. Think of it as the passenger compartment of a car. Just like you can take more people to dinner in your four-passenger vehicle than in a two-seater, a larger number beside the Meg or MB (megabyte) means you can run more programs at once, and also that you can run bigger programs.

When you start or run a program (a Web browser, a word processor, or anything you make the computer do), it is using memory to temporarily "hold" and use information while it does what you told it to do. This is different from the hard disk, which is permanent storage (see below).

"40 Gig"—Hard Disk

The hard disk (sometimes also called "hard drive") is permanent memory storage where the programs are saved, much like a library where you store books. Or, again using the automobile analogy, it's like the trunk of your car. The bigger the gig, or GB (short for gigabytes), the more things you can save on the computer—clip art, photos, educational software, and everything else.

"CD-ROM, DVD-ROM, CD-RW"—Huh? Almost every computer sold today has a CD-ROM (or sometimes called just "CD") drive in it. It is used for playing music CDs, as well as loading software from CD-ROM disks (like music CDs but with information and programs on them instead).

One upgrade to a CD drive is called a "DVD-ROM" drive (also called simply "DVD drive"). DVD stands for digital versatile disc, and it is a new type of CD that holds a lot more (about six times that of a regular CD), which is why they can put entire movies, and huge software collections, on DVD. Though it will be a few years from now, DVD-ROM drives will eventually replace standard CD-ROM drives, at least in PCs. Also, a DVD-ROM drive can do everything a CD-ROM drive can do, and more.

The other upgrade from a CD-ROM is the CD-RW, which is a read/write CD drive. You can buy blank CDs for under $1 apiece and use a CD-RW drive to make copies of other CDs or to back up your word processing. Also, if you are producing your own local newspaper on the computer, a very efficient way to both store it and to get it to your printer is by saving it to a CD.

"19" Monitor"—The Screen

The computer screen, also known as a monitor, is what you look at—sometimes for many hours in a row—when you are using the PC. Similar to a TV, this is your most important interface with the computer, so it is something to pay close attention to when you go to purchase one. You'll get a better image and have less eyestrain if you get one with .28 dot pitch or smaller. This number represents the size of the pixels that make up what you see on the screen.

Purchasing the Hardware

When looking for computer hardware, make sure whatever you get is industry standard, Windows-compatible equipment. There are now devices such as "Web TV" and "e-mail devices" that are not truly computers. These will serve some basic functions, but you will quickly reach the limitations inherent in these systems. If your local is broke or you are part of a rank-and-file group with little cash reserves, a good option is used equipment, available in most urban areas or on online auctions.

Whether new or used, how do you proceed once you decide to take the plunge? You can look in computer magazines for mail-order companies or stroll into a neighborhood computer store or go on the Internet to find what you want. It would be in your best interests to bring along a computer "geek" from your membership or a knowledgeable person from your circle of family and friends when you get serious. Computer salespeople, especially in the retail stores, may try to sell you items you don't need or possibly leave you underequipped.

• *Processor:* For the low-end, a Celeron 600 MHz is about the slowest computer that you should even consider buying these days. Priced at around $750, it will take care of most of your basic needs, as well as some desktop publishing and other tasks. The difference between these and higher-end units is price and speed. The Pentium II, as well as slower Celerons, will soon be nonexistent on the new computer market, but are still available used and sometimes new at great prices ($300 to $500). The next step-up in speed and price is the Pentium III, at 700 MHz and faster. Street prices on these are around $1,200 to $1,400 new. Top of the line currently is the Pentium IV, 1 GHz or faster, priced anywhere from $1,600 to $2,000. The improvement in chip design makes the Pentium IV-class computer faster and more powerful than a Pentium III of similar speed, so a Pentium IV at 1 GHz is going to perform a lot better than a Pentium III at 1 GHz. If your budget is no concern, go with the Pentium IV 1.5 GHz or better. This will not be obsolete for quite awhile.

Any of the current computer options on the market, from the Celeron 600 on up, are great for educational programs, word processing, desktop publishing, getting on the Internet, playing games, and so forth. However, the faster the processor, the better the performance you will get. Depending partially on your connection to the Internet (phone line, DSL, cable modem), a faster processor will help Web pages come across more quickly. If you're planning on higher-end computing such as Web page design or graphical/ photo editing, then a faster processor will make those functions speed up a great deal.

• *Memory:* As with the processor speed, the more memory you have, the more current your computer will remain. You can do fine with the units containing 64 or 128 megs. They will run most programs just as well as the larger 256 meg units. But if you want to run Web page design software, process photos and clip art on your PC, or produce a thirty-page newspaper with your own digital photos, the more memory the better. Also, in three years, the 256 meg units will be much more current, though you can always add memory yourself at a later date. Memory upgrades currently run about $1 per meg.

• *Hard Disk:* As of this writing, 20 gigs is the minimum you should look for. That is changing, however, as software grows and creates larger files; 30

or 40 gigs is better and will keep you more current. About $100 per 10 gig upgrade is about what you should expect to pay.

• *Monitor:* Basic 15" monitors (15 inches measured diagonally from the top-right corner to the bottom left corner of the screen) are fine for general use, but they are quickly becoming obsolete. A 17" or 19" monitor is worth considering; this will help reduce eyestrain and allow more than one person to watch the screen at the same time. Current monitor prices range from $150 for a 15" to $400 for a 19".

• *Input/Output Devices:* Standard items on all PCs are the 3.5" floppy disk drive, mouse, and keyboard. Variations such as the Microsoft Natural Keyboard and the Trackball style mouse will help with repetitive motion disorders. These are worth considering if time spent on the PC will be more than a few hours a day.

• *Printer:* Ink jet or laser? Those are your basic choices. Ink jets are inexpensive, they produce nice quality printing, but the consumables (the ink cartridges) are pricey and don't last long, so if your organization is doing a good deal of printing, they are not cost-effective. Laser printers are available in both black and white and color, and they are great both for printing large quantities and for more professional-looking print jobs. Ink jets range from $100 to $400 and laser printers, from $800 to $2500.

Software Considerations

Software is the word used to describe the programs that make a computer do what it does. Following are some suggestions to help you get up and running.

• *Windows ME vs. 98:* As of this writing, Windows ME (Millennium Edition) still has too many problems to receive a positive recommendation, but in most cases, you will not have a choice. If you can, instead get Windows 98 Second Edition, and you would be better off. Don't even think about Windows 2000 unless you are already a full-fledged computer nerd.

• *Desktop Publishing:* Microsoft Publisher 2000, available by itself or with the Microsoft Office 2000 package, is the easiest of all to learn, and it has some of the power you can get from much more expensive desktop publishing programs. It has the added advantage of being very inexpensive: approximately $100 retail. Adobe PageMaker is also used for doing newsletters and flyers, but the learning curve is very steep, as is the price tag: about $600. Do not attempt to use a word processing program such as Microsoft Word to handle desktop publishing jobs.

• *Word Processing:* Microsoft Word is the overall standard, having unseated WordPerfect many years ago. They can read each other's file formats, so either way you go on this, you will do fine. Either has a current street price of $150 or so.

• *Web Page Design:* Microsoft Publisher, listed above, can do basic Web page design pretty well. If you want to get more advanced, then consider Microsoft FrontPage (about $150 street) or Adobe PageMill ($100 or so). Of these two, FrontPage has a steeper learning curve but can do more.

• *Accounting/Database Software:* For databases, there are several companies marketing software for local unions to keep track of just about anything. Do a simple "Yahoo" search to find them, using the search term "union membership software." For accounting, QuickBooks is unbeatable, and priced at around $150 street.

Stepping Beyond

Now that you have your computer system and boxes of software, what do you do with it all? It doesn't make sense to invest that kind of money and then spend months trying to figure out how to make it all work.

Some international unions may have people who can help train your staff in the use of computers. You might even find a rank-and-file member of the local who can help with staff training; many people are buying computers and learning about them as hobbies in their spare time. You can check with the company you bought the items from and see if they have classes, or hire a consultant to set everything up and train your people.

But the main thing is to find someone, even for a couple days, who can install your system, show the key people how it functions, and make it do what it's supposed to do while training others. Regarding manuals: Most hardware and software manuals are pretty thick, and very hard to wade through, because they are written by techies. The best way to learn a program is to jump right in and play with it. You won't break anything, and you'll know what to do when someone says, "Can you change that font to bold?"

Once you get everything going and your computer system is humming along, cranking out labels and producing flyers for the latest meeting, you can start to think about expanding the use and productivity of the investment you've made. Some ideas on expanding your scope:

• Web pages, along with the rest of the Internet, are a great source of information for activists. Most international unions, and many locals and nonprofit organizations, have Web sites with information that can be copied and used in your publication or on your Web site. While there is a lot of trash on the Internet, there is also a lot of useful information if you know how to look. Consider attending a class on using search engines and getting around the Net.

• As you begin to use e-mail to communicate, start gathering your own "networks" of people to exchange information with. In most e-mail programs you can set up groups to which people may be assigned. This will enable you to, for example, e-mail everyone who signed-in at one of your rallies, or contributed time/money to a political candidate.

• Scanners can be used to store, change, and improve photos and clip art that you may want to use in your local's newspaper or on your Web site. Some of the scanners to consider: any of the HP Scanjet models (4300, 5300, 6300) are great, and some of the Visioneer scanners are good units also.

• Digital cameras have come a long way; some (e.g., Sony Model FD-75 are relatively inexpensive, and others (e.g., Sony MVC-CD1000) are much pricier but loaded with features. Most use floppy disks to store the pictures; the MVC-CD uses a mini-recordable CD that can be read in any CD drive. Unless you are technically inclined, stay away from the digital cameras that use an interface cable to download pictures.

With the right hardware and software, and armed with the knowledge to make use of it all, computers are wonderful tools in the hands of labor activists. As informed local union members, officers, and staff, we can put them to good use for the benefit of today's labor movement.

---

13. Avoiding Shams, Scams, and Spam as You Journey the Information Superhighway

Bill Ringle

As with all human endeavors, labor's use of the Internet entails unnecessary risks and serious pitfalls, some of which are cruelly mean-spirited. Over 50,000 viruses, for example, were active in 2001, and about 300 new viruses appear every month. Fortunately, many of these problems can be avoided, or at least countered.

Help is available in the form below of concrete advice from a longtime Internet user and consultant. His essay tackles such questions as:

• *How can you avoid identity theft?*
• *What is dangerous about an e-mail chain letter?*
• *Can e-mail viruses be thwarted?*
• *How can you detect an Internet hoax early enough to avoid harm?*

- *How can you detect a bait-and-switch Web site?*
- *What is a ring trap, and why should you care?*

Ten protective ideas are shared that can substantially help increase your chances against the "shams, scams, and spam" we are all up against.

It happens every day, yet never ceases to amaze me: Perfectly reasonable, perfectly intelligent people leave common sense behind as they take to their keyboards and wander out onto the Internet. And then moan and complain when they inevitably run into trouble. You've heard this sad story from friends and coworkers, too, haven't you?

I've been using the Internet for about twenty years. By luck, circumstance, and curiosity, I got aboard early—long before the World Wide Web, before AOL, before business transactions were even allowed. From my perspective, it was like watching a small town go through an enormous boom in prosperity: Growth can be good in some ways, and not so good in other ways. Opportunity attracts all kinds of attention.

At one end of the spectrum you'll find contributors who wanted to shepherd the direction of certain technologies and visionaries who wanted to do amazing things, like provide telemedicine links between doctors at the Wilmer Eye Institute at Johns Hopkins and doctors performing operations by kerosene generators in the heart of African bush country. At the other end of the spectrum, you have people looking to make a buck regardless of how much (if any) value they add through their products or services, and those who simply want to create a sensation for bragging rights.

The information economy is largely about attention—who is paying how much of it to whom for what reason. No matter how fast our computers or networks get, you and I still only are allotted 1,440 minutes each day. Let's explore ways to shift attention away from the hucksters and back to those who add value.

Think Risks

Whether you use a dial-up account to AOL on a computer so old that your high school children refuse to touch it, or have the sleek, titanium-shielded, jaw-dropping laptop that makes your airplane companions stare with envy, or something in between, you are at risk the moment you set foot on the information superhighway.

Think broadly about what risk means for a moment. If you type a letter on your computer to another union member, for instance, you are risking the time and energy expended between the time you start and each time you press the SAVE command keys. Whenever you pick up your computer, you are risking dropping it and damaging it—the loss of the hardware is almost insignificant when compared to the hours of work stored on many hard drives. Regular backups are an important way to reduce exposure to this risk. And these are only a few of the ways you can mess things up yourself—just think what it means to connect to the Internet.

People connect to the Internet to connect with other people and with information resources. We do this primarily through e-mail and the World Wide Web. To access e-mail, you need an e-mail client, such as Eudora or Outlook on your computer. E-mail messages that come from people unknown to you pitching a product or service (from ink jet refills to Internet service hosting providers to a kit on how to spy on anyone using the Internet) is called spam. You didn't ask for the message, you may not want or need what they're offering, but you get it anyway.

To access the Web, you need Web browser software such as Internet Explorer or Netscape Navigator. The vast majority of the Web pages available provide just what you expect. Some, in the seedier off ramps of the information superhighway, dish out nasty surprises.

What to Watch Out For

When you connect your computer to a network that includes at least 80 million other people around the world, you've got to admit that not all of them have your best interests at heart and that perhaps a few individuals are capable of unscrupulous behavior. Here are six of the most insidious, malicious, and frequent potholes that you'll encounter on the information superhighway.

1. *Identity theft.* Some days we have a hard enough time remembering the names of the people we see in the shop or around the office each day. Think of how many people whose e-mail arrives in our in-box that we've never met. How do we know they are really who they say they are? Interesting, huh? Now flip it around. How do they know that you are really you!

The barrier to identity theft is so minimal that any advanced beginner with e-mail could pull it off by simply changing their return mail address and name in their e-mail client software under the Preferences window. Click here, type a few words there, and poof—you're the president of your union. From this point, you could send a message to all the members promoting your agenda and raising or lowering dues, depending on who you're mad at.

2. *E-mail chain letter.* Okay, now let's see how someone could take it to the next level and get other people to join the pitch of suckering others in. The scam artist makes up a new e-mail identity and sends out a sob-story

message (or get-rich-quick scheme) that asks for the recipients to send it out to at least five of their friends within the next hour to avoid breaking the chain and incurring bad luck. This is the essence of a chain letter.

Two variations include: (1) Adding addresses that "roll off the top" and urging everyone to send five or ten bucks to the person listed at the top, then forwarding the list to your friends and wait for the money to come rolling in when your name hits the top spot. (2) Asking each recipient of the chain message to send an e-mail to poor Tommy with this dreadful disease who really could use a pick-me-up of messages of hope from around the world.

Guess what—I'll bet you dollars to donuts that there is no Tommy (or Sally or whomever), and by sending a message to the e-mail address listed, you've just added your e-mail address to a list that's sold to other spammers.

3. *E-mail virus.* The subject line read, "I love you," and it was from the association executive based in Phoenix where I had presented just two days ago. Of course I opened the-mail. I couldn't wait to read the details behind what prompted such comments. Who could resist follow-up feedback like that! As soon as I saw the brief message and attachment, though, you could hear my hopes deflate all the way down the hall from my office. Nothing in the message indicated the personality of the sender. She would never have sent something with a "Check this out" message.

My internal suspicion alarm went off. I checked mail again. Sure enough, fourteen other e-mails with the identical subject line and internal message came pouring in, though from different people I know. This particular e-mail virus attacked each person's system when the attachment was opened, or launched, like a rose with poison perfume—inviting, but hazardous. Once launched, the virus looked for the Microsoft Outlook e-mail package and then took it over, mailing a copy of the same message and attachment out to every person and group in Outlook.

The point of this benign virus was simply to propagate: to see how far it could get before it was stopped. Some e-mail viruses, however, are designed to erase files on the hard drives it infects, or other serious harm.

4. *Internet hoax.* Say, did you hear about the woman who was charged $250 (when she thought the charge was $2.50) for the Neiman-Marcus chocolate cookie recipe, and now encourages everyone to distribute it widely on the Internet to get back at the company?

These and other stories that circulate on the Internet are sensational fiction. They're known as "urban legends." They pique your curiosity, but don't let them disturb or distract you. And before you feel compelled to warn everyone in your address book, count to ten.

If you're curious about whether something is legit, visit www.urban legends.com for the lowdown on the latest hoaxes circulating. If you want more sources to check, come visit the www.BillRingle.com Web site. I've got links to about a dozen sites that debunk myths and misinformation. Don't get suckered in by Internet hoaxes.

5. *Bait-and-Switch Web sites*. These are typically Web sites that operate in two ways: indirect and direct subterfuge. The purpose of bait-and-switch sites is, of course, to draw you into either paying attention to something you wouldn't be drawn to if given the chance, or handing over a credit card number (or personal info) to someone who you wouldn't give it to ordinarily.

Here's an example of the first type of bait-and-switch Web sites: an adult-content site took the domain name "whitehouse.com," counting on the fact that a lot of visitors would simply type "whitehouse" into their Web browser, hoping to arrive at "whitehouse.gov," which is the anticipated destination. "Ha ha, fooled you," the porn site owners say every time someone shows up this way.

The reason the owners find this tactic to be successful is that every visitor is exposed to their advertising, and the more people who see it, the more valuable the property. Eyeballs = attention = income from a strictly capitalistic perspective, regardless of the person connected to the eyeballs.

Suffice it to say, this has been a real thorn in the side for primary and secondary school educators directing their students to perform government research online. Direct bait and switch is even more dangerous. It is like being mugged in a dark alley because you are lulled into a false sense of security by a popular brand name, typically, and then lured to place an order or respond to a questionnaire.

The problem is that where you are sending your data is not where you think, and because the site is hosted somewhere halfway around the world, you will be hard pressed to prosecute the offenders, were they ever to be apprehended. Your best bet if you discover you've been had this way is to immediately suspend or cancel the account, credit card, or calling card. If you've given away your social security number along with other personal information, you've got a good chance for a world of trouble ahead.

6. *Web traps*. Like Venus fly traps, these are Web sites that won't let go. The idea behind this scam, when it is done well technically, is that a group of site owners collaborate and agree that they'll form a ring trap. Site developers add code to the Web pages that make them like the prank birthday candles that can't be blown out—instead every time you attempt to leave the site, another window pops up with another page of the site or the home page of a related site.

It is a maddening experience the first time you encounter this because you feel like you've truly lost control of your computer. It's like upgrading to Windows 95 all over again, only worse. For many people who have run out of both options and patience, their last resort is to pull the plug and completely reboot their computers. These Web trap sites are a tremendous energy drain and time waster for this reason. And yes, in case you're wondering, porn sites and racial hate sites are among the most common employers of this technique.

What You Must Do to Protect Yourself

Unfortunately, the countermeasures to use against these scams fall into two distinct categories: the blazingly obvious and the nonintuitive. Once you are aware of a particular trap, you know not to step into it. Common sense dictates that you be careful about who you share personal and financial information with, and to be familiar with the extent of your exposure and coverage in the event of fraud. Check your credit card policies as a minimum. Some card companies offer additional protection against online abuse.

Now here are some ideas to support your effective and safe exploration of the Internet. To increase your chances of success with the following strategies and tactics, work with a knowledgeable buddy or consultant who can help steer you in the right direction.

- Establish multiple e-mail accounts. Designate at least one "public" and one "private" account. Distribute the public one anytime a Web form asks for your e-mail or there is a chance it will be passed on to others. Use the private account for work correspondence. Perhaps have another "personal" account for communicating with family and friends.
- Learn to use e-mail filters or rules. They help sort out your messages automatically, based on who sent it or where it came from. Participants in my "Take Back Your Inbox" seminar rave about how much time this feature saves each day in cutting through the clutter. Eudora, Outlook, Lotus Notes, Netscape, and many other e-mail software packages support this functionality.
- Learn to recognize a fake e-mail address. Jklm009@hotmail.com is unlikely to be used by a legitimate user. Act accordingly.
- Verify attachments by checking with the sender. Delete attachments that are unexpected.
- When you send an attachment, include all the relevant information about how to open it. Describe the software needed to open it, including the version, and what the user should expect to see. For instance, "Here's the slide set for the introduction to the labor rally, Frank. I used PowerPoint 98 and stuck to the installed font set. Good luck!"

- Visit www.Norton.com to learn more about viruses, worms, and Trojan horses. You should have a basic understanding of how each of these types of malicious software can affect your computer.
- Invest in antivirus software such as Norton Antivirus. It is available for both Windows and Macintosh users, and they update their virus definitions regularly. The peace of mind you get is well worth the price.
- You cannot prevent being shuttled to an unexpected Web page, but you can decline to participate further if you encounter a suspicious activity. If in doubt, bow out. Use the order by phone or fax option instead.
- Shop securely. Before sending your credit card information over the Web, check to make sure the connection is secure as indicated by the SSL padlock icon on most Web browsers. Be familiar with how yours works.
- If you get caught in a Web trap, go under the Preferences of your Web browser and turn off the following features: Visual Basic, Java, and JavaScript. The next time you attempt to leave the Web site, the tricky code will not be able to control your Web browser.

Hopefully, this information will make you more savvy and your experiences safer from shams, scams, and spam on the information superhighway. If you find something useful, be sure to pass it on. That's how we all learn.

III. How to Manage E-Mail and List Servers

If everything you try works, you are not trying hard enough.
—Gordon Moore, Intel engineer (father of "Moore's Law")

Our lives have been changed forever by the tsunami we know as the e-mail system, a 24/7 source of stress and power alike. While the Postal Service struggles to deliver 570 million pieces of mail daily, the Internet blithely transmits 1.47 billion e-mail messages every twenty-four hours—and that is just in this country (Romita 2001)!

Home users in America receive about thirty-five e-mails a week, while people at work get about 150 per week (Farmer 2001). Employees feel obliged to read 75 percent of their messages and finally think only about half are actually worth their time (Tejada 2001), which is all the more reason for labor to exercise care and craft in the use of this remarkable new communication tool.

Typical of the progressive use being made is the program of the Metropolitan Washington Council of the AFL-CIO. Since 1997, the D.C. AFL-CIO has built a database of 7,000 people, with 4,000 receiving e-mail newsletters and 1,000 getting information via fax. A simple Microsoft Access program is used. Chris Garlock, coordinator for the 150,000-member Washington Council, explains there is no real cost to the effort, and it gets information quickly to members and activists: "That's the huge attraction of it."

Garlock, a former journalist, says the key for his labor organization's online efforts is keeping the information brief and important so the e-mails aren't seen as junk mail or spams. He and council president Josh Williams hope to expand their list to 10,000 by the end of 2001(Sunnucks 2001).

Cathy Howell, North Carolina state director for the national AFL-CIO, met with Garlock in February 2001 and hopes to use databases and e-mails to better coordinate the group's 125,000 members. "In a way we need it more because we are so spread out," Howell says. She agrees access is a challenge, as many of her members are poor and far flung across rural areas.

But, in places such as North Carolina, where some unions and locals are sorely lacking in technology, the state and national AFL-CIO will work with them to purchase fax machines and to use members with Internet access to distribute the labor information they receive to those who are not online (Sunnucks 2001). Not surprisingly, the D.C. Labor Council's use of e-mail and faxes to distribute information has rapidly become a model for other unions—regionally, nationally, and internationally.

Consistent with this model, this source of still-better ideas, five essays follow below that make a point common to the entire handbook: We know a good bit about how to get the job done, and how to get it done with flair and effectiveness.

The first essay clarifies several crisp "rules of thumb," closing with a cogent hunch list well-worth pondering. The second clarifies the legal situation where union use of an employer's e-mail system is concerned. The third explores the many rewards possible from a focused list serve. The fourth offers a case study of success here. And the fifth, albeit wry and brief, teaches a valuable lesson about expectations of list servers. Taken all in all, the essays demonstrate the appeal, ease of operation, and payoff possible from e-mail and list servers—two *very* valuable new labor aids.

References

Farmer, Bryan Edward. "A Week on the Web." *Business 2.0*, June 26, 2001, p. 74.
Romita, Tessa. "Internet at a Glance." *Business 2.0 Com*, February 6, 2001, p. 102.
Sunnucks, Mike. "Unions Using Tools of New Economy to Build Support." *Washington Business Journal*, May 25, 2001, p. 3.
Tejada, Carlos. "Work Week" ("Electronic Hassle"). *Wall Street Journal*, May 8, 2001, p. A-1.

---

14. How-To's and Why Not's: A Quick Guide for Union E-Tool Use

Donna Jablonski

Although organized explicitly around ten vital matters, this essay actually ranges far and wide, closing in a sprightly way with cogent rules of thumb worth thinking about at length. Answers can be found to such questions as:

- *What's happening?*
- *What might a local's mission statement resemble?*
- *Why avoid abstract statements?*
- *What does "mapping" a Web site mean?*
- *How can we measure effectiveness?*
- *What is the real value of e-mail, and what has the AFL-CIO learned thus far from its use?*
- *What is an append process, and, so what?*
- *How serious are copyright laws where the Internet is concerned?*

Above all, what sorts of tips and tricks really heighten the likelihood you can create, maintain, and steadily improve a computer-aided communications system that warrants ample support and enthusiastic use.

As the AFL-CIO has developed an e-tool operation that has become a cornerstone of our overall communications program, we've learned a few things. Here's a sampling that can be helpful in planning and implementing e-tool use at any level of the union movement.

E-Tool Use

1. Go for It!

Electronic communications tools such as e-mail, Web sites, and online communities have revolutionized the way we are—or could be—doing our work for working families. Not since the invention of the printing press has there been such a massive and fundamental change in the tools available to communicators.

We estimate that 65 percent of union members are online—slightly higher than the general public, probably because union members make more money than nonunion workers, so they can spend more on computers. That figure is growing, so never assume your members are not likely to have computers. In fact, the Internet has penetrated America's homes faster than any other medium in history.

Here's how long it took various media to infiltrate 60 percent of U.S. households: telephone, thirty years; radio: ten years; television, five years; cable television, twenty-seven years; VCRs, ten years; computers, fifteen years; Internet, two years (Holsendolph 2001).

Internet access is influenced by household income, whether children are in the home or not, and age. But even seniors, the least-connected age group, are getting online. Internet access among older Americans, in fact, is growing faster than in any other age group.

2. Get the Big Picture

In planning your use of e-tools, it's important to first know what you want to get as a result. It would be a good idea to write a mission statement for your organization's use of e-tools. These are your organization's goals, the "big picture" results you want to gain over time. Unlike objectives (more on that later), these do not have to be measurable, but they should be concrete enough to help guide your planning.

Your mission statement also should be something the stakeholders in your e-tool effort can buy into. If your president or secretary-treasurer has a different idea of what the mission should be, for example, you've got a problem.

Sample Mission Statement for E-Tool Use

Local 234 will use new electronic communications media to further our mission of improving life for working families in our community, state, and country. We will employ a Web site, e-mail, and related tools to:

- *Inform* our members about developments in our relationship with our employer;
- *Educate* our members about working-family issues and political candidates' positions on those issues;
- *Mobilize* our members to support organizing, bargaining, and working-family-friendly candidates;
- *Empower* our members by providing online access to union, community, and government leaders.

To ensure that our members are not victims of the digital divide, we will inform them about discount computer and Internet service available for union members, and we will place at least four computers with Internet access in the union hall, available for members' use.

Remember, a mission statement isn't something you do once and never think about again. When you have a mission statement that really reflects your union's goal, its commitment, that's a living document.

Get your decision makers to agree on a mission statement. Then use it. Stick in on the wall above your desk. And when an e-tool project comes along, ask yourself, How does it fit with this mission statement? Is it consistent with our goals? If not, how do I make it consistent? Or should I be doing this effort at all?

3. Set Objectives Before You Build

You should begin by identifying exactly *who* it is you are trying to reach, *what* it is you want them to do as a result of the communication, and *which* e-tool or tools you think is most likely to prompt that audience to do that desired thing. Think of the desired action as your objective—and you'll want it to be measurable so you can gauge your success. That means you'll want to use specific and concrete terms to define your desired actions, rather than abstract words or phrases.

For the AFL-CIO's Executive PayWatch site (www.aflcio.org/paywatch), for example, an *unmeasurable* objective would have been: We want people to know how much those CEOs make! A measurable objective would be: We want at least 1 million people a year to visit pages that divulge what individual CEOs are getting paid.

These Phrases Express Measurable Objectives:

- The site will attract at least 50,000 unique visitors monthly
- Visitors will view an average of ten pages within the site
- At least 20 percent of e-mail recipients will click on the link provided

These Phrases Don't:

- Visitors will learn more about the topic
- The site will attract heavy monthly traffic
- The e-mail will increase traffic to the site significantly

For a Web site, a good objective could be the number of unique visitors coming to the site each month. For an e-mail campaign, it could be the percentage of people taking a measurable action as a result of receiving your e-mail. For an online community, it could be the proportion of your intended audience that participates.

4. Choose "Effective" Tools

The measurable objectives we just discussed will enable you to determine whether an e-tool use is effective—that is, whether it prompts the intended audience to do (or think or feel or consider) what you want it to.

For every kind of e-tool, multiple tactics influence effectiveness. Some of these you can only figure out by testing and carefully tracking results of your own e-tool efforts with your particular audience. But common sense will give you some general guidelines. A public Web site, such as the AFL-CIO's Executive PayWatch, for example, is an appropriate tool for reaching broad segments of the general public and membership with information of broad interest. But it's passive and just building it doesn't mean anyone will come.

So to reach activists and engage them in a specific activity at a specific time, an e-mail campaign that drives recipients to a linked Web site where they can take a specific action (e-mailing Congress, for example) can work. When you need to get somewhat sensitive information to a targeted group of people, though, a private e-mail community can be the right way to go.

5. Map Each Web Site

Before building a Web site, it's important to create a clear, logical structure that will accommodate growth of the site. Too few Web folks bother to take this step—and it's crucial. You've probably visited Web sites where you can't figure out how to find information, or you hit dead ends with no way to continue through the site, or you're aiming at what you thought was a page about bowling, and you end up with a recipe for green bean casserole.

Someone didn't plan those sites well. The Web editor probably had a neat piece of information and put it up. Then he or she found another neat piece of information and put it up. And so on and so on. And what we end up with is the online equivalent of a house built with no blueprint. The front porch may be there, but you have to go through the chimney to find it.

Remember that Web sites are *nonlinear*. They don't proceed in a straight line down a page as a news story or feature does, or neatly travel panel to panel as a pamphlet does. A well-designed Web site has several points of ingress and egress—several ways to get into, through, and out of the site.

A map can be set up like an organization chart—put a topic in a box, then draw lines to boxes that contain subtopics, and so on. Or it can be a detailed outline. Whatever type of mapping system you choose probably will make your Web work much, much easier and more effective; you'll have something that can grow as new elements come along, and you'll be able to build on it because you have a solid foundation. And the Web site will make sense to visitors.

6. Give E-Mail the Chance to Change Your Life

Much of the AFL-CIO e-tool work—and most of our e-tool successes—have involved e-mail campaigns. We've discovered that we can get remarkable results from e-mailing union members—results significantly better than industry averages, which themselves are encouraging.

On Thursday, March 1, 2001, the AFL-CIO sent out a mass e-mail to about 40,000 addresses. The e-mail included links to two pages on our Web site (www.aflcio.org) asking recipients to send messages to Congress. One link urged opposition to President George W. Bush's millionaire tax-cut proposal; the other prodded Congress to preserve the federal rule protecting workers from repetitive stress injuries such as carpal tunnel syndrome. Five days later, 16,032 e-mails, faxes, and letters had been sent to Congress as a result.

Think about it: A successful direct mail marketing effort might get a 1 or 2 percent response—400 to 800 returns—over the course of weeks and at considerable expense. The AFL-CIO's Web site and e-mail effort took about two hours to produce and—because the infrastructure and staff already were in place—cost basically nothing.

A Web site can have the greatest information in the world, but it's not very helpful if few people know about it. You can have a killer action campaign online in hopes of getting hundreds or thousands of people to a rally, or to contact Congress or your state legislators about a key vote that's coming up on Monday. But if people don't wander to your site until Tuesday, you've wasted your efforts.

E-mail is an instant, relatively inexpensive, and effective way to alert your members who are online to something they need to do or to know right away. A large e-mailing can be used to drive people to specific Web pages within hours. In our experience e-mail works like nothing else.

Here's a good example: For the week of Labor Day 2000, the AFL-CIO developed a major Online Labor Day Festival. It featured online games such as Smash Corporate Greed, a cinema with videos, an art gallery, streaming music, fun features for children (including an online coloring book), booths set up by national and local unions, the opportunity to tell and read stories about what Labor Day means to working people, and much more.

Our traffic-building promotions included inserts into 800,000 union members' credit-card statements; 1 million Internet banner ad views; 500,000 fliers to hand out at Labor Day events; 25,000 direct mail letters to union leaders; T-shirts, flying disks, can holders, and temporary tattoos featuring the Web address; airplanes pulling banners advertising the site flying over major Labor Day events (as Dave Barry says, "I am not making this up"); ads in the AFL-CIO's *America@work* and in affiliate publications; and two e-mail efforts to 20,000 total addresses. Only one promotion effort produced *measurable* results: e-mail.

The first e-mail effort, to 11,579 addresses, urged recipients to visit the festival site. It received a click-through rate (the percentage of people receiving the e-mail who clicked into the site as requested) of 27.3 percent. The second e-mail encouraged 8,497 addresses to view a Labor Day Web cast featuring then-Vice President Al Gore, ALF-CIO President John Sweeney, the Reverend Jesse Jackson, and others. The click-through rate was 27.9 percent!

These e-mails were customized by union, and each recipient received an e-mail with his or her union's name in the "From" field. Click-through rates varied by union, with some exceeding 40 percent, a rate never before seen by the affinity e-mail marketing specialist who sent the e-mails for the AFL-CIO. So, clearly, e-mail is an e-tool loaded with potential for the union movement. Unfortunately, almost no one in the union movement has collected much in the way of e-mail addresses.

7. So Collect E-Mail Addresses!

Considering the power of e-mail campaigns, the dearth of e-mail addresses is really a crisis for the union movement. The AFL-CIO is working to develop movement-wide solutions to collecting and managing e-mail address lists, but while we're at that, everyone can start building some e-mail bases. When someone asks, "How should we collect e-mail addresses?" my response is always, "Every way you can!" Worksheet 1 at the end of this section will help you get going.

We have been so excited by the potential of e-mail that we dream of finding the magic, quick method to suddenly have a huge list at our disposal. So far, get-rich-in-e-mail-addresses-quick plans haven't worked for us. In an effort to bolster e-mail communications during the 2000 political season, for example, we experimented with the "append" process for collecting e-mail addresses. We provided a vendor with a list of names and addresses of Michigan union members and paid for these to be matched to a master list of e-mail addresses.

The resulting lists, one a statewide list and one of union members in Michigan's Eighth Congressional District, each received two e-mails designed to drive traffic to political material on the www.aflcio.org Web site. The first e-mail included generic political information about candidates; e-mail to the eighth district recipients included targeted information specific to their races. The second e-mail invited recipients to click to receive an online greeting card urging them to vote.

More than 10 percent of recipients unsubscribed—asked to be deleted from the lists. The e-mail with generic political content had a 1.1 percent unique user click-through rate from the eighth district list and a 0.9 percent unique user click-through rate from the statewide list. The E-Vote Card e-mail had a 1.8 percent unique user click-through rate among eighth district recipients and a 2.1 percent rate among the statewide recipients. The cost of using the append process generally runs between 90 cents and $1.10 per e-mail address. The cost for append generation of an opt-in list can range from $5 to $15 per address.

Around the same time, the AFL-CIO sent two e-mails to a national e-mail list collected through ongoing e-activism efforts rather than the append process. The first asked recipients to click to receive their E-Vote Card. The second contained a generic get-out-the-vote message and clicking through was not its primary call to action. The E-Vote Card e-mail received an 8.1 percent rate of unique users clicking through, compared with the 2.1 percent rate from the Michigan append list. The generic get-out-the-vote message received a 2 percent unique user click-through rate.

At the AFL-CIO we'll keep exploring jump-start opportunities to build e-mail lists—but meanwhile, we're going to do the day-to-day hard work of having people at meetings fill out cards and of featuring multiple collection opportunities on our Web site.

8. E-Mail with Care

A few words of caution about e-mail efforts. First, if you want to use your e-mail list as part of your political work, you probably need to be able to identify who the union members are and who the nonmembers are, because some laws and rules limit our political messages to people who aren't union members.

Second, big e-mail mailings might be considered spam, or unsolicited mass e-mail. The Internet has a system of very active spam police who don't miss anything, and they can make your life miserable up to and including getting you kicked off your Internet server. The most important way to avoid having your e-mails labeled spam is to make sure the people on your list have opted in, that they have responded to something and positively replied that "yes, they want to receive e-mail messages from you." None of us wants to become the online equivalent of those sales people phoning during our dinner about cemetery plots—so on every e-mail you send, give people the opportunity to "opt out," to get off your list.

These and other legal issues, like what kind of privacy policies you have about how your e-mail list will be used, whether you'll let any other groups use it, and so forth, require care. I'm not a lawyer, but once you have plans for e-mail and other e-tool use drafted, your union's lawyers or outside counsel definitely should review them all with this in mind.

9. Now Plan Some More

Once you have objectives, a clear idea of which tools you want to use for which intended audiences, mapped Web sites, and a plan for e-mail collection, put it all together in a coherent plan for e-tool use that builds in accountability—who is responsible for doing what and when. Worksheet 2 at the end of this section may be helpful.

10. Keep in Mind These Rules of Thumb

I can't give data to "prove" any of these rules of thumb. But I love them and rely on them. I hope they will be helpful for you, too. As you use and learn more about e-tools, and follow the literature and talk to other e-tool users, add your own.

Web

1. *You have to work to build traffic.* Just because you build it doesn't mean they'll come.
2. *Put your Web address everywhere.* On handouts, publications, T-shirts, caps, your building sign. . . .
3. *In design, aim for a low common denominator.* Don't assume users have the most current browser or fastest modem.
4. *Keep load time low.*
5. *Get links.* Ask others to link from their sites to yours.
6. *E-commerce won't make you rich.* It works best as a supplement to a "brick-and-mortar" sales operation.

E-Mail

1. *Collect e-mail addresses everywhere.* At meetings, rallies, in publications, over the phone. . . .
2. *Use opt-in names.*
3. *Allow people to opt out, or unsubscribe, at any time.*
4. *Use e-mail to drive traffic to the Web site.*

Online Communities

1. *Seed communities*—line up people in advance to take part.
2. *Monitor comments.* Disallow the offensive ones.

Security

1. *Remember the Web is public.* Don't put info about sensitive strategies or tactics on your public site.
2. *Security for private areas isn't foolproof.* It's best to assume that
   some day, someone who doesn't like you will enter a protected area.
3. *Assume e-mail may be read by unintended eyes.* Misfires happen,
   and many employers monitor employee e-mail use.

Events

1. *Online events get more traffic on demand than live.* Let people tune
   in after the actual event.
2. *Streaming media ain't perfect.* Video and music streams are often
   interrupted by net congestion.

Rights

The Internet is subject to the same copyright rules as print media. Don't run
photos, words, music, or other protected work without having the proper
rights.

Summary

Adding e-tools to your communications arsenal can change the way you do
business. I don't mean that e-tools will or should replace print publications
or any other communications medium. But think about it: You can make a
brochure or newsletter that's effective. You can make a video that's effective. You can create a Web site that's effective and send an e-mail that's
effective.

But when you put all the tools you use together to leverage one another
and build on one another in a coordinated communications campaign effort,
well, then, you *really* have something that can make a difference.

Resource

Holsendolph, Ernest. "Study Says Americans Are Using Internet at Ever-
Increasing Rates." *Atlanta Journal-Constitution*, February 19, 2001, p. 1-A.

Worksheet 1: Template for Planning E-Mail Address Collection

E-mail addresses will be entered into: _____
(Common database or address program)

1. *Outreach*
        Collection Method
        Assigned To
        Events/Meetings
        Sign-in sheet
        Cards collected
        Other_____

2. *Publications*
        Tear-out sheet to mail back
        Insert card to mail back
        Solicit sign-up on Web site
        Solicit sign-up by phone
        Offer incentive/bonus (e.g., T-shirt or magnet)
        Other _____

3. *Mailings*
        Insert card or page to mail back
        Solicit sign-up on Web site
        Solicit sign-up by phone
        Offer incentive/bonus (e.g., T-shirt or magnet)
        Other _____

4. *Phone Calls*
        Ask all callers for e-mail address
        Ask all callers for e-mail addresses of other members
        Other_____

5. *Web Site*
        Online form to submit addresses
        Design regular online actions and capture addresses when action
           taken, with permission
        Allow user to send sign-up form page to other members via
           e-mail
        Other_____

6. *E-mail*
        Advise recipients to forward to other members

7. *Other*

        _____

Worksheet 2: Template for Creating an E-Tool Communication Plan

Project:

Audience/s:

Desired action/s:

E-tool:

Editorial schedule:

Production schedule:

Assigned to:

Audience:

Audience:

Audience:

Action:

Action:

Action:

Draft:

Review:

Final:

Staged:

Review:

Final:

Writing:

Production

Review:

Approval:

15. Union and Employee Access to Employer E-Mail Systems Under Federal Labor Law

Stuart W. Davidson, Esq., and Eric M. Fink, Esq.

Given how recent is the age of the Internet (circa 1995), it is understandable that in our litigious society much remains uncertain where the law and relevant administrative rulings are concerned. We have only just begun to sort out legalities, and much remains problematic and volatile. All the more valuable is the sage counsel below from two labor lawyers who are closely following fast-breaking developments. They provide sound advice for union activists wondering about using an employer's e-mail system.

As electronic means of communication, including e-mail and the Internet, become more prevalent, issues will inevitably arise concerning the right of employees and unions to make use of employers' computer systems to communicate about union matters. While the National Labor Relations Board (NLRB) "has not yet adopted any unique doctrines governing employees' right of access to the employer's electronic equipment to communicate with each other about unionization,"[1] the Board has begun to address these issues in terms of existing legal principles. This article will review the most significant statements of the NLRB in this area, and offer some guidance to unions and their supporters seeking to use electronic communications as organizing tools.

Discriminatory Restrictions on Access

One principle that appears reasonably clear is that an employer's rule or practice that prohibits employees from using the company e-mail system to send pro-union messages, while permitting other types of personal, nonwork-related messages, is discriminatory and therefore unlawful.[2] Even if the employer's official policy is facially nondiscriminatory, the employer may still run afoul of the law if, in practice, it allows nonunion-related personal messages but prohibits union messages or notices.[3]

If a union believes that an employer's e-mail policy discriminates against union messages, the union should file a charge of unfair labor practices. If the Labor Board finds that the employer's e-mail policy, either facially or as applied, discriminates against union-related messages, the remedy will be a "cease and desist" order, requiring the employer to treat union-related messages the same as other nonwork-related messages under its e-mail policy.

The decision of the NLRB in Lockheed Martin Skunk Works[4] is instructive in that it suggests some affirmative steps that a union should take where it believes that an employer is discriminating against pro-union messages on its e-mail system. In Lockheed Martin Skunk Works, the employer maintained a policy prohibiting solicitation during working time and prohibiting the distribution of literature in working areas or during the working time of either the person distributing or the person receiving the literature. The company also maintained a policy regulating the use of its electronic mail system.

Occasional personal use of the system was permitted during nonwork time, provided that was "of reasonable duration and frequency," did "not interfere with or adversely affect the employee's performance," and was not "in support of a personal business." Employees commonly used the company's e-mail system to send personal messages without being subject to discipline. However, the company had previously disciplined employees after receiving complaints about certain "inappropriate" uses of the system, such as running a personal business, administering a pornographic Web site, and sending "off-color jokes and ethnic comments."

A bargaining unit member filed a decertification petition with the NLRB. In support of the petition, that member, along with other employees, sent six mass e-mails to the entire unit of 1,100 employees. The union objected to those messages, and asked the company to put a stop to the use of the company's e-mail system for decertification campaign messages. The company assured the union that the messages would stop; however, the company did not order employees to cease using the e-mail system for such messages. The union then requested permission to send up to three e-mail messages over the company's system "to remedy the discriminatory manner in which [it] has been used to date." The company granted that request. However, the union sent only one mass e-mail message over the company's system.

The NLRB found that the union was not placed at an unfair disadvantage relative to decertification proponents. Even assuming that the pro-decertification mass e-mails violated the employer's policy, the employer was not responsible for the union's failure to make greater use of the e-mail system. The company never precluded the union from sending e-mails over the system, but granted the union's only request for access. It was the union's own choice not to avail itself fully of the access that the employer granted to its e-mail system. Accordingly, the NLRB concluded, the union could not complain that the absence of additional pro-union messages was discriminatory.

The lesson for unions from Lockheed Martin Skunk Works is twofold. First, unions should be alert for anti-union messages circulated over the employer's e-mail system. Where the union learns of such messages, it should immediately request that the employer clarify its e-mail policy. If the employer responds that its e-mail policy prohibits such messages, the union should demand that the employer put a stop to the offending use of the e-mail system. If the employer responds that such messages are permitted under its e-mail policy, the union should encourage its supporters to make similar use of the system.

Second, the union should request equal access to the e-mail system to send its own messages. If the employer refuses, while permitting others to circulate anti-union messages, the union should file a charge of unfair labor practices protesting the discrimination.

An interesting side note in the Lockheed Martin Skunk Works case is a disagreement between the NLRB majority and its dissenting member over the relative efficacy of e-mail over other means of communication. In her dissent, NLRB member Wilma B. Liebman asserted, "It is by now beyond dispute that e-mail is a most effective means of communication. It is a particularly powerful organizing tool. Fast and easy to send, e-mail messages are immediately accessible to their audience and have a more direct impact than messages sent by other means."[5]

The majority, however, noted that there was no evidence to show that "the distribution of campaign materials by e-mail is inherently more effective than distribution by more traditional means."[6] In some cases the union may wish to offer expert testimony or other evidence to demonstrate the particular efficacy of e-mail as a means of communication. For example, where a group of employees rely heavily on e-mail for their routine communication, the union will want to emphasize that fact in proceedings before the NLRB.[7]

Nondiscriminatory Prohibitions

While an employer may not impose or selectively enforce rules so as to discriminate against union communication, it is less clear whether an employer may impose and enforce a nondiscriminatory blanket prohibition on all nonbusiness uses of its electronic mail system, including messages relating to union issues. Two distinct and conflicting lines of analysis have emerged in this area. It remains to be seen which line the Board ultimately will adopt.

One line of analysis holds that employers should have the right to prohibit outright any nonbusiness use of employer-owned electronic mail systems, on the grounds that these systems are the private property of employers.[8] In this view electronic mail is analogous to more traditional communications devices, such as photocopiers, bulletin boards, telephones, or internal mail systems.[9] The NLRB has held that employers may prohibit the use of such company equipment for nonbusiness purposes, including communication about union matters.[10] Employer advocates argue that the same principles should apply to electronic mail and other computer-based communications systems.

The property rights theory has found some acceptance within the NLRB. In one case, the NLRB General Counsel's office opined that an employer could lawfully discipline an employee for using the employer's computer and printer to produce pro-union literature, where the basis for the discipline was the employee's misuse of company equipment and not the pro-union nature of his communication.[11] In another recent case, an NLRB administrative law judge applied the doctrine pertaining to bulletin boards and telephone systems to uphold the validity of an employer rule prohibiting nonbusiness use of the company computer system, including electronic mail.[12]

A contrasting approach rejects the absolutism of the property rights view and instead analyses electronic mail within the established framework that the Board applies to employer restrictions on "solicitation" and "distribution" in the workplace.[13] A distribution is a one-sided communication that is effective so long as it is received and can be retained for later consumption. In contrast, a solicitation is any communication inviting a spontaneous response or reciprocal conversation. The hallmark of solicitation is the immediacy of the communication. Solicitation may include nonverbal communications, such as the circulation of union authorization cards that invite the recipient to respond in some timely manner.

An employer may limit both distributions and solicitations to nonwork time. However, while an employer may outright prohibit distributions in work areas at any time, an employer must permit solicitations in work areas during nonwork time. An outright ban on solicitation is unlawful even where alternative avenues of communication are available. In contrast, the availability of nonwork areas for distributions renders a blanket ban on work-area distributions presumptively lawful.

The NLRB and various legal commentators have analyzed employee and union access to employer e-mail systems in terms of the solicitation-distribution framework. For example, in Pratt & Whitney,[14] the NLRB General Counsel opined that an employer's blanket prohibition on all nonwork use of its e-mail system was overbroad and therefore facially unlawful. In that case the employees spent the majority of their time on computers, and e-mail was their primary means of communication. For these employees, then, the computer, including the e-mail system, was a "work area." The legitimacy of the employer's rule against any nonbusiness use of the e-mail system thus turned on whether the prohibited communication constituted distribution or solicitation.

In some respects, employee e-mails resembled distribution, the General Counsel conceded. Like traditional literature distributions, which may cause litter in the workplace, e-mail messages may take up valuable space on the employer's computer system. Like a traditional leaflet, an e-mail message can be preserved to be read at a later time.

However, at least some employee e-mail communication could be classified as solicitation. The General Counsel noted the ability of an e-mail recipient to "talk back" in direct response to a message, and observed that the employees at Pratt & Whitney engaged in real-time e-mail conversations about union issues. In these respects, e-mail communications possess the hallmark of immediacy to render them solicitations. Because the employer's rule precluded any nonbusiness e-mail, even those that resembled solicitations, the rule was overbroad and unlawful.

The Pratt & Whitney analysis will be most applicable in workplaces where employees rely heavily on e-mail to communicate with one another. In settings where employees make little or no use of e-mail in the performance of their work, the company e-mail system is less likely to be deemed a "work area," and thus less likely to fall within the solicitation-distribution framework at all (and also less likely to be of value as a means of communicating with employees about union issues).

Assuming that the solicitation-distribution framework does apply to employee and union access to employer e-mail systems, unions and their supporters should tailor their messages accordingly. Where an e-mail message invites a direct response from the recipient, it is more likely to be treated as a solicitation, which the employer must permit during nonwork time. In contrast, where a message simply announces some information, without calling for a response, it is more likely to be treated as a distribution and thus subject to outright prohibition by the employer. The interactive capabilities of e-mail and the Internet make these modes of communication especially suited to solicitation-like messages, and unions and their supporters should take full advantage of these capabilities, both to maximize their right of access to the employer's system and to maximize the effectiveness of their communications.

Unresolved Issues

The General Counsel's memo in Pratt & Whitney expressly left certain issues unaddressed. First, the General Counsel noted that the "the lines between working time and nonworking time may be even more blurred and doubtful with regard to professional and quasi-professional employees whose work involves extensive use of computers."

Second, employee access to employers' electronic bulletin boards may not fall within the same distribution-solicitation framework as e-mail communication. Third, the right of employees to access an employer's e-mail system during nonwork time for solicitations does not guarantee that nonemployees (including unions) have a right of access to employee e-mail addresses to send such solicitations.

Finally, while employers may not prohibit employees outright from using e-mail systems for solicitations, employers may be able to impose "reasonable rules limiting E-mail to narrowly address particular problems," such as interference with the functioning of the e-mail system.

The NLRB will likely confront these and other issues in future cases, as the use of e-mail for intercompany communication continues to grow. In the meantime, unions and pro-union employees should continue to explore the use of company e-mail systems as a means of communicating with employees about union issues and encourage the Labor Board to develop clear guidelines on the right of employees and unions to access company e-mail systems to circulate such messages.

Notes

1. Mid-Mountain Foods, 332 NLRB No. 19, 2000 NLRB LEXIS 638 at *21 (2000) (Member Wilma B. Liebman, dissenting).

2. See E.I. Du Pont de Nemours & Co., 311 NLRB 893 (1993).

3. Ibid.

4. 331 NLRB No. 104, 200 NLRB LEXIS 463 (2000).

5. 200 NLRB LEXIS 463 at *28.

6. Ibid. at *17, n. 14.

7. See Pratt & Whitney, 1998 NLRB GCM LEXIS 40 (General Counsel Advice Memo 1998) (citing evidence that e-mail is principal means of communication among employees).

8. See, for example, Susan S. Robgfogel, "Electronic Communication and the NLRA: Union Access and Employer Rights," 16 *Labor Lawyer* 231 (2000).

9. Ibid. at 236–37.

10. Champion Int'l Corp., 303 NLRB 102 (1991) (copy machines); Eaton Tech., Inc., 322 NLRB 848 (1997) (bulletin boards); Honeywell, Inc., 262 NLRB 1402 (1982) (bulletin boards); Churchill's Supermarkets, Inc., 285 NLRB 138 (1987), enf'd, 857 F.2d 1474 (6th Cir. 1998) (telephones); The Cincinnati Enquirer, Inc., 279 NLRB 1023 (1986) (company mail system). Union access to company bulletin boards is a mandatory subject of collective bargaining. *NLRB v. Proof Co.*, 242 F.2d 560, 562 (7th Cir. 1957), cert. denied, 355 U.S. 831 (1957).

11. National Tech Team, 2000 NLRB GCM LEXIS 30 (Gen'l Counsel Advice Memo 2000).

12. Adtranz, 200 NLRB LEXIS 80 (ALJ Dec'n 2000).

13. See Stoddard-Quirk Mfg. Co., 138 NLRB 615 (1962); Le Tourneau Co. of Georgia, 54 NLRB 1253 (1944), enf. denied 143 F.2d 67 (5th Cir. 1944) rev'd 324 U.S. 793 (1945); Republic Aviation Corp., 51 NLRB 1186 (1943), enf'd 142 F.2d 193 (2d Cir. 1944), aff'd 324 U.S. 793 (1945).
14. 1998 NLRB GCM LEXIS 40 (NLRB Gen'l Counsel 1998).

---

16. Lessons from Pioneering in Union Uses of the Internet

Ed Czarnecki

Pioneers have special lessons to share, lessons learned the proverbial hard way. Refined over time and after many revisions, their guidelines have unique value, especially for those of us open to learning from both the mistakes and the "eureka" moments of others long on the job.

The essay below is authored by possibly the first, and probably the longest-lasting, editor of a labor-oriented, computer-based Internet newsletter. Answers are offered to such questions as: What might you do when labor leaders ignore the case you are making for computer uses? What are some of the major weaknesses today in labor's use of the Internet? Contrarily, what are some of the major strengths? Above all, what is the ultimate value of the Internet to organized labor . . . as seen from the vantage point of a very experienced user.

No one I know of has had as long an experience (six years so far) as I have issuing a *Labor Education Newsletter.* Art Shostak, one of my subscribers, invited me to "mine" this for lessons to share with unionists eager to make better use of the Internet, and that led to the short essay below.

Getting Started

Computers came to the AFL-CIO in the late 1980s, and the Education Department, where I was the Assistant Education Director (having worked for the AFL-CIO since 1977), was hooked up early in the 1990s.

I had had a computer for many years, and I was already impressed with the potential to access information from a wide variety of sources. I subscribed to various new services, such as Delphi, Prodigy, AOL, and CompuServe, that initially provided connections to news, sports, entertainment, weather, and so forth, and then eventually provided connections to the Internet.

By my retirement in 1993, the AFL-CIO was just beginning to develop its own LaborNET service. The AFL-CIO George Meany Center had a bulletin board operation. The Institute for Global Communications (IGC) in California had its own LaborNET and had sponsored a first-ever conference on unions' use of the Internet, with strong contributions from European unions. The Canadian Union of Public Employees (CUPE) was setting up the Solinet network—the first major attempt to develop a central location for unions working with computers.

Stepping Forward

In retirement I became increasingly impressed with the wealth of information the Internet offered to unions, but it was going untapped. So two years later, in 1995, I initiated pointed discussions with some labor educators, hoping some unions would assign a staffer to search the Web for resources helpful to all the unions.

To be sure, few unions at that time had Web pages, and few used computers extensively. Their primary use, beyond tracking dues and benefits data, was to categorize collective bargaining trends and practices, and compile statistics on organizing and arbitration activities.

No one volunteered. And so, in the beginning of 1996, with the technical assistance of my family, I set up my own Web-based *Labor Education Newsletter.*

Finding My Way

I scoured the Internet for Web pages and articles of possible interest to labor educators who had neither the time nor, in many cases, the computer access to find it. Each issue of my newsletter gave a very brief description of about a dozen items, complete with Internet links when available. Shortly thereafter, Workers Education Local (WEL) 189 provided some limited financial support, so I could "pay" for my technical support, and the newsletter also became the home page for WEL 189.

The number of people who visited the site was quite small—ranging from 200 to about 500 visits per month. However, since individuals had to learn about the site basically by word of mouth, and since there were and are only about 600 labor educators in the U.S., I was satisfied with the totals. A useful niche on the Internet had been established, and it continues to this very day.

Missed Opportunities

Now, six years after I got started, I believe the potential for labor using the Internet has barely been scratched. Five major weaknesses particularly vex me—all of which labor should and could soon remedy.

1. In many areas—arbitration, organizing, minorities and women in the workplace, and even politics—unionists will find that resources on the Internet are few and far between.

A labor educator, for example, teaching about sexual harassment in the workplace should be able to easily find references to the law, court cases, arbitration cases, management positions, approaches by others in the field, maybe a list of speakers in the area. And even some useful teaching techniques, such as role-playing examples, icebreakers, brainstorming suggestions, and so forth. This is the potential of the Internet. But it has not even been approached.

2. Exchanges of labor education course material and course outlines could be facilitated, thanks to the Internet. But very little of this actually takes place. Good and innovative teaching techniques that others may appreciate are not reported. To date the labor ed community has still not developed an exchange of requests or answers to problems that members may have.

3. Union mailing lists do occasionally get inquiries from rank-and-filers. But those who answer are often not fully competent to reply. Questions, for example, dealing with collective bargaining, labor law, political positions, and national union policies are sometimes given erroneous answers—based primarily on the personal experience of the respondent (if one waits long enough, however, the correct answer often does appear, thanks to input from others).

4. Internet labor education programs that workers could access online are few and far between. This, despite the fact that distance education seems a perfect fit. There are about 30,000 local unions in the United States (according to Cornell's Catherwood Library) with over 100,000 local union officers and perhaps 300,000 (rough guess) local shop stewards. Traditional labor education programs only reach a very small fraction of this audience.

Most labor education subjects—such as collective bargaining, steward training, labor law, organizing, safety and health—could be adapted to the Internet. Union members could take courses in their homes or, better yet, at the union hall. The potential here is almost unlimited.

5. Outside of a few unions, far too many put little effort into utilizing the Internet as a way to provide members with information. Some do not even have a way to exchange e-mail with officers and staff, and most unions do not list the e-mail addresses of their own department heads.

Realized Opportunities

Five positive gains help me keep smiling—and help me keep going:

1. I have gone from mailing out my newsletter to putting it on a Web page (czarlab@erols.com). Since beginning this in 2001, I have already gotten more than 500 subscribers (mostly members of UALE—the United Associa-

tion of Labor Educators), and perhaps down the road it could even be more widely distributed.

The availability of automated mailing lists, or list servers, provides an inexpensive opportunity for someone like me, with limited technical expertise, to "publish" a newsletter and have it e-mailed to many people.

2. Another major gain involves the ability to mobilize in support of a strike, boycott, protest, or rally. Almost daily there are requests via the Internet to support some local union at a crossroads with its employer. Oftentimes the appeal includes suggestions as to how best to help out—with letters, e-mails, and contributions. Lately some more sophisticated Web sites let you send a support letter "automatically" by following simple instructions.

3. Needless to say, the demonstrations around the world involving global financial institutions—World Trade Organization (WTO), International Monetary Fund (IMF), World Bank—would not have been possible without the Internet. Besides the call to action, when these groups meet, the Internet provides a valuable educational function. More unionists and activists now know how these groups operate, their function, their shortcomings, and so forth. From a labor educator's perspective, this is an immense accomplishment.

4. Similarly, international campaigns against particular companies—such as Nike, GAP, and Kohl's—could not have accumulated the pressure for their positions without the Internet. How could anyone learn about the practices of these companies in Asia, Mexico, or Africa without the ability of the Internet to instantly report on local working conditions?

5. Several major labor list servers provide strategic information nowhere else available to unionists in this format. I am especially impressed with list servers that disseminate articles dealing with labor issues that appear in the major U.S. newspapers from sources like the Associated Press, or Reuters, or offer job openings within the labor movement. Or alert members to items of direct interest (Industrial Relations Research Association). Or offer a weekly summary of events in a particular geographic area (Washington, DC). Or disseminate articles to support a particular political viewpoint (third party). Or provide opportunities for individuals to concentrate primarily on labor issues in one country (Canada).

Pulling It All Together

A serious Internet problem that applies to such publications as my monthly newsletter, but also applies to mailing lists like Labor-L H-Net Labor History, is that the information is transient—it disappears as soon as it is issued.

So by putting all of the "best" resources on one page, there is permanence to the information. My Web site now is a place I hope labor educators will turn to when they want to find a Web link dealing with labor education. The only other such site that has a similar approach with links is that of the American Federation of State, County, and Municipal Employee (AFSCME), which is one reason I use so many of their references on my page. (See www.afscme.org.)

In trying to publicize my newsletter, I contacted hundreds of local unions affiliated with the International Brotherhood of Electrical Workers (IBEW), Communications Workers of America (CWA), American Federation of Teachers (AFT), and AFSCME and viewed their Web sites. Regrettably, I found most were little more than a list of officers, with links to their national union and a few other sites. Fortunately, many others had very interesting sites, complete with information on their contract, activities of their local, and minutes of their locals' executive board and monthly meetings. It gave them an opportunity to keep the membership up to date on what was taking place.

My many years trying to make a difference have me persuaded this is *the* ultimate value of the Internet—a way to have everyone with a computer know what is going on within the organization.

Though I have no knowledge of how effectively this is taking place, I would have us honestly reflect on traditional ways information has been transmitted within a local union. There is the membership meeting (which hardly anyone attends). There is the local union newspaper (which, if published at all, no one reads). And there is the person-to-person workplace communication network (which is ad-hoc, noninclusive, and often misinformed).

The Internet, from a labor educator's viewpoint, at least offers the potential to do a far more effective job in making the union member feel an integral part of his union: Helping to "organize the organized" remains a task the United Auto Worker's legendary Walter Reuther tried to get us to understand was *the* most important challenge of all.

---

17. The MODEM Experience:
The Moderator's Views on Some Questions

Brian Mitchell and Cheryl Mitchell

Brian and Cheryl Mitchell, the authors of the unusual report below, are the moderators of a model "electronic community" list server, one I am hoping you will consider replicating for yourself and for your own union brothers and sisters.

I helped create this service several years ago as part of my ongoing twenty-six-year stay guest-teaching at the AFL-CIO George Meany Center for Labor Studies in Silver Spring, Maryland. After a few early years there enjoying a two-week-a-year schedule, I felt unionists needed an unofficial electronic medium for anything they cared to share with others when off-campus fifty weeks of the year.

Brian and Cheryl pick up the tale below and highlight some very valuable advice for anyone drawn to follow. Note especially their clear answers to these critical questions:

- *How might you get started?*
- *How often should your new list server be used?*
- *What sort of contribution—dialogue or information-sharing—is most likely?*
- *Does this require funding?*
- *Is it vulnerable to hackers?*
- *Are responses expected?*
- *Is censorship necessary or advisable?*
- *How prominent a role should the moderator play?*
- *What does the blind cc contribute?*
- *And, how much work really falls on the list moderator?*

Focused and exclusive list servers of the type explained below can help build a very special twenty-first-century sort of electronic "solidarity." Cutting across parochial union boundaries, and allowing for lightning-fast messages or threaded lines of discussion that can go on for years, these list servers have a powerful contribution to make.

What follows is an e-mail message from Art Shostak describing the roots of MODEM and the intentions of its creators. We believe the e-mail was intended to neither flatter nor critique. It was written in response to a number of questions about the origins of MODEM. It is necessary to include this e-mail at the beginning in order to give a sense of history to the brief essay that follows. It will attempt to answer more of the questions that have arisen since Art's original e-mail:

Several years ago I had the good fortune to meet Jim Benson, an especially competent student of mine at the Meany Center and an early user of e-mail. He stood out in his appreciation for what "solidarity" could and should mean among union brothers and sisters. We put our heads together, and

Jim created MODEM, an acronym that stood for Meanyites Online Doing E-Mail, or some such thing.

Over the many intervening years, thanks to the Mitchells, who have generously filled in after Jim's tragic and premature death, MODEM has grown to be a low-key, high-value part of the Internet lives of many alumni and a few Meany Center staff and faculty. Nothing earthshaking, and certainly not a burden on anyone—either senders or receivers.

Instead, much as Jim and I envisioned at the outset, MODEM helps Meanyites stay in touch, share some relevant thoughts, highlight some new Web sites, and occasionally grapple with questions of wide interest.

MODEM is unique as a list server in that we all have in common our love of our time at the Meany Center. Our concern that it's high quality persists. And our desire to turn our Center learning—both of the classroom and the more informal variety—to Labor and America's best advantage.

Absolutely unofficial, and completely independent of Center officialdom, MODEM is a grass-roots operation, a labor of love, and a forerunner—we hope—of many more such "electronic communities" that Organized Labor needs to keep the "soul" in the Movement.

Quiet sometimes for days on end, and seldom the carrier of more than a few good messages a month, MODEM is an ally in our effort to make better sense of these dizzying times. It is a partner in our shared effort to renew and empower Organized Labor. And it is a booster of our Alma Mater, the Antioch College/National Labor College of the AFL-CIO George Meany Center for Labor Studies. MODEM welcomes your membership . . . and especially your voice.

The number of MODEM members, when Jim's torch was passed, was about forty, only four of whom were staff or faculty involved in the College Degree Program. Over the last three years that number has slowly grown to 128, in large part because Art and others at the Center continue to mention MODEM to new students and graduates.

Only three people out of 128 have asked to have their names removed from the MODEM list. One complained that he simply received too much e-mail from too many sources and could not absorb everything. The second objected to the anti-Republican (Bush) bias Meanyites exhibited during the 2000 election/recount controversy. The third offered no explanation at all. About twice that many people have been removed from the list after they abandoned their e-mail address. Still, a total loss of less than ten people says a little something about MODEM's usefulness in its current form.

As the number of members has grown, so, naturally, has the number of messages we receive. So as not to overload e-mail boxes, however, we have adopted a policy of not forwarding more than two messages per day. We had received some complaints about the volume of e-mail, so the limit made sense. Exceptions are made to accommodate time-sensitive material, such as a request for immediate action on an issue.

We do not wish to create the impression that MODEM has been a great vehicle for dialogue. It has not. Besides the 2000 elections, only the changes in policies concerning the College Degree Program of our alma mater regarding admission, curriculum, class schedules, and graduation exercises have generated any real dialogue strings. MODEM's forte is information sharing.

Why so little dialogue? We believe the reasons are actually part of a description of how and why MODEM works.

First, the most time-efficient system for computer-exchanged dialogue is the real-time forum. These things have been around since Q-Link and the Commodore 64. But MODEM is an e-mail list only, not even a bulletin board. All messages are sent to a single address and spammed to all members from there.

Second, maintaining dialogue strings requires an active Web site or bulletin board that must be monitored and maintained. This includes, minimally, dedicating a server, or a computer to act as one, on constant hookup to a reliable ISP. But we are talking about an ad-hoc organization with *zero* budget. MODEM operates from a desktop PC. In this manner MODEM also avoids hackers.

Third, MODEM messages are generally not designed for opening dialogue through MODEM itself. Most messages share timely information, such as Ike Gittlin's daily accounts of activities in Seattle surrounding the World Trade Organization's meetings there in 2000. In such cases we do get the occasional "Great stuff!" responses that let us know people actually do read MODEM.

Fourth, since most of what is shared through MODEM is work-related, readers tend to use the information on an as-needed basis. No response is offered; none is necessary. If someone accidentally replies to MODEM instead of to an intended individual, we gladly forward the message and advise each of the action. No one has ever complained.

Fifth, there has never been more than a handful of regular contributors to MODEM. While a dozen or more people have offered letters on more than one occasion, most members have remained silent in the forum. Let us offer special thanks here to Katie Callan and Paul Plaganis, Karin Hart, Mike Clarke, Hal Sutton, and, of course, Art Shostak, for their continuing contributions. What they offer is both timely and unique.

Contributors have been evenly divided, male and female. Those in private industry outnumber those in public employment, though the trend, as the membership, is shifting. We have not attempted to account for age, ethnicity, or specific union affiliation . . . and like to believe we have a healthy spread along all of these lines.

Now, for some advice (as requested by Art):

1. *MODEM does not hold to any rigid rules of communications, as some commercial systems do. We have had no need for censorship. We edit almost nothing.* However, MODEM moderators do have the advantage of adding editorial comment to the beginning of each message, though we seldom do. So far, we have done so only to clarify the content, to identify the source, to define the issue, or to add thanks or congratulations. We believe the best moderators are those who can remain relatively anonymous.

2. *MODEM does one thing that many individuals should do with their personal mailing lists: the blind cc.* Thanks to Microsoft-knowledgeable MODEM members, we have found a way to avoid those annoying e-mail address lists that appear at the top of so many messages by using the Outlook Express e-mail program. Just put your list of addresses in a Group. You can invent a Group the same way you do a New Folder, only you do it in the Address Book. Send your message only to the Group using Outlook Express. Select the FORWARD button, then Tools from that menu bar, then Select Recipients. The next screen shows all your addresses, including your Groups. Highlight the proper Group, then click on the BCC box, and bingo! All that is left to do is hit the SEND button. Your readers will appreciate it.

3. *MODEM works. It works because it does what it was intended to do, share information and ideas.* There is very little fluff, no overkill, and almost no demand for extra work in MODEM's e-mails. It works because its members share the common experiences of the Meany Center and the College Degree Program (CDP). No fancy subject titles are needed to catch people's attention. It works because MODEM members are all actively committed to the labor movement.

4. *MODEM works because it is not work at all. Nor is there much labor involved, at least not for the moderator.* Reading, forwarding, and clerical details such as changing e-mail addresses and saving files takes only six to eight hours a week. The moderator gets the first look at all the information, a wonderful incentive. We also get to be the first to respond. To us it is well worth the effort for these reasons alone. But we also believe that MODEM helps to keep committed activists informed and that MODEM members read and use much of the e-mail we forward.

5. *The moderators are the least important link in the chain. Besides the minor time commitment, only a few skills are necessary to do a decent job.* A working knowledge of e-mail systems, like Outlook Express, is important. Understanding editing in Microsoft Word is helpful. A strong will to resist the temptation either to continually edit others or to send all your own stuff to members is a prerequisite. We guess there are several MODEM members who would be willing to carry that torch, and would do it well.

6. *Could others emulate MODEM? Could you? We think so. Any relatively homogeneous group could.* MODEM's continued existence will depend, however, on active vocal support from the Meany Center and the College Degree Program. As well, it requires the commitment of a few good members who find the best information in the interest of labor and send it to the moderators for forwarding.

To some extent, perhaps, MODEM is what the AFL-CIO had in mind when it created LaborNET. That system's demise is unfortunate. For a while it performed an info-sharing function. But it was cost prohibitive for that purpose. Its dialogue strings too often took on a soapbox quality, and flaming became far too common. The LaborNET issue has been worthy of much discussion, and we hope labor has learned much from its shortcomings.

7. *Will others rush to emulate MODEM? We doubt it.* Most sizeable labor organizations already support their own Web sites and e-mail systems. For them, MODEM does not represent a particularly attractive alternative info-sharing vehicle. Seemingly simple questions of internal politics, like who keeps all the e-mail addresses and who decides what and when to edit and post, become sensitive issues of power.

What, then *is* the future of MODEM and its imitators? Organs that exist outside the formal structure of union leadership, as does MODEM, require a solid base of support, both ideological and geographical, in order to continue. In other words, one needs to know whom he or she is talking to and where the base of support lies.

To all those bases, we offer our system/structure as a field-tested and proven model of Internet information sharing—a twenty-first-century way to stay together even when apart . . . a new way to craft (electronic) solidarity.

---

18. The Natural Life Cycle of Mailing Lists

Kat Nagel

Humor is far too rare a component in handbooks of this type, and that error is highly regrettable. A vital aid to our effort to stay sane, and a most revealing commentary on our foibles, humor can make possible the telling of certain truths otherwise too painful to hear.

The very short essay below readily makes up in insight what it lacks in bulk. Read with appropriate care, it provides a heads-up message one can turn to keen advantage: It would seem to recommend a readiness to adapt to each of six major stages through which mailing lists are likely to pass. Knowing ahead of time what is coming next, unionists can get out ahead and thereby find the turmoil there a bit less dizzying than otherwise likely. The tongue-in-cheek essay also suggests that retention of an appreciative subscriber pool is quite possible, albeit getting there from here may prove something of a trial as well as an adventure.

Every list seems to go through the same cycle:

1. Initial enthusiasm (people introduce themselves, and gush a lot about how wonderful it is to find kindred souls).
2. Evangelism (people moan about how few folks are posting to the list, and brainstorm recruitment strategies).
3. Growth (more and more people join, more and more lengthy threads develop, occasional off-topic threads pop up).
4. Community (lots of threads, some more relevant than others; lots of information and advice is exchanged; experts help other experts as well as less experienced colleagues; friendships develop; people tease each other; newcomers are welcomed with generosity and patience; everyone—newbie and expert alike—feels comfortable asking questions, suggesting answers, and sharing opinions).
5. Discomfort with diversity (the number of messages increases dramatically; not every thread is fascinating to every reader; people start complaining about the signal-to-noise ratio; person 1 threatens to quit if "other" people don't limit discussion to person 1's pet topic; person 2 agrees with person 1; person 3 tells 1 & 2 to lighten up; more bandwidth is wasted complaining about off-topic threads than is used for the threads themselves; everyone gets annoyed).
6a. Smug complacency and stagnation (the purists flame everyone who asks an "'old" question or responds with humor to a serious post; newbies are rebuffed; traffic drops to a doze-producing level of a few minor issues; all interesting discussions happen by private e-mail and are limited to a few participants; the purists spend lots of time self-righteously congratulating each other on keeping off-topic threads off the list).

OR

6b. Maturity (a few people quit in a huff; the rest of the participants stay near stage 4, with stage 5 popping up briefly every few weeks; many people wear out their second or third DELETE key, but the list lives contentedly ever after).

IV. How to Provide a Web Site

Life is painting a picture, not doing a sum.
—Oliver Wendell Holmes, Jr., jurist

With over 1 billion Web sites up as of June 2001, and 100,000 new ones coming online every week, it is imperative to honor a basic argument (Helperin 2001): "Human attention has become our scarcest and most precious resource" (Labarre 2001). Accordingly, union activists intent on making a success of their labor Web site must attend to Lesson Number One: "If you want to get any attention, you've got to give attention" (Labarre 2001).

A good example of what is meant here by "give attention" is provided by the contents that labor educator William Puette, a contributor to this handbook (see Part XI), has put online for the Hawaii State AFL-CIO (www.hawaflcio.org/). The major sections of the labor site are entitled: Who We Are; Affiliates; Officers; Staff; Committee on Political Education; Steward's Corner; Labor's Bookshelf; Community Services; Union Yes!; Frequently Asked Questions About Unions; Online Newsletter; AFL-CIO State Director's Page.

The Union Yes! pages are meant to help people with the issues and procedures of organizing a union and to assist workers who are thinking of forming or voting for a union in a representation election. A major link can take a user to the Web site of a university labor education center (www.uhwo.hawaii.edu/clear) that features extensive information on the state, applicable federal labor laws, and descriptions of center classes, video collections, and the center's archive. Plainly, sensitive attention *has* been paid to the needs of Hawaii's labor movement, and high usage reflects this.

Along with emphasizing focus, it is important to accent two limitations of Web sites, lest expectations of them be unreasonable or even counterproductive.

For one thing, nothing can substitute for labor's calling card, its ace-up-the-sleeve, its single greatest strength—namely, face-to-face contact. Web sites can supplement, but cannot completely substitute for sound, familiar approaches, especially in-person encounters. They are meant to strengthen and enhance, rather than to compete with the "high touch" ways of seasoned union activists.

Second, Web sites are costly to design and launch, demanding in their maintenance and upgrade requirements, and uncertain in their payoff. They are not to be employed casually or with naiveté. Locals are well advised to try out e-mail and list servers long before going onto the Web, and only then after considerable study and honest reflection.

These cautions notwithstanding, Web sites can substantially reward—and not incidentally, also be a helluva lot of fun! They give their sponsors a chance to put their best artistic foot forward, experiment with scores of glittering options, learn a lot from and about site visitors, help "get business done," and, at the end of the day, have a special feeling of satisfaction from having a sterling presence in cyberspace.

The better to help labor get more from its Web sites, five essays follow that are strong in tips and tricks: The first sets out some starter points. The second shares how-to reflections from two experienced webmasters. The third stands apart in daring to ask aloud some deep-reaching and challenging questions. The forth returns us to the webmasters for further hints from the frontline. And the fifth, while brief, accents two vital points: A site must have special appeal if it is to stand out, and labor sites must consider audiences beyond its own ranks.

Taken all in all, the five essays teach a critical lesson: The idea of Web sites is here to stay, and those of organized labor can and must get better . . . rapidly, creatively, and endlessly,

References

Farmer, Bryan Edward. "A Week on the Web." *Business 2.0*, June 26, 2001, p. 74.
Helperin, Joanne R. "The Outernet Is Coming." *Business 2.0*, June 26, 2001, p. 38.
Labarre, Polly. "Attention Readers!" *FAST COMPANY*, July, 2001, p. 50.
For sharp criticisms of Web sites that reduce to pointless, zero-content sludge, see
    http://www.tuxedo.org/~esr/html~hell.html

19. Unix? Linux? How Do I Even Begin to Create My Own Site?

Matt Seng

Getting started can be scary, and often has us blink, falter, and find some-thing else to do. All the more valuable, therefore, is my stepson's guide be-low to eight easy steps in creating a Web site.

Answers are offered to such questions as:

- *What might be THE hardest task in getting started?*
- *How do you register a domain name?*
- *What sets one ISP off from another?*
- *What options are desirable—Visitor counter? Guest book? Message board? Search engine?*

Coursing through the entire essay is the writer's conviction that you can *master this challenge (as have many rank-and-file contributors to this vol-ume).*

How should unions regard the Internet, arguably the most powerful pub-lishing medium ever invented! A union's Web site can be listed in hundreds of search engines and grouped with 101 others containing related content. But while this sort of awesome outreach is very impressive, and is expand-ing rapidly, making effective use of the Internet is no small task.

I propose to tackle eight fundamental aspects of the challenge and share some advice based on many years of loving (and sometimes cursing) this crazy and wonderful set of communication possibilities. While I make my living at this sort of thing, and would not do otherwise, I have no illusions about the permanence of my advice. I urge you to understand it as a launch-ing pad, a starting point to help you get going: Reach out to nearby pro bono advisers in your rank-and-file, and especially to their youngsters, to help you keep current. Above all, take the first step . . . and, enjoy!

1. Begin by asking what kind of Web site do you really need? Will it be as simple as a contact sheet of phone numbers, officers, and addresses? Or a database hosting pages of dialogue between your members and international affiliates? Deciding what you want from your Web site is always the first

task and perhaps the hardest. Begin building only after you've defined your goals as clearly as possible.

2. Next, register a domain name. You want something that is short and self-evident, or closely representative of your local's name or number. Art Shostak uses a very simple Web address to help people like you keep up with cyberunionism—http://www.cyberunions.net (I designed and maintain the site for him).

You may wish to register several similar domains and direct them all to the same site. For example: You are Union Local 319, Keyboard and Monitor Technicians of America. Different names that would make sense for you to register would be www.local319.org (or .com). Also www.319.org, www.319kmta.org, or www.kmta.org.

Currently (summer 2001) the cost of registering Web addresses runs from about $15 to $35 a year, depending on whom you use to register your name. InterNIC is the organization in charge of managing the millions of Web site addresses in the world. Its Web page (www.internic.com) has a useful listing of accredited worldwide registrars.

There are three primary domains that you might want to consider when buying your presence on the Web: com, org, and net. The other suffixes—gov, edu, and mil—are reserved for government agencies, schools, and the military respectively. There are efforts under way to create other suffixes (including that of .union), but for now, focus on getting a dot com or dot org suffix. Dot com is the better of the two choices, since many Web browsers automatically append any unfinished address in a browser window with dot com, making it simpler for users to reach your Web site.

3. Locals using Internet service providers (ISPs) will find it easiest to set up Web sites on the ISP's servers. Often this means you won't need to pay extra for a Web address name. For example, a local ISP in Oakland, California, called Lanminds Internet Service, offers 25 megabytes of hard-drive space to anyone who signs up for a dial-up account with their company. With this arrangement you won't have your own full domain name (though your own domain generally can be implemented at little cost). Instead, your Web address would be something like http://users.lmi.net/local319.

Remember, though, that you most likely intend for your site to expand as the number of site users does. Will your ISP have available space for you to increase the size of your site? How much would the company charge you to have more than the freely allocated amount? Never underestimate how quickly your site can grow, especially as you yourself grow in knowledge about what it can hold.

There are countless ISPs; all you need is one with a local dial-in number. The company hosting your site should be using something stable, *not* experimental. Generally speaking, a Unix or Linux server running Apache Web server software is less likely to crash than would other setups. You could even ask for the uptime listings of the company's currently hosted sites. Many service providers will guarantee that your site is up a certain amount of time—99.9 percent, for example. If they can't come up with the numbers, it's possible the numbers aren't good.

4. Consider adding such options as a visitor counter, guest book, message board, and search engine. These add-on scripts (known usually as CGI scripts) are like extras on a car; you could live without a CD player, but it makes the ride so much more enjoyable. Also, databases for your records need to be set up in different ways depending on the system (an Apple server manages databases differently than does a Unix or Linux server). Make sure the people who are creating your site understand the system you would be using.

An added benefit to using a popular server/software configuration is that there is a plethora of resources already available on the Web. Sites like www.webmonkey.com or www.worldwidemart.com/scripts/ offer free or shareware versions of guest books, visitor counters, and bulletin boards. (These downloads will need minor tweaks to get them to function for your particular site, and the system you are running must be able to understand the scripts.)

5. You will also want to know about "redundancy" concerning the ISP's network connection to the Internet. The usual standards are either T1 or T3 lines. The more connections a server has to the Internet, the less likely there will be an overload on any one line. Or, even scarier, the less likely is it someone can cut just a single line to disable your Web site.

6. Most companies have weekly backups of their servers. When would your host company perform theirs? Are there nightly backups? It can be very satisfying to know you won't be likely to lose all the data that is being collected by your polls or membership data because of an electrical spike or a tree falling on the server (It can happen!).

7. Who could design a site for you? As of this writing, there are hundreds of Web designers currently unemployed and looking for work. You could probably use the yellow pages, or go to any coffeehouse or friendly local bar, throw a stone, and find one. I know of three different types of designer options: individuals, teams, and firms. Usually the pricing increases as you move from an individual to a design firm. Naturally, there are benefits to all three. While individuals may take longer to design and implement a site, I have found many charge sometimes half as much as local firms for the same work.

Teams are good because they usually have designers, coders, and a wider idea of ways to implement your site. My partner and I, for example, enjoy handing parts of the site design back and forth because we each specialize in different parts of Web design. Design firms, while very expensive, have more resources and employees to bolster your site. I have seen quicker turn around when a larger company works on a site. They often have more hard-core coders at their disposal, individuals who can implement extensive databases.

8. Lastly, remember your site should be dynamic and constantly updated. If someone finds the same stuff repeatedly, they will quickly stop visiting. Freshening could require hiring a full- or part-time staffer who is Web savvy and dedicated to keeping the site appealing, although many locals have hobbyists (or their teenage youngsters) willing to work pro bono (at least for a while). If you do what you can to keep your site catchy and helpful, your union brothers and sisters will keep coming back.

More locals are launching Web sites every week, and more unionists are finding cyberspace to their liking everyday. I hope my eight tips help you start or upgrade your Internet adventure, and I wish you every possible success.

---

20. What a Web Site Should Offer

Linda Mathews and Mike Wisniewski

Two very experienced labor webmasters share some pointed and informed advice below, advice grounded in many years of learning-by-doing. They tackle such questions as:

- *What sort of material really belongs on a union Web site?*
- *What do shop stewards appreciate finding on a Web site?*
- *Is editorial control by a webmaster advisable?*
- *Can pressure be usefully put on an employer by posting current grievances on the local's Web site?*
- *What are the gains and risks of interactivity (back-and-forth communication)?*
- *Why are chat rooms one of the most difficult forms of Web communication to use effectively?*
- *How might the Internet be used to share existing contract language?*
- *Can certain uses of the local's site during negotiations influence results for the better?*
- *In what smart ways can Web sites boost organizing campaigns?*
- *How might a labor Web site reach out to the whole community?*

Taken all in all, this unique dialogue rewards in many ways, not the least of them being the example of two dedicated and thoughtful cyber activists.

MIKE: Drawing on nearly ten years of combined experience and learning from our site visitors, the kind of information that is most usefully presented on a Web site includes constitutions; collective bargaining agreements; health and welfare; legal plans, and so forth that can be considered the backbone of the site. Where possible I have created searchable indexes for these documents.

Current events can include negotiation updates; job postings; memos from officials; news about union activities; and links to news resources, particularly if they are focused on unionism throughout the world. I have links to local papers, TV, and radio, a link to LabourStart, AFSCME Cyberactivist, Campaign for Labor Rights, and the soon to be renovated Labor-OnLine.

I also offer a history of my local, photo albums, the AFSCME stewards handbook, and information titled "How to Contact Your Steward."

LINDA: Information I have found to be most useful on a local's site is first and foremost the contact information. Beyond that, the possibilities are endless.

Through strategically worded interactive forms, we're able to help workers think about specific issues, as well as gathering information from them. Our negotiations survey was available on our site and could be filled out and sent electronically or printed and mailed. We have featured a Member's Attitude form allowing members to give the leadership anonymous feedback.

The electronic mail list provides an easy way to make announcements on monthly updates and new features that have been added to our site. Our photo album, for example, generates a lot of member interest. People like to see themselves on the Web.

Pages dedicated to officers, volunteers, and committee members allow the opportunity for us to give recognition to the too few who are willing to devote their time and efforts toward the cause. Their pride in being featured generates additional activity and promotion of our site.

A recent addition to our district site is a page titled "A Moment in History." It contains links to several streaming video clips that I was able to tape at our recent International Utility Conference. I would like to continue to expand this feature and work on perfecting our video capability. I believe this could develop into a tremendous tool for communication, as well as for educating and training our members.

A site search engine helps visitors easily locate specific items on our site, including the collection of articles in our library section. The reports that I receive on key words that have been used in the search engine helps guide me in supplying the type of info that our visitors are looking for.

The links to current labor news, labor laws, and other sites have helped our members view the labor movement outside of our small inner circle and encourage networking with other union members and labor activists around the world. Several years ago, dialogue among our members was primarily related to job- and company-specific issues. We now have a significant amount of discussion regarding labor issues around the world and how they relate to our industry and us. I attribute the majority of this transition to the communication that has become possible with Web access.

Our stewards section contains our current steward list, a comprehensive steward manual, grievance forms, and our contracts that can be searched with key words. It has been used by a number of locals as a training resource.

With e-mail, members and leadership can communicate more efficiently, and our free Web-based e-mail allows members to send and receive e-mail without it crossing the company's mail server. Our members use e-mail as frequently as the phone when contacting the union hall and officers. It reduces the opportunity of playing that irritating game known as "phone tag."

Our boardroom, chat room, and guest book add additional interactivity. I've approached some of our members about submitting articles, and several have taken on the challenge. Each one that has been submitted has been featured on our site.

I have editorial control over the contents of our site, and occasionally editing is required due to subject controversy. Although this is sometimes a time-consuming process, it's proven to be well worth the effort. I've noticed that when we feature members' articles and pictures, the site hits increase significantly.

We have a section on our site that lists current grievances that has been a big hit with our members. We haven't used it to add pressure on the company over a particular issue, but that will happen, I'm sure, and it is the idea behind why we publish this info.

Labor and industry news as well as action requests from other unions and labor activists are circulated through our mail list. There are now instances of ongoing dialogue and cybersolidarity between our members and other union members on the Web.

MIKE: Interactivity is an area where Linda is way ahead of me. There are two reasons for this. First, I have tried to be the complete designer and keeper of the site. By this I mean I have not gone out to other Web sources to supply interactivity features.

For example, my guest book is entirely contained on my site. With the help of FRONTPAGE, I was able to design the .asp that operates it. On the other hand, my Web host has had trouble keeping up with my demands. I should be able and hopefully will soon be able to supply e-mail addresses.

Interactivity is a very important factor that needs to be more fully developed. Its main drawbacks are that certain types of activity, chat rooms, for example, can be very labor intensive. Open posting of comments, while welcome, can cause great problems. Remember, you not only get the good, but also the bad, and in some situations very determined adversaries can overwhelm your postings.

I have even had to delete things from my guest book because they were inappropriate (political announcements or worse). Since my site is paid for by a union, I have to use my judgment about the politics of the situation. Yes, I do need to be somewhat undemocratic. I wish that weren't so. I enjoy a good exchange, but it isn't my place to get sucked into one.

LINDA: Actually, chat rooms are one of the most difficult forms of Web communication to use effectively. They have the same failings as union meetings. That is, that they require a number of people to be at the same place at the same time. Unless you have a very heavily visited site, the chances of success are not very high. For general use and communication, the easiest and most useful tool is group e-mail, known as a list server.

Guest books and discussion boards both require monitoring and maintenance. For example, online support for an organizing campaign can be a tremendous tool. In fact, having our organizing information on the Web to help plant the seeds of interest in unorganized workers offers us an opportunity to [attract] people that we would have never had access to without this technology.

Unfortunately, it offers the same opportunity to our opponents. We have our work cut out for us in harnessing and utilizing this power. Strategic planning and procedures need to be put into place in order to assure that this tool works for us, rather than against us. Proper administration is needed when interactive communication is used on an official Web site. Rules of conduct need to be stated up front; constant monitoring and the ability to edit or delete any slanderous or illegal information is a necessity.

The ability to collect Internet Protocol (IP) addresses should be utilized in case they are needed for proof of company intervention or interference. And online "salts" are necessary in order to maintain a consistent flow of useful and positive information.

I have made some tremendous allies through the Internet, thanks to the abundance of communication tools at my fingertips. It is wonderful to be able to exchange ideas, strategies, failures, and success stories with brothers and sisters across the world. It has given me the ability to become acquainted with people that I would have otherwise never had the pleasure of meeting.

During contract negotiations, or when I have needed suggestions or guidance on difficult issues that we are facing, an abundance of information and experience from others who have faced those same situations is only a click away.

Our negotiation research committee used some of these contacts to request information on existing contract language. Through requests via e-mail, we arranged for contract book exchanges with a wide variety of local unions for research purposes.

Wouldn't it be awesome to have a huge database available to us with examples of existing contract language? It could include notes on each article of challenges and arbitration along with the findings of each. Of course, it would need to reside within a secure area, requiring password access, but what a tool that would be!

Our Web site and e-mail played a major role in our negotiation sessions. When our negotiations got rocky, we started a related campaign and carried the theme over onto our Web site. Each negotiation session was followed by an online update. While not giving out specific details that could have a negative impact on our strategy, we were able to capture the atmosphere and relay general information.

As things continued to heat up at the table over issues surrounding job security, our site gathered a following of interested activists from around the world who were encouraged to leave feedback for us in our guest book or on our bulletin board. As messages of solidarity and demands for the company to bargain fairly accumulated on our site, we had as many management people following the online saga as members.

The impact on the company was obvious. We had power over them as we had never had before. The ability for us as unionists to connect to one another in a show of solidarity gave us a greater strength in numbers that we could never have had on our own.

The Web also lends us its power for organizing. Though it can never replace one-on-one organizing, it provides an awesome support and communication tool. It gives us the ability to reach the unorganized worker in the comfort of their living room and away from the company's prying eyes and pressure tactics.

When that person is up late at night, unable to sleep, and searching the Web in desperation for help in dealing with his crummy boss, lousy work environment, and inadequate pay, the Web gives us the ability to reach out to him. I've been witness to this ability. But a Web contact has to be followed by a personal contact; otherwise, we have failed in our duties.

We could learn a lot from those who have had successful campaigns using the Web as a major support system. For example, the SPEEA (Society of Professional Engineering Employees in Aerospace) set up a simple Web site for employees at Boeing in Wichita, Kansas, where employees had access to Downloadable Representation Authorization Cards that could be filled out and mailed in. They had the ability to contact representatives online with questions and concerns, and frequently updated information kept them informed about the campaign. The organizing campaign was a success, adding approximately 4,000 new technical and administrative workers to the union.

In their effort to organize workers in the computer industry, the CWA [Communication Workers of America] developed a Web site for a campaign at IBM. It is one of the most innovative Web sites I've seen yet. Impressive in the fact that they posted for public display the contract for IBM's boss, Lou Gerstner, with his $1.1 million a year pension and $1.5 million a year salary—a very strategic move.

But, most significantly, you can join the union online. That's right—not write in for more information, not request a membership pack that will be-mailed to you "in due course." They do have a form that you can sign and mail in, but they have taken it a giant step further. They have a secure online form, where you can request that your employer deduct your dues or pay dues by credit card or a debit from your checking account, and where you can duly authorize the union to represent you: a true online authorization card. That is certainly proof that the Internet offers us tools that we cannot afford to ignore! (See Alliance@IBM—www. endicottalliance.org/.)

Overall, where organizing and Web sites are concerned, my recommendation is that a Web person be used as a support system in organizing campaigns. Our organizers cannot be in both places, in the field and on the Net, and do justice to both. They need our support, and the online network we are building is just what we need in order to rally the troops and keep the ball in our court.

MIKE: I believe ideally our sites would be of use not only to our members, but to the whole community. Our sites should draw people in and capture them. Unless we find a way to do that we will, for the most part, be preaching to the choir. We need to bridge the digital divide not only for our current members, but also reach out to the unorganized. We must drag our membership, or more pointedly, our leadership, into the future.

From my perspective the best way, outside of content, of doing this is to keep the sites fresh and at the cutting edge of technology. We must form and maintain alliances between the union movement and other like-minded socially progressive groups. We must compete with the dot coms for the attention of the world.

---

21. Crucial Questions for Union Webmasters

Mindy Pines

Pablo Picasso once dismissed computers as of no interest to him because they only provided answers. He was interested in questions, the more challenging the better. Picasso might have found the unusual essay below quite to his liking. Questions follow rapidly, one after another, pressing the reader to dig deeper than usual. Enriched by a brief case study, the essay stays grounded thereby in actual experience. Its questions warrant careful pondering and a very creative response.

Creating a Web site forces a union to focus on what it's doing that's worthy enough to inform members (and the public) of and to reflect upon how to become a better union.

The crucial questions are: What is the union doing that's important enough to make the site worthwhile? How should readers feel about the union upon viewing the site? Will the site be interactive? Will it portray an inclusive organization? Or will it merely disseminate information without opportunity for visitors to respond? Will it feature rank-and-file members or just the officers and staff?

Though maybe not as crucial a task as negotiating good contracts, winning grievances, and organizing new members, creating a union Web site is both important and rewarding. It is more than an economical way to disseminate information, to bring members closer together, and to promote a positive image of the organization. A Web site reflects the organization for which it's created. When you create the site, you must look at the organization in ways you might not otherwise.

As a union webmaster, you have to engage leaders, staff, and members in discussing the characteristics and qualities of the organization that they want to portray. What do you want viewers to think about your union upon visiting the site? How do you want them to feel about the work your members do, how your union feels about its members, and the way in which your union is run?

In designing a site you need to know what will make the site fresh or dynamic. What will make your members want to visit regularly? What new and changing features will your site include? What needs to be updated on a regular basis? Will there be a monthly calendar, resource links, staff and officer directories?

Who will be mainly responsible for managing the site? Will it be one person or a team of reporters, photographers, artists, and others? What degree of computer access does the membership have? Do they have slow connections and old, slow computers with little memory, or do they have slick machines with speedy DSL or cable modem connections?

There already exists a plethora of materials both in print and online on how to design and produce Web sites. So I'll spare you those details here except to recommend a couple of online Web site resources that are functioning at the time of this writing:

- Communications Workers of America—Guide to establishing and maintaining local Web sites: www.cwa-union.org/about/local_web_manual/overview/intro.asp
- Putting your union on the Web: www.afscme.org/publications/puttc.htm

And, of course, the articles by Matt Seng, and by Linda Mathews and Mike Wisniewski, that appear in this book are tremendous resources.

Two years ago, as a technology teacher at Lakeshore Alternative Elementary School in the San Francisco Unified School District, I proposed a Web site design for my union, United Educators San Francisco (UESF). UESF represents approximately 7,000 teachers, nurses, psychologists, counselors, and paraprofessionals who work throughout the school district.

At my school, my coworkers ran the gamut from being computer savvy to somewhat technophobic. Many did not own new and fast computers. They used slower, older models with slow dial-up connections that dictated the need for a simple, low-tech Web site without bells and whistles that, when the connection is slow, lead to slow downloads or worse, computer crashes. (It's amazing how much you can do without having to have slick animations, sound, video, or other flashy graphics.)

My coworkers wanted updates on negotiations, quick and easy access to the union contract, phone numbers to call when help was needed, and answers to the more generic question, "What is the union doing for me?" Additionally, they wanted links to education and teaching resources that could help them in their daily work.

Staffers, stewards, and activists wanted links to legal and political resources as well as education policy issues. They also requested calls to actions such as letter-writing campaigns with mail links to legislators and the school board. They also wanted the Web site to become an additional resource for downloading applications and other relevant documents.

I already had basic computer and Web design skills, so the design and execution of the site were not difficult. The most difficult part, particularly because I am a rank-and-filer who doesn't work in the union office, has been developing some systematic way of having information flow so that I can get it in a timely enough manner to make the Web site newsworthy and relevant.

How do you get members, officers, and staffers to submit information, ideas, photos, articles, and other items of interest? Sound familiar? The main difficulties in executing a union Web site are the same as those in building a strong union, period! How do you get members to take enough interest to spend time participating?

Another difficulty is determining what the posting procedure will be. Will there be a committee who must approve content before it's posted? Is the webmaster free to post without approval except for when legal expertise or fact checking is needed? If an approval process is desired, how long a delay in posting of information will this process cause?

Of course, communicating via a Web site should in no way replace the more important human contact or even printed communications. A union Web site should merely supplement them as a part of an overall communications program. However, the site can more cheaply and expediently deliver information on a timely basis if your members have access to the Internet and are in the habit of checking the site. Moreover, by using e-mail hyperlinks, a Web site can more expediently and cheaply receive input from members as well.

Working on my union's Web site (www.uesf.org) has certainly helped me to form a more positive relationship to my union, and I hope and believe that in some way it helps to form a more positive relationship between the union and the rest of the membership. It has been a dynamic process that has come to involve more people with time.

I also hope that some of the questions posed above will help get you started in doing the same. Good luck.

----

22. Web-Site Lessons

Linda Mathews and Mike Wisniewski

Two frontline webmasters share a frank dialogue below about the ups and downs of their ongoing experience. Answers are offered to such questions as:

- *Do all the locals in the same council use the Internet the same way?*
- *If not, so what?*
- *Is a computer upgrade a sure source of Internet gain?*
- *How does use of a union's bulletin board at work compare with use of its Web site?*
- *How can hardware help with the challenge of reaching non-Web members?*
- *Is a site that has become dormant better or worse than no site at all?*
- *What sort of hazards do unofficial sites pose to official ones?*
- *How might unions best aid locals eager to do more here?*
- *How smart is it to employ a top-down structure of support?*

Note especially the contention that the majority of the labor Web movement is being built in the same fashion that the labor movement itself was born . . . from the bottom up, and that is the very reason it has grown so strong, and that is what makes it such a powerful tool.

MIKE: Linda and I daily maintain Web sites for the purpose of educating, involving, and enlightening visitors about our unions in particular and unionism in the larger sense.

We met at a Labor On Line conference in New York City in 1999, and have carried on a long-distance friendship and working relationship since then. At that time she already had a site up, and I was just looking for information and guidance.

LINDA: Our local's site has been a work in progress now for seven years. We are a very small local, but we have built a large presence on the net (http://ibew1613.org). Our local, through our Web site, has gained a lot of attention across the country. I also maintain our district site (http://ibew11th.org), which has been online about a year now.

I own and maintain the domain CyberSolidarity.com, where I developed the first Cyber Greeting Card Service for labor and human rights activists. This site is dedicated to helping activists get their message on the Web and to hold their hand and guide them through cyberspace. It's a great frontier as they work toward claiming their space on the Web.

Last and least, I have a small, but well visited personal site titled Solidarity Forever (http://home.earthlink.net/~solidarity) where our local's Web site was actually born. It is not updated often due to time constraints, but because it has been in existence the longest it has a fairly high traffic rate, and it gives me the opportunity to direct visitors to the other sites as well.

MIKE: At the 1999 Labor On Line conference much was made of the idea that labor needs to establish its presence on the Web. Upon my return I found support from my local union and then from the district council to which we belong. So I began to develop a site.

Apart from design considerations I followed my prime rule in life: "When in doubt, do the obvious." My plan was to set up individual areas for each local and active department of the district council under the umbrella of a district council domain. In each of these areas I would present the information that was most immediately useful to the local or department in question. This meant gathering the content from the various groups involved.

The Health and Welfare Foundation jumped right in, seeing this as an opportunity to make the usual complex information readily accessible to the members. The largest local also jumped on the bandwagon. For some the site is indispensable. The Council Health and Welfare Fund has every bit of information about their benefits up. The council president regularly sends me new things to post.

But then I ran into a wall: Many of the other locals couldn't see the need to spend time giving me what they already had. If you look at my site today, most of the locals have nothing other than a home page. For the most part it is a matter of time for them. There's just one more thing for the overworked union rep to do. Some still don't see the need. Some see it as a threat.

I have been working on the sites, in their various incarnations, for a couple of years now. I had no experience when I started, so site development and skill development proceeded hand in hand. One drives the other. My site is always in a state of change: If I am not adding new content, I will be tinkering with the design and trying new tools.

I started out trying to build a site for my local. When I put it up on my personal space, it was a disaster. I bought some space from Linda and set it up there. As a trial it worked pretty well, and I convinced the district council to fund a site with a domain name. This is when I switched host, so I could take full advantage of programming that wrote the HTML code as I designed and allowed me to directly edit the site.

The council was in the middle of a computer upgrade, and I thought that this could be a great opportunity. It didn't work out that way. The vendor who was installing the server also sold them an ISP and created another council site with a domain name and e-mail service. So there are actually two council sites: mine, which they own completely, and one that is owned by the vendor who installed the server, which they have no control over. Fortunately, the vendor put a redirect up to the real site. If you want to see the basic look of my first site it still exists on the rogue Council site.

LINDA: We, as well as other unions who represent clerical and technical workers, have a unique tool at our fingertips. Direct access to our members is normally readily available through e-mail on the company's server. Although not suitable for confidential communication, it is certainly a link that should be utilized. Recent arbitration cases have upheld the union's right to use e-mail communication on the company's server, as protected activity. Great news for us!

The next logical step was to expand our use of the Web for a communication tool. Our site began as an online newsletter. It's purpose, to provide labor information, news, and education to those we were not reaching through our monthly membership meetings. Regular mailings were a cost we couldn't afford, and since the majority of our members would soon have Internet access at work, the Web was an intriguing economical resource for us. I had quite a few years of experience with desktop publishing, but knew nothing about the Web.

I signed up for an Internet service that offered free Web space and started learning the process of Web publishing by trial and error. Once our site was up and running, I started telling our members about it, sharing my vision of its future potential. I gave out the address to everyone I talked with, and submitted the address to as many search engines and other labor sites as I could find.

When the primary employer of our members decided to implement a corporate intranet (a system confined only to the corporation), there was a lot of discussion about who would have access to the Web as well as the intranet, and who would be restricted to the intranet only. It was finally determined that the majority of our jobs would be enhanced by having the ability to access industry information that was available on the Web. A liberal guideline was put into place on Internet usage.

I sent a request to the department head who instituted the intranet, asking him to put a link from the intranet to our local's site, and supplied him with our address. A couple of days later he sent a message saying our site was very impressive, and agreed that a link should be added. Needless to say, I was both flattered and excited. Shortly after, a page appeared on the intranet with all three bargaining units listed, along with general information on each one. Our local's information included the link.

Once this was accomplished, our members felt more comfortable with the fact that viewing our local's site on the company's computer was really okay. I compare it to the use of our union bulletin boards at work. No one has ever received a warning for occasional brief visits to the board to see what has been posted. And it's certainly okay to spend your breaks and lunch reading through the board postings. But if you frequently visited that board and stood there staring at it for an hour or more every day during work time, we would probably have a real issue on our hands! Fortunately that has not been the case with either the bulletin boards or our Web site.

For each monthly update we send out a notice to our membership by e-mail. It gives a quick overview of any changes, additions, feature articles, and actions that may be requested, along with a link to each item listed. Members are encouraged to submit labor book reviews, articles, suggestions, and comments on site additions.

We also ask that they print out the pages and distribute them to union members who do not have easy access to the site, are not utilizing their access, or who are still a bit leery of the Web. One of our members prints out each page on her color printer and pins them up along the outside of her cubicle. That hallway looks like a living memorial of Local 1613! Actions like this create pride and strength among our members.

The amount of information that the site contains is limited only by sufficient time to get it all published. The work that I do on all of my sites is from home on evenings and weekends. Over time, our site has transformed into a powerful tool that provides an abundance of labor information—a feat we could never have accomplished without Web technology.

I want our sites to provide the information and resources that are needed whenever they are needed, twenty-four hours a day, seven days a week, but more than that, I want to help build the network we need to make a tremendous impact. To help our unions mobilize our members and hold policymakers more accountable.

There is more information out there than there is time to find it all. That is one more reason why each organization needs to develop their own sites. I believe that our job is to provide our members and visitors with the articles and links to relevant information about our particular industries and organizations. We should be acting as guides to the abundance of research material and information that is available. The Internet offers a cost-effective way to increase member knowledge and awareness, and by acting as the portal to the vast amount of information, we are offering a service that helps to make more efficient use of their time.

I think that the IBEW has taken a very positive step in that direction, and I am proud of the fact that we were the first international union to sign up for our own private portal under the AFL-CIO Working Family Site Project. It is still a work in progress, but the potential is very promising.

MIKE: The primary audiences for my site are the members of the district council, its affiliates, and subordinate bodies. Like Linda, I try to provide material of interest to them and open their eyes to the world around them.

This material can be static or offer immediate updates passed on to me. I have links to all the local media, labor, unions, and women's resources.

Basic to my design philosophy is that as much as possible should be available from a link on the home page. I also believe I need to constantly upgrade my skills to keep the site looking fresh and technologically up to date.

Because I receive some financial support for my work, I have been able to experiment. As I said earlier, I used software that wrote the HTML as I designed. This software, in conjunction with a server that supported it, also allowed me to do some fairly complex things rather easily (guest book, interactive questionnaires, etc.), all completely under my control.

At some point I realized that there was more to put on the home page than I could possibly fit without scrolling. But my design philosophy includes eliminating scrolling if at all possible, especially left to right. I had to find a way to compress the info but still have it all fit on the page.

I obtained new software that allowed me to build more complex pages to fit my need to compress the info, and I was able to create drop-down menus that allow access to most of the site from the home page. If I wasn't thrilled about writing HTML, I certainly wasn't going to write scripts to do this. My searches for existing scripts gave me a mixed bag of results.

On a daily basis I try to improve the site. Often I need to put new info up, and I do it as quickly as possible. I send out an e-mail to let the members know that there is something new.

At this point Linda and I diverge to a degree. Not because of any philosophical difference, but because of the way we operate. Linda does this entirely without compensation, while I have been lucky enough to receive support from my district council. And thus it behooves me to spend more time on the site, and it also allows me to invest in new programming.

Let me be the first to say that her graphic instincts are much better than mine! My site tends to look as if it were designed by an erstwhile engineer using only a straightedge. To that end Linda regularly changes the look of her site as well as the content. I am constantly just tinkering with mine.

Be that as it may, I believe that there is nothing worse than a site that has become dormant. Better to have no site at all.

LINDA: Along that line we have a bit of a philosophical difference. I know mine is not the popular belief, but if you give it some thought, you may decide to agree with me on this one.

I have been preaching to our locals that they need to get their site out there, and when they say, "Yeah but . . . It is so much work to keep it updated. Who's going to do it, and without someone to do it, we've been told we are better off not even going there." My response is, "Yes, in order to keep your site alive and of interest to your members, the information needs to be updated on a steady regular basis." However, anybody who is anyone needs to have their site out there, even it if is strictly a one-page ad for their organization.

My reasoning on this is that the Web has become to many, as it has to me, an online "yellow pages," if you will. If they cannot find you through a search engine or at the very least, obtain your contact information, you will be viewed by many in a negative light. I would much rather find a listing of some type with an address, phone number, mission statement, and other basic information than to find no site or listing at all.

Add to that the fact that in the absence of an authorized Web site, there are many unofficial sites popping up daily. If there is no official site in place, then the unofficial ones will be the ones listed and found by not only the members, but your audience-to-be at large. This will make for a difficult transition once the local does take a step into the twenty-first century and tries to establish its presence online.

Between the various sites I administer, I am constantly receiving messages and requests for more information. Some are from other activists. Some are students looking for research information. Some are workers asking about labor laws and union representation. And, sadly, many are union members who come to our site looking for information because their locals are not on the Web. As use of the Web continues to grow, so is the number of our visitors, seeking the information and guidance that only we can give.

MIKE: Yes, but what usually happens is that in some spurt of energy a site is created, probably without a domain name, time-sensitive material is put out there and forgotten about. At some point somebody stumbles across the site and sees some old info and decides that unions are still backward.

A prime example I can give happened when the city unions in Philadelphia were negotiating last year. MSNBC linked to my site and to another local's site in the other district council. The other site had no news about the negotiations. It just sat there like a lump.

The other problem with the personal union sites is that they get listed in groupings, like the list that the AFSCME International site has, and then disappear. Trying to keep up with those massive sets of links could be a full-time job. If you are suggesting that somebody take on the role to coordinate sites setup, I'm all for it.

LINDA: There are still many who have not gotten on board, or that have become stagnant and slow in development. While the logical thinking may be that they could or should be handled in a centralized manner, I submit to you that the opposite is true.

As you know, most of the labor Web movement has been built in a typical grassroots manner, from the bottom up. That is the very reason that it has grown so strong, and that is what makes it such a powerful tool. It is being built in the same fashion that the labor movement itself was born.

Many unions have experienced the development of the Web with the rank and file leading the pack, while the upper layers were dragged along kicking and screaming in denial and blindness behind them. Some have tried ineffectively to stifle the growth because of the perceived threat to the comfortable structure they have become accustomed to.

I am proud to be in a union that has been open to growth and potential, allowing for development to take place from both ends of the structure (though probably not as quickly as it should have been but we are continuing to grow in this area and seem to be picking up our pace).

The largest drawback and hindrance from the bottom is the same as with any movement in this day and age: the lack of time, energy, and resources to devote to the cause. Most of us who have been pioneers in this endeavor have done so at our own expense and on our own time. And it has taken a considerable amount of time and effort to lay the foundation and prove the worthiness of this tremendous tool. So where do we go from here in order to fully utilize the power of the Internet?

We need to invest in order to grow. Not by ripping up the roots and transplanting them like seedlings into an artificial environment. But by watering and fertilizing the roots in order to help them grow in their own natural environment—just like organizing.

My vision is to have an individual to work with each district office to help get them online, with backing and encouragement from the international union to invest financially in developing their Web presence "for and within" their own district. Leadership by example if you will. Ideally, the sites could be hosted on the international union server, with room for expansion to include space for locals to be added as subdomains if needed, or as an economical alternative to an external host. With the proper (and necessary) financing, the district would have the ability to maintain and grow their site. Each district has specific territories, constituencies, and needs unique among themselves that are most properly dealt with from within.

If this responsibility were centralized, we would be utilizing a cookie-cutter approach, which only gives the illusion of being on board. The result of this method would be a top-down approach. Easier to administer, maintain, and control, but a method that strips away the key element that we are trying to build—the pride of ownership and individuality, which comes with building your presence online.

Nothing new here, the same is true in how a local is successfully run.

Lead from the side and build upon the power of the group as a whole, or lead from a top-down structure that take away the need or drive of the members to participate. The latter is a common downfall for labor.

If each district were to assign Web responsibilities to a rep within the district, their responsibilities could be to build and maintain the district site, and to grow from there by becoming an ambassador within the district for development on the Web: teaching locals about the resources and tools made available to them with the Web; offering training and support to the staff or designated officer(s)/member(s) who will take on the responsibility of the local's site; educating them on the legal pitfalls and how to avoid them by developing guidelines and the necessary approval process for Web publications; offering priority status assistance (acting as a resource/consultant to develop or help with online support) to locals involved in organizing campaigns, rocky negotiations, strikes, local political actions/activities, and so forth.

This again would be an act of leadership by example and at the same time would afford the opportunity to prove the validity and usefulness of new technologies. As its usefulness is proven, there would be a natural increase in the number of locals willing to make the needed investment for development and expansion of their own sites.

My ideas for building our interstructure may not be *the* way to go, but if it helps get us thinking along these lines, so much the better.

As far as design, it is true that I have devoted a lot toward monthly and bimonthly designs, usually based on the season or holiday of the month. Whether or not this has driven more traffic our way could probably be debated. However, our local site has become so large over time that it has become very difficult and awkward to do complete makeovers on a regular basis. I plan to do a new look much less often and spend more time focusing on current events, news, and indexing.

MIKE: I wasn't suggesting centralized control of the sites, just an entity that would show the way to do it. There is one other problem here. If I as a union activist decide my local should have a site and set about creating one using my own resources, do I have the right to claim some direct variant of the local's name as a domain name? I think not. I guess if I called it *Mike's Local Union . . . org* it would be okay, but that raises problems with searching.

I would certainly argue that putting up a rogue site, no matter how bad the union might be, under the union name is dishonest. Putting a site up to spur the leadership in the right direction is a good thing to be sure, but the fine lines of good judgment can get really blurry.

What is so compelling about this technology? What is so different about it that we are willing to invest so much time and effort on it? Simply put, it is potential. As long as the Internet remains unrestricted and open to anyone, we have the opportunity to put our ideas up right next to any rival in an open forum.

However, we need a structure of support for development. There are ways to minimize the time necessary to keep up the basic site, but people don't know how. Linda has her "cybersolidarity" site, which she operates on her own time and at her own expense. The AFSCME International has a "Webmasters Corner." But there is no full-time and fully supported site for all union Web developers or potential developers to get together. We can and must find a better structure so we can work smarter, not harder.

---

23. Finding and Holding a Web Audience

Robert Kolb

Well known in the world of labor Internet users, the essayist below continues to pioneer in offering a wide array of communication services to union activists. His essay underlines the strategic necessity for labor to market its message and to pursue Web users beyond the ranks of union regulars.

A sheet-metal worker of local 73 Chicago, I operate grassroots Web sites and operations primarily from 73online at http://www.73.org, which was founded in October 1998. I administer about 100 domain names, over 100 opt-in online newsletters and groups, most of which are labor related, and also over 10,000 e-mail addresses. As well, I manage tens of thousands of banner exposures through Microsoft LinkExchange and other banner networks, including paid-to-surf surfbars, fax-o-grams, on-exit scripts, on-exit exchanges, drop-down menu bars on thousands of sites, and some e-mail blasts.

As for sharable advice, I want to make two points in particular: First, you have to be *very* dynamic if your site is going to stay useful. And second, we have to aim our message at the general public, not at the "choir," if labor is soon to gain any new members.

1. I urge you to recognize that, in general, a Web site, an activist group, or any campaign is usually short-lived. People get on the Net, get involved until they lose interest, and then they move on. If you would hold onto your

audience, you must continually offer gimmicks—freebies, controversial stunts, and special effects—that will set you out from the rest.

You may even offer services considered unethical if handled by an official organization. You might take the enemy's position in order to infuriate and inspire retaliatory activist support, using jokes and even racy material that will be forwarded by recipients to friends, and best of all, thereby take advantage of free services provided by the same companies that wish to crush organized labor. You must be prepared to constantly change and adapt to conditions.

I have learned through trial and error to offer an amalgamation of computer/Internet information and labor topics. The computer/Internet information includes things like free downloads, hacker and virus alerts, and privacy and security information. The labor topics are directed to all of my labor groups, regardless of whether they directly or indirectly affect them, as I have found that, over time, each and every issue facing a particular union does in fact affect all at some point.

Using the above strategy, I have achieved a longer retention of visitors and subscribers. My dual approach breaks the monotony for activists of exclusively labor-related material, While those who came to my sites only to investigate computer/Internet-related topics are exposed to pro-union–related material, either directly or subliminally.

2. The biggest mistake labor makes is to spend funds on promotions and campaigns targeted only at our own members or activists. Most of these brothers and sisters already know the issues, and they are probably three steps ahead of labor, as many union bureaucracies operate very slowly in adapting or reacting to any new thing.

Union funds should be used, instead, to target the general population. Example: Instead of giving out free Union-YES! T-shirts to the members, take out a Union-YES! one-page ad in *Sports Illustrated*. Or place a Union-YES! billboard above a high-traffic roadway. Or have a public bus wrapped in a Union-YES! design. Or place Union-YES! ads on the Web sites of major Internet search engines.

Never forget: The presence of online labor-related material can stimulate interaction with the general public, serve as a medium of communication with members and nonmembers alike, and help invigorate union democracy. It can also counter negative stereotypes of unionists, especially images of us that maintain brothers and sisters are not "with it," that we do not compute— when a good many of us certainly do!

V. How to Become a CyberUnion

Nothing will ever be attempted, if all possible objections must first be overcome.
—Dr. Samuel Johnson, English writer and critic

Just about everything that comes to my attention inspires me to ask, "How might organized labor make use of this?"—which, in a nutshell, explains the origins of this handbook, my latest attempt to share a lot of good advice from over forty union activists with 16 million other unionists.

Going back to 1986, when I wrote *Robust Unionism: Innovations in the Labor Movement*, I have been preoccupied with three ideas: First, that labor is too insular and would profit from adapting bright ideas field-tested elsewhere. Second, that many sound innovations within the labor movement fail to get the attention and adaptation they warrant elsewhere in the movement. And third, that unless and until labor risks more and adopts bolder innovations, its progress will continue to seriously lag.

In articles and books since *Robust Unionism,* I have tried to highlight scores of promising reforms for labor's consideration, ranging from A to Z—from alternative dispute resolution options to zip code–based software for superior distribution lists. Increasingly, I have focused on computer-based options, as I have become convinced they offer more for less than any other available resource—save, that is, for one-on-one contacts among caring human beings.

All of this came to a head in my 1999 book, *CyberUnions: Empowering Labor Through Computer Technology*. With the help of ten very able contributors, I laid out in that volume a three-fold typology of contemporary unions and locals busy trying to come to terms with the computer revolution, and I suggested what might be a better-than-ever hypothetical model for labor to consider adapting.

1. *"Does Not Compute."* The first model, which I call Cyber Naught, involves a minimum employ of computer potentialities. These organizations generally hesitate to go beyond staid reliance on computer-based bookkeeping. Put starkly, these unions and locals use computers only to get through the day, and do so in a flat and uninspired way. They settle for inertia and quietism. Intent primarily on keeping things (deceptively) calm, Cyber Naught leaders patch over organizational ills with cosmetic "band-aids," and leave in their wake fatally wounded unions and locals.

2. *Galloping Off in All Directions.* The second model, Cyber Drift, involves labor organizations that move first in this direction of computer use and then in that one, unable to maturely guide their own efforts. Crippled by unthinking adaptation of incompatible, if glitzy and trendy hardware and software, Cyber Drift unions and locals disappoint unionists eager to believe labor has much to gain from sharply focused computer use.

Cyber Drift unions or locals move aimlessly, like a cork bobbing on a turbulent sea, though with far less likelihood than a cork of staying afloat. Lacking an information technology (IT) officer, and available for "seduction" by a never-ending series of slick-talking vendors, these organizations are crippled by incompatible software, hardware, and infrastructure components. Hardly anything works together, and frustration runs rampant.

The problem here appears especially rooted in gullibility: Susceptibility to the siren song of unscrupulous vendors has far too many Cyber Drift labor leaders preferring flattery to function, promises to results, and glossy brochures to demonstrated rewards. Intent primarily on keeping things hopping, Cyber Drift leaders substitute dust raising for ground breaking, and can leave in their wake one hell of a mess.

3. *"And the Oscar Goes to . . ."* The third model, Cyber Gain, wins accolades for its state-of-the-art accomplishments where computers are concerned. In contrast with Cyber Naught and Cyber Drift types, Cyber Gain unions and locals today make much of computer possibilities. Officers, staffers, and activists alike enjoy adapting gains made elsewhere in and outside of labor. Indeed, this handbook may become something of a major resource for these organizations, and many of the essayists in its pages are proud to think themselves Cyber Gain enthusiasts.

However, before too glowing an impression is given, it should be noted that Cyber Gain unions and locals have many costly weaknesses. Especially telling is that they remain frozen in the first generation of Internet use. Their

Web site typically offers their logo and basic facts, a static display that critics dismiss as "brochureware" or "billboards." Their e-mail and list server messages are characteristically uni-directional, going only from top to bottom. They hold back the e-mail addresses of their leaders lest members attempt to finesse the hierarchy and go directly to the top. And they frown on unmoderated chat rooms and bulletin boards lest matters get "out of control" (read—the officers come under heated attack).

Cyber Gain unions fail to understand or decline to value the fact that second-generation computer applications are quite different: These advances emphasize the dynamic participation of all of the parties, rather than only of some, and champion a feisty culture rather than one that promotes passivity.

Back to the Future

Transactional computer approaches would take American labor back many decades to its heady and turbulent origins in open debate. In those early raw decades the likes of Samuel Gompers, William Green, Philip Murray, James Carey, Walter Reuther, and other now legendary pioneers in democratic unionism gave as good as they got in meetings and on the convention floor. In illuminating debate with the Loyal Opposition, these labor leaders openly explored bold new ideas, and labor thrived on the give-and-take of alternative plans, values, and visions.

While the Cyber Gain model is clearly superior to Cyber Naught and Cyber Drift options, my argument is that it will not suffice. By failing to take the potential of transactional computerization into account, by failing to grasp its ability to re-energize dialogue within the house of labor, Cyber Gain organizations do not so much deal with the future as they streamline the past. Only a far more ambitious and freewheeling use of computers will enable labor to do the job necessary if the movement is to survive and thrive.

Which is what this and the next four parts of this handbook are all about: They make a case for helping unions and locals to soon achieve the four distinctive strengths of a CyberUnion—the computer-based ability to forecast, to innovate, to provide new services, and honor traditions (FIST). FIST sets the CyberUnion far apart from its Cyber Gain forerunner.

Each of the FIST strengths is explored fully in an ensuing part of the handbook. So, instead, attention is best paid below to an engaging short introduction to the transition process. That is, to tips and tricks which a local can use to go from Cyber Naught to Cyber Gain status—the better to peer beyond and weigh the appeal of a beckoning CyberUnion model.

24. Bridging the Cyber Gap

Peggy Myrie

If unions and locals are soon to grow beyond Cyber Gain status and move toward CyberUnion stature, it will be in large measure because of the faith, effort, and sacrifice of union activists like the essay writer below. Her essay helps explain the necessary motivation and "smarts" of pioneers, along with an upbeat "can do!" attitude without which nothing ever gets done.

During my year 2000 week in residence at the National Labor College, after previewing a documentary film, *Labor Computes: Union People, Computer Power*, developed by Art Shostak, I wondered about the involvement of my union in computer technology.

When the film ended, I went to the George Meany Center's computer lab and clicked www.uaw.org and hunted for my Local 652, Lansing, Michigan. I could not find it, but I did find local UAW 602, another Lansing General Motors local, and several GM UAW locals from neighboring Flint, Michigan.

On my return home I went to my union's financial secretary to inquire about a Web site for the local. He seemed only aware there was quite a cost to having a Web site, but one with which our union should have no problem.

I then went to Plant 3, where I worked before I entered the UAW's Educational Opportunity Program (EOP), to the local union office to speak to my committeeman. The office was smoke ridden, and the computers that were on showed a screen of solitaire. I knew this was a Cyber Naught holding pattern, and as a member, I was no better off. I finally got the go-ahead to create a local Web site from another union representative, one who holds a position somewhat out of the loop of the local union hall leaders.

I have since been looking at many Web sites to examine the pros and cons of their offerings, using the objectives from *CyberUnion*, the book by Shostak that I used as a text at the National Labor College.

I know that creating a Web site is more than listing the officers' names, placing a photo of the union hall across the page, or keeping it up to date. On the book's advice I signed up for a class on creating a Web site and a class on the use of a digital-video camera. The more members that I have since talked to, the more ideas I have received about the content that unionists and Netizens are interested in.

Most difficult is focusing "beyond the present." However, incorporating the FIST model from the *CyberUnion* book will help.

My local's Web site will need a mission or vision, and a means to present the traditions of the UAW. I recently viewed a documentary, *The Great Sit Down*, about the Flint, Michigan, 1936–37 strike in. This was a great history lesson, of great heroes, one that can relay the "soul" of unionism. The film reaches out to women as well, with their contributions in the Emergency Brigade and the Women Auxiliary. I thought, "How great these clips would be for viewing on the Web site!"

I know the local's Web site should offer the ability to exchange skills and services of members to one another. It should offer volunteer or service opportunities and promote union-made products. Educational workshops, training, and skills updating can be available, as well as the memberships' chance to become more politically involved. The Web site needs to inform. People are starved for information, and we need to get the word out with better communication and exchange of ideas.

CyberUnion also stressed the need to hire a full-timer to maintain a site by keeping it current and full of merit. We should ask young people to help us with the high-tech technology that they are so comfortable with. Adults should not be embarrassed, but should take advantage. Retirees are also valuable assets. Many with computer interests are more than happy to lend their spare time contributing to or maintaining a Web site for their union.

As well, so-called out-dated computers are being tossed away, no doubt by many union members. It would seem that these computers could be channeled to those Americans who are "have-nots" via offers through the local's Web site, thus helping to increase membership.

Once my local's Web site is up and going, members can be proactive on issues around the world. We can help out other workers many miles away by putting pressure with a click of a button on firms to honor health and safety issues. It will be easy for us to gain ideas already in practice by other global unions. And this cross-fertilization will be very valuable in building union strength and solidarity.

Unionists must communicate, must become actively engaged, and must seek the high-tech talent of members to accumulate new power. We need to look to the future, plan ahead, and find "grand ways" to use computer technology to its full potential.

VI. How to Employ Futuristics

We're just beginning to glimpse what we have.
And it makes feasible a world of possibility.
—John Ellis, author

The best way to predict the future is to invent it.
—Alan Mckay, computer programmer

Even before launching into a discussion of tips and tricks for forecasting, it is vital to explain that the four major strengths of a CyberUnion—its computer-based prowess at forecasting, innovation, services, and honoring traditions (FIST)—are *not* exclusive to it. Any Cyber Gain labor organization can also profit from use of these resources, and it is my fervent hope that all will soon do so!

What sets the two models apart—CyberUnion versus Cyber Gain organizations—is that the former are defined by the FIST components, while they remain optional interests of the latter. CyberUnions have FIST at the center of their being, while Cyber Gain organizations can make the mistake of ignoring, scorning, or underemploying any of the "big four."

This said, the ideas below and in the following three parts help promote the computer-based employ of forecasting, innovation, services, and tradition-honoring practices.

Futuristics

Those in organized labor drawn to improve their use of the art form known as futuristics recognize that union activists are natural futurists: They are always second-guessing what the boss, the company, the industry, and the economy—to say nothing of their spouse and children—will do next. It is not possible to live within a framework of labor contracts that must be renewed every three years, union elections that shake the organization every two years, and other such cycle traumas, and not be an organic "futurist."

Increasingly, union activists stressed by forecasting needs ask how they might get beyond guesswork, speculation, and industry gossip in planning for the near future. They understand that unionism goes where you imagine it. Many envy forecasting tools *already* part of the arsenal of big business and government, and some intend to transfer and use those tools (National Conference of State Legislatures 2000).

Committee on the Future

To get started, a small voluntary Committee on the Future, possibly a subcommittee of the executive board, should be established. This should be either at the initiative of elected officers or of the staff, but always with official status and a small, though adequate, budget. This imprimatur helps establish legitimacy early on for a venture that might otherwise be wounded from the outset by suspicion and/or ridicule.

Members of the committee should agree to serve pro bono, above and beyond their regular duties, out of sheer love for the intellectual venture and the excitement of helping to explicitly shape the organization's future. They should also agree to stay with this for at least five years, and train their successors for two years before turning over their seat.

The new committee should expect to quickly pick up key norms in forecasting, for example, drop the words "will" and "will not" from one's vocabulary; likewise, the words "never" and "always." Remain tentative and keep an open mind. Understand that the more certain we get about the alleged details of the future, the greater the likelihood that we are wrong. Keep in mind that whatever we expect to happen in the future, we must also anticipate that it won't. Note that history suggests the "most likely" future really isn't that likely at all.

The committee can have a wide variety of functions, as outlined below.

1. Gathering Ideas

Among its many tasks, the committee should be charged with using a form to scan the literature, the World Wide Web, and all other sources of relevant forecasts. (Contact info@wfs.org.)

A call should go out for volunteers from among the rank-and-file (and family members), and a scanning form should be posted on the organization's Web site and e-mailed to all in hopes of drawing more into the venture. (See www.wfs.org/bookstore.) Major forecasts of relevance to the rank-and-file, and also to the organization as such, should be culled, assessed, collated with others, archived, and acted on.

2. Employing Methods

The committee could hire professional futurists to teach it how to employ a bevy of field-proven methods for forecasting and shaping the future. Prime candidates include scenario writing, trend analysis and extrapolation, computer modeling, brainstorming, simulation and gaming, the interviewing of experts, polling, intuition, and the search for lessons in history, science fiction, and the environmental sciences (May 1996).

3. Employing Talent

The committee might want to recommend the hiring of young hackers as an indispensable aid to keeping the use of computer power as futuristic as possible . . . and also because some influential hackers are busy inventing a "free, raucous, engaging new civilization" labor will want to share in (Katz 2000, 206).

Hackers thrive on solving problems with hardware and software beyond the ken of ordinary mortals. They take joy in exploring the nooks and crannies of the Net to build anew (versus a tiny bloc of scorned "crackers," who break the law and most other things). Hackers revel in redefining what is possible, in trying to invent the "next big thing," and in bewildering the adherents of the status quo. Many are anti-authoritarian, and have "an instinctive hostility to censorship, secrecy, and the use of force or deception to compel responsible adults. And they are willing to act on that belief." (Raymond 1999, 236)

Hackers are increasingly in short supply, especially those of a pro-labor bent ("hacktivists"—see the Introduction to Part XI), and labor has much to learn about how to attract and hold onto these valuable information age digerati (Katz 2000).

4. Exploring Forecasts

The committee should pay special attention to work-life forecasts; for example, the estimate that an American who boosts his or her working time by 10 percent, from 2,000 to 2,200 hours a year, tends to raise his or her future earnings by about 1 percent for each such year. Many workers, however, would prefer to spend more time with their families. CyberUnions could sponsor Internet-based debates and dialogue designed to help members think through the trade-off (Koretz 2001).

CyberUnions could assess the worth and significance of such workplace-related forecasts as:

- "For the United States, as a whole, between 25% and 30% of workers are in nontraditional arrangements—and that percentage will grow" (Malone, in Rosenfeld 2001).
- "By 2007, the average U.S. corporation will have 30% more of its workforce in non-U.S. countries" (SAP America 2001).
- "It's estimated that by 2010, there will be 10,000,000 fewer workers than jobs in the U.S. alone" (SAP America 2001).
- "Blue-collar workers have much higher mortality rates than white-collar workers. An increase in the retirement age for Social Security, which the Bush Social Security Commission is considering, would have a sharply disparate impact on blue-collar workers" (American Academy of Actuaries 2001).

Forecasts, in short, could scrutinize demographic changes in the labor force that the union and/or local draws on, and help develop plans in advance of changes. Forecasts could enable labor to test the warring claims of antagonists in public debates that beckon labor to take sides, as in the global warming or energy embroilments. Forecasts could enable unions and locals to better anticipate training upgrades for members and continue thereby to distinguish dues-payers from less well prepared nonunion competitors.

5. Exploring Scenarios

The committee could study and "mine" scenarios, written by its members, rank-and-filers, and/or retained professional futurists. An example of how rich they can be in ideas is available in this imaginary picture written by Miguel Abrantes Antunes, a young college student of mine:

> Fresh out of college five years ago, in 2000, I was eager to use my new computer skills. My dad, a longtime activist in the Electrical Workers Union, told me labor might soon be doing something big, really big, and that caught my interest.
> I began by helping my old man overcome his own fears in the matter. Up until then Dad had no use for computers. Hell, he had only gotten me

one to help me in school. But when I actually sat him down, someone he trusted, and when I showed him some of the possibilities, he became an overnight fan.

Soon after, a bunch of hotshots took over his union. They hired computer technicians, programmers, and software designers, myself included, and let us lose to digitize the entire shebang. Almost overnight we created a Web site for every local, including my old man's, and we provided free updates and maintenance. The international union (IU) also decided everyone should have a free home computer, and free email and Internet access, a helluva new fringe benefit the members liked a lot!

We began to start carrying personal digital assistants, the fancy kind that are voice-activated, the kind that kinda talk with you, rather than at you. Some also carry Microsoft's wireless Tablet, a gadget you just scribble messages on and they flash away as e-mails. We were never out of touch, and had 24/7 access to everything you would want in the field. We could bring our laptop in from the car, plunk it down on the kitchen table, and be online instantly. It was like you never left the office!

This really kick-started a "Webolution," and it spread. Locals of other unions were falling over one another to copy us, and within two years every part of the labor movement, and I mean every part—city councils, state, feds, everyone!—was digitized.

Labor overseas tried to match us. Outfits in Sweden, France, Germany, Finland, and Spain began to do some clever things, as did some in South Korea, Japan, and Taiwan. We were not too proud to learn from them, and everyone kinda smiled at the friendly rivalry.

At about the same time many of us, here and there, asked, "What if we could get everybody, the world's labor movement, really linked—really?" There had been sporadic international labor Internet conferences in the late 1990s, but few got any attention or made a ripple. Most involved big-shot leaders or academic types. We wanted to reach everybody.

Within a few months we took a global vote via e-mail, and labor federations around the planet decided a Webcast would be the best first way to go. It would be like attending a local union meeting or an IU conference. But it would be online, and it would bring us together, the entire labor world, from pole to pole, everybody! You would be able to sit at home and watch, listen, and even talk back to labor leaders from France or Japan or anywhere, and you could have a running translation on your monitor's screen.

We decided the conference would go for half a day to allow members in distant time zones to speak live, rather than just play back a prerecorded message. We wanted the entire labor world to broadcast live, for that would add excitement to the whole affair.

I have to get down now to the local where a bunch of us are going to take this in together, you know, with popcorn and beer. Now that my old man and his buddies have gotten excited about computer power, there's hardly any limit to what we can imagine doing. Watch out, world, labor's a player!

Maybe someday soon such a conference will actually happen!

6. *Visioning*

Another major contribution, arguably the first, second, or third most important, would have the committee tackle the vision challenge. As explained in Chapter 11 by Nancy Bupp:

> Victory does not always go to the largest armies, the best deployment, and the most firepower. It goes as often to the smaller force with the greatest imagination, flexibility, and boldness, with the vision to make something happen.
>
> Every vision of the future sets off its own feedback loop. One prepares for what one believes will happen. At the same time, that preparation makes it more likely that this particular future will happen. Ask ourselves what future does the union really prefer? Ask ourselves what is our union preparing for? It is not enough to do our best at figuring out what is likely to happen and then only react to it.

Particular attention should be paid to ensuring the visioning project remains sensitive to the increasing diversity in the ranks, as this is likely only to expand in fact and political significance: Between 1990 and 2000, for example white males as a percent of all union members declined from 53 percent to 49 percent. Women increased their share from 37 percent to 41 percent. Foreign-born workers in 2000 constituted 10 percent; in 1995, only 8 percent. Black men's share fell while black women's rose. Asian and Hispanic men and women's share all increased (Hirsch and Macpherson 2001). All of these subgroups see and desire a slightly different future, and accommodations *must* be worked out.

Summary

A labor Committee on the Future could usefully do all that was outlined above, and also the following: (1) Discuss the process and forecasts in the organization's paper and on its Web site. (2) Create an e-mail list server of members especially interested in the committee's work. (3) Exchange ideas about process upgrades with similar future committees in other unions and locals, within and across union boundaries. (4) Attend the annual meeting of the World Future Society; caucus there with other labor futurists. And (5) keep the process going by steadily improving its results and their application.

The better to help this all along, two essays follow, the first exploring the teaching of futuristics, and the second taking a very brief look at computer possibilities. It never ceases to amaze me to think that if auto technology had kept the pace at which computer technology operates, "a new car might cost about $2 and go 600 miles on a thimble of gasoline . . . ," but enough of this wishful thinking, and onto some brass-tacks forecasting matters. (Henderson 2001)

References

American Academy of Actuaries, press release, from Jeffrey Speicher, June 11, 2001 (202-785-7870).

Ellis, John. "Digital Matters." *FAST COMPANY*, June 2001, p. 74

Henderson, Carter. "How the Internet Is Changing Our Lives." *The Futurist*, July–August, 2001, p. 38.

Hirsch, Barry, and David Macpherson. *Union Membership and Earnings Data Book.* Washington, DC: Bureau of National Affairs, 2001.

Katz, Jon. *Geeks: How Two Lost Boys Rode the Internet Out of Idaho.* New York: Villard, 2000. See also Warren Bennis and Bob Thomas, *Geeks and Geezers: Partnering Across Generations.* Boston: Harvard Business School Press, 2001.

Koretz, Gene. "Why Americans Work so Hard." *Business Week*, June 11, 2001, p. 43. The research is from a recent National Bureau of Economic Research study by economists Linda A. Bell and Richard B. Freeman.

May, Graham H. *The Future Is Ours: Foreseeing, Managing, and Creating the Future.* Westport, CT: Praeger, 1996.

National Conference of State Legislatures. *A Practical Guide to Futures Study.* Washington, DC: NCSL, 2000.

Raymond, Eric S. *The Cathedral and the Bazaar: Musings on Linux and Open Source by an Accidental Revolutionary.* Sebastopol, CA: O'Reilly, 1999.

Rosenfeld, Jill. "Free Agents in the Olde World." *FAST COMPANY*, May 2001. The quotation is from Thomas Malone, a professor at MIT's Sloan School of Management.

SAP America, Inc. ad in *Workforce*, February 2001, pp. 24, 28.

---

25. Seven Guidelines from a Futures Course for Unionists

Arthur B. Shostak

If CyberUnions are soon to take full advantage of the subject matter available in futuristics, they might want to collaborate with the very few academics earnestly trying to get the subject offered more widely and often in the nation's 3,500 colleges and universities, to say nothing of scores of labor

education centers. Pointers in this regard are offered below, along with in-
sights into how labor might readily raise consciousness about, and make use
of, a resource that has always been part of its toolkit . . . albeit in an uncon-
scious and thereby underdeveloped way.

Having now introduced and taught what is probably the only course in
futuristics ever offered in labor education, I have a few tips to pass along to
anyone drawn to offer a lecture or course in this vital matter.

Background

In 1974 the AFL-CIO opened the nation's only union-directed residential
college-degree program, which is housed at the George Meany Center for
Labor Studies, on a 240-bed campus in Silver Spring, Maryland. Each year
the students of the National Labor College are resident on-campus for the
weeklong start of a course with a six-month interval in between their next
on-campus session. They do an impressive amount of intense course work
on a correspondence basis in the interval.

Despite carrying a full workload, and trying to maintain a decent family
life, most matriculates (average age, thirty-five) successfully complete the
program in three or so years. (Many start with a year or two credits for life
experience.) To the great pride of their immediate families and their union
employers (and sponsors), over 600 Meany Center alumni now boast a
bachelor's degree in labor studies.

One year after the center's college-degree program began, I was invited
to teach a basic sociology course and another in industrial sociology, an honor
I have enjoyed for over a quarter-century ever since. Quickly impressed with
the eagerness of my working-class colearners, I received permission in 1988
to introduce a third elective, an unprecedented college credit course in
futuristics.

Teaching Strategies

Drawing on ten previous years of offering the course on the campus of my
primary employer, Drexel University, I employed seven major tools, all of
which have earned endorsement in course evaluations.

First, I encouraged hope by highlighting historical matters of which the
students had little or no prior knowledge, such as the covert role of the AFL-
CIO in winning the Cold War. To counter the bleak view with which many
begin the course, I review the extraordinary progress we have made as a

species in extending our life span, raising the level of well-being, and strengthening the infrastructure of governance and civility.

Taking care not to ignore painful gaps in equity and the atrocities that daily mar the front page, I help my students process their many grievances with runaway capitalism and other mortal threats to the world's welfare.

I go on, however, to emphasize my belief that more has been gained than lost in recent centuries. I think we have it in our power to extend this trend line for time indefinite—provided we find the will power, creativity, and capacity to care enough about one another.

Second, I review well-known successes of major unions in recent organizing drives or political campaigns. I emphasize the long-range planning entailed in such campaigns and identify such planning as a key component of futuristics. I also discuss how Fortune 500 companies and all major branches of federal, state, and local government make extensive use of futuristics.

I note corporate *and* labor union successes in introducing new products and services they are familiar with, and in this way, underline the powerful potential of forecasting applied to payoff matters. This establishes the many significant rewards possible from our academic subject and whets their appetite for bringing this new tool—long-range planning—back to their union sponsor.

(I mention here my success over the years in bringing top union leaders in as panelists at the annual meeting of the World Future Society. These powerholders generally earn strong applause from initially skeptical, if not hostile, attendees, once the unionists make plain their respect for forecasting as a serious component in running the labor movement. I also talk about my occasional consulting with this union or that eager to explore ideas with a professional forecaster.)

Third, I refer over and over again to the democratic dimension in futuristics, emphasizing thereby the students' responsibility for becoming major players in helping to decide our future(s). I rail against nonvoters and other demonstrations of apathy. I explore the sources of class consciousness, class rivalry, and the power monopolies that undermine individual participation. I get them to tell of their own voter-registration efforts, of their local union meetings to debate policy issues, and of many such labor efforts to make a difference—and I link all this to futuristics.

I reject the notion that there is any one future to be predicted, as in the absurdity of the newspaper's daily horoscope column. Instead, I work closely with the class in explicating probable, possible, preferable, and preventable futures. We assess the weaknesses of each, but only after first uncovering and weighing the major strengths and values underlying each.

We make the future in the present, I maintain, either through acts of commission or omission, but the responsibility—especially in one of the most advanced democracies the world has ever known—is fundamentally ours!

Fourth, I put special emphasis on mind-boggling matters, the better to get unionists to reassess their unexamined assumptions and to struggle to take an open-mind approach. Futurists, I explain, are not optimists or pessimists so much as they are possibilists. I use this to segue to science-fiction notions that challenge much conventional and political correct thinking; for example, I discuss cyborgs, terraforming Mars, interplanetary travel, and so on, paying special attention to what computer-power gains were key enablers.

Lest my colearners privately dismiss this as dreamy fiction, I also note science-fact developments that are almost as fantastic as those dreamed up by writers Isaac Asimov, William Gibson, Ursula LeGuin, and their creative peers. We explore biotech "miracles," cloning prospects, the nanotechnology revolution, the possible impact on our lives of wearable computers and Personal Intelligent Agents, and so forth and so on.

Fifth, I explain the tools we have in futuristics for gathering data (Delphi polls, expert-genius interviews, large-scale polling projects, computer processing of massive data banks, etc.). I also discuss the tools we have for assessing the impacts of developments, for example, technology-assessment techniques, social-indicators research, computer simulations, and so forth. Special attention is paid to tools we have for evaluating forecasts and for learning from their fate. Above all, however, I focus on the values inherent in this tool or than one, and to the transferability of any of the tools to the special forecasting needs of organized labor.

Sixth, I take great care in my choice of literature. Trial-and-error has taught me that the books must be engaging, clear, short, and relevant. As well, it helps if they are available in an inexpensive paperback edition.

From the outset I used a great utopian novel, *Ecotopia*, by Ernest Callenbach. While written in the mid-1970s, it remains creative and prescient. Better still, it offers a plausible upbeat scenario for America's thoroughgoing overhaul, a blueprint my students find fresh and inspiring. A successor-of-sorts, *EarthFuture*, by Guy Dauncey, uses short fictional stories to update the subject, and is quite a helpful paperback. I have also experimented with using *Beyond Humanity*, a 1997 paperback by Gregory S. Paul and Earl D. Cox, easily the most mind-stretching book in futuristics I have come across in years (now, alas, out-of-print). They forecast what they call an Extraordinary Future, one predicated on the securement soon of mind-boggling advances in computer-empowered artificial life (far beyond artificial intelligence), very advanced robotics, and nanotechnology.

I prepare my own chapter-by-chapter, true-false, open-book, take-home quizzes to accompany my texts. The men and women in the class thanked me for this in course evaluations, as it helped highlight what I wanted them to focus on, and they took pleasure in getting high scores week after week (all of which I plan to place someday soon on the course Web site). Each quiz features two write-in questions that ask what surprised or pleased or dismayed or puzzled the student the most in the assigned reading.

Finally, in closing the course I make a point of connecting it to one overarching possibility that could just make labor's renewal a better-than-ever prospect. I call this scenario the CyberUnion Prospect, and use it to pull together many strands of the semester's work. A CyberUnion stands out in its employ of futuristics (a perspective), infotech (cutting-edge tools), services (the quid pro quo for dues), and tradition (a commitment) (Shostak 1999).

Naturally, I have each class do an anonymous evaluation of every aspect of the course, especially the books and the essay assignments that guide their learning over the six-month interval between the two weeklong on-campus sessions. I take their assessments quite seriously, so much so that I have no hesitation about considering my adult enrollees as colearners with me in a joint intellectual (and spiritual) adventure.

An elective course, futuristics generally gets a full enrollment and in the hallway scuttlebutt apparently ranks very highly. It would profit from more attention to utopian thought, and also from computer-based exercises in modeling social systems (such as a local and its growth possibilities), simulating mediation processes, researching trends in relevant industries, and so on—computer exercises for which labor cannot soon enough help to get code-written and shared (Shostak 2001).

Overall, I believe trade unionists are organic "futurists," devoted as they are to grievance-resolution, collective bargaining, and political influence, each a profound exercise in making the future in the present. All the more important is their matriculation in a college-level course that surfaces much that they need to know if they are to strengthen their record as future-shapers. I am very pleased to pioneer here, and I hope to soon learn of many more such efforts wherever free trade unionism is struggling to help create a world closer to our heart's desire.

References

Callenbach, Ernest. *Ecotopia.* New York: Bantam, 1977.

Dauncey, Guy. *EarthFuture.* Gabriola Island Beach, British Columbia: New Society Publishers, 1999.

Paul, Gregory S., and Earl D. Cox. *Beyond Humanity.* Rockland, MA: Charles River Media, 1997.

Shostak, Arthur B. *CyberUnion: Empowering Labor Through Computer Technology.* Armonk, NY: M.E. Sharpe, 1999.

————, ed. *Utopian Thinking in Sociology: Creating the Good Society.* Washington, DC: American Sociological Association, 2001.

---

26. A New Society Gives Birth to a New Union

Bob Marino

The advances labor must make in the information age hinge in part on the awareness that union activists maintain of fast-breaking possibilities. The very brief essay below attests to the effort some are continuously making, and it models what all of us must undertake.

At the beginning of this century a technology revolution introduced us to . . . the telephone. Computers and associated information technologies have now set the stage for the next big revolution in communications. A new society is being built, a new society based on science and technology.

One recent tool—the modern computer—has the capacity to create more impact than all the others now combined. It has the ability to support and unite labor as never before, though it is not a panacea. Instead, it is a conduit through which remarkable new and creative solutions can be realized and shared.

Information is the key to having the competitive edge. Organizations that control information will control the world. Unions have vast amounts of information to share, but as of now no structured system in place to share it.

Unions have been cautious with expenditures, primarily because they lack surplus funds. But today the cost of computers has dropped dramatically, and this allows unions, union members, and their families to become part of the new "information revolution."

Communications is *the* key to organizational survival—communication anywhere, anytime. I foresee the use of handheld devices that will allow for instantaneous global communication, possibly through wireless or satellite connection or a new media we haven't yet seen (one possibility for this new media might be photonics, now that scientists have been able to temporarily exceed the speed of light).

I envision ultra-high-speed ubiquitous communication access, 1 gig per sec, and hardware that is thin and light, allowing for data streaming, true voice recognition (not what is passing for voice recognition now), and data storage. Most computers today have hard drives that can store approximately 10–20 gigs of data. Not long from now we will be storing 100 times that in the same small handheld computers people are using today.

Some components of organized labor have been able to get by with a basic understanding of computer technology. But far deeper knowledge is increasingly required to function and persevere in this new society. Labor, particularly in New York State, is committed to leading the way in promoting the use of new technologies to its members.

VII. What Innovations?

> *As a rule, I always look for what others ignore.*
> —Marshall McLuhan, communications theorist

The notion of *innovation* refers to a process by which CyberUnions try this, that, and the other thing in pursuit of ever better processes, services, and so on. As early adopters of cutting-edge items, their members look to them for advice when considering testing a novel option themselves. Innovation marks the CyberUnion as self-confident and forward-looking, intent on boldly making, rather than meekly inheriting a future.

Especially vital for CyberUnions is what consultant Rosabeth Moss Kanter calls an "e-culture." Much like improvisational theater, it places a high value on creativity, recognizes that the end hasn't been written yet, and expects the players to have great confidence in one another's abilities. "Players" (union activists) enjoy going where few have yet gone, and "audience" members (dues-payers) enjoy novelty that pays off. On this dynamic stage, bringing along rewarding innovations is the key to ensuring a long run (Angel 2001).

Symbolic here of labor's dynamic new "stage" is the recent conversion of the *AFL-CIO News*, a bland, prosaic, and mind-dulling house organ that John Sweeney inherited in 1996 on assuming the presidency of the AFL-CIO. Much to his credit, his aides quickly turned it into a bright, brassy, and hip publication now called *America@work*. Nearly every colorful issue has a page devoted to Internet sites and cyberspace tools worth union attention.

Tips and tricks in connection with three labor-relevant innovations, the first two up and going, the third one barely glimpsed, merit brief mention below before we turn to three essays focused on some better-known cutting-edge matters.

1. *Daily Online "Newspaper."* The Internet's only American labor daily online paper, *Workday Minnesota*, draws on volunteers across the state to feed it news of labor and labor-related events. Backed by a three-year commitment from the AFL-CIO State Federation, and managed by the Labor Education Service of the University of Minnesota, the paper boasts a thoughtful mix of content: national labor news, state labor news, op-ed essays, letters, overseas labor news, "Today in Labor History" box, labor cartoons, reviews of books and videos, and other material (see www.work dayminnesota.org).

Anyone drawn to create the second, third, or fourth such online paper is advised by Howard Kling, the editor, to first line up support from your state labor federation. Ask for a three-year commitment, at the very least, and for $50,000 to $100,000 per year to cover one full-time person and many auxiliary expenses.

Then seek support from the nearest labor education center, as it may agree to manage the project, and it can provide academic freedom and objectivity.

Next, recruit volunteers, especially from the state's largest cities, and school them in exactly the topics and style of material best for the paper. Explain that the right to monitor material must be reserved by the editor, and encourage an endless search for material and other writers.

Above all, protect the integrity of the online paper, and do not let it become a mere house organ of the state federation, since this will drive away readers suspicious of getting propaganda under the guise of news.

2. *Webmasters Community.* Arguably, the single most significant American labor innovation in 2001, where computer use is concerned, was initiated by Linda Mathews, a contributor to this handbook (see Chapters 20 and 22). She created a Web site to fill a serious gap, and thereby set us all a model of what innovation can accomplish.

Linda's welcome message to all those who create and manage labor Web sites explains:

> While the online movement has grown by leaps and bounds, there is a major component missing that is a hindrance to us all. That is a lack of any type of formal structure where we can turn to share online strategies, success stories, blunders, and technical support. This community is my attempt to help build that type of structure. The success will be dependent on us all. It will require participation and organization to build this community, and to realize it's full potential. Please join me in the promotion of this community, and recruitment of members to the list. (www.cybersolidarity.com/join.html)

On joining, you get a message that suggests that "the resources in this community will provide us with a method of sharing support, tips, and tricks on

Web authoring, and will help each other with the strategic planning and effective use of new technologies to benefit our cause."

Now, that appears one really smart innovation!

3. *Free Software Movement*. Organized labor could carefully explore what role, if any, it thinks it should play in the titanic struggle under way between two socioeconomic philosophies of innovation in general and software ownership in particular.

Ranged on one side are giant for-profit companies, led by Microsoft and Apple, that profit from keeping their operating-system code very secret. On the other side is a loose coalition of about 1,000 digerati types (hackers, but not law-breaking "crackers"), intent on giving away the secrets of any code they develop. Once released, it costs next to nothing to copy and modify, and this is what makes such programs (Linux, Free BSD, etc.) a credible threat to the established order.

The open-source movement sees itself as standing "in opposition to a world where cash is king, greed is good, and money is power" (Wayner 2000, 1). Its supporters, a small band of talented, passionate warriors, think sharing might help make the world a better place. Many believe they are fighting for the information age equivalent of "liberty, equality, and fraternity" (Wayner 2000, 306).

Popular with very talented programmers ("geeks") who actually enjoy writing code, and endorsed now by IBM and some of the world's most serious scientists, the main product of the movement—Linux—already controls more than half of the Web. Its graphical user interface for drawing windows and icons is thought much better than the competitive product from Microsoft. Not surprisingly, the movement's code of sharing, caring, and curiosity utterly bewilders many hard-boiled corporate titans.

While the outcome of the contest between the two sides is far from clear, at least one close student forecasts an eventual win for the geeks over the suits, but only after a bloody war more costly than any expect (Wayner 2000, 292). Peter Wayner expects the free software movement to "grow in strange leaps and unexpected bounds until it swallows the world . . . [because] in the end, information just wants to be free" (Wayner 2000, 307).

Organized labor can continue to watch from the sidelines and meekly accept the ultimate outcome. Or it can soon decide that the innovative free software crowd is ideologically aligned with labor movement values (such as the principle of lower costs, open debate, broad circulation, easy access, and complete disclosure), and thereby merits a helping hand. In which case, unions and locals could reach out to area Linux user clubs and ask for workshops and online distance learning courses to help labor adapt open-source movement products.

Now, that would be an innovation of major proportions!

While other candidates for innovation projects rush to mind—Hawaii, for example, has a local that has innovated in creating its own Internet access company (a very successful venture!)—it is time to shift to the longer discussions below: The first essay explains how to achieve honors rapidly in Web site innovation. The second calls for "virtual" local meetings in cyberspace and offers a successful example. The third hails a unique labor newswire and explains why this innovation is truly a "big deal." Taken together, the essays make plain the indispensability of risk taking, a high order tenet of cyberunionism.

References

Angel, Karen. "Old E-News." *Business Week*, June 11, 2001, p. 24E6. The book reviewed is Rosabeth Moss Kanter's *Evolve! Succeeding in the Digital Culture of Tomorrow*. Harvard Business School Press, 2001.

Wayner, Peter. *Free for All: How Linux and the Free Software Movement Undercut the High-Tech Titans*. New York: HarperBusiness, 2000. On the political implications of open source software, see www.tuxedo.org/~esr.

---

27. Revitalizing a Union Through Cyberspace

Larry Johnson

When scholars years from now try to piece together the history of how unions and locals in the 1990s made their way onto the Internet, the sort of essay below will be very helpful. An engaging account on innovation by a pioneer, it explains how he helped his local get online and create its first (of several) Web sites.

The essay answers such questions as:

- *Do nonunion workers visit union sites? If so, with what results?*
- *What kind of Web site has special appeal to the unorganized?*
- *Does upgrading a site really pay off?*
- *What is exciting about Internet radio network possibilities? And video possibilities?*

Above all, the essay illustrates how an innovative local can lead its own international union to make creative use of computer possibilities, rather than passively wait for the international union to take the lead.

In January 1998 I purchased my local union's first computer. I could only do this after much coaxing to convince my membership that computers would be vital to the success of our union. Originally the computer was supposed to be used for recordkeeping, such as grievance logs, financial records, and an address list that coordinated with the local union newsletter I would produce with it.

I not only used my GMP (Glass, Molder, Pottery) Local 238 computer for these uses, but I also signed up for the Internet. My experience there was a surprising one. I discovered virtually hundreds of union Web sites, both international and local sites, with a wealth of information. I was surprised to learn my international union had no presence on the Web. I talked to several officers but couldn't really find out why the international wasn't on the Internet. After searching, I also discovered there were no Web sites for any GMP local unions.

I decided that if my local was going to grow and gain allies, we had to have a Web site—not only to communicate with our membership, but also to gain allies within the labor world. I had to once again tackle my members and convince them that we needed a presence on the Internet, and that we needed to do it the right way if we were to be successful. I gained their approval and set out to build a Web site that would meet their needs.

First I assembled a committee of my local union members to review various labor Web sites with me. We sent e-mails to several that we liked, asking how their union had benefited from having a Web site. The responses were positive, as we learned of how one union used their Web site to gain support while on strike, and how others used their sites to develop a network of labor support during contract negotiations and help keep their members informed of contractual issues.

I searched hundreds of union Web sites for ideas on how to make our GMP Local 238 site one that people could learn from and one that would promote the Glass, Molders, Pottery, Plastics, and Allied Workers International Union. I sent e-mails to several union Web sites asking advice, and I received some very good tips.

I received advice, for example, on first making the Web site attractive, so when someone finds the site they will be drawn to the look and want to search through it and possibly return often. I was also told to have items of interest that would appeal to the average worker, and to also keep the site updated so visitors wouldn't lose interest.

I contacted James Rankin, the GMP international president, about my Web site and how our international needed to develop a presence on the Internet. He was very open and supportive, as he had taken over as president only a few months before, and he was looking for ways to build the union.

In September 1998 my GMP Local 238 Web site was unveiled, the first for any GMP union (www.gmp238.org). While its design was very basic, the site contained a description of the GMP International Union, links to several labor Web sites, a Web version of *Hotline* (my Local 238 newsletter), and a labor news page.

Little did I know, but my local site was beginning to attract viewers that I never had considered before—contacts from workers seeking a union in their workplace. I called them and found out the histories of their workplaces as well as what the issues were. I then sent the data to the international president, who had our representatives in the region meet with the contacts. We started developing an organizing program based on my e-mail leads.

Since I was getting several such contacts every month, I put a page on the Local 238 Web site for workers seeking a union. It described the benefits of having a union, the rights of workers to form a union, a biography of the GMP International Union, and a contact page for workers seeking help in forming a union to get in touch with me.

This organizing page brought in even more contacts, and the GMP International Union decided to start up a full-fledged organizing program, as our previous one had been disbanded under other administrations. The international began its own Web site as well, a great start in reaching out to the members with technology. I firmly believe this will help strengthen the bond between the international union and the rank-and-file member.

In July 1999 I was notified that the GMP Local 238 Web site had been given the second place award for local union Web sites from the International Labor Communication Association, a division of the AFL-CIO. This award was significant in providing evidence to my membership that our Web site was important and that we were making new allies through the Internet.

In December 1999 I unveiled a newly designed GMP Local 238 Web site. It had a more colorful look, new features, an expanded organizing page, and more resources. This new look brought in still more viewers, and we grew from 150 visitors in the early stages of the Web site to 40,000 per week in early 2000.

I continued to get dozens of organizing contacts each month from workers seeking a union in their workplace, and realized that if I could get such leads on my Local 238 Web site, I could get even more with a Web site devoted entirely to organizing. My thinking was if you go to a search engine and type in "union organizing," you will get hundreds of union Web sites, because most have something on their pages about organizing. I thought that if we had a separate site for organizing, the search engine would go to it before it would go to regular union Web sites.

In July 2000 the GMP Organizing Center Web site (www.gmporganizing. org) was launched with features such as workers' right to join a union, how a union works, testimonials from workers who have let the GMP organize their workplace, benefits of GMP membership, and a contact page. It also has a link to my Local 238 Web site so visitors could see a GMP union Web site, a frequently asked questions page, an account of the union advantage, and a description about the GMP International Union.

The GMP Organizing Center has brought in more contacts than I had ever thought possible, and international president Rankin is now able to build an organizing program around that Web site.

There are currently five GMP local union Web sites and hopefully more will be starting soon. Statistics show that a site should be redesigned each year so it will remain fresh to viewers. I am once again redesigning my Local 238 site with more features, such as an e-mail newsletter written by experts in the field of labor. I am also adding a comprehensive "step by step" on how to design a Web site for other local unions to use so they can have one site at little cost. I am also establishing a GMP e-mail service for those who sign up so they can have e-mail at a GMP address.

The thing I am most excited about is a new feature called the GMP Internet Radio Network. We are in discussions with the GMP international union about creating a radio show on the Web site that will have timely features of interest to GMP members and the entire labor world as well.

As GMP locals develop a presence on the Internet, we can add the GMP radio show to their Web site, as well as have the GMP radio show on the GMP International Union Web site. The radio show will be updated regularly, and I believe we can use it to recruit new members as well as help in our campaigns against sending product parts made by GMP members to Mexico to be made into finished products, which is costing GMP jobs.

I also plan on expanding the GMP Organizing Center Web site to include features that will better attract new contacts. I hope to use video technology as a means to draw nonunion workers to contact our Organizing Center. We can also use the organizing Web site to let GMP organizers, who are located in different areas, talk free of charge to each other through the Web site, seeking ideas and help on their respective campaigns (and, not incidentally, saving the international a lot on phone bills).

I have obtained many contacts with the Local 238 Web site. Unions from all over the world have contacted me through the Internet, and I have developed allies should my union need help during contract negotiations or strikes, or possibly to provide information on companies we are trying to organize.

In January 2001 LabourStart (www.labourstart.org) named the GMP Local 238 Web site as Web site of the year for the year 2000. This was quite an honor as LabourStart is widely viewed. I have received numerous new contacts from Labourstart viewers who have been at the forefront of labor struggles and who have offered help should my local union ever need it.

My GMP Local 238 Web site now averages between 70,000 and 93,000 viewers per week (as of January 2001). We started small and soon found that not only could we find allies throughout the labor world, but we discovered the biggest gold mine of all, which was organizing prospects.

Soon we will be using video technology on the GMP Organizing Center to attract new members, and the GMP Internet Radio Network will make our union more effective as we move toward being a CyberUnion.

I have discovered in my own local union that until people understand how beneficial computer technology can be to their work lives, unions risk becoming stagnant. I credit my international president for taking steps toward becoming a CyberUnion, but we all need to do more.

If every local union, no matter how big or small, would develop a presence on the Internet, they would see opportunities for advancement beyond their imagination. If local unions push to create a CyberUnion of their own, it could force international unions to follow suit—and then organizing possibilities would be endless.

Recently I was reminded through an e-mail from Arthur Shostak, labor educator and professor of sociology, of a quote by Ralph Waldo Emerson that states: "This time, like all times, is a very good one if we but know what to do with it." Unions, including my own, need to embrace the meaning of the aforementioned quote if we are going not only to survive, but to grow. We can win strikes, launch worldwide boycotts, and organize workers far better by using the Internet. The future is ours, if we just make the most of cyberspace possibilities.

---

28. Virtually Meeting: How the Internet Can Open Up Union Meetings to All the Members

Sam Stark

Interest grows steadily in labor's ability to make the most of the opportunity to hold "virtual" meetings in cyberspace. Proponents expect greater than ever participation, possibly even of a higher-than-usual quality. Skeptics worry

*that the digital divide will take a toll, and that the lack of face-to-face con-
tact will undermine the quality of dialogue.*

*All the more helpful, therefore, is the rare report below of an ongoing and
revealing experiment, a thoughtful effort to reach a membership that rarely,
if ever comes together. Attention is paid to questions of format, impact, values, the opposition, and ultimate worth. Coming from a long-time union activist quick to admit his early doubts about certain uses by labor of computers,
the essay carries special weight, and casts valuable light on a fascinating
possibility.*

I used to sneer whenever union discussions shifted to talk of cyberspace,
e-mails, and dot coms. To me, it sounded like one more justification for some
activists not to interact with real live human beings. I've changed a lot since
then. Now I even find myself offering advice to others in something called a
CyberUnion Handbook.

My conversion is genuine, I can assure you that, and it's not a conversion
of convenience, either. Although I do appreciate any machine that doesn't
require you to insert a piece of coated paper and hit the same wrong key over
again to erase a mistake.

Today, I am a strong advocate of the Internet even as I watch it turn more
and more into a capitalist tool, just like radio, television, and local cable
before it. As a union and social activist for thirty-six years, I have come to
appreciate that, like any tool, computers and the Internet can be used for
either good or evil.

Here's how I think these tools can help union activists do good—mobilizing people, expanding democracy, and debating with all workers about what
kind of world we want.

The Southeast Michigan Unit of the National Writers Union (SEM-NWU), United Auto Workers (UAW) Local 1981

SEM-NWU has a membership of nearly 150 freelance writers in the Detroit
and Ann Arbor areas. The national organization has over 6,500 members and
is one of the fastest growing local unions in the UAW or anywhere.

The typical NWU member works alone at home or as an isolated individual in a nonunion work environment. As members of a collective organization of workers, they were just as isolated when our unit was first organized
several years ago. From another perspective, that of the SEM-NWU steering
committee, the NWU membership was nothing more than names on a mailing list.

We had to figure out how to reach out to this membership we rarely, or never, see. Mass mailings meant communication going out one way and not coming back. One or two phone messages signified a busy month for our voice-mail system. In reality, our steering committee was as isolated from the NWU membership as they were from us. Despite regular notifications, hardly any rank-and-filers ever attended monthly union meetings.

People-to-people contact through phone trees and local union-sponsored workshops and social gatherings helped, but such interactions were few and far between. Given people's busy work schedules and family responsibilities, our phone tree collapsed.

What we needed was our own union hall, water cooler, or break room. We lacked a central place where people could gather daily to exchange information, chat, or debate union policy. A local union Web page and list server eventually became our city square, union bulletin board, and hangout.

Although the results cannot be termed overwhelming, union involvement has visibly increased since we went online. Every steering committee meeting seems to attract at least one and sometimes two new members every month. The Web page and list server keep members up to date with the local's business and issues.

One cyberspace debate over a bylaws question emerged because of a steering committee notice of an upcoming union meeting. Modeled after the national's, our local bylaws called for our union cochairpersons to automatically attend the NWU's annual Delegate Assembly, the highest decision-making body of Local 1981. Several members initiated a debate challenging the assumption of automatic representation. They argued this procedure was inherently undemocratic. The e-mail exchange was so lively and persuasive, with voices heard on both sides, that the Steering Committee voted to revise our bylaws, requiring every member, including the top officers, to run in an election for assembly delegate.

It occurs to me that it isn't just local unions of dispersed and isolated freelance writers that could benefit from entering the computer age. Even industrial local unions with several hundred or several thousand members often hold membership meetings where there are the barest of quorums.

The Internet can be a two-way communications tool, a means to expand democracy, and an opportunity for members to participate in the business of their union. Before every meeting, local unions could post the agenda on a local union Web site or through an e-mail list server to interested members.

At a bare minimum, such meeting notices would remind everyone of upcoming membership, executive board, or standing committee meetings. But these notices should contain more than the formal Robert's Rules of Order agenda. It should include the real substance of the old and new business to be discussed.

In that way members could "speak out" on the issues from home on their own time and at their convenience. I realize some traditionalists in the labor movement will scoff at the idea. I have heard it said many times over the last thirty years that if the members want to know what happening "they should come out to their union meetings," and if they don't, then "they should keep their mouths shut."

The effectiveness of such hard-line attitudes is evidenced by the ever-decreasing numbers of members attending union meetings or even caring about their union. The days when workers live near their workplace and their union hall went out when urban sprawl came in. Attending union meetings today often requires workers—who have already put in six-day, ten-hours-a-day workweeks—to drive back maybe twenty, thirty, or more miles on a Sunday morning to the union hall. Why should we make it harder for people who are burdened with heavy overtime schedules to participate in their union and exclude them from having a voice when we—and they—have the tools to include them?

Many, maybe most, union members have personal computers at home and are computer-literate enough to write messages and send e-mails to the president or executive board. Based on what I have witnessed with our own NWU unit, allowing people access to the union through the Internet doesn't necessarily mean lowered meeting attendance or less interest in the union. On the contrary, it cannot help but heighten people's interest. With our Web page and list server, everybody in the Southeast Michigan Unit can keep up to date on union issues and business. If people are included, they will take a greater interest in their organization.

After arousing people's interest in union affairs and making them feel a part of the union, then it is very possible that a twenty-mile ride once a month might begin to look like time and effort well worth the trouble.

---

29. Beyond the Web Site: The Experience of LabourStart's Labour Newswire

Eric Lee

Eric Lee is the pioneering author of The Labour Movement and the Internet: The New Internationalism *(Pluto Press, 1996), the first major book on the subject, an invaluable and seminal guide. He shares below an exciting progress report about an innovation of major significance, one that finally puts labor on an equal footing with the corporate world where newswires are concerned.*

This innovation enables labor to move beyond the Web site and "engage in solidarity work of a kind that was previously unthinkable." Note especially Lee's appreciation of grassroots enthusiasm for the breakthrough and his intriguing challenge to the American labor movement to soon emulate it.

It's one thing to have a Web site that a few hundred or thousand members of your union visit. It's quite another to have a newswire service of your own with your content appearing simultaneously on dozens—or hundreds—of other Web sites. That's the idea behind the Labour NewsWire, launched by LabourStart (www.labourstart.org).

I should begin by saying that the idea of creating a newswire was by no means original. Quite some time ago I briefly used the newswire being offered by the Excite Web portal. A company called 7am.com was also an early promoter of a Java-based scrolling newswire that can still be seen on small Web sites to this day.

But the breakthrough, at least for me, came when Netscape launched its "channels" for the "My Netscape Netcenter" in March 1999. Netscape used something called Rich Site Summary (RSS)—based on a new extensible markup language (XML) that allowed individuals to set up their own customized home pages with their own "channels." If you liked sports, you could have a sports news feed. If you liked politics, you picked a political news feed. Best of all, if you wanted to create a news feed of your own, Netscape told you how. My world has never been the same since.

What was previously possible only for giant corporations was now available to anyone who could make head or tail of Netscape's instructions. Unfortunately, not all of us can do things like create a properly formatted RSS file. Fortunately, I know two people who can.

Chris Croome and Bruno Postle are architects who have turned their talent for Web site design into a business called, appropriately enough, Web Architects. Based in Sheffield (England), they have been behind some of the more interesting things happening on the fringe of the labour movement's use of the Internet. Chris and Bruno saw a way to use the new RSS format to create a news feed for LabourStart's daily online news service for the trade union movement.

But let me step back a moment and explain another change that made this possible. LabourStart was originally a simple Web page, updated every day, with new links to trade union news stories that had appeared on other Web sites. But in April 1999—coincidentally, a month after Netscape launched the RSS format—we switched over to a dynamic database, using a free software system called dbman, produced by Gossamer Threads in Vancouver, Canada.

The switchover from a hard-coded HTML page to a dynamic, online database was done to make life more convenient, but it also opened up new and unexpected possibilities. One was the creation of a global network of volunteer correspondents who could update the database remotely, logging in with their own user IDs and passwords. The other possibility was to write a script that would read through the database and generate properly formatted RSS code—allowing the Labour NewsWire to be born.

Let me review the three stages of how this works:

1. Volunteer correspondents from around the world log on to LabourStart's online database and add links to news stories (that appear on other sites) concerning working people and their unions. This occurs in real time.
2. Webmasters at other trade union sites who want to use those news stories copy and paste a single line of code (available on LabourStart) to their own sites. That line of code—written in JavaScript—calls up a Perl program on LabourStart's server that generates the newswire code in properly formatted HTML. This is a one-time only job and will take a webmaster under a minute to accomplish.
3. Visitors to the Web sites that use the service see the latest five or ten headlines from their own country, or globally, in their own language, in nearly real time.

It didn't always work this smoothly. The first version of the Labour NewsWire required webmasters to install a script, written in Perl, in their cgi-bins. This proved to be an insurmountable challenge for most of them, and use of the first version of the NewsWire was quite limited.

But when Chris and Bruno came up with their one line of code, everything changed. Here is the code: <script language="JavaScript"src="http://www.labourstart.org/rdf/labourstart.js"></script>.

All webmasters need to do is to copy and paste that line from our Web site into the source of one of their HTML pages. And that's it.

As a result of this change, interest in the Labour NewsWire skyrocketed. As I write these words (late May 2001) there are more than 210 trade union Web sites using the newswire. According to a recent estimate by one Harvard academic studying trade union use of the Web (Richard Freeman) there are 2,700 trade union Web sites around the globe. We are therefore rapidly approaching the point where one in ten use the Labour NewsWire.

We were quickly able to customize the newswire to offer up news from individual countries, regions, and sectors of the economy and in different languages. National newswires are now available for the following countries: Australia, Belarus, Canada, India, Ireland, Korea, New Zealand, Russia, South Africa, the UK, and the United States. Regional newswires exist for Africa and the Caribbean.

In January 2001 LabourStart announced plans to expand beyond the English language and aimed to be producing online labour news in a dozen languages by the end of the year. (By way of comparison, the Global Unions Web site, launched by all the major international institutions of the trade union movement, still appears only in English.)

As new languages were added to LabourStart, new newswires were created in those languages. The Labour NewsWire now works, in addition to its English versions, in Spanish, French, Dutch, Portuguese, Norwegian, Swedish, and Turkish. The Norwegian version has proved to be the most popular of all, with no fewer than fifty-two local trade union Web sites relying on it for a news feed.

At the request of Australian trade unionists we also created our first newswire for a particular sector of the economy—the information and communications technology (ICT) sector—in May 2001. We will be able to create future newswires for other sectors and for particular campaigns.

Web sites using the newswire range from official, mainstream trade union sites to dissident, marginal, activist sites. National trade union centers using the newswire include the Congress of South African Trade Unions, the General Federation of Nepalese Trade Unions, and the Dutch national trade union center FNV. Regional organizations of national trade union centers are also key users of the service—such as several regional bodies of the Norwegian LO and the Northern Regional Council of the Trades Union Congress in Britain. Several national unions have adopted the newswire as well, including the giant MSF union in Britain and NKF in Norway. But the greatest enthusiasm seems to be at the grassroots level, with scores of local trade union Web sites jumping at the opportunity to provide national and even international labour news to their visitors.

For LabourStart, the launch of the Labour NewsWire has been a real boon. We've been able to get trade union news out to a much larger audience than ever before by not compelling people to find and visit our Web site. This has allowed us to engage in solidarity work of a kind that was previously unthinkable. For example, when striking hotel workers in Jakarta need to get an urgent message out to the trade unions of the world, one of the best ways now is to ensure that their news appears in LabourStart's Labour NewsWire. That means that for tens of thousands of workers around the world, visiting their own union's Web sites, the news goes directly to them.

I think there are lessons to be drawn for the broader labour movement, and I'm actually surprised that the example of our newswire hasn't been emulated. Surely national trade union centers like the AFL-CIO issue statements, appeals, press releases, and calls to action that could also be posted directly onto local and regional trade union Web sites throughout the United States.

And international trade union organizations, such as the International Confederation of Free Trade Unions and the dozen or so international trade secretariats, would benefit greatly from the ability to directly disseminate information to their millions of affiliated trade unionists—and thereby, perhaps, mobilize them.

For LabourStart, the combination of a global network of volunteer correspondents and a network of Web sites offering up the Labour NewsWire has completely transformed our project. The impact of our efforts has been multiplied many-fold by these new tools.

We've moved beyond the Web site, and your union can too.

VIII. What Services?

When people are serving, life is no longer meaningless.
—John Gardner, educator

The word *services* refers here to the use of computer power to help the membership in ways not always reached by the terms of a collective-bargaining agreement. While Cyber Gain organizations may get involved in these matters, CyberUnions are always involved.

Advice in this regard is quite varied, and only a very short and illustrative list, including some relevant Web sites, follows (for more sites, see the Internet Resource Guide, p. 299 of this volume).

1. *Help Lower Expenses.* Members may appreciate tips on how to spend less, get more, and wherever possible, buy union. Scores of helpful Web sites can be located by a union or local, assessed, and spotlighted via e-mail that is "pushed" out to members who volunteered to receive this service. Or they can be highlighted on a Web site. As the popularity of this service grows, rank-and-filers can be encouraged to send in their own nominations. Typical is a new site, GasPriceWatch (www.gaspricewatch.com), which uses 30,000 volunteers in the United States and Canada to be able to tell users where the cheapest gasoline is within a 20-mile radius of any zip code. It also tracks the price of heating oil and marine fuel.

To find consumer-oriented how-to advice on buying life insurance, dealing with your HMO, and avoiding insurance fraud, see www.consumer action.org. To learn what it would take to support your family should you die today, see www.life-line.org/life/life_value.html (the Human Life Value Calculator). And to help with grassroots activist efforts in labor's best interest, coast-to-coast efforts to control costs and reform the insurance industry, see www.consumerwatchdog.org/insurance.

Representative of even more specialized dollar-saving sites is one that covers about 1,000 state and federal benefit programs available for older Americans. They and their families and caregivers can get a report of available benefits and how to claim them by completing a confidential survey on the site at www.BenefitsCheckUp.org.

Far more novel is our ability "to use our home computer to control the sprinkler system, turn on the bug zapper at night, or even fire up the electric barbecue around dinnertime"—all at some handsome savings in dollars and stress. Home automation systems use your computer and your home's electrical wiring to communicate with other electrical devices (see www.x10.com, or for MAC, www.mousehouse.com) (Komando 2001).

As for buying union, BuyUnionNOW (www.BuyUnionNOW.com) double-checks that all its products are union-made and U.S.-made. Each product is accompanied by the name of the union that organized its production facility. Recertification is required every three months, and certifications are double-checked with the unions cited. Consumers can notify the Web site of a union-made product by e-mailing to products@buyunionnow.com or by calling (314) 638–9900 with the name of the product, its manufacturer's name and address, telephone number, and a contact.

Also worth calling to the attention of members are these sites:

* www.hereunion.org/hotelguide/union hotel guide
* www.ilafl-cio.org/unionstore.htm union grocery stores
* www.union-contractors.com/ union contractors
* http://cflonline.org/printers.html union printers

Finally, for labor music, books, videos, posters, buttons, and note cards, see the Labor Heritage Foundation site at www.laborheritage.org.

2. *Help Improve the Workplace.* Members may appreciate tips on how to live better at work. For example, Safety Online is an excellent source for life-saving tips, and can be found at www.safetyonline.com. RISKS is a new e-bulletin from the Trade Union Congress in the United Kingdom. Weekly issues are posted to a Web site, but you can also subscribe by e-mail. A recent issue covered health and safety developments at work in the United States, Australia, Canada, and Britain (www.tuc.org.uk).

From another angle entirely, members may appreciate learning they have a right to be told beforehand about their right to deny their employer access to Internet-based credit information about them. These notoriously inaccurate reports are, offered to companies for a nominal fee over the Internet (see www.equifax.com)

3. *Help Aid Current Events "Smarts."* Members may appreciate learning

they can click on one Web site and chose from among 700 categories of news gathered from around the world. They can request daily news in any of the categories via e-mail or have the news feed appear on their union or local's Web site (www.moreover.com/categories/category-list.html).

Similarly, American unionists may profit greatly from clicking on daily sources of overseas labor news, as from the very popular labourstart site (see Chapter 29). Its creator, Eric Lee, believes more and more overseas labor stories are now getting distributed in a "viral" manner, appearing first on a local trade union site somewhere, then getting picked up by LabourStart and by others: This kind of interaction is beginning to create something new in the trade union movement—a sort of global consciousness growing daily (www.labourstart.org).

To learn more about African-American concerns, members of all racial identities may want to access www.blackradicalcongress.com. It features articles, commentaries, and reports that, according to its coordinator, try "to get people talking about issues that really matter." He contends that for activist groups, the Internet may be the best invention to come along since the bumper sticker (McGee, in Steiner 2001).

To help monitor issues of corporate accountability, members may want to access CorpWatch, an online activism center and e-zine for those concerned about the effects of corporate globalization (see www.corpwatch.org). Similarly, Common Dreams News Center draws from both wire services and many progressive magazines and Web sites (www.commondreams.org).

4. *Help Promote Good Deeds.* Members may appreciate learning how their computer may help others in need. For example, a medical project is seeking donated spare time on idle PCs (www.fightaidsathome.org). A similar request comes from a joint effort of Oxford University, the National Foundation for Cancer Research, the Intel Corporation, and United Devices, Inc. (www.intel.com/cure).

Stranger, but no less intriguing for all of that, is the SETI@home program. It harnesses the unused power of PCs to look for signs of extraterrestrial intelligence. Begun in 1999, it signed up its user number 3 million in May 2001 and is now "the most popular public computer project of all time" (Biersdorfer 2001).

From a different, but related angle, members may welcome learning how they can recycle their computers and help close the digital divide. The average life span of a computer is now much less than three years, but less than 15 percent are being recycled. IBM charges only $30 to take back any manufacturer's computers and peripherals, then it renews them and helps get them to schools, agencies, and homes that would otherwise go without (www.ibm.com/ibm/environment). Gateway offers rebates toward future purchases (www.gateway.com/recycle), while Hewlett-Packard charges a variable fee, and denotes working equipment to charitable organizations. See also Share the Technology at www.sharetechnology.org.

The list could go on and on, and the back inside page of nearly every issue of the AFL-CIO magazine, *America@work,* features new additions of strong appeal. What with over 1 billion Web sites already available, along with an untold number of list servers, the choice of service resources appears endless.

The point already seems clear: Computer power makes possible *n*-number of new services for labor's dues-payers. This is an option Cyber Gain organizations should do more with—and one that helps define the very essence of the CyberUnion.

Further light is shed on labor's new service opportunities by the three essays that follow: The first explores how to provide especially good electronic design and layout, two underrated services. The second calls attention to ways minorities can counter prejudice and help one another through new "high touch" services of the Internet. And the third shows how to conduct corporate campaigns, a type of computer-based service with very special rewards.

Taken together, the essays underline the notion that computer power can make 101 familiar labor services better, and it can also support 101 sparkling new services . . . if only labor would reach out.

References

Biersdorfer, J.D. "Q&A." *New York Times*, May 24, 2001. p. G-4.
Komando, Kim. "Many Uses for Retired Computers." *The [Albuquerque] Sunday Journal*, June 3, 2001, p. C-7.
Steiner, Andy. "New Media Heroes." *Utne Reader*, May–June 2001, pp. 77–79. Art McGee is profiled on p. 78.

---

30. I Came, I Saw, I Digitized—A Union Editor's Guide to Electronic Design and Layout

Brandon Weber

Having grown up accustomed to the appeal, the versatility, and the feel of paper, many of us (particularly those born before 1970) are in no hurry to give up its use. Rather, we welcome steady improvements, as with no-smudge ink, brighter colors in our newspapers, lower prices, and recycled tree-sparing content.

All the more valuable, therefore, is the straightforward how-to guide below for upgrading desktop publishing in general and, in particular, laying out a labor paper in an electronic format.

Answers are provided for such questions as:

- *Why bother? Can significant amounts of money be saved?*
- *What software packages are best? Worst? Why?*
- *How does one make smart use of a scanner? A digital camera? Color clip art? Colors? Imbedded and standard fonts? Zip disk or CD-ROM?*

Especially valuable is the air of "can do!" that courses through the essay, written as it is by an activist who has learned—much as we all can—to do just that!

Software for desktop publishing has finally grown up. It used to be extremely difficult to lay out your own newspaper, using cumbersome software that often didn't work correctly, even though there were one or two programs, such as Ventura Publisher and Aldus Pagemaker, that could get the job done after you learned a complex system of hoops and hurdles. Even before those days I remember using "press type" to create flyers—staying up until the wee hours scratch-scratch-scratching the plastic on one side to put another letter in the title at the top of the flyer.

Fast-forward to today, and our local, UAW 889, has just completed the first totally electronic layout of our newspaper. Modern software tools make it very easy to edit and publish your own newspaper, newsletter, or flyer. In our local we used Microsoft Publisher 2000, which is extremely easy to learn and has some nice extras that help when dealing with your printing company. We scanned most of the photos and used a digital camera for others, chose our own clip art, used the colors and fonts that we wanted, and tweaked the desktop publishing software to make the *White Collar News* look professional and to allow our printer to receive the publication on a CD and run it straight from there.

By doing this, we saved many thousands of dollars in layout costs, which enables us to have the publication printed in color with glossy pages. In addition, the money the local has saved will mean that some of the editorial staff can attend more workshops on improving writing and editing skills.

There are other packages on the market: Adobe Pagemaker is very powerful but is more than six times the cost of Publisher and has a learning curve that is too steep for many to get beyond the opening screen. Quark Xpress, also pretty costly, is widely recognized as one of the most powerful tools, and also is frequently the publication format that printing companies prefer. Some less expensive packages include Printshop and Corel PrintOffice.

Whatever software you decide on, there are some tricks to creating your publication electronically that will help immensely when you take it to your union printer on floppy disk, Zip disk, or on a CD. Please keep in mind that you should verify all of the following with your specific printing company before charging ahead: These are generalizations based on experience in the southeast Michigan area, but the industry is such that most of the tenets here will apply elsewhere.

Photos and Graphics

If you are using a scanner, make sure to set your resolution to 300 DPI (dots per inch) or better. Full color is preferable, unless you are scanning black-and-white line-drawn clip art. Use a photo editing package (the best is Adobe Photoshop) after scanning to improve the picture, color, and brightness, and to resize, crop, and otherwise change the appearance of your scan.

Almost all printers want the scans to be in four-color format, or CMYK (the initials stand for cyan, magenta, yellow, and black). Make sure that whatever desktop publishing program you use allows you to insert links to the scanned pictures instead of actually placing them inside the publication. Another hint is to use the photo-editing software to change the size of the image, instead of resizing it within the publication.

Possibly the most important tip: After all processing and changes have been made, make sure you save the final image as a TIFF, sometimes called TIF (tagged image file format), a standard that was developed in the 1980s and is widely used today for high-quality images.

If you will be using photos from a digital camera, be aware that since they usually store the image in a JPG format, those photos need to be converted to TIFF. Also, the color usually needs to be changed from RGB (red, green, blue) to CMYK.

Some digital cameras store the images in an extremely large physical size but with less "pixels per inch" (PPI, a term used interchangeably with dots per inch). For example, the Sony MVC-CD1000, when saving pictures at top quality, stores images at 22 by 17 inches, 72 pixels per inch. You must change the image size to make it the same as it will be in your publication (3 by 4 inches, for example). When you make that change, also change the pixels per inch to 300 or better so you don't lose quality.

If you have color clip art, whether scans or images from a CD, you will also need to convert the colors to CMYK and the image type to TIFF. However, if the image is black and white or shades of gray, it will cause problems if you go with CMYK; these should be converted to "grayscale" in your photo-editing package, and then all color levels should be turned to zero, so that nothing but black comes through. This will make sure there are no small bits of blue or red or green that are hard to see on the screen but will be picked up by the printing process.

Colors

When dealing with colors, you should realize that what you see on the screen, or on your laser/inkjet printer, is not always what you get in the final, printed product. In fact, it can be dramatically different. We found that out the hard way with our last issue; what was supposed to be a nice combination of sky blue and navy blue turned into a sort of blue-green with a sort of purple, though the color laser printer "proof" that we made looked just fine.

One of the best ways to make sure it will come out exactly as you want it is to have the local invest in a "Pantone Color Swatchbook" (www.pantone.com). This book gives you the exact levels of red, green, and blue that go into any color you wish to use when dealing with four-color and other printing processes.

Most desktop publishing programs allow you to tweak the colors of fonts, backgrounds, clip-art, and so forth. Try it on the software you use; there should be an area where you can change the percentage of red, green, and blue for an object. You will see the color itself change as you tweak the percentages. If you have the swatchbook, you can then see exactly how that color will turn out once it's printed.

Another option if you don't want to purchase the Pantone book is to sit down with your printer and have them show you the color swatches, decide on your color scheme, and write down the percentages of red, green, and blue that go into the colors you want.

Embedded Fonts and Standard Fonts

Talk to your printer about what fonts are best for its process. For the printing company we work with, the fonts Arial, Helvetica, Century Schoolbook, Bookman, and Palatino are what fit best with its printing process. Palatino is closest to one of the standard Windows fonts, Times New Roman.

Also see if your desktop publishing software can perform what Microsoft Publisher calls "Pack and Go"—pack all fonts, colors, borders, and any other items. into one file so that everything is embedded. Printers love that—it makes their job a lot easier.

Run It!

When you have taken care of all of the above, of course you then have the most difficult job of all—editing the paper. Or you may only be responsible for the layout and desktop publishing aspect. Either way, one of the big advantages of doing all of this yourself is that, as my coeditor told me when we first started doing it this way, "We can now see exactly what we are going to get before taking it to the printer."

Indeed, this is a major benefit of doing the entire publication on the computer; if you are a perfectionist like me, you can make thousands of subtle changes, looking at the results both on-screen and fresh from your laser printer, until you are as close to 100 percent happy as an editor can get.

Once you have reached that point, it's time to store the publication so that your printer can read it from disk. The only real options now are Zip disk or CD-ROM. Zip drives allow you to store either 100 megabytes or 250 megabytes of information onto a disk slightly larger than a floppy disk. You will need that kind of space if your publication is beyond a few pages, because the photos and clip art alone will eat up a lot of disk. If you have a CD-R/CD-RW drive (also known as a CD writer, burner, copier), you can make a CD-ROM with your publication and images on it, which is safer and more standard than Zip drives. Most printers will give you either option. When you are ready to go, save the publication and the images/clip art to whatever media you choose, and that's it. If your software can perform the Pack and Go feature, then it's even easier.

Stop the Presses

Wait! Have you gone over all of the details above (CMYK? TIFF? Pantone colors?) with your contacts at the printer to make sure they are on the same page as you? Have you asked your printer what software it's equipment can read files from?

These are important details. Not all printers will accept publications in all formats. Some will only accept the big guns (PageMaker and Quark Express). Some are more flexible. If you are wed to a particular desktop publishing package, as I am to MS Publisher, and your printer doesn't deal with that format, I suggest you politely, but firmly, ask them to adapt and accept whatever it is you use. It is in their best interests to open up their repertoire anyway, but in addition, *you* are the one paying *them* to do the job for you. I will go as far as to suggest that if your union printer will not accept the file format you prefer to use, shop around. Some other union printer will.

---

31. The Virtual Union Hall

T Santora

The essay below explores the valuable contribution that use of the Internet is making to help integrate marginalized communities into the labor movement. Answers are offered to such questions as:

- *How can the Internet weaken the hold of "all the ignorant and hateful 'isms' of our society"?*
- *In what ways can marginalized communities find a safe haven in virtual union halls?*
- *What is Pride At Work, and how is it helping organized labor?*
- *How did Al Gore and Ralph Nader profit from the help of Pride At Work during the 2000 election process?*
- *How did the Internet aid the campaign to get the Boy Scouts of America to change a major position?*
- *Where on the Internet can unionists find material in support of domestic partnership benefits (DPBs)?*
- *Why is caution in order when a gay worker considers using an employer's computer drive to visit a gay-related Web site, as in thirty-nine states where it is still legal to fire workers based solely on their sexual orientation?*

Especially valuable is the essay's ability to counteract the impression that computer uses are all cold and impersonal: For "in the right hands, with the right motives, new technologies can transcend these flaws."

The Internet and e-mail have revolutionized the way trade unionists communicate in the United States and around the world. I do not use the word "revolutionized" lightly. Others have waxed eloquent about its potential for organizing new workers into the labor movement. In my capacity as communications coordinator for several contract campaigns, I have used Web pages, e-mail, and chat rooms to mobilize workers engaged in collective bargaining struggles. But these examples point only to the obvious utilitarian aspects of Internet technologies.

For hundreds of thousands of people the Internet has become a refuge, a place to share ideas and be yourself, where all the ignorant and hateful "isms" of our society become irrelevant. Not surprisingly, LGBT (lesbian, gay, bisexual, transgender) people, persons with disabilities, and other marginalized communities were among the first large constituencies of the Internet.

LGBT people are likely to use the Internet more frequently, for longer periods of time, and conduct more online financial transactions than their heterosexual counterparts, according to the results of a survey by Harris Interactive. These findings were part of a larger study about consumer behavior and attitudes of adults related to Internet use. The survey was conducted online between January 11 and 15, 2000, with 2,525 adults responding. Of these, 137 people (6 percent of the total sample) identified themselves as LGBT.

Within the labor movement, these communities have turned the Internet into a virtual union hall—a safe space where strategies are developed, actions are debated, elections are conducted, and resolutions adopted. A place where those among us who have been left out and isolated can fully and freely participate as equals, where our work schedule, even our time zone, becomes irrelevant. Our virtual union hall is where we can simply "hang out" with our colleagues in the struggle and "carry on" about anything from world events to labor issues to home cooking recipes.

As in any union, there are members content to enjoy their relative security, but there are also those others who prefer to push the envelope to expand the benefits, broaden the agenda, raise the consciousness, and increase the membership. In his 1999 book, *CyberUnion: Empowering Labor Through Computer Technology*, Arthur B. Shostak describes the CyberUnion as one that aggressively takes advantage of the enormous potential of new technologies and the Internet.

Clearly, many activists are ahead of their unions in this regard.

Pride At Work, the AFL-CIO's newest constituency group for LGBT workers, fits the CyberUnion model. Because LGBT workers have been so maligned in our society, many of us gravitated toward the Internet's relative anonymity as a safe vehicle to reach out to others in our community.

It follows that LGBT unionists, many of whom have felt unwelcome in their own unions, used their comfort and skills with computer technologies to organize online. It is ironic that from the isolation of the closet emerged one of the nation's most sophisticated and powerful political forces. Pride At Work members use these technologies to mobilize previously shut-out members to fight for equal rights, equal compensation, and access to union leadership.

There are hundreds of examples of how Internet and e-mail have facilitated the development and growth of Pride At Work. Most of our communications are electronic. We rely almost exclusively on list servers, Web pages, and e-mail to conduct our business.

However, unlike many labor organizations, our group has become accustomed to a more freewheeling discourse of issues and ideas. Top-down or one-way communication from the leadership to the members is not an option at Pride At Work. This is just the way we like it, and the fact is, having built the organization this way, there is no turning back now.

Ideas, Discourse, and Debate

During the 2000 presidential election cycle, many lively discussions were generated over so-called third-party candidacies. A significant number of liberal to radical-left members emerged to challenge the conventional wisdom of labor's endorsement of Democratic Vice President Al Gore. Not surprisingly, heated e-mail debates ensued between unionists supporting Gore and those supporting Green Party candidate Ralph Nader.

As the polls narrowed to razor-thin margins and it became clear that Nader votes could tip the scales toward Republican George Bush in certain areas, both sides searched for a compromise. Much press was generated on the phenomenon of vote-swapping initiatives that played out on the Internet as a result of these debates. Pride At Work members actively participated in this exchange of ideas and votes.

A Green Party member from Seattle forwarded an article he found endorsing Nader to members of the Pride At Work executive board. An angry reply from a member in Washington, DC, was sent to all recipients of the original e-mail along with several others. This exchange escalated into a full-blown debate within Pride At Work as the recipient list grew and more people felt compelled to add their own views.

Ultimately, a consensus emerged. The election of Bush could spell disaster for both the LGBT and labor movements. At this point, many of those in safe districts, such as Washington, DC, agreed to vote for Nader to help garner the 10 percent vote the Green Party needed to earn matching federal funds. Those in less safe districts, such as in the Midwest or South, agreed to vote for Gore.

Another issue that generated equally heated discussions among unionists followed the controversial U.S. Supreme Court decision in *Boy Scouts of America v. Dale*. In its 5 to 4 ruling on June 28, 2000, the Court allowed the Boy Scouts of America (BSA) to exclude gay youth and adult members.

Given the history of close ties between the labor movement and the BSA, the Court's decision represented a terrible dilemma. However, the reaction from Pride At Work and the larger LGBT movement came swift and clear.

The BSA policy was roundly condemned. This issue, even more than the presidential election contest, would test the limits of solidarity among unionists. Although the leadership at the AFL-CIO was inclined to distance themselves from the controversy, it swirled around them. Could the labor movement remain silent and hope to sustain credibility in the civil rights community?

Many unionists, spurred on by the leadership of Pride At Work, began to demand a response from AFL-CIO president John Sweeney. E-mails were flying across the country asking when Sweeney and other union leaders would address the issue. Reports of Central Labor Councils, United Way, and other organizations that did speak out against the BSA were funneled through Pride At Work to the Civil Rights Department of the AFL-CIO to underscore the point that labor's leaders were not leading.

In my role as copresident of Pride At Work, I take responsibility for broadcast communications to our members. In order to broaden our efforts, I turned to other list servers, including one [MODEM; see Chapter 17] started by activists from the National Labor College at the George Meany Center. As an alumnus, I sent the following message:

> Subject: AFL-CIO Versus Boy Scouts of America
> Sent: Sunday, October 29, 2000, 3:01 P.M.
>
> As I'm sure you know, the Boy Scouts of America (BSA) has adopted a formal policy that excludes gay boys and men. The Supreme Court ruled that BSA was a "private" organization, thereby exempting them from most nondiscrimination laws. Since that time, hundreds of public and private organizations from across the country have cut off funding or suspended BSA's ability to use their facilities.
>
> What has received less attention, but which is just as wrong, is the fact that the BSA also discriminates against atheists and agnostics.
>
> Despite a growing backlash against the BSA, Labor has not yet taken a stand. Thousands of union members and their children are involved in the Boy Scouts, and this has created a bit of a dilemma for many unions and their leaders. Although most unions, and the AFL-CIO, have adopted very specific nondiscrimination policies, they have remained silent.
>
> The time for silence is well past. Pride At Work has requested that the AFL-CIO sever all ties with the BSA until such time as they drop their discriminatory policies. Letters with a similar request have been sent to most major unions.
>
> The AFL-CIO Executive Council will be meeting on November 28 and

will likely take up the issue there. Although an internal task force that reviewed the P@W request has recommended severing ties, AFL-CIO President John Sweeney chose not to issue a statement, at least not before the Nov. 7 elections.

Your union's leadership needs to hear from you. You can bet they will hear from those who believe in the BSA's policy of exclusion. Please contact your Local and international union officers and encourage them to stand up for our gay, atheist, and agnostic union brothers.

Your union can be very influential on the AFL-CIO Executive Council. If your union condemns the BSA, the AFL-CIO and others will likely follow suit. Act now to end Labor's complacency in the face of ignorant and bigoted discrimination.

"An injury to one is an injury to all."

Within two days the first reply was posted on the list server. Sadly, but not surprisingly, the brother who responded did not immediately see the connections. He wrote:

Sent: Tuesday, October 31, 2000, 1:35 P.M.

Labor shouldn't take a stand on this issue. We fight for jobs and a 40-hour work week. Not a persons' sexual choice or whether or not they can become part of some group. My personal view or yours gets distorted when we look outside of what our focus should be on issues.

Whether I am pro-choice, support gun laws, or agree with someone's view of being gay and in the Boy Scouts, takes me away from my focus of representing the Labor movement. Example: Thousands of union members and their children are involved in the Boy Scouts, and are glad that a gay or lesbian are not teaching their children. Are they wrong for feeling that way? It's the same with gun laws. The same party we are trying to elect is also trying to limit our usage or choice of owning guns. Are they right or wrong? The Democratic party generally stands for a women's right to choose. Are they right or wrong?

We are a Labor organization, not a special interest group. Fight for JOBS. Without a job would we really care about the other issues? NO JOB, who needs choices? They are made for you.

I would hope my Union keeps the course of securing me a high-paying job with the right to bargain my wages and benefits.

My reply:

Sent: Wednesday, November 1, 2000, 2:10 P.M.

The brother's tunnel vision is very disturbing. Or, maybe he doesn't understand that jobs are central to the issue with the Boys Scouts of America

(BSA). People have been fired or denied employment from the BSA not only because of their sexual orientation, but because they are agnostic, or atheist. Even if you choose to look the other way on the issue of banning volunteers from the BSA, as a unionist, you cannot turn a blind eye to the employment discrimination there.

The brother poses the question, "Are parents wrong for being 'glad' that their children are not being taught by lesbians or gays?" Of course they are wrong! They should be concerned with what is being taught and how, not irrelevant personal aspects of who is doing the teaching. After all, I'm sure there are lots of parents who would prefer that their children's teachers weren't union members either. Are they "wrong"? Shouldn't we be concerned about the teachers and their jobs?

When my union brothers and sisters are attacked and marginalized in the way the BSA has, you bet I'm concerned about it. Every union member would do well to remember our motto, "An injury to one is an injury to all." I expect my union to stand up for jobs. In fact, I demand it!

The writer did not respond again. However, I received many more e-mails that were not posted to the list server. They were overwhelmingly supportive. Several people simply copied me the e-mails they sent to their union executive officers.

I know that many minds were left unchanged on this issue. However, the discourse illustrated the point that there is more here than meets the eye. It is dangerous for unionists to dismiss any issue of discrimination without viewing it from a worker's point of view. Whether or not unionists are ready to believe that sexual orientation is not a choice, they must come to terms with the reality that LGBT people are workers and union members too.

Bargaining for Equality

Shortly after I joined the staff of the Communications Workers of America (CWA) in 1993, my staff union entered negotiations for contract renewal. One of the items I submitted as a bargaining demand was to add domestic partnership benefits (DPBs).

Trying to assist the bargaining team by researching the issue and providing them with cost data, usage statistics, and sample contract language was no easy task. I had to make several calls before I found an organization that would mail me information upon receipt of a formal written request. The information they sent was hardly comprehensive, but I photocopied the relevant data and mailed it to the bargaining team. Now such information is readily available on several organizational Web sites, including Pride At Work's.

Doing this kind of research has dramatically improved in the past few years, thanks to more sophisticated Internet search engines. A good illustration of this came about in the 2000 negotiations between the Office and Professional Employees International Union (OPEIU) and the International Brotherhood of Teamsters. A Teamsters employee represented by OPEIU Local 2 e-mailed a request to Pride At Work for cost data on DPBs. Her bargaining team had informed her that Teamsters management was resisting adding the new benefits because of concerns over potential healthcare cost increases.

Within hours of receiving the request, Pride At Work staff was able to direct the member and her bargaining team to the most current information available on the subject. The National Gay and Lesbian Task Force has a publication entitled *The Domestic Partnership Organizing Manual for Employee Benefits* by Sally Kohn (Kohn 1998) on its Web page (www.nglft.org). It is one of the most comprehensive and accessible studies of DPBs available, and it is free to download in Adobe Acrobat (PDF) format. It was the perfect resource for the OPEIU bargaining team.

Another example of how bargaining is enhanced by the use of instant communications presented itself when a colleague in contract negotiations with a national high-tech firm called me from the bargaining table. She had just sent me an e-mail from her laptop computer with a draft of a newly revised non-discrimination clause attached. She was very excited to have achieved the inclusion of sexual orientation in the clause and asked me to review it before she signed off on it. The document had arrived before we ended our brief conversation. The language prohibited "all forms of illegal discrimination based on race, creed, gender, marital status, disability, or sexual orientation."

Many people are unaware that in most communities, it is still perfectly legal to discriminate on the basis of sexual orientation. It hadn't occurred to my colleague that prohibiting only illegal forms of discrimination would be meaningless for most gay members.

I sent her an e-mail with a suggestion to drop the word "illegal" and visit the Lambda Legal Defense and Education Fund Web page (www.lambdalegal.org) (Lambda 2000) with her management counterparts. By contacting this Web page, they could see if sexual orientation discrimination was permissible by law in any of the communities in which the company did business.

As it turned out, the company headquarters and the bargainers themselves were located in just such a community. The managers were just as surprised about this as my colleague. Because they were still at the bargaining table, the counterproposal was agreed to and signed that same afternoon.

Conclusion

The skeptics among us will be hard to convince. Some will deride the newer technologies as cold and impersonal or too easily manipulated. Certainly, these characterizations can be accurate. However, in the right hands, with the right motives, new technologies can transcend these flaws.

The enemies of labor and other progressive movements are taking full advantage of these technologies. Our colleagues who may still need motivation are encouraged to visit the Web pages of the National Right to Work Legal Defense Foundation. (www.nrtw.org) or HateWatch (www.hatewatch.org), a Web-based nonprofit group that monitors the evolving threat of hate groups on the Web. Many of these hate groups, including so-called religious right organizations, have openly embraced traditional labor organizing tactics to pursue their political goals and increase their membership. They have relentlessly exploited new technologies and communications vehicles to spread their message. At the very least, labor should be equally armed.

Regardless of the issue of the day, the speed and reach of the Internet in providing workers with real-time access to information and opportunities to share ideas cannot be matched. Our ability to arm our members with useful data and mobilize them to action should not be underestimated. For those of us who serve in labor leadership roles, providing a vehicle for members' ideas and feedback will keep us well connected with the grassroots of our movement and, ultimately, far more accountable to those we are privileged to serve.

A cautionary note may be in order as I close. Even though 257 of the Fortune 500 companies maintain a written nondiscrimination policy that includes sexual orientation, these policies are not necessarily embodied in collective bargaining agreements. Such policies are therefore subject to unilateral changes.

Further, it is still legal in thirty-nine states to deny employment or fire workers based solely on their sexual orientation. That's a reality gay workers must take seriously when surfing or communicating on the Internet. The temptation to join with other gay workers and activists in our virtual union hall using workplace computers may be risky. For example, cookies or temporary Internet files can be deposited on an employee's computer drive after he or she visits some gay-related Web sites. A snooping coworker or supervisor who may reach his or her own conclusions about the employee's sexual orientation could easily access these. The degree to which one should worry about privacy issues is directly related to the degree to which that person feels vulnerable to workplace discrimination, bias, or even violence.

References

FindLaw for Legal Professionals. *Boy Scouts of America and Monmouth Council, et al., Petitioners v. James Dale*, n.d. <http://caselaw.lp.findlaw.com/scripts/getcase.pl?court=us&vol=000&invol=99–699> (downloaded November 2000).

Fox, Kara. "Poll: Gays More Likely to Use Internet; Survey Shows Gays Are Online More Often Than Heterosexuals." Washington, DC: *The Washington Blade*, The Washington Blade Online!, February 23, 2001 <http://washblade.com/>.

Kohn, Sally. *The Domestic Partner Organizing Manual for Employee Benefits*. Washington, DC: Policy Institute of The National Gay and Lesbian Task Force, 1998.

Human Rights Campaign. *HRC WorkNet Employer Database*, February 2001 <www.hrc.org>.

Hunt, G., ed. *Laboring for Rights: Unions and Sexual Diversity Across Nations*. Philadelphia: Temple University Press, 1999.

Lambda Legal Defense and Education Fund. *Boy Scouts v. Dale Online Press kit*, n.d. <www.lambdalegal.org/cgi-bin/pages/documents/record?record=613> (downloaded October 2000).

Lukenbill, Grant. *Are Privacy Issues Coming Out on the Web for Gay Consumers?* New York: OnMoney, OnMoney Financial Services Corporation, n.d. <www.onmoney.com/Editorial/plan/luken/gaypriv1.html> (downloaded February 2001).

Pride At Work. *Pride At Work Calls for AFL-CIO and Affiliates to Condemn the Boy Scouts of America*, November 21, 2000 <www.prideatwork.org/news.html> (downloaded November 2000).

———. *Domestic Partnership Benefits & Union Bargaining*, n.d. <www.prideatwork.org/story.html> (downloaded February 1999).

Shostak, Arthur B. *CyberUnion: Empowering Labor Through Computer Technology*. Armonk, NY: M.E. Sharpe, 1999.

---

32. A Clipboard, a Cell Phone, and a Laptop: What Every Organizer Needs

Will Collette

The service we know as labor's strategic corporate research is more efficient and effective today than ever before, thanks to the wealth of information available on the Internet. Guided by the informative essay below, even the most experienced researcher is likely to pick up a new tip or trick.

Among the questions tackled are these:

- *How much relevant information do companies share?*
- *Is there reason to search the general press? Government portals?*
- *If so, which ones?*
- *Are investor Web sites worth a look?*
- *Are relevant free sites switching to a fee basis, and if so, so what?*
- *Above all, is it best to hold off? Or to jump in? And if the latter, how is this best done?*

In today's organizing climate, union activists *must* be computer literate and *must* be online. At the AFL-CIO Building Trades Department, we make a conscious effort to promote computer literacy. Several affiliates promote that cause as well: At Sheet Metal, much of their organizing and corporate research training curriculum is contained in a self-teaching program on CD-ROM. The Asbestos Workers have equipped their organizers with state-of-the-art laptops and Internet access. The Ironworkers and others use a tailor-made organizing software program to facilitate house calling and member tracking.

For over a year now the Building Trades Advanced Organizer Training Program has included a two-day module on strategic corporate research, where more than half of the class time is spent in the computer lab doing hands-on work investigating actual union organizing targets online. We work on the principle that to answer basic questions about targeted employers—for example, "who *are* these people?"—organizers must use computer technology and Web-based resources. Otherwise they are wasting members' dues money by being inefficient.

Some participants in our training had never sat in front of a computer. Locating the on-off switch is step one. A few have asked why the letters on the keyboard are all screwed up ("Hey, what's with this QWERT stuff?"). The computer "newbies" need and get special attention. They often reward us by their rapid learning curve.

We teach basics, like how to use a search engine. Current favorite: www.google.com, followed by www.dogpile.com. These are meta-search engines, meaning they are search tools that use other search tools. Starting with an exercise of having participants plug the name of their target company into these search engines (to see what there is to see), we introduce trainees to the wonderful world of corporate research on the Web.

Usually, the target company's Web site pops up right away. Increasingly, businesses of interest to union activists will have Web sites. We walk participants through these company sites, and I always get a kick out of how surprised our trainees are at the level of information companies will reveal about themselves. Typically, a company will describe itself, its subsidiaries, its structure, its business plan, its major projects, and its locations.

Next we show these activists how to search published news accounts to see what, if anything, has been written about their targets in newspapers, magazines, trade press, and business journals. Many, probably most, of these publications are online. Nearly all allow you to see their current issue and to search their archives. Unfortunately, more and more are shifting to either pay-per-view or subscription for full services, especially archive search. Even so, this line of research is far more cost-effective than the old-fashioned paper chase.

Use media meta-search engines to begin shopping around (e.g., http://ajr.newslink.org/news.html, www.metagrid.com/, and www.newspapers.com/npcom1.htm).

Many regulatory agencies, especially federal, have searchable databases that allow activists to develop a "rap sheet" on target companies. You can check out their safety record, environmental compliance, labor law violations, and so on. To compare how your target rates, you can use federal, state, and, increasingly, local government online resources to look at industry standards. You can compare wage rates, unemployment, and benefits for your target versus the industry at the national, state, and, often, county or municipal level. You can use these sources to evaluate the outlook for the industry in which your target operates. Some convenient portals to government information include www.pac-info.com/, www.library.vanderbilt.edu/romans/fdtf.html, and www.fedstats.gov/.

More government sources are coming online and more such sources already on line are expanding and improving. These include secretary of state corporate records for states, local property and tax records, court dockets, court decisions, and local regulatory bodies (e.g., health department inspections). In many instances these postings tell you a file exists on a target, but you still need to go and look at that file to make the best use of the information.

Nearly all state laws, and many local ordinances, can be searched online. One great meta-search engine to help you get started is www.findlaw.com.

While the amount of free government information is rapidly expanding, some agencies are shifting to pay-per-use. There is no consistent pattern at the moment. For example, you can get lots of great, free statistical information from the Bureau of Labor Statistics (www.bls.gov), while the Department of Commerce requires a subscription fee and per-use charge for similar data. The state of Florida provides tons of free corporate information, while, by contrast, states like Indiana and Massachusetts provide a paltry amount at high pay-per-view fees. Go figure.

If a target company is publicly traded on the stock exchange, the volume of information skyrockets. Companies must file detailed public reports with the Securities and Exchange Commission (SEC), and you can view this material online at www.freeedgar.com and www.tenkwizard.com. These services are edging toward paid subscriptions, so use them now while they are free.

SEC reports by target companies contain detailed financial information, executive compensation, ownership, markets, subsidiaries, lenders, business strategy, litigation, and much more, all in the companies's own words. A must-read for any activist.

In addition, public companies are watched, analyzed, and reviewed by dozens of investor-oriented Web sites, most of them still free. These sites will digest information for you and create simple summaries and reports that might take hours or days for you to do for yourself, especially if you are new to this. Try www.investorama.com (you need to apply for a free membership) or www.corporateinformation.com/ to begin looking at the wide range of investor Web sites.

Using these portals, you can then decide which sites are most useful to you. Through them you can get capsules, financial information neatly digested and arranged, all the kinds of business information found in SEC filings in digested form—institutional ownership, insider ownership, trading, and just about everything but the CEO's shoe size.

The universe of free Web sources is changing. As the dot-com bubble has burst, many Web sites are turning to user fees and subscriptions to stay alive. Some of my favorite sites are going this route, such as www.companysleuth.com (which allows you to track your own special list of target companies for many important subjects, including some more obscure ones like patent and trademark applications) and www.lionshares.com (which is one of the easiest sites for tracking which banks, pension funds, mutual funds, and other institutional investors own shares of any given public company).

This shift to pay-for-service makes the premium subscriptions more attractive, though no less pricey. The best known premium service is Lexis-Nexis, long the favorite of the AFL-CIO, and extraordinarily expensive. Lexis-Nexis packages legal, corporate, and media records together and allows you more depth of material than anything you can find on any free site. However, a useful, free source for legal research into Lexis-Nexis offers a nice collection of complete decisions: www.lexisone.com/index.html. Westlaw (www.westlaw.com) offers similar depth of material, but is now trying to win accounts away from Lexis-Nexis by offering better prices and package deals.

Generally, I recommend that activists start simply and cheaply, and build from there. You can more easily justify the expense of paying for service or even subscribing to the premium services when you are confident in your ability to use computer research to actually help your organizing work go better and more efficiently. Whether you go to the max and buy access to these services depends on your needs and capabilities.

But whether you ever reach that stage is less important than starting to use the Web to help you build organizational power. Do it now. Today. Right now. Go to www.google.com and type in the target de jour. Where that leads you is up to you.

IX. How to Honor Traditions

When the legends die, the dreams end.
There is no more greatness.
—Shawnee proverb

We are shaped and fashioned by what we love.
—Johann Wolfgang von Goethe, German poet

Traditions refers to the intention of Cyber Gain unions and locals in general, and CyberUnions by definition, to honor their culture and lore, their founding dream and their core values. CyberUnions recognize in traditions a key opportunity to emphasize the parity in their culture of "high touch" with "high tech" matters.

Traditions basically highlight stories worth recalling, pondering, embellishing, and retelling over and again, stories worth cherishing for their unique ability to illuminate empowering truths. Their relationship to power—a key concern of modern unions—is considerable, if commonly under-recognized: "Those who do not have power over the story that dominates their lives, power to retell it, rethink it, deconstruct it, joke about it, and change it as times change, truly are powerless, because they cannot think new thoughts" (Rushdie 1991).

An insightful assessment of our times traces much of our "modern melancholy" to a lack of empowering stories and celebrations: "We live in an age of unprecedented wealth, but in the realm of narrative and symbol, we are deprived. And so the ache for meaning goes unrelieved" (Delbanco 1999). Labor union traditions offer welcome balm, some overdue relief, stimulating thoughts, and a heady lift to our spirits. Thanks to computer options, we are now in a position to gain more from labor traditions than ever before.

Many tips and tricks are available to help, a small sample of which follows as an introduction to two fuller accounts of key tools in this regard—labor education (this time for gaining computer skills) and labor videos (this time as part of a world-wide cyberspace screening system).

1. *"Mine" the past.* New members could be invited (required?) to take a digital camera on loan and interview some of the oldest living members of the local. Questions could explore timeless lessons hidden away in the origins of a local and in the sacrifices and gains of its pioneers. Old-timers whose lives were transformed against a backdrop of industrial conflict often have for the asking insights of lasting value.

A well-financed and quite deliberate effort might be made to create an oral and video record of reminiscences, complete with archival storage. It is important that new members learn about certain key deceased members. For if, as German playwright Heiner Muller suggests, the level of culture is fixed by the way in which society interacts with its dead, so also is the quality of a labor organization set in a like manner (Breytenbach 1996, 158).

2. *Recreate the past.* Key aspects of the history of the organization might itself be recreated by actors and actresses, videotaped, and placed permanently on the union or local's Web site. Many relevant labor songs, anecdotes, and historic speeches might be added, along with streaming video celebrations of special days and events in the organization's past. In this way the story might get told honestly—that is, with fairness to working people—possibly for the first time (Oscar Wilde argued that "the one duty we owe to history is to rewrite it." [Doyle 2001]).

Too much, however, cannot be made of the point that explorations of labor traditions must keep faith with historic truth, however great the temptation may be to do otherwise. Labor has a rare opportunity to set the record straight where a lot of misunderstandings, errors, deliberate deceptions, and just plain foolishness have crept in. Using its new cyberspace sites, labor can regain the high ground in telling its story, knowing that anything less is disastrous in the information age: As Sun Microsystems CEO Scott McNearly explains, "On the Internet, even more than other areas of our lives, trust is the real currency. Squander what you have, and you'll find out how hard it is to get more" (McNealy 2001).

Tom Katona helps show the way with this excerpt from his essay, Chapter 42: "After you create a site for your union, consider creating another one about a union-related topic. . . . Here's an example: I created a Web site for a local event in labor history that was fading away into the mists of time. In less than two years, the Italian Hall Disaster Web site (www.ih1913.eg.st) had over 1,100 hits! That's close to three visits per day. I hope that the site not only helped to preserve the memory of this event, but also that it was able to lift the consciousness of at least a few of the visitors. Naturally, the site carries the union label. Make sure your sites do, too."

Similarly, Peggy Myrie explains in her essay, Chapter 24, the appeal of using labor history: "My local's Web site will need a mission or vision, and a means to present the traditions of the UAW. I recently viewed a documentary, 'The Great Sit Down,' about the Flint, Michigan, strike in 1936–37. This was a great history lesson, of great heroes, one that can relay the 'soul' of unionism. The film reaches out to women as well, with their contributions in the Emergency Brigade and the Women Auxiliary. I thought, "How great these clips would be for viewing on the Web site!"

Why bother? Because, as labor historian James Green explains, "Historical narratives can do more than just redeem the memory of past struggles; they can help people think of themselves as historical figures who, like those who came before them, have crucial moral and political choices to make" (Green 2000).

3. *Mine the present.* Members could be encouraged to take a digital camera on loan and cover present-day labor events for immediate sharing (via still photos or streaming video) with the entire rank-and-file and everyone else who cares toview it.

Typical here was a June 18, 2001, rally, when over 150 home-care workers and consumers in Oakland, California, converged on the Alameda County Administration Building to demand a living wage from the board of supervisors. The workers brought a series of photographic posters that depicted the struggles and joys of personal care attendants.

A group of the workers had taken the photos as part of the Service Employees International Union (SEIU) Local 616 project "Picturing Change," which taught them photographic and storytelling techniques. The workers presented their photos along with the accompanying stories, printed in English, Chinese, and Spanish, to the board of supervisors at the public hearing. Thereafter, labor list servers carried the story through cyberspace to every corner of the globe.

4. *Mine professional resources.* There are various state labor historical societies eager to ally with locals in celebrating key aspects of labor history, and many have welcoming Web sites. For example, learn about the rich tradition of labor history in Illinois at the Illinois Labor History Society site (www.kentlaw.edu/ilhs/index.html).

As well, much can be learned from the new Labor Arts Web site at (www.laborarts.org/). Labor Arts is a virtual museum designed to gather, identify, and display examples of the cultural and artistic history of working people and to celebrate the trade union movement's contributions to that history.

In the spring of 2001 it featured digital exhibits titled Parades and Demonstrations (past and present); Workers at Work; Strikes; Cartoon Art (on labor themes); Bread and Roses (selections from the poster series); Buttons, Badges and Ribbons; and selections from the Wagner Archives. The Resources section here lists over 30 additional Web sites related to workers' art and culture.

The staffs at various museums are available to custom-tailor tours or even create virtual visits in cyberspace to celebrate labor traditions. Museum portals include. http://museumspot.com, www.musee_online.org, www.MuseumNetwork.org, and www.museumstaff.com.

Also valuable, and especially fun when attended in person (albeit also available in a cyberspace version), is the annual LaborTech conference, a gathering of labor digerati involved in computers, radio, video, film, and communications in general. Sponsored outside the purview of the AFL-CIO, it has a zesty counterculture air reminiscent of the 1970s, along with a focus on the future that expands the horizon of all.

The first LaborTech conference in 1990 was organized in part to provide basic education to the labor movement about how to use technology and the media for labor. Other LaborTech conferences have been held since in Minneapolis, Madison, San Francisco, Vancouver, and Moscow, and a LaborMedia conference is held in Seoul, Korea, every November. As explained in Chapter 34 by Steve Zeltzer, a founder, these intense and info-rich conferences "have provided a critical vehicle and spark in bringing labor media/computer technologists together from around the world to build, network and strengthen our activities."

5. *Keep up alliances.* Major support for labor traditions comes from the rich diversity of the rank-and-file. Locals gain much from participating in celebrations of ethnic and racial pride such as a Christopher Columbus Parade, a Polish-American fete, or a memorial service for Dr. Martin Luther King, Jr.

For example, on March 31, 2001, the first anniversary of Cesar Chavez's birthday as an official state holiday—the first state holiday in the country honoring a labor leader and the first for a Latino—the United Farm Workers held an interfaith service and big parade in San Francisco. Won as the result of a campaign by labor to honor one of its own, the holiday and parade were expected to generate a tremendous amount of public attention, participation, and media visibility.

CyberUnions could supplement all of this with a major Web site constructed for the occasion, complete with a quiz contest about Chavez, the history of Hispanic American labor relations, facts and forecasts of value to concerned union activists, and, naturally, live coverage of the celebration.

This list could be extended quite far, but the point would seem already adequately made: Traditions can receive a substantial boost from the sensitive and creative employ of computer power. The two essays that follow underline the point, the first by offering tips and tricks where education is concerned, arguably one of labor's oldest traditions, and the second by heralding the arrival of new video possibilities, a promising source of many new traditions.

References

Breytenbach, Breyten. *The Memory of Birds in Times of Revolution.* New York: Harcourt Brace, 1996, p. 158.

Delbanco, Andrew. *The Real American Dream.* Cambridge, MA: Harvard University Press, 1999, p. 107.

Doyle, Rodger. "Rewriting History." *Scientific America,* May 2001, pp. 24–28. The quote from Wilde is cited on p. 26.

Green, James. "Historians as Allies of the Labor Movement." *The Chronicle of Higher Education,* July 28, 2000, p. B-4 (autor's e-mail: james.green@umb.edu).

McNealy, Scott. "Absolute Privacy Shutters Web's Window." *The Sunday (Albuquerque) Journal,* June 3, 2001, p. B-3.

Rushdie, Salman. "One Thousand Days in a Balloon." *New York Times,* December 12, 1991, p. B-8.

---

33. Designing and Delivering Internet Instruction to Labor Unions: A Practical Guide

Deborah Joseph

As in almost every new such venture, progress hinges on how rapidly and surely labor helps a critical mass move over the starting line and gain more momentum all the time. Pivotal here are labor education specialists, many of them "cybrarians," coast-to-coast, busy helping rank-and-file unionists become computer users.

The essay below by one such specialist helps answers these questions:

- *How popular with unionists are workshops for learning how to use the Internet?*
- *What should a course instructor learn early on about enrollees?*
- *How might an instructor best prepare for these courses?*
- *Why is more less? Why is it smart to go slow? How does walking around the room help the learning process?*

- *Why is it smart to have online material available in alternative forms?*
- *What tips and tricks really help in these courses? Why?*
- *Does distance learning have a role to play?*

Note especially the experienced teacher's conclusion that "most unionists, regardless of age or gender, are knowledgeable, willing, and ready to learn."

On a recent winters' morning I was jarred awake by the all-too-familiar sound of my trusty travel alarm clock. I was in a dark hotel room in the middle of midtown Manhattan—my third such visit to that particular hotel in the past six months.

I have perfected the art of packing in ten minutes or less, have developed a built-in radar allowing me to wake in a strange hotel room in the middle of the night and, without the benefit of light, find my way to the bathroom. I know where the best candy store in Rochester is, I have the Buffalo Sabres box office phone number memorized, and I can give you exact directions to Pagliacci Ristorante in downtown Albany.

I have developed these amazing skills and knowledge as a result of my position as traveling Internet trainer (or to be more precise, Outreach Services Librarian) for the Martin P. Catherwood Library, of the School of Industrial and Labor Relations at Cornell University in upstate New York. Over the course of the last three years, I have headed up Catherwood Library's Labor Outreach Program, teaching Internet workshops to labor union members across New York State and in Washington, DC. In this capacity I have traveled roughly 4,000 miles, taught over thirty workshops on a variety of topics, and have trained more than 500 union members in the process.

The School of Industrial and Labor Relations, founded in 1945, is dedicated to the study and teaching of workplace issues. Areas of study include collective bargaining, labor history and law, labor economics, human resources, and organizational behavior. The school also has an Extension Division, with six offices throughout New York State offering a wide array of classes to both students and professionals in the field.

Catherwood Library has long been involved with training union members by working in partnership with the Extension Division. These offerings usually take the form of one- or two-hour sessions on the Internet and/or the use of other library tools during the course of an Extension class held on-campus in Ithaca. While participating in these training sessions, union members repeatedly told reference librarians that additional training on the Internet would be beneficial. That feedback provided the impetus for creating the Labor Outreach Program.

The program's first workshops, aimed at labor union members in central New York, were offered on the Cornell University campus in June of 1998. These were soon followed by sold-out workshops in New York City, Buffalo, Rochester, Albany, and Washington, DC. While the extension office handles the administration of the workshop, including publicity, registration, and pricing, the Outreach program develops and teaches the classes.

Much has been written about the importance of the Internet to labor, and the topic is adequately covered elsewhere in this volume. Rather than repeat what others have written about most eloquently, I have chosen instead to focus this essay on the lessons learned in designing, promoting, and presenting Internet training workshops for union members. Using the Catherwood program as a model, I hope to share some of my experiences and pass along some tips for others endeavoring to offer similar training.

Assessing User Needs

Before beginning any instructional program, it is important to know your audience by adequately assessing and understanding their needs. This can be achieved in a variety of ways. If the training is for a local union, invite members to an informal brainstorming/information session. If the intended audience is based across a large geographic area, surveys can be used.

When the Labor Outreach program was created, letters were sent to labor councils and local unions throughout upstate New York, inquiring into their perceived needs for Internet training. This method was later replaced with a more formal survey addressed to meet the needs of both past and potential future participants. The survey (Figure 1) will be launched on the Labor Outreach Program Web site as well as mailed out to a targeted audience. It addresses issues such as specific program offerings, workshop time (day, evening, weekday, weekend), and workshop location (on-site, in a specific city, etc.). Gathering as much information as possible beforehand is vital to planning and presenting a successful workshop.

Designing the Workshops

Once the needs of the audience have been determined, it is time to start formulating the design of the workshop. Most of the Labor Outreach workshops are full-day sessions with morning, lunch, and afternoon breaks. The day is broken into segments by topic, with each segment focusing on specific Web sites. For instance, when teaching Corporate Research Online, the morning section is divided up into one-hour segments devoted to company profiles, researching nonprofit organizations, obtaining financial information and other relevant subjects. Specific Web sites are demonstrated for each of these segments.

Having a lesson plan or outline for the workshop will help the day flow more smoothly. I find it useful to make an outline for each segment I am presenting. In my outline I list the Web sites I am showing as well as the searches I plan on conducting within each site. This outline is for myself only, though participants are given an agenda for the day. It is also important to walk through all of your material at least once. This will ensure that you don't meet with any surprises, such as Web addresses that no longer exist.

Assessing Computer Literacy

All Labor Outreach workshops are held in computer labs. It is very important when presenting Internet training to provide participants with the ability to follow along on computers. Allowing participants the opportunity of hands-on training results in a more complete understanding and better retention of the material being presented. If your union does not have a computer lab, explore partnerships with other unions or your local labor council.

The use of computer labs does raise the question of how to ascertain the computer literacy of incoming participants. One of the main challenges of teaching Internet workshops is the ability to create courses in which the level of technical knowledge is neither too simplistic nor too sophisticated for participants. While the demographics are changing, many Labor Outreach participants are over the age of forty, have not been in a classroom since high school, and have had very little computer experience.

In most programs there is at least one participant with no typing skills and/or who has trouble handling a mouse. The simple act of typing in a Web address, something most Web users do without thinking, can become a frustrating experience for these first-time computer users. At the same time, many participants are increasingly at ease with computer technology and research. Designing and pacing a class to address different levels of expertise can be a challenge.

When the Labor Outreach workshops were first offered three years ago, we attempted to determine the level of computer literacy among participants through a mini-questionnaire included in the registration brochures. Participants were queried as to general computer usage, Internet access, the use of e-mail, and so forth. In addition, they were asked which type of computer user they would describe themselves as: beginner, intermediate, or advanced.

This last question proved to be the most difficult; many users who identified themselves as intermediate level users were actually judged to be begin-

Figure 1. **Survey—Internet Workshops**

1. What is your position in the union?
   Member
   Steward/Committee Person
   Officer
   Staff

2. Have you taken Cornell-ILR computer-based workshops in the past?
   Yes
   No

If so, which of the following workshops have you attended?
   Labor Unions and the Internet: Basic
   Labor Unions and the Internet: Advanced
   Corporate Research Online
   Creating a Web Site for your Union
   New Communication Technologies for Unions

3. Which city did you attend these workshops in?
   Albany
   Buffalo
   Ithaca
   New York City
   Rochester
   Washington, DC

4. If you have attended either Labor Unions and the Internet: Basic or Labor Unions and the Internet: Advanced, which of the topics has proven to be most helpful?
   Starting Points
   Corporate Research
   Search Engines
   Statistical Sites
   Legal Sites
   Using the Web Browser Effectively
   Political/Campaign Finance
   Safety and Health

5. Which of the following topics would you like to get additional Internet training on:
   Collective Bargaining—Contract Language
   Collective Bargaining—Wages and Statistics
   Collective Bargaining—Researching the Employer
   Organizing—Researching the Employer

Organizing—Anti-union Campaigns
Privatization—Corporate Research
Labor Law
Politics and Campaign Finance
Worker Safety and Health
Finding Information on the Internet (Search Engines and
    Directories)—Advanced
Creating a Web Site for Your Union (Construction and Design)
Other

6. What format would you find most useful?
    One-Day Workshop
    Half-Day Workshop
    Two-Day Workshop (Web Page Design and Construction)

7. What time of year is most convenient?
    Fall
    Winter
    Spring
    Summer

8. What day of the week is most convenient?
    Monday
    Tuesday
    Wednesday
    Thursday
    Friday
    Saturday

7. What time of day is most convenient?
    Morning
    Afternoon
    Evening

8. Which location is most convenient?
    Downtown (name of city)
    Other

9. Would your union be interested in "onsite" Internet Research training customized especially for your union/group?
    Yes
    No

10. Additional Comments

ners during the course of the workshop. On the other hand, many who considered themselves beginners were often quite advanced in their ability. This form of self-assessment became a loose marker at best, and the issue of evaluating competency levels prior to workshops is still being addressed.

More Is Less

Deciding how much material can be realistically covered in a reasonable amount of time is crucial. Often covering less material in greater detail is better than skimming over a large amount of material. This is a philosophy instructors often have difficulty embracing. As we all know, there is an overabundance of information on the Internet, and there are a multitude of Web sites that are of use to labor.

The temptation, therefore, is to cover as much material as possible. However, the human brain can only take in a certain amount of information in any given day. It is infinitely better to concentrate on a few areas thoroughly than to cover a wider range of materials more quickly. Think carefully about which Web sites would be most useful for your session and plan your time accordingly.

The workshop Labor Unions and the Internet has a section covering statistical Web sites. Initially I walked participants through seven Web sites. While it was possible to cover these (albeit briefly) in the time allowed, it left very little time to get to know any one site well. After feedback from participants, the number of statistical sites was reduced from seven to four, thereby allowing for more time on the chosen sites.

Adequately timing workshop presentations is an art form, and one that comes with experience. As a model, try the following example: Suppose you are devoting one hour of your workshop to government information sites. Pick about five good Web sites. Draw up your outline and then clock the amount of time it takes to walk through each site. Once you have determined the amount of time needed, add at least another five minutes for each site.

Remember, many participants are going to take longer to reach the site through lack of typing skills or familiarity with the technology. In addition, once you have displayed this wonderful new site, nothing is more frustrating to a participant than suddenly being whisked off to visit another site. Build in enough time, not only to display the site and its features, but also to let the group spend a few minutes looking around the site on their own.

You may find that you don't have time to get through all four sites. That is fine. It is better to pad your presentation with a few extra sites in the event that one site is down or that participants are faster learners than expected. However, be prepared to drop some of these extra sites due to an unexpected number of questions concerning a particular site or due to slow Internet connectivity or other computer problems. In other words, be flexible.

The Internet is an unpredictable beast. Nothing is worse than having slow response time or, even worse, having the whole network go down unexpectedly. Always prepare to present the online material in alternate forms. Initially I made overhead transparencies of every Web page I showed. This soon became expensive and unmanageable. These days I prepare for emergency contingencies by arming myself with handouts and a white board or flip chart to illustrate talking points.

I find I can often talk about a specific topic or Web site for several minutes without actually having the site up in front of me. Asking and answering questions can also cover "down time." Participants never feel there is enough time for questions. Take advantage of this time to answer questions or engage the members in a discussion of material already covered.

Teaching the Workshop

It is extremely important to become familiar and comfortable with your teaching environment before the workshop. If possible, visit the computer lab a day beforehand and keep the following points in mind:

Become familiar with the layout of the room and the technology available. Ask for temperature adjustment if the room is too warm (nothing puts participants asleep faster than a semidark computer lab that is too warm). Learn the log-on procedures for each computer (often a computer needs to be rebooted during the class and a password may be required). Familiarize yourself with the browser being used, as some navigation features vary from browser to browser.

Get to know the information technology staff. This is *very* important. When the network crashes midday, you will want these people on your side!

Provide an Agenda and State Expectations

Whether we care to admit it or not, most of us learn best in a structured environment. Prepare a detailed agenda for the day and review it with participants. At the beginning of class, point out the location of bathrooms, water fountains, and telephones (and while at it, request that cell phones and beepers be shut off for the duration of class). Point out break and lunch times. If lunch is not included in the workshop cost, be prepared to provide directions to nearby restaurants.

Explain any case studies or quizzes to be given during the class. Providing these details before the class is important, as it will help to avoid unnecessary interruptions throughout the day. In addition, while some of these points may seem minor, such information is appreciated by participants and presents an image of a well-prepared instructor.

Provide hard copies of training materials whenever possible. Most of us still prefer to have paper documentation in front of us when processing information. All Labor Outreach classes include a manual containing annotated Web sites, a glossary, and other relevant information. This manual is often supplemented with additional handouts. While class materials are available and updated regularly on our Web site, participants still like to have a hard copy of the materials.

Start every workshop by taking a few minutes to have participants introduce themselves, tell which union they are from, and express what they hope to get out of the workshop.

Engage participants by breaking the classes into small teams for quizzes or case studies. Not only does this provide a way to draw out the shyer members of the class, it also allows for very valuable networking between the participants. This is particularly important when participants are from various unions, as it allows them to share thoughts, ideas, and experiences.

Go Slowly

The material being taught is often very familiar to those teaching; therefore, there is often a tendency on the part of the instructor to be three layers into a Web site while some participants are still struggling with the Web address itself. Asking participants if they are keeping up with you is not always a good indication whether or not everyone in the class is really following along. Often participants are hesitant to admit they are lost.

For this reason it is beneficial to both the participants and the trainers to have more than one instructor in the classroom. While one person is presenting the training material, the other is free to move around the room to assist participants as needed. When trying to determine whether everyone is keeping up, rely on discreet signals from your copresenter working the room or, if alone, step away from the podium and walk around the room to ensure that everyone has reached the page you are on.

This approach takes extra time and, therefore, patience. When an instructor has timed his or her presentation precisely, a few extra seconds can seem like ten minutes. Build in more time than initially expected for each Web site displayed to cover this eventuality.

Walk around the lab as much as possible, even if a second instructor is in the room. This helps eliminate the artificial barrier imposed by a podium or elevated workstation. Walking around the room also allows for better eye contact and an overall better connection with your participants. While on the topic of exercise, make sure participants have ample time for breaks and stretches. Even the most experienced computer user falls victim to a stiff neck or sore back after sitting hunched over a computer for a few hours.

When teaching computer workshops, it is important to be as empathetic as possible. Many beginning participants are intimidated by both the research and technology (I recently had one participant walk into the lab and compare it to entering a torture chamber). It is therefore very important to present the classes in a casual, encouraging, and unthreatening atmosphere. Participants are often nervous or unsure of themselves when they come into the class-room, and a friendly, nonjudgmental instructor can make all the difference in their workshop experience.

A supportive, light-hearted tone, along with a generous dose of empathy, are important components of my teaching. It is equally essential to maintain a sense of humor, to not take yourself too seriously, and, most important, to find a way to connect with your class.

I recall one particular incidence when I was substitute teaching for an evening labor class. The participants had not met me before and knew noth-ing about me as an instructor. All they knew was that their regular instructor wasn't there and they had a relative greenhorn standing before them. As I earnestly started going over my materials, four men in the back of the room started talking loudly about football, indifferent to the fact that I was speak-ing. I could have tried to ignore them, though their voices were distracting to the rest of the class. I could have lost my temper or demanded their attention (don't bother trying this technique—it never works).

Instead I tried to find something we had in common. I know nothing about football, but this class was taking place during the end of the 1999 baseball season, more specifically during the series between the New York Mets and Atlanta Braves, leading up to the World Series. I am a lifelong Mets fan, and I guessed that at least some of the workshop participants followed baseball. I stopped my lecture long enough for the men in the back to realize I wasn't talking any more, and once I had their attention, I struck a deal with them. If they would settle down and let us get on with class, I would make sure we ended early enough for everyone, including myself, to get home in time for the start of the televised baseball game that night. It may not have been the most orthodox way of controlling a class, but it worked wonders and gave me instant rapport with the class.

Assessing the Outcome

Accurately assessing the outcome of your workshop will ensure success for future programs. There are two types of assessment that should be conducted

Figure 2. **Corporate Research Online: October 27, 2000**

Catherwood Library is committed to providing the highest quality work-shops for our outreach program and as such, your feedback is very valu-able to us. Please take a few minutes to answer the following questions on the workshop you have just attended.

1. The instructors were well prepared.
   a. Strongly Agree
   b. Agree
   c. Neutral/Undecided
   d. Disagree
   e. Strongly Disagree

2. The material was presented in a clear, understandable, and organized manner.
   a. Strongly Agree
   b. Agree
   c. Neutral/Undecided
   d. Disagree
   e. Strongly Disagree

3. The instructor was approachable and available for help when needed.
   a. Strongly Agree
   b. Agree
   c. Neutral/Undecided
   d. Disagree
   e. Strongly Disagree

during and following any workshop, one being a participant evaluation of the workshop. Constructive criticism can often give an instructor a close assessment as to whether or not training goals have been met.

The Labor Outreach program provides each participant with an evalua-tion form to complete at the end of the workshop (Figure 2). Participants are queried on the content of the program, the usefulness of the information learned, the ability of the instructor, the amount of time allowed for ques-tions, and suggestions for improving the workshop. Each of these evaluation points is based on a statement (i.e., the instructor was well prepared) and ranked on a scale from strongly agree, agree, neutral, disagree, and strongly disagree. Each statement has space provided for additional comments.

---

4. The handouts were useful.
    a. Strongly Agree
    b. Agree
    c. Neutral/Undecided
    d. Disagree
    e. Strongly Disagree

5. There was enough time for questions and answers.
    a. Strongly Agree
    b. Agree
    c. Neutral/Undecided
    d. Disagree
    e. Strongly Disagree

6. As a result of these sessions I now have a better understanding of corporate research on the Web.
    a. Strongly Agree
    b. Agree
    c. Neutral/Undecided
    d. Disagree
    e. Strongly Disagree

7. How did you hear of this program?

8. What did you find most useful about these sessions?

9. What changes would you suggest?

10. General comments

Workshop evaluations proved very useful for the Labor Outreach Program's first offering, Labor Unions and the Internet. One lesson learned early on was the importance of keeping information practical and to the point.

Initially the morning session of this workshop was a very comprehensive and detailed introduction to the Internet. It included such topics as a history of the Internet, an introduction to Web browsers, and a technical section addressing how the Internet works. Subsequent evaluations reflected a lack of interest in a history of the Internet or other basic background information of how the Internet works.

This feedback resulted in a redesigned workshop in which some of the basic information regarded as superfluous was dropped. Feedback from Labor

Unions and the Internet participants also included suggestions for additional class offerings, resulting in new workshops such as Corporate Research, New Communication Technologies for Unions, and Designing Web Sites for Local Unions.

While evaluation forms can be a good measurement of participant satisfaction, they must also be taken with a grain of salt. If an instructor is likable and sympathetic, participants are less likely to express negative comments regarding the workshop, even if they were disappointed in certain aspects of the class.

The second measure of a successful program is the determination of how much the participants learned. This is a very difficult measurement to obtain in a one-off classroom situation. One method of at least partially determining this is by the administration of quizzes throughout the day. These exercises, which include using actual Web sites, are always offered in a nonthreatening manner and are presented to the participants as a way to "have a bit of fun" with the information learned.

Surprisingly, evaluations have shown that the quizzes are very popular with participants. They feel that such exercises provides them additional time exploring Web sites and allows them to test their understanding of the material covered.

Marketing and Promotion

Since the Labor Outreach program is offered in partnership with the ILR Extension offices, that office handles most of the marketing and promotion. However, for those offering workshops independently, there are several ways to market and promote offerings:

1. Create a brochure or flyer advertising the upcoming classes. These can be mailed to labor councils and local unions in your area.
2. Contact the local media and arrange to have the workshops mentioned in an "upcoming events" listing.
3. Arrange for publicity by interesting a local newspaper or television station to feature your workshop offerings in a news story.
4. Write a letter to the editor of your local newspaper announcing upcoming workshops and why they are important to labor.
5. Take advantage of the Internet. If your organization has a Web site, announce the workshops on the site. Include workshop descriptions, sample agendas, and training materials. Beware, however. Once this is undertaken, your Web site must be kept current—a task that can prove time consuming. Have someone on staff dedicated to handling information on workshops.
6. List program announcements on labor list servers.

7. Maintain a mailing and e-mail list of past participants and send future workshop announcements to them.
8. Network and spread information by word of mouth.

Keeping Up to Date

With any instruction, the individual teaching the workshops must keep abreast of the newest tools and be willing to constantly adapt training to meet the changing needs of the user. Teaching union members requires an up-to-date knowledge of the issues affecting the labor movement, monitoring the Internet for new Web sites, and the ability to anticipate and respond to a variety of technical and legal questions concerning the Internet.

What Comes Next?

After the workshop has ended, endeavor to stay in touch with participants. Build an e-mail database of past participants and keep in touch by offering e-mail updates of new Web sites or other items of interest. If you plan to do this, get the participants approval beforehand to send e-mail. Many people view unwanted e-mail with the same disdain they hold for telemarketers. This database can also be used to inform past participants of upcoming workshops that may be of interest to them.

How will workshops evolve in the future? As more unionists become computer literate, the need for face-to-face training will be less necessary. The Labor Outreach program is already beginning to adapt some of our offerings to distance learning by means of online subject tutorials. Many universities and other teaching institutions are now taking advantage of more sophisticated technology, including streaming video and audio links to offer "live" online training, something labor should be taking advantage of.

The Role of Organized Labor in Internet Training

John Sweeney, president of the AFL-CIO, has taken a strong stance toward the necessity of providing unionists with access to computer technology. Many local labor councils are now working with statewide unions to offer computer training, a case in point being the New York State AFL-CIO Workforce Development Institute, which works in partnership with local labor councils to provide training to union members. Despite this, many local unions still do not embrace the technology available to them. It is hoped that some of these initiatives will pave the way for introducing a greater number of unionists to the benefits of the Internet.

Conclusion

So just what lessons have I learned in developing and teaching these programs?

While most of our participants are middle-aged males, this demographic is rapidly changing, with younger men and more female participants attending. While no real learning differences have been noted between males and females, males do seem more willing to explore the Internet on their own.

Younger attendees tend to be more comfortable and learn easier, a natural result of having been exposed to the technology at a younger age. But again, this is in flux, with many more of our older union members coming into workshops with a greater knowledge of the Internet, e-mail, and other computer technology.

Most unionists, regardless of age or gender, are knowledgeable, willing, and ready to learn. They engage in online research quite easily once they have mastered the technology.

All attendees are attracted to the amount of free information on the Internet as well as the relative ease in obtaining such information. Most are not interested in a lot of unnecessary introductory information concerning the history of the Internet or technology. They are eager to plunge straight into the research itself.

In general, participants are drawn to the chance of having a whole day devoted to exploring the Internet, and are therefore anxious to have as much hands-on time as possible. They also enjoy the chance to meet with members of other unions. Attendees often spend breaks and lunchtime discussing and comparing their union's recent organizing campaigns and other matters.

I personally take great pleasure in working with union members, and I have built up an easy camaraderie with them, often resulting in a continued working relationship with participants after workshops end. I make a point of always keeping the door open for any questions or research help my labor colleagues may need.

These programs have also offered an unexpected and (certainly from my point of view as a librarian) an unanticipated plus—a new view of librarians and the services they provide. As stated earlier, many participants have not had exposure to instruction or libraries for a number of years (or in some cases, decades) The stereotype of the aged female librarian, hair in bun, ubiquitous glasses posed on the end of her nose, perpetually stamping out books at a circulation desk, still seemed to hold for some of our participants. It therefore is an added bonus of teaching to be able to enlighten some of our attendees not only as to what librarians are really like, but also what a treasure trove of information libraries have to offer labor.

I relish some of the comments I have received on evaluations and close this paper by sharing a few: "Well worth the time—extremely educational. Distilled a daunting subject into user-friendly elements." "I had a lot of experience searching the Web blindly. This was the perfect workshop to help me organize and focus my Web searches—and my use of the Web in general."

And two of my favorites: "Wow, I didn't know you guys knew all this stuff! You have definitely changed my view of the library. Librarians Rule!" "Thank you for all of your help. . . . I appreciate all that you have done to help our local union in finding information that will help in our organizing efforts. Keep in touch, and if there is ever anything I can help you with, please feel free to call at anytime. Just don't call for any advice on computer skills cuz I ain't worth a damn at that."

---

34. The Power of Digital Media and Technology for Working People!

Steve Zeltzer

Video, especially as a computer-aided tool, is steadily emerging worldwide as a factor of consequence. In a few years, when millions of union households are using broadband and DSL, labor will have a powerful 24/7 media through which to share its message.

Among the many related questions tackled by the video-focused essay below are these:

- *What are independent media centers, and how do they help labor?*
- *How does live video make a difference?*
- *How close are we to having an international Labor Video News Program, and what impact might it have?*
- *What does the Korean union struggle teach about dueling videos?*
- *How do the LaborTech conferences help in the growth of this medium?*

As it is vital that labor soon do more here, the essay's message warrants creative and rapid employment.

One of the most important developments out of the Battle of Seattle, the November 1999 protest against the World Trade Organization, was the formation of the independent media centers. These centers have brought together hundreds of writers, computer workers, videographers, and video editors to break the corporate media blockade, using new technology and a democratic structure for free speech.

Since Seattle, with a small budget and the use of the Internet, dozens of independent media centers have been established not only in the United States but around the world. The Union Producers and Programmers Network (UPPNET), as well as other labor media activists, are now encouraging trade unionists to begin to publish their stories and news online at the independent media sites. In Chicago, and in the San Francisco Bay Area, at www. indybay.org, not only have labor pages been established, but live labor video is now being broadcast on a regular basis. From the "living wage" struggles to how the Free Trade Area of the Americas Act (FTAA) will harm working people, these sites have the facts and are increasingly becoming necessary instant news sites.

The new digital technology that allows one not only to shoot the video but to stream it on the Web is allowing workers, environmentalists, and human rights activists to get their story out by the Web broadcasting of their material. Imagine the many locals who face a battle to prepare their members and the public about the issues they face: They can now not only develop written information, but also interview their members about the real conditions and struggles that they face, and then stream it on the Web.

While most workers do not have high-speed access through cable or DSL, this is on the agenda, and we need to be prepared for it now. This will be an exciting and powerful media weapon if we grasp the tools and make this a high priority within the labor movement.

One key to this is that we work with other labor media/computer activists in the independent media centers. They can help us and we can help them. A concerted effort by labor councils and locals around the country could help establish the centers in nearly every city of the country and begin to train ourselves and other workers to get their stories out in a powerful way.

During the Seattle demonstration, we at the Labor Video Project taped the labor march and protest, and we were able to stream it on the Web the following week. We were getting over 300 hits a day from Belgium, Turkey, and many other places around the world. It added up to 12,000 hits, and this is only the beginning.

We are also using www.labornet to help build up this labor video. The potential for an international labor video news program is growing by the day. We are accumulating labor video not only from throughout the United States but internationally, and this again can be made available to millions. This is *real* content that we will not see on ABC, CBS, Fox, NBC, CNN, MSNBC or other corporate-controlled news sources.

In fact, one of the most powerful examples of this media technology struggle is in Korea. Labor News Production, an independent labor media cooperative, has trained hundreds of workers how to shoot and edit, as well as to stream labor video. Rail workers, shipyard workers, hospital workers, and auto workers now have their own media units that are recording every struggle and digitally editing their powerful video.

In the ongoing labor struggle at Daewoo, the workers and their union, the Korean Metal Workers Union, won a court order that they had the right to their union offices. In Korea most union offices reside in the plant. The police, however, tried to prevent the workers from going into the plant. The union attorney said that the police were violating the court order and that the workers had the right to gain entry. Police videographers edited the comments of the lawyer to indicate that the lawyer was calling on the workers to attack the police who were blocking the entrances to their plant and union offices.

Not only did the police manipulate the video, but they also streamed it on the Seoul Police Web Site. In response the Daewoo Auto Workers Union put the uncensored video on the Web. Also, the Korean Confederation of Trade Unions launched a national campaign to show the tape to 10 million people. Some of this powerful worker-produced video can be seen at http://cast. jinbo.net/english/special_daewoo.html. In the same struggle, dozens of workers were seriously injured when they had a sit-down. Angry police battered them as they sat peacefully on the street with no shirts on. This is also available on the Web.

This example of dueling videos from labor and the police is obviously at a much higher level of communication than in the United States, but the tools are here for working people to get their streaming video on the Web. In fact, there is even a tutorial program on how to do this, located at www. indybay.org/tutorial.php3.

Education and Linking Together Is Critical

The first LaborTech conference in 1990 was organized in part to provide basic education in the labor movement about how to use technology and the media for labor. The use of multimedia is critical to get our labor material out in a popular and powerful way. Since the first conference, other LaborTech conferences have been held in Minneapolis, Madison, San Francisco, Vancouver, and Moscow.

Now, a regular LaborMedia conference is held in Seoul, Korea (http://lmedia. nodong.net) every November in conjunction with the Korean Confederation of Trade Unions' labor cultural commemoration for Chun Taeil. (For more information on the Korean conference, contact Myoung Joon Kim at lnp89@chollian.net.) These conferences have provided a critical vehicle and spark in bringing labor media/computer technologists together from around the world to build, network, and strengthen our activities. For working people, internationalism and global solidarity are making new gains using the tools of information technology and multimedia.

X. Promoting Union Democracy

The American labor movement was built on realism,
persistence, and democratic values.
—Jimmy Carter, former U.S. president

No one put it better than Lane Kirkland in 1980, when, as president of the AFL-CIO, he explained: "Unions can no more live without democracy than a fish without water" (Bollen 1983, 95). Today, thanks to empowering uses of computer power, the prospects for internal union democracy appear better than ever.

As for tips and tricks independent of the three essays that make up this part of the handbook, seven warrant special mention, along with the gentle reminder that all such advice cries out for adaptation, not cloning.

First, it can help to learn alongside change agents who are committed 24/7 to the Cause (as made clear in Chapter 37). Useful in this connection is face-to-face attendance at the annual meetings of the Association for Union Democracy (AUD), subscription to their newsletter, use of their Web site, exchanges with their staff via e-mail, and study of their considerable shelf of books and pamphlets. (For more information, see Chapter 37.)

Second, it can help to dialogue with other union activists wrestling with the same or similar questions. They can be located on the Internet with the help of search engines, or within labor list servers (such as PubLabor), or by posting questions on neutral list servers (such as MODEM, as explained in Chapter 17) or Web sites (see chapter 23 for several operated by handbook contributor Robert Kolb).

Third, it can help to learn quietly ("lurk"), if you also learn attentively from the cyber sidelines. That is, you can join certain list servers and then silently follow the e-mail dialogue as others wrestle with vexing aspects of internal democracy in their own organizations. Especially helpful in this regard are Web sites listed at the end of Chapter 7, as their existence outside the labor movement provides useful distance from certain aspects of labor culture that can cloud matters (such as historic rifts between skilled and semi-skilled workers).

Fourth, it can help to explore how the computer can secure survey answers from the membership, and thereby get the organization beyond very subjective (and self-serving) guesses about the attitudes, opinions, and wishes of the rank-and-file. Computer-based surveys sent into the homes of members via e-mail can inform the leadership as never before. Sharing the unvarnished findings of such surveys can significantly aid internal democracy, especially if the Loyal Opposition is free to attach its own questions to all such official surveys and monitor data collection techniques.

Fifth, it can help to create a cyberspace chat room (possibly even unmoderated) as part of your organization's Web site. Some of these are advisably password-protected for use only by members. Wide-ranging discussions can help the rank-and-file make up their own mind about key issues within the organization, and Chapters 22, 36, and 37 offer wise guidelines for keeping up the quality of discourse (e.g., no anonymous postings, no scurrilous personal attacks, etc.).

Sixth, it can help to assure the Loyal Opposition equal space on the organization's official Web site, along with equal use of the official e-mail postings. Incumbents, by modeling fair play, can make a vital contribution to rank-and-file consciousness of democracy's tenets.

Finally, when all else fails, it can help to create an unofficial Web site and list server to air grievances members may have with alleged governance failings. It may be necessary to fight misguided incumbents to restore a democratic ethos, lest a labor body sink to the level of autocratic organizations common elsewhere in the (nonunion) world of work.

Thanks to the three essays that follow, the challenge here is a bit more manageable: The first highlights how an activist, as a low-keyed webmaster, can add much to a local's democratic culture. The second explains how a union can opt for a democratic chat room, keep it useful, and learn much of value from it. And the third essay, by a staffer from the AUD, teaches much of value about the intricacies of the subject, even while sharing sound advice for advancing the entire matter.

Reference

Bollen, Peter. *A Handbook of Great Labor Quotations*. Lynnfield, MA: Hillside Books, 1983.

35. A Simple List Serve and Union Democracy

Charles H. Laskonis

As helpful as the Internet can theoretically be, it remains vital to learn whether or not its use actually pays off as desired. Labor depends far more on its verifiable accomplishments than on glittering possibilities, and reports from the field are what counts at the end of the day.

All the more valuable, therefore, is the low-keyed but also high-powered essay below. Valuable answers are offered to such questions as:

- *What sort of contribution can an unofficial Web site make to a local's well-being?*
- *How complicated is setting up such a site?*
- *Can a local's job referral service profit from such a site?*
- *How is internal union democracy impacted? And, so what?*

In closing, the essay underlines the urgency that courses through the entire matter—either labor gets on with it, or labor gets left behind.

List Serves can make a great difference, as union messages are sent instantly and are free from the corporate media spin that was largely the way most workers received ideas prior to the Internet.

My union, the International Brotherhood of Electrical Workers (IBEW), has a "free exchange" unofficial List Serve with close to 450 members. Brothers and sisters "meet" who, without this technology, might never have had that chance. Our international president and secretary-treasurer, as well as local union leaders and rank-and-filers, share ideas to help make the union stronger.

Two years ago my local started an IBEW Local 364 List Serve, of which I am the creator and moderator. Today 148 out of 1,000 members participate, and to the best of my knowledge it is the largest unofficial List Serve of any IBEW local.

The way I operate it is simple. Every member who wishes to be included sends me his or her e-mail address. When any list member sends a message to an e-mail account that I had set up exclusively for the List Serve, I send it out to every other member. No anonymous messages are allowed, and members are asked to use proper language and to make sure what they are sending is accurate. There is talk we will soon set it up on a host server so messages will be sent automatically and instantly.

Our list serve has contributed to some changes from the way union business used to be conducted. Prior to the list serve very little information was discussed between monthly union meetings. Now the list serve aids in the exchange of many ideas and opinions, adding to the debate on our union meeting floor.

We are a multi-employer construction local, and because of that the availability of electrical work constantly fluctuates, which leads to a high turnover of manpower. The local runs a job referral book out of our hall to insure that job referrals are given out fairly. Prior to the list serve every member who was interested in obtaining a job referral had to call a nightly telephone recorder message that contained the daily job calls. For many people who do not live in the same city as the union hall that meant a long-distance telephone call everyday. Now daily job calls are also sent over the list serve.

The list serve also dynamically changed the democratic process of our local union in regards to the election of local union officers. During the last election of officers three years ago, one effective campaign tactic was to send out a letter close enough to the election date so that the other candidate could not send out a letter in response before the day the ballots were cast. Now, with the advent of our list serve, that tactic is no longer effective because any candidate can respond almost instantly.

Another positive aspect concerning the election process and the list serve is the fact that debate can happen at all. In previous elections there was really no means to discuss and debate union issues between the monthly union meeting when nominations took place and the subsequent monthly union meeting day when the elections took place. Now, with the list serve, it is not only possible, it is happening! The list serve is having a major influence for the better in our local union election process.

As a delegate to our central labor council, I am currently working on setting up linked list serves and Web pages for all our member unions. This way we can communicate between the entire local labor community. Each local's list serve moderator will be part of yet another separate list serve. That moderator can then determine if a particular message pertains to his or her local, and whether or not it should be sent to his local's list serve members. Hopefully we will accomplish this in the next few months.

We have made great strides, but we need to have more participation by local unions and members. Hopefully that will happen as more members purchase computers and become familiar with the technology. We have a long way to go to reach our potential, and it is imperative that we do so as soon as possible.

36. One Union's Leap into Cyberdemocracy

Rick Inclima

The field report below can help settle some common doubts about the impact of letting members speak out. Among the many questions tackled are these:

- *Will members sign up for a fire-wall–protected "membership forum"?*
- *What sort of ground rules make sense?*
- *How do members use the forum? Wisely? Recklessly?*
- *Does the forum actually influence union policies?*
- *How might a forum police itself?*

Based in actual experience carefully processed, the essay goes far in affirming the confidence of those who believe Internet support for union democracy is a major gain for organized labor.

The Brotherhood of Maintenance of Way Employees (BMWE) is a rail labor union representing approximately 50,000 railroad workers who construct, repair, inspect, and maintain the tracks, bridges, and structures of all of North America's major railroads. As guardians of virtually every mile of main-line railroad track in the United States and Canada, BMWE members are widely disbursed throughout the North American continent. They are often required to "follow the work" hundreds, and sometimes thousands, of miles away from home.

Keeping up with even the most routine family and personal matters from hundreds of miles away is a constant source of tension and emotion for these workers. Under such trying circumstances, where access to regularly delivered mail and other forms of communication are severely limited by the nomadic work-life of a track worker, keeping up with family life is difficult, and keeping up with current union issues and events is virtually impossible.

During the early 1990s, the leadership of BMWE recognized the Internet's potential to improve communications between all levels of the brotherhood—from the guy on the track all the way up to the international president. Although it was anticipated that, at some future point in time, the Internet would become an integral part of our world's communications network, its rapid proliferation surprised many. Not surprising, however, was how society, especially business, industry, and government, quickly recognized its potential for opening new and effective lines of communications.

BMWE, like many other unions, recognized the Internet's potential to create new and effective lines of communications, both within individual unions and among organized labor as a whole. The question was how best to utilize this potential for the betterment of the union movement and its ideals.

Early on, while it was still somewhat cutting-edge, BMWE established its first Web page and began posting union news and other items of interest. Shortly thereafter, all the officers and staff of the BMWE International (Grand Lodge) were issued e-mail accounts as a means of improving both internal and external communications. E-mail addresses for all Grand Lodge officers and staff were thereafter posted on our Web page and published monthly in our union newspaper, the *BMWE Journal*.

At first, utilization of this new technology was met with general resistance and bore plenty of frustration. As the Internet matured and technology advanced, however, things slowly but steadily improved as people grasped the technology, society accepted the technology, and the union creatively harnessed the benefits of the technology.

Members and officers alike steadily increased their utilization of the Web, accessing BMWE's Web page for updated information and corresponding with each other via e-mail. New features and "links" were built into our Web page to make it more useful and user friendly, and we soon realized many of our officers and members were becoming astutely computer literate.

However, the leadership of BMWE also recognized that private e-mail has its limitations, and something needed to be done to enhance and improve communication and dialogue among all levels of the union regarding issues affecting the lives of our members. That's when the idea of a fire-wall–protected, members-only forum came to light.

In a sort of technological *Field of Dreams*, BMWE realized that "if we build it, they will come." BMWE established a fire-wall–protected membership forum on our Web page. Members and officers were encouraged to sign up for access to the members-only site. Upon verification of being a BMWE member in good standing, individualized passwords were issued and access to the membership forum was opened.

The ground rules for BMWE's membership forum are simple and direct: No political campaigns for union office, no malicious attacks against another member or officer, no illegal activity. However, no work-related or union-related subjects are taboo, and every participating member is free to express his or her opinions or criticisms on any issues without censorship from the union. Freedom of speech and freedom of association are key components and unalienable rights of BMWE's cyberdemocracy, and we have become a stronger, better informed, and more effective union for it.

Providing an electronic forum where geographically disbursed members can post views, opinions, and responses on virtually any issue is an incredibly powerful medium for union building and union democracy. Many important and complex issues confronting the rank-and-file are openly discussed and debated in this forum by members from throughout the United States and Canada.

The forum has become a virtual cyber union hall, with lively and intelligent discussion of issues in an open and democratic way. Every member is entitled to voice his or her opinion and raise issues they deem important. In fact, the membership forum has become a virtual "issues advisory site," often utilized by union officers and activists to get a sense of the membership regarding significant issues.

If a member or officer wants to know what their fellow brothers and sisters think about an issue, all they need to do is log on to the membership forum and read the postings or voice an opinion. In fact, many of BMWE's recent "priority issues" have been influenced, at least in part, by the views and opinions voiced in the membership forum.

This is not to say that all the users of the membership forum do so for constructive reasons. Occasionally, a member with an ax to grind will post views with a clear attempt to discredit the union or one of its officers. Such malcontents are generally tolerated by other users of the forum because it is accepted that the forum belongs to all the members, and everyone is entitled to his or her opinion. Whether the issue be about the union's handling of a particular item, the union's actions or inactions, government and politics, legislative, safety, legal, or social policy issues, the forum presents a platform for all ideas to be expressed.

The forum is also somewhat self-policing in that outrageous positions and clearly bad ideas are exposed and reputed by other users in an open and democratic forum. Thus, while every user is entitled to his or her opinion, those who disagree will make it known, and each user's opinion eventually lives or dies on its merits.

In general, serious questions or opinions are given serious consideration and debate; absurd questions or opinions are considered, debated, and exposed for what they are. This occurs in a free and uncensored environment, out in the open and without interference from the union.

The membership forum has provided our union with an ability to keep its fingers on the pulse of the membership and to understand its priority issues and concerns. The forum also provides our membership an opportunity to keep its fingers on the pulse of the union, thereby assuring union governance "of the people, by the people, for the people."

This union-sponsored forum, which openly encourages freedom of association and freedom of speech among all its members and officers (both supporters and detractors alike), has evolved somewhat into a cybersystem of checks and balances, making officers more accountable and members more responsible for the direction of the union. Cyberdemocracy is alive and well within the BMWE, and we are undoubtedly a more effective, responsive, and inclusive union because of it.

---

37. Matters of Human Debate: Using the Internet for Union Democracy

Matt Noyes

Easily one of the most exciting aspects of labor's use of computer power involves its ability to help improve democracy inside union bureaucracies. Labor, an idealistic social movement (a "town hall") as well as an "army," is either robustly democratic or it is fatally wounded. Only as rank-and-filers feel comfortable in their membership, confident in their officers, and capable in the exercise of their citizenship rights within labor will they exhibit the loyalty and even enthusiasm labor needs to regain density and win critical fights.

Prodemocracy grassroots activists are able now to use e-mail, list serves, and Web sites to forge bonds. To spread the word. To refine their thoughts and actions. To make plans. To expose harm. To propose reforms. And, in 101 other ways, to help reclaim locals and unions for the quality of unionism that does everyone proud.

The essay below, from someone engaged daily and directly in the struggle, begins with a wide-ranging case study. It makes clear why rank-and-filers have to fight at times to remind local and union officers to whom the union really belongs and to "do the right thing." Highlighting the many types of literature and individuals often relevant in a dispute concerning internal union democracy, the case study gets the essay off to a thoughtful and challenging start.

Answers are provided thereafter to such questions as:

- *How can a Web site help in educating members about the struggle?*
- *What are the major gains—and limitations—where the use of the Internet is concerned?*

- *How are three levels on which workers organize—structure, culture, and participation—impacted by prodemocracy uses of the Internet?*
- *What sort of guesstimates can be attached to types of participants in union democracy struggles?*
- *How does the "digital divide" figure into union democracy efforts?*
- *How can the challenge of the Lone Ranger activist and the use of "flaming" best be handled?*

The essay ably illustrates how Internet options empower rank-and-filers struggling to promote a democratic culture that honors us all.

"The Internet makes it easier for union members to form rank-and-file caucuses in their unions. Is that a good thing? I don't know, but it's true, and there is nothing that unions can do to stop it," said Nancy Brigham, at the LaborTech 2000 conference.

Across the United States and the rest of North America (and, of course, internationally) more and more rank-and-file workers are using the Internet to advocate and organize for union democracy and reform. The already well-established "new technology"—e-mail, list serves, Web sites—has become an indispensable tool in the hands of union activists seeking to make their unions more democratic and powerful. To quote Martha Stewart: "It's a good thing."

It is not that union organizing in democratic ways happens now in some kind of mysterious cyberworld, but that the Internet provides workers a way to do much of their organizing work more quickly, more easily, with greater reach, and at a lower cost. The Internet amplifies and extends two of the fundamental pillars of union democracy—freedom of speech and freedom of association—and brings workers into contact with a host of tools and resources they can use to build democracy in all its aspects.

Through the Internet workers have dramatically enlarged the existing democratic space in unions and created new forums for cross-industry, cross-union, international reform discussion and activism. This new arena of rank-and-file activism is being built by workers in nearly every industry: flight attendants, factory workers, pipe fitters, stationary engineers, carpenters, clerical workers, and more. There are limits—the Internet does not win union elections, get better contracts, or back down abusive supervisors—but in the world of union politics and activism, it is a great equalizer.

This essay is intended to answer the following questions in a cursory fashion, the hope being that readers will be tempted to explore the world of rank-and-file Internet activism on their own. Who are these activists using the Web? How do they use the Internet, and what two main tools have they developed or adopted (Web sites and e-mail)? How does online work relate to off-line activism/organizing? What does the new activism mean for the movement for union democracy and member control? The essay concludes with reflections on some limits and possibilities of online activism.

For the purposes of this chapter, "rank-and-file activist" is used loosely to include workers who are not officers or staff members of unions, and the groups these activists form. The success of some organizing has meant that some rank-and-file groups now include officers and staff, but by and large, there is still an identifiable rank-and-file activist layer in the union movement. Excluded from this discussion are official union Web sites and list serves, though some are fine examples of rank-and-file–oriented Internet use. The sites from which this essay draws are all listed on the Association for Union Democracy Web site, under rank-and-file links (www. uniondemocracy.org).

"By union democracy" means both the struggle to achieve and enforce democratic rights in the union, and the active use of democratic methods by unionists to pursue their collective aims. (More on this below.) Finally, this essay assumes that union democracy is good for the labor movement.[1]

In order to see what the struggle for union democracy can look like, and how valuable a tool is the Internet, we should first consider what it is that union democracy activists do. The term "activist" covers a wide range of unionists, from the experienced and highly organized cadre of a group like Teamsters for a Democratic Union, to the disgruntled member who refuses to be silenced or shut out. Any activist group contains workers all along this spectrum, and rank-and-file Internet activism reflects this range as well.[2]

To see what activists are up against and how they organize, let's take a fictional scenario that condenses a number of typical problems.

Gisela's Story

A worker, let's call her Gisela, finds out that she and her coworkers are being paid less than the contractual rate. She goes to the steward to file a grievance but is told that there is nothing that can be done and advised to keep quiet and stay out of trouble. Gisela asks the steward for a copy of the contract between the union and the employer and is told that only official union representatives are allowed to have copies.

Gisela speaks with her coworkers. Some are angry about the situation, many complain about the steward, who seems to be friends with a supervisor, but only a few come to the meeting Gisela calls for at the end of the shift. They decide to write up a petition to the union business agent demanding a copy of the contract and asking for elections for a new steward.

The business agent ignores the petition at first, but finally replies, giving them an unsigned, outdated version of the contract. The business agent informs Gisela that stewards are appointed, not elected, and tells her that the union will not change the steward.

Gisela's coworker draws a cartoon making fun of the steward and the business agent. The business agent asks around about who drew the cartoon and tells workers to stay away from Gisela and the other troublemakers. At this point Gisela begins to receive warnings and is written up by management for imaginary infractions. Again, the steward says there is nothing he can do.

When Gisela goes to a union meeting to protest, she finds that most of the people there are either union officers or appointed staff, plus a handful of members who are their friends and supporters. The meeting consists mostly of reports from the various officers. In the president's report it is announced that the officers have decided to increase members' dues in order to pay for salary increases for the officers. Everything the executive board proposes is approved by a voice vote.

Gisela tries to get the floor, but the officers use Robert's Rules (or their own version thereof) to close the agenda and then adjourn the meeting. One guy tries to pick a fight with Gisela after the meeting, accusing her of being a management spy.

Fed up with the way they are represented, Gisela and her small group of coworkers decide to run for union office. They have four candidates, not enough for a full slate, but enough to run for all the top officer positions. When nominations come around, the president informs them that they are ineligible to run because they have not attended the required number of union meetings over the past two years. Gisela writes a letter of protest to the international union, which she circulates to her coworkers. The union officers charge Gisela with violating the union's "oath of membership" and expel her from the union without a hearing.

Gisela's story shows how union democracy problems emerge and develop, and the different levels on which workers struggle for democracy. We will look at three levels on which workers organize—structure, culture, and participation—and see how they are using the Internet on each level.

First, though, we should note that problems of union democracy are usually rooted in problems with the employer. In Gisela's case the struggle with the union emerges because the employer is paying substandard wages. The struggle for democracy is fundamentally shaped by the conflict with the employers, who, after all, control the greatest autocracy of all, the workplace.

It is not surprising that challenges to the authority of the union officers usually flow from issues of power on the job, and go hand in hand with challenges to management. The interests of workers and those of their employers rarely coincide, and the union is a great potential vehicle for defending workers' rights and interests. As central as the task of enforcing their rights may be, activists inevitably fight for more than internal democracy.

Navigating the Structures

Much of the work of activists is aimed at enforcing, using, and changing the structural aspects of the union: the offices, rules, procedures, and institutions of union governance and administration. In addition to the internal union structures, there is the workplace regime and its rules and structures (mostly defined in the collective bargaining agreement), and the surrounding legal system, with the various government agencies and the state and federal court system.

Readers familiar with the rights of workers on the job and in the union will have noted in Gisela's story a series of obvious violations and several probable violations requiring further investigation. But for a worker experiencing the situation for the first time, there is a desperate need for information and resources.

Gisela and her coworkers need copies of their current contract, including all side agreements, to know if they are being underpaid and to know what recourse they have through the grievance procedure, or even what the procedure is. They need to know if they have a legal right to see the contract, and how to enforce that right, including the agencies to contact, the evidence needed, and the procedures to follow.

To know what the steward's duties are, whether workers have the right to elect and recall stewards, and their own rights as grievants, they need the union constitution and bylaws and they need information on the duty of fair representation, which is enforced (more often not enforced) by the National Labor Relations Board.

To know whether the union representatives have the right to advise workers to stay away from Gisela, discipline her for her letter to the international, or expel her without a hearing, she needs to read the union constitution and find out her rights under the Labor Management Reporting and Disclosure Act (LMRDA). If they want to intervene in a union meeting, workers have to learn Robert's Rules of Order.

To know if the disqualification of candidates for failure to comply with meeting the attendance rules is legal, the workers need to know not only the letter of the law, again the constitution and LMRDA, but how it has been interpreted and applied by the Department of Labor and the courts. They may also need to consult an attorney familiar with union democracy law and willing to take on such a case, or at least give advice. For all the legal questions, they need to know their rights on paper and how they work in the real world.

Gisela and her coworkers will also want advice and information on the politics and history of this particular union and its officers, and this employer. Experienced reformers know when they need more information and where to go to get it. They have learned that to deal effectively with the structures and institutions of the union, workers need access to a wide range of information and resources.

How is the Internet helpful? Think of what Gisela and her coworkers would have to do to get all of the documents and information described above without using the Internet: Repeated visits to the library, calls and visits to local (or regional) government offices, government agencies, and other organizations. That's after they get over one of the biggest obstacles—simply knowing what to look for. They also need to consult other union activists and supporters who know the history and have experience in this type of organizing.

Now consider the resources available online, on a Web site like that of the New Directions caucus in Transport Workers Union Local 100.[3] This is just some of the information available to transit workers via links from the home page:

- The complete text of the contract, including the "hidden agreements";
- The full text of the "freedom degrading" Taylor Law (covering New York State public employees);
- A full list of union officers;
- Civil service exam applications;
- The "letter that brought in the Department of Labor on credit card scam in Local 100";
- A "news update on the Pension Reform Bill."

There are links to government agencies, prolabor groups, and information on various laws. In addition, there is contact information for New Directions, for workers who want to get in contact with other activists.

Jim McGough's remarkable, if overwhelming, Laborers for Justice site goes even further, offering a comprehensive collection of documents and resources for members of the corruption-plagued Laborers Industrial Union of North America (LIUNA).[4]

Some of the links:

- LIUNA 2001 election rules, including protests and decisions;
- International salaries and expenses (LM-2 forms in PDF format);
- Links to locals, councils, and departments of the international union;

- Collective bargaining agreements;
- Constitutions;
- Work referral rules;
- Ethics code and disciplinary procedure;
- Independent hearing officer decisions;
- Court cases;
- Transcripts, affidavits, statements; trusteeships;
- Funds (welfare and pension);
- Newspaper and magazine articles about the Laborers.

A good rank-and-file Web site offers workers a kind of specialized library, tailored to their interests and needs, and also serves to connect activists in one location with workers in any part of the union, including their own local.

Seeding a Culture of Democracy

The Web makes it vastly easier to find and distribute information and resources that help workers address the structural side of unionism, but it also serves in the cultivation of a democratic culture. Harder to pin down than the structural side, the culture of the union is a vital element of union democracy.

A union election that is fair and democratic in its procedures may simply be a contest between different camps of an entrenched leadership, neither of which is interested in promoting union democracy or member control; the simple democratic form may be just a moment of transition in the bureaucracy.

This should not lead us to minimize the importance of democratic procedures, but should guide us to understand that union democracy is also seen in the way people talk, feel, and think about the union and their role in it. In Gisela's story you see the culture of the union in the way workers complain about the steward, in the cartoon and conversations, and in the union meeting. There is a dominant culture of exclusion and authoritarianism, and a struggling rank-and-file counterculture.

How are activists using the Web to build a democratic culture? The most obvious example of culture in a union is the official union magazine and its rank-and-file rivals. Let's see how the Internet contributes to workers' ability to generate an independent culture in the union.

Gisela's official union magazine comes to her home in the mail. It is forty pages or so, with glossy, full-color printing, and the kind of professional design you see in commercial magazines.

The content is carefully selected and edited to put the union's (for most union publications, the union equals the current leadership and its supporters) best foot forward.

The cover profiles a successful campaign and often shows workers and staff in action. In the first pages she finds a letter from the president and selected letters to the editor. There are many photos of the leadership and write-ups of the fine work they are doing, along with exemplary campaigns, causes, and candidates the union leadership has endorsed. Generic material published by the AFL-CIO is often interspersed. As she gets to the back pages, she finds an educational segment, obituaries, and lists of resources.

The magazine comes out regularly and is distributed to all members at their home address, nationally. It reflects the officers' control of resources, their domination of union affairs, and their ability to put their message in the members' hands.

Union reformers, operating with bare-bones resources and even more limited time, are simply never in a position to put out a print publication that rivals the official union magazine in format, design, quantity of content, and distribution. The standard best practice among activists continues to be the four- to ten-page black on white newsletter printed on a computer, reproduced at a copy shop, distributed locally, and mailed to a few supporters or contacts.[5]

In a few cases, well-organized rank-and-file groups have managed to publish regular newspapers, for example, *Hell on Wheels* published by Transport Workers Union Local 100, or *Convoy Dispatch*, published by Teamsters for a Democratic Union.

Now look at the rank-and-file Web sites. To begin with, there may be more than one. In some union locals there are several independent rank-and-file Web sites, and perhaps fifty sites in a union like the UAW. For example, there are at least three independent sites in Local 30 of the International Union of Operating Engineers (IUOE)—Honest Union, Local 30 Members First, and the Unity Slate Caucus.[6]

(I have found it difficult to determine how many rank-and-file Web sites actually exist as they are often denizens of the "deep Web," not easily picked up by search engines. The various "rings," such as the postal union ring, provide one form of access to the less known sites. See the Uncensored Auto Worker, Local 594 Dissenter [http://uawlocal594.com/] for a UAW site with links to many others.)

Most members probably access the Web from their home but can do so anywhere they have computer access. Workers in some industries have regular computer access on the job and use the Internet from work. (This is an area where rights and freedoms are presently being fought out. Some activists liken Web use to other forms of joint activity on the job and argue for the same protections. See "Company E-mail Rules: Are They Illegal?" by Robert Schwartz in *Labor Notes*, June 2001.) In any case, it is generally better to avoid using company or union computers when possible.

Unlike print newsletters, Web pages are full color, with photos and other features. The are often well designed and employ the best technology, rivaling in every way the production quality of the official union Web site (if there is one).[7]

The content of rank-and-file sites is also generally superior to the official union sites. Many official union Web sites are born as online billboards for the union, then grow to be the equivalent of the union newspaper, operating within the same political and cultural constraints. Rank-and-file sites, on the other hand, tend to sprout up as expressions of dissent and grow into vehicles for free give and take of ideas, challenges to authority, wide dissemination of information, and an orientation to action. This makes for lively content and an engaged readership.

Because Web sites are constantly online and can be frequently updated, they can provide up-to-the-minute information on union events to a degree unmatched by any other medium save television or radio. As one IUOE Local 30 webmaster told me, "Before the officers can get from the union meeting back to their desks, we've posted our minutes of the meeting!"

The circulation of important and time-sensitive union information about negotiations, spending, bylaws changes, and elections has been expanded dramatically. It's as if every conversation, meeting, or action were broadcast. During a strike or a union election campaign, workers can get the latest news from the Web site and spread it directly at work or on the picket line, rather than waiting for word to come down the chain of command. Rank-and-file webmasters are usually not great respecters of protocol.

All in all, with the Internet it's as if every rank-and-file member were given equal access to the means to produce and distribute a regular full-color, glossy magazine and the license to put their free speech to use for a mass audience.

Web sites differ fundamentally from print publications in that they contain hyperlinks to other sites and sources of information, not only the crucial legal rights information described above, but links of particular interest to workers based on the nature of their jobs or other shared interests.

One operating engineers' site has a prominent weather report link on the front page because the union's members depend on the weather to do their jobs. GRUNT, a Web site for members of the boilermakers union, provides an array of links for information on technology and machinery of interest to workers in that trade and many photos of workers on the job.[8] Many sites also link to sources of international labor news like LabourStart, or general labor information sites like Internet Labor Resources.[9]

It is easy to see the advantages of a rank-and-file Web site for workers seeking information and resources or wanting to participate in the cultural and political life of the union, but it is worth pausing to take note of what that implies. Articles on unionism and union democracy circulate, workers find links to organizations like the Association for Union Democracy, magazines like *Labor Notes*, and more. They learn about other unions, both the official story and the word on the shop floor. They see activism under way all over the country and internationally.

On rank-and-file Web sites the relationship between readers, writers, and editors is very fluid and egalitarian. Workers become not only passive viewers of information, but correspondents, experts, and editors. Recall the old line about how the history written by hunters is different than the version that would be written by the lions. Well, the lions are online and at the keyboard, and they outnumber the hunters. Tapping and clicking away after work, they are shifting the culture of unions and the union movement.[10]

Activists create a democratic culture by putting out newsletters, flyers, and other publications. They shape the culture through the jokes they tell, the languages they speak, and the way they talk about and to their fellow workers, union representatives, and employers. Speaking (and listening) one on one and in their own meetings and activities, they cultivate an atmosphere of debate and exchange of ideas.

Lest this sound too dreamy and Platonic, real living cultures of democracy often sound and look more like a riot than a symposium. There's a lot of shouting and arguing involved in building a culture of democracy out of an autocratic status quo.

Who Does the Thinking, Deciding, Questioning, Answering, Proposing, Planning, and Organizing?

However much activists master union structures, promote ideas and principles, and practice a democratic culture, their project will run aground if they cannot find ways to make their activism into a vehicle for increasing the participation of other workers. The purpose of union democracy is to organize the collective power of members in the union in a way that ensures accountability and member control. The kind of participation we are taking about here differs from mere mobilization of members in what are essentially top-down actions, and it goes beyond "consultation" or "input," to include participation in setting goals and assessing risks and opportunities— all the elements of strategic planning. The distinguishing feature of democratic participation is the power to make informed decisions. Our case study of Gisela is also a case study of participation: At every step she and her coworkers assessed, planned, and acted.

The experience of collective action, the security of knowing the truth about one's rights and how to defend them, and the ability to find information and secure resources all contribute to a worker's confidence and willingness to participate in more activity. The best rank-and-file activists look for every opportunity to involve their coworkers in discussion, decision making, and action, not simply as "troops" but as developing activists and leaders. They do this in one-on-one discussions, in meetings and job actions, in union elections and contract campaigns.

The Internet is not simply the online equivalent of magazines, newsletters, or reference libraries. It also offers spaces in which workers can participate in discussion, debate, and planning, analogous to a union or caucus meeting. Again, the contrast with off-line activities is instructive. Many union meetings are wooden, tedious exercises in disempowerment that members quite rationally avoid. They are effectively antiparticipatory and reinforce the top-down culture of the union power structure, down to the way people are seated. In the worst cases, they are hostile or even dangerous places for dissenting unionists.

Official union meetings are not the only game in town. Most rank-and-file activists organize their own meetings, discussions, and workshops, providing an alternative venue for workers to gather to share information and ideas, exchange resources and contact information, learn skills, and plan activities. These unofficial meetings provide an important forum in which members can begin to participate and develop the skills of democratic activism.

The official union meeting, though, has a crucial status in the politics of the union and in the eyes of the law. Membership meetings are the highest body of the local union (between union conventions) and are the terrain on which some part of the struggle for union democracy must inevitably be waged. So activists advocate that their coworkers participate in the official meetings, trying to advance their agenda by asking questions, making motions, offering proposals, and demonstrating by their actions that democracy is possible, even if unpopular.

When it comes to meetings, like newsletters, rank-and-file activists work in an often hostile environment with meager resources of time and even space. As working conditions are eroded and unions restructure into larger units, conflicts of shifts and work locations become even bigger obstacles. Imagine trying to hold a regular independent meeting in a local that covers three states and has members in hundreds (or more) of workplaces, on all manner of shifts and schedules.

Here again, the Internet is a valuable tool, (though not a substitute for off-line meetings). Rank-and-file Web sites provide a common space—across shift and work location—for workers to share information and ideas, exchange resources and contact information, and (to a lesser extent) plan activities. By submitting articles or reports on meetings or other events, writing "letters to the editor," and posting notes on message boards and bulletin boards, workers can be active participants in the content of the Web site and can bring the internal workings of the union to a broader audience.

Sites like HERETICS, for hotel and restaurant union members, and REAP, for members of the food and commercial workers union, serve as a kind of jumping-off point for members to get involved in activism.[11] The webmasters and other activists respond promptly to inquiries and work to connect workers to resources and other activists.

This is where e-mail comes in. Workers use e-mail for one-on-one communication, for broadcasting information or questions, for communication in or with a group. (For reasons of space, I cannot address here the uses of e-mail as a tool for pressuring the employer or union directly.) The freedom from limitations of space (one mile is the same as 1,000 miles to an e-mail message), time (the message can be read, and responded to, now or later), and cost makes e-mail a great tool for communication across shifts, geographic distances, and other hurdles.

To manage this form of communication, activists have developed several techniques and tools. To begin with, activists have their own address books and lists of other activists and contacts with whom they correspond for various purposes. This can be used to notify people of events or the latest news, new features on Web sites or lists, or to ask questions or seek advice. It can be used to organize job actions, like sick-outs or other protests. The interchange of messages and responses and the flow of information to and from mailboxes forms a kind of continuous online discussion. Chats and instant messages are also used, though many activists find the technology still too awkward and stilted.

One way to organize e-mail discussion is by creating list servers, in which participants send messages to a central hub, which then distributes them to everyone on the list. Lists like Gangbox and Carpenters Discussion List are good examples from the building trades.[12] The lists can be moderated or unmoderated, and can be password protected or open to all. Workers often take messages they receive on one list and forward them to other lists, creating a cross-list dialogue. Again, the nature of the medium is to go over boundaries. Much of the e-mail correspondence is cross-local and cross-union. It's as if there were hundreds of ongoing rank-and-file labor council meetings.

E-mail lists can also take the form of message boards, bulletin boards, or guest books located on Web sites.[13] Many activists have added online polls to their repertoire. These polls present a question or series of questions on which workers can vote, and then immediately tabulate the results, which the voter can see.

All of this activity contributes to a culture of unionism that is based on dissent, debate, and exchange of ideas, opinions, and information on every topic of concern to union democracy activists. It is not channeled into the top-down structures of the union meeting or official magazine, but rises up wherever a member figures out how to set up a site or list server, send an e-mail message, or surf the Net. The experience of doing all this "from the safety of your own home" makes a worker's entry into activity easier and less threatening. Once in dialogue with activists, there is room to develop trust and confidence that can lead to increased participation on and, hopefully, off line.

Putting It All Together

Towards the end of the AUD/CDU (Association for Union Democracy/Carpenters for a Democratic Union) National Rank-and-File Carpenters Conference in early 2000, one carpenter called out a question to his brothers and sisters: "How many of you are online?" Out of 100 working carpenters, most middle aged, all but two had regular Internet access and used it.

This suggests the degree to which Internet access has the potential to become a staple of rank-and-file activism and a feature of working-class life. (It would be interesting to know the percentage of the carpenters union members with Internet access, and the proportion of nonunion carpenters as well.) Computers and Internet access are increasingly available and affordable. Many activists buy computers for their families or children, only to discover the value of the computer for their own work.

Carpenters union activists, who operate at all levels of the union, from the local to the international, have developed a tiered structure of e-mail and online communication. The first tier consists of Web sites run by local groups such as the Piledrivers in Local 34 and the Canadian Carpenters Union of British Columbia.[14] These sites provide local and international news and the typical array of legal rights and other information, resources, and links.

The second tier of communication is that of the various list servers like Gangbox and Carpenters Discussion List. These are open lists, readily accessible to all carpenters (and others) that provide wide-ranging discussions on an impressive array of topics. Mostly used for discussion, they can also be used to spread information and advertise upcoming actions or events.

At the next level, an international rank-and-file group might have a password-protected list server for their members only and an additional separate list for the steering committee or core activists. The Carpenters for a Democratic Union International have such a structure and have experimented with chats and polls. They found that chats were good for informal conversations, but not useful for serious decision making, for which they use phone meetings and many e-mail exchanges. They have used online polls for informal "straw poll" purposes, but not for binding votes. Distrust of electronic media for secret ballot voting runs deep in many union members.

In the buildup to their national union convention in Chicago, carpenters across North America circulated copies of resolutions, coordinated delegate elections, and organized for the protests that were held in and outside of the convention center. They built up lists of contacts that they used to coordinate tours of activists who met with local members across the country. At the convention, the union democracy activists were outnumbered and outmaneuvered; to quote Eugene Debs, they were "crushed but not destroyed, defeated but not conquered."[15]

The key to organizing in the carpenters union, as in others, remains the same: One-on-one contact, discussion and debate, practical activity on the job and in the union, and off-line activity is still primary. However, it is clear that the Internet is valuable across the range of activism: from access to information and resources to publications and communications to personal development and group activity. Using tools like e-mail and Web sites has enabled carpenters union activists to boost the reach and quality of their organizing.

More research is needed, but we can imagine that on any night, there are thousands of workers, some activists, some just curious or desperate, sitting at home in front of the computer, searching Web sites, writing to a message board, learning to create a PDF version of a flyer, or puzzling through HTML code. The Internet has also brought out in workers the skills for design, planning, and organization that are typically ignored and undervalued at work, and has encouraged the kind of self-expression that is routinely suppressed. In all of this activity, workers demonstrate the capacity for self-organization that the labor movement so badly needs.

Limits, Possibilities, and Further Research

The Internet should be labeled like a car's side mirror: "Objects may be closer/farther, larger/smaller, faster/slower, more accurate/less accurate, more representative/less representative than they appear." For all the virtues described above, it is unclear just how big a phenomenon union democracy Internet activism is, and what impact it is having in the daily life of unions.

Limit One: Is There Anybody Out There?

The first major limit to the Internet as an organizing tool is simply that very few workers probably use it for this purpose. The proportion of rank-and-file activists (e.g., caucus members who attend meetings, write leaflets and newsletters, edit the Web site, etc.) in a union with a lot of rank-and-file activity is usually under 1 percent, with a much larger layer of more passive reform supporters (e.g., members who will vote for reform candidates), at times surpassing 50 percent of the membership, but more typically around 20 percent. (These percentages are unscientific estimates based on discussions with activists in several rank-and-file reform groups. Participation online, like the off-line type, varies with the surges and lulls in the movement, and probably varies by industry, income, and other factors.)

The number of activists who use the Internet in their organizing is, optimistically, on the order of 30 to 50 percent. It is difficult to estimate the number of reform supporters and general members who use the Internet. But, if the proportions are similar to off-line activism, we can guess that the proportion of union members involved in rank-and-file activism online—via Web sites, lists, and e-mail exchanges—is probably no greater than 10 percent of the total union membership at best. At times of great turmoil and debate, the number may leap much higher, but the norm is probably fairly low.

This means that in a union of 50,000 members, with 60 reform activists that have 5,000 to 10,000 supporters, something like 2,000 workers may occasionally visit a rank-and-file Web site. Hundreds may subscribe to a list server on which probably one-third of the subscribers regularly post messages. Thirty or forty activists would use the Internet intensively for their activism. (Note that these numbers would describe a union with a very active internal political life.)

In addition, there is the digital divide, chiefly defined by geography (infrastructure), time, and income, but also by language, race, and generation. The contours of the digital divide in the world of union democracy activism have yet to be defined. There is also the divide between union and nonunion workers. While we can be confident that the level of worker access to and use of the Internet is rising, it is important to take into account the unevenness of workers' access to it.

A review of the rank-and-file Web sites on the AUDLinks page of www. uniondemocracy.org suggests that rank-and-file Web activists tend to be higher-wage workers in manufacturing, construction, and transportation, though there are (lower-paid) clerical and food-processing workers. With few exceptions, the only language used on the sites is English, even in unions with large numbers of recently arrived immigrant workers.

While the numbers are impossible to know, experience shows that employers do surf rank-and-file Web sites and have infiltrated discussion lists in an effort to learn what workers are up to and put a stop to it. Union officials surf the lists and sites for their own, often legitimate, reasons. There is no space to rehash here the arguments about why free speech is worth it, even if it means that the employer gains access to information it can use against the union and its members.

It should be sufficient to point out that the same objections have been raised in the past about rank-and-file newsletters, meetings, and other activities. As advantageous as they may be to power-hungry officials, secrecy and unquestioning loyalty to authority are not paths to democracy or member control. Workers who want to limit the damage can use passwords and oblige the user to agree to certain conditions in order to enter the site.

Workers enjoy strong legal protection from overlapping sources in their online activity. In addition to the union member bill of rights in the LMRDA, there is an emerging body of Internet free speech law based on the 1968 Wiretap Act and the Clinton-era Communications Decency Act. If the employer or union take legal action against a Web site or its owner, editor, or contributors, the First Amendment on the freedom of speech also applies. The boundaries of speech and association online are still being drawn, but rank-and-file workers are staking out some valuable terrain by asserting their rights and defending them against employers and union officials. Note: It is not wise to use computers or resources belonging to the employer or the union. (Public Citizen's Internet free speech project is a valuable resource in this area: www.citizen.org/litigation/briefs/internet.htm.)

Limit Two: Organizing Is Organizing

The same basic dynamics of organizing and personal relations that apply in the "real world" also apply in cyberspace. People bring their vices with them when they go online, not just their virtues, and find new tools for both. There is another essay on this subject, but it is more important here to touch on some of the basic problems that impede effective use of the Internet for union democracy.

The first problem is posed by the one-man (usually a man) band, the activist with lots of answers and few collaborators, the Lone Ranger. This courageous soul is unsatisfied with half steps and decides to go it alone, drawing up a particular list of reforms and complaints—often quite legitimate, often quite long—that he has cobbled together over the years. The Web provides a perfect hothouse for the cultivation of this type of solo activism, starting with the fact that the user can spend hours alone in front of the computer, apart from his coworkers.

On the Web, the Lone Ranger activist creates what we can call a webmaster-centered Web site, one that reflects in its content and presentation the interests, ideas, pet peeves, grand solutions, and extended analyses of its creator, with little or no reference to who the audience is or what they may want, need, care about, think, and so forth.

Such sites may end up resembling one of those crazy Dr. Seuss musical instruments, with fifteen different horns all emanating from one mouthpiece attached to a frazzled pajama-clad figure who puffs away enthusiastically while he struggles to hold the contraption up. You find on such a Web site: hundreds of links, and links to more links, countless articles, documents, pages and pages of testimony from court cases, animated chimpanzees, banners, music, waving flags, blinking beacons, pop-up windows. (The Steward www.thesteward.net is a great example of this phenomenon. The site opens with a picture of the Lone Ranger, accompanied by the *William Tell* Overture, and, yes, includes chimpanzees. The site also proves that even an idiosyncratic site can be a valuable resource for workers in need of information.)

You have to appreciate the unique contributions of these sites and take from them what you can, but this is no model of organizing. The point is obvious but, like many truths of organizing, worth emphasizing: Do not let the Internet—or any other tool—become a diversion that results in withdrawal from day-to-day collective activism in the workplace and union hall.

There is a second vice that plagues organizing that has thrived online: flaming. Free speech is an unruly thing. Like off-line rank-and-file meetings, rank-and-file lists and message boards are often the site of reckless accusations, baseless slanders, and even fighting words.

Some of this is attributable to the "Caliban effect." (Caliban was the slave in Shakespeare's *Tempest* who "profited on" the language taught him by his master to curse and insult him.) It is no surprise that people who have been denied a voice or treated as inferior, stupid mules may, when finally provided a space for free expression, come out swearing and cursing. E-mail exacerbates this effect by providing a medium that allows for easy expression, but hides the body language and intonation on which we all depend to show irony, sympathy, modesty, and other expressions. The result is a host of blistering attacks and counterattacks. When the problem is of the Caliban variety, the proper form of response is patience and support, along with some positive examples.

It is a more serious problem when the person doing the flaming knows better but chooses to indulge. This kind of behavior is terrible for organizing; it sidetracks serious discussions or prevents them from getting started and repels new participants. In one local, where a rank-and-file webmaster set up an unmoderated message board, the board became consumed with anonymous personal attacks followed by attacks on the webmaster for setting up the message board. The webmaster responded by shutting down the board for some time and then reopening it, in an effort to clear the decks of the abusive speech and endless debate it provoked.

Some webmasters address the problem by having a moderator who will convert four letter words to comic book symbols, or even edit messages to lower the heat. Those who choose to weather the storm of unmoderated speech should provide disclaimers and, better yet, participate frequently in the discussion to keep it focused on real issues. Swearing is not the only way to drag down a discussion. Rhetorical posturing, misinformation, and bluffing are all effective means of disruption.

Some Limits Are Also Possibilities

There is another, more fundamental, way in which free speech poses a problem and an opportunity. The struggle that union members sometimes wage to create democratic structures and a democratic culture blends into a struggle in which workers use democracy to defend their rights and advance their interests. Activists often neglect this difference between the two, as if every struggle were a life-and-death question of union democracy, or as if union democracy were just another way of describing their particular agenda for change, their own set of goals.

There is a difference between fighting for union democracy and using union democracy to fight. Democracy is a clear goal when basic rights are being violated, and it provides a framework of broad principles. But union reform also involves much discussion and action where the choice is not simply democracy versus autocracy.

As W.E.B. Du Bois observed, "There are in this world, here and there again, great partings of the ways—the one way wrong, the other right. . . . On the other hand, it is also true that the usual matters of human debate and difference of opinion are not so vitally important or so easily classified, so that in most cases there is much of right and wrong on both sides."[16] This is why the culture of democracy is always a culture of debate and discussion.

The objective of union democracy is for union members to define their own goals and pursue their interests, using democratic means. To create and cultivate a culture of democracy, activists need to model democracy in the way they organize; it is not just what they stand for that matters, but how they handle debate and discussion in their own groups. It bears repeating that committed, honest advocates of union democracy can, and will, have serious disagreements over the most important questions of union policy and strategy that nonetheless fall within the boundaries of democratic unionism. Most discussion on rank-and-file sites reflects this kind of seriousness of purpose and willingness to debate.

While Web sites and list serves are prone to Lone Ranger isolation, flame wars, and sectarian disputes, they are facilitating the creation of a model of multiparty democracy in the old one-party system that defines the typical union.

The independent clerical workers union, CUE (Coalition of University Employees), is a model of this kind of functioning, with more virtues than vices. The CUE Web site provides members with information on their rights and union activities and has links to the two rival caucuses, CUE Power and CUE2000.[17] CUE activists also make extensive use of e-mail. The union Web site and e-mail list are open to all candidates during election campaigns. There is a fair share of flaming, and accusations of flaming, but there is also a culture of debate and discussion that puts most unions to shame.

Unions should both open official publications and meetings to different points of view and encourage members to develop independent Web sites, newsletters, and even caucuses, and provide links to them on the official union page. The Massachusetts Institute of Technology has launched a project to put all course materials online, free of charge. Rank-and-file activists are already working in this spirit of openness and cross-fertilization; their unions should follow.

Conclusion

Through the Internet workers are dramatically enlarging the existing democratic space in unions and creating new forums for cross-industry, cross-union, international reform discussion and activism. They are setting up list serves, meeting in online chats, publishing Web pages and online newsletters, running debates and polls, and more. They are setting up Web sites of higher quality and sophistication than the official union sites, and charting new terrain for union reform, for workers rights, and for the labor movement.

Union democracy has always depended on the "lone reformers" battling in relative obscurity against institutionalized power. The new technology is bringing the reformers together and shedding light on their daily struggle for democracy and power—on the job and in the union.

The Internet amplifies and extends two of the most fundamental general tools and pillars of union democracy—freedom of speech and freedom of association. Will using the Internet result in more workers forming caucuses to exercise and expand their democratic rights? Let's hope so.

Notes

1. For arguments in favor of this position, see *Democratic Rights for Union Members* by Herman Benson (New York: Association for Union Democracy, 1979); *Democracy Is Power* by Martha Gruelle and Mike Parker (Detroit: Labor Notes, 1999); and the *Transformation of U.S. Unions* edited by Ray Tillman and Michael Cummings (Boulder, CO: Lynne Rienner, 1999). An instructive exchange also took place in *Dis-*

sent magazine (New York, Summer 1998, Winter 1999); see Steve Fraser's "Is Democracy Good for Unions?" and Herman Benson's reply, "Is Democracy Good for Intellectuals? Democratic Rights for Union Members."

2. Contrast the following three Web sites: SEIU member Annie Gabston says, "These pages contain little bits of my day-to-day life at home and at work (two distinctly different environments!)," http://anniegabston.homestead.com/660 newsletter1.html; Teamsters for a Democratic Union is "a grassroots organization with chapters from coast to coast in the U.S.A. and Canada," www.tdu.org; and the railroad workers who publish Snakebites, a print and online newsletter that "blasts the carriers, the unions, friends and enemies alike. We're not politically correct or any other kind of correct, for that matter," www.snakebites.org.

3. New Directions, www.newdirections.net.

4. Laborers for Justice, www.thelaborers.net.

5. Some of these newsletters are available online in PDF format and can be downloaded and printed by the workers who visit the site. See, for example, Snakebites (cited above); autoworker Caroline Lund's The Barking Dog/El Perro Labrador/Ang Asong Kumakahol at http://geocities.com/abarkingdog/; and carpenter Tom Crofton's The Kerf, http://forthemembers.tripod.com/documents/kerf/june00.htm.

6. Honest Union, www.honestunion.homestead.com/main2.html; Local 30 Members First, www.local30.com; and the Unity Slate Caucus, www.iuoe30.com.

7. For example, IAConnect, a page for members of the International Alliance of Theatrical Stage Employees (IATSE), http://free.freespeech.org/iaconnect/connect.htm.

8. GRUNT, www.grunt.org.

9. LabourStart, www.labourstart.org; Internet Labor Resources, www.lib.berkeley.edu/IIRL/iirlnet.html.

10. For readers who object to the use of the term "hunter" for union officials, I refer you to John L. Lewis, who once described workers as birds, radical union staffers as dogs, and himself as the hunter. "Who gets the bird? The hunter or the dog?" For all his contributions, Lewis was no great champion of union democracy.

11. HERETIC (Hotel Employees Restaurant Employees to Insure Change), www.heretics.net; REAP (Reform Education Action People), www.reapinc.org.

12. Gangbox, gangbox-owner@egroups.com; Carpenters Discussion List, www.onelist.com/subscribe/UBCMEMBERS.

13. The 21st-Century Postal Worker Message Exchange, www.21cpw.com/, and Rank and File 25 (for IBEW members), http://rankandfile25.com, offer good examples of message boards.

14. Piledrivers in Local 34, www.geocities.com/pdl_34/union.html; Carpenters Union of British Columbia (my one departure from the exclusion of official union sites), www.carpentersunionbc.com/enter.html.

15. *Eugene Debs Speaks* (New York: Pathfinder Press, 1984).

16. John Brown (New York: International Publishers, 1996).

17. Coalition of University Employees, www.cueunion.org. The two caucuses were formed around the last statewide election and may not represent the current level or pattern of organizing: CUE Power, www.geocities.com/cuepower; and CUE2000, www.homestead.com/vivalocapolitica/files/home.htm.

For more information, contact the Association for Union Democracy, 500 State Street, Brooklyn NY 11217. Phone: 718-855-6650; e-mail: aud@igc.org. Our Web site can be found at www.uniondemocracy.org.

XI. Promoting Union Militancy

If you can find a path with no obstacles,
it probably doesn't lead anywhere.
—Frank A. Clark, educator

Fewer unionists experience a strike nowadays than ever before: "In any given year between 1950 and 1975, approximately 1.5 million persons were involved in strikes in the U.S. By comparison, today [2001], when the work force is twice as large, there are on the order of 100,000" (Thieblot 2001).

Or, to put this another way, in 1947, when the Federal Mediation and Conciliation Service (FMCS) was formed to ease labor-management conflicts, there were 270 strikes idling over 1,000 workers. In 2000, the number was only thirty-nine. The FMCS, which had as many as 315 mediators in the late 1970s, was down in 2001 to 218 (Chen 2001).

Last year, however, labor was reminded (once again, as so often over its history) that it must never let its guard down. Thirty-nine major work stoppages began in 2000, idling 394,000 workers and resulting in 20 million workdays of idleness. Comparable figures for 1999 were only 17 stoppages, 73,000 workers idled, and 2 million days of idleness (BLS 2001).

This is not all that surprising, given the inability of many blockhead employers to see merit in sharing, rather than in hoarding power. Unlike many other advanced industrial nations, America has consulting firms specializing in union avoidance and decertification campaigns. We have law firms specializing in how to defeat organizing drives and weaken strikes. And we have anti-union industry groups and businesses falling over one another in their eagerness to serve as pallbearers at labor's funeral.

All the more reason for labor to employ computer power to boost its prowess at fighting back. Advances here of late are many. Some are obvious, as in labor's ability to use e-mail and list servers to rally the troops, assign and monitor pickets, share picket sign art over the Internet, collect and counter rumors, share fast-breaking news, stroke exemplary behavior, discourage defeatist attitudes, prop up morale, keep headquarters and the front lines in touch 24/7, and, in 101 other ways, bolster conventional strike matters.

Other gains are far less obvious, as in using the Internet to research the company balance sheet, wage a corporate campaign against a targeted company and/or its key power-holders, coordinate a series of protests at nationwide locations or functions of the company, rally consumers to withhold sales support from the business, seek the support of unions overseas able to exert some useful pressure.

Still other computer-based weapons remain hypothetical, but no less vital for all of that. It is possible, for example, that unions or locals could soon begin to provide online training programs for picket line captains, for example, in advance of any strike (thereby sending a message to the company about the local's earnestness). Similarly, the Internet could host virtual reality scenes of picket line confrontation with police and/or scabs, a visual exercise that might help improve the readiness of those new to industrial conflict. Streaming video coverage of earlier or similar strike victories might help boost morale, as might also daily live TV/computer-based interviews on the picket line with enthusiastic strikers.

More intriguing yet is the possibility that a new agent of change may soon emerge to alter industrial conflict in far-reaching ways. Known as a "hactivist," this individual combines hacker skills with social issue concerns. He or she is available to employ cyberdisruption tactics on behalf of social cause gains. Two academics believe it "inevitable that hactivists sympathetic to labor will invent and circulate widely usable cyberequivalents of such traditional working-class strategies as sabotaging, working-to-rule, and striking" (Cloward and Piven 2001, 92).

These academics point out that computer-savvy workers can use either home or even work computers to join in cyberdisruptions. While they believe unions per se will shy from the matter out of fear of harsh legal repression, they expect unofficial tactics to grow: "Increasingly, workers will, without union sponsorship, do such things as support strikes by disrupting employer communications. And there is every reason to believe that cyberdisruption will spread" (Cloward and Piven 2001, 93).

Consistent with this expectation of more and smarter militancy, the three essays below attest to growing sophistication in labor's use of computer power. The first recounts a creative effort to use e-mail to ready a union for a possible strike. Especially noteworthy are transferable lessons about the place of an Internet chat room. The second essay explains what it means to create an online paper as a weapon during a newspaper strike. The third essay shares the strategy of a union required to respond quickly to the loss of e-mail contact with members dependent largely on the employer's Internet services.

Taken together, the three essays offer valuable tips and tricks you will want to store away—for the day (anytime soon) when it might be your turn at the (Internet-informed) barricades. Bytes, not bricks; better-than-ever cybercommunications, rather than clubs and curses; and possibly even the spooky aid of underground hactivists—all of this may soon combine to shorten a strike's duration, lessen its toll, and heighten labor's gains.

References

Bureau of Labor Statistics (BLS). *Major Work Stoppages in 2000* (February 9, 2001) (http://stats.bls.gov/news.release/wkstp.nr0.htm).

Chen, Kathy. "Government's Labor Mediators Branch Out." *Wall Street Journal*, May 31, 2001, p. B-1.

Cloward, Richard A., and Frances Fox Piven. "Disrupting Cyberspace: A New Frontier for Labor Activism?" *New Labor Forum* (Spring/Summer 2001), pp. 91–94.

Thieblot, A.J. "The Fall and Future of Unionism in Construction." *Journal of Labor Research* (Spring 2001), p. 305.

---

38. Using Cyberspace to Enhance the CyberUnion

Anthony W. Zumpetta

The first act of a drama casts a long shadow, especially when the number of ensuing acts and the play's conclusion cannot be known. Similarly, the act of preparing to strike can actually be of great significance to what follows, strike or otherwise.

The preparatory phase sends messages minutely read for clues by many concerned parties: Management, for example, looks for evidence bearing on the local's unity and firmness, the popularity of pro- and anti-strike factions, and the seeming resolve of the rank-and-file to "stay out one day longer." Ambivalent members do the same, as do the family dependents of the potential strikers. And hovering in the shadows, the media searches for leads with which to slant the news, while local politicians put a finger in the air to suggest what should be their public position today.

Advice about gearing up for battle is a feature of the essay below. It explains how a union met the challenge posed by a hard-boiled manage- ment that scrutinized the union's Internet messages, controlled e-mail ac- cess to the union's members (which it threatened to immediately cut off should a strike occur), and was thought thoroughly frightening by many in the rank-and-file.

You will find answers to questions such as: What are now regarded as flaws in the union's response strategy and its execution? How useful are chat rooms, and why? In what ways do messages outshine messengers? How is the rumor mill effected? And, what does it mean to struggle to keep e-mail in perspective?

Ralph Waldo Emerson once remarked, "This time, like all times, is a very good one if we but know what to do with it." Those of us who have been intimately involved with job actions, whether it be management or union, know too well that those times can turn into disasters if we but don't know what to do with them. The lack of action is action, which will too often spell organizational chaos, failure, and eventual demise.

We also know that "getting our heads together" for collective planning, evaluation, and implementation is at times damn near impossible. Even if we can agree on committing ourselves to a time and place to meet, it is not uncommon for ego's and attitudes to come in the way of sound planning and unified action. The strategy and tactics of a successful job action go far be- yond textbook planning.

My essay offers some tips on mobilization, especially during periods of crisis when time is more important than money and a collective job action is imminent. It involves the use of cyberspace, and the added bonus many of us share at work called e-mail.

The value of communicating through e-mail became quite apparent dur- ing my union's last negotiation for a new contract. The Association of Penn- sylvania State College and University Faculties (APSCUF) represents over 4,500 faculty members working in the State System of Higher Education (SSHE), which is composed of fourteen state-funded universities serving over 95,000 students.

Our contract with the SSHE was due to expire on July 1, 1999, and the initial feelers from Harrisburg, the state capital, were most discouraging. The proposed new contract had a more-than-usual increased workload along with frozen salaries. Also included were salary cuts, a decrease in benefits, and surcharges for any item published while being an employee of the state university system. This was nasty. There was even a rumor circulating that

Governor Tom Ridge would try to break APSCUF if we did not accept the state's offer.

But we were surely doomed as a faculty union if we did accept. The state's "last best offer" had a polarizing effect, and it sent a message to the rank-and-file that this negotiation was the most serious any of us had experienced since joining the state university system. We knew this would be a hard fought battle.

Our union's initial efforts at mobilization were fairly successful. Our first meeting, in the summer prior to the beginning of classes, had a fairly good turnout. Members were recruited by the union leadership to act as a steering committee to coordinate major efforts, such as communications, press liaison, pickets and signs, relocation of offices, and so on.

At that meeting we agreed to use our e-mail system as much as possible to communicate with one another to share ideas, progress reports, and bulletins. We all had e-mail accounts on the job, and most members of this steering committee had e-mail at home on a separate system. Little did we realize then how valuable a tool was this electronic wonder of the new millennium.

The global address list on the university system made it easy to establish a server list. But this would be effective only as long as we stayed on the job. If there were a job action (a.k.a. strike), access to e-mail via any university facility would probably vaporize. Obviously, we would be denied access to our offices as well as other university locations with computer access, including the library, student union, and computer center. In addition, using e-mail at any time posed a security risk. Not only could management deny us use of this service, it could also eavesdrop on and monitor staff transmissions.

To counter each of these disadvantages, a separate list server was established using members' personal Internet addresses at home. For members who did not have Internet service at home, a telephone call list was established with respective individuals assigned to make calls to the non-Internet members when needed.

This system, even with its flaws and cautions, yielded many great benefits. Among them were the following, each of which can serve as a lesson for *any* union facing a conflict situation:

1. *No need to copy, fold, and address notices.* With e-mail, once the list server is established there is no need to copy, fold, address, and mail notices. Just identify the address list, type the message, and hit the send command. There is no need to type a new distribution list ever again. Changes can be quickly made to the list to add or delete names as needed.

Finding a copy machine when it's "business as usual" may be rather simple. But during a job action these means that we too often take for granted will become scarce. Of course, there are private office supply outlets that will make copies. But consider the time it takes for travel and turn-around time, then the folding and mailing routine.

2. *Instant delivery.* Once the send key is activated, notices arrive at their destination at the speed of one's microprocessor. If someone has an outdated system, the message may take a few nanoseconds longer, but the time delay will be seconds before the message can be received as opposed to hours or even days. Union members involved in the job action will get into the habit of checking their e-mail not just daily, but hourly. With laptops, you can take your mailbox with you.

3. *No lost notices.* Consider the number of times you have placed notices in the interoffice mail system and they didn't get delivered, or those that took longer to make it to the next building than across the country. This won't be a problem with e-mail.

4. *Chat rooms become committee meetings.* Chat rooms can be established in which committee members can exchange ideas and make decisions. This option would probably be best to utilize via home-based systems rather than one at the office due to increased confidentiality. In addition, if committee members had to be at the office to be at their computers, it would be just as easy to meet as a group in a more traditional manner.

But to be working at home in a chat room provides access to files and documents one may have at home that can't be taken to a meeting. It also provides total personal comfort. Your home office is what you want it to be, smoking or nonsmoking, not too hot and not too cold, and your most appreciated beverage in hand. Late evening meetings can become productive forums.

5. *Messages become more important than the messenger.* Have you ever been in a meeting dominated by one or two people whose message becomes second to their annoying method of delivery? Or perhaps there are certain union brothers and sisters you have had clashes with to the extent that you reject their advice and influence based purely on personality differences?

Even during times of crisis some situations don't change. We're all human and capable of frailties associated with that status. E-mail won't become the Prozac of communications, turning us all into mellow, understanding comrades. But it will do a great deal to bridge the gap between message and messenger, emphasizing the message portion of that equation.

In my experience with this situation, I found individuals who were noted for adding colorful illustrations, bravado, and drama to their message when on center stage dropped the theatrics when it came to putting the message into written form. With e-mail the sender is playing to the same audience but in a far different manner. In the worse-case scenario, the receiver can still elect to just skim messages received from a verbose sender and file them away or hit the DELETE key.

6. *Communication has few limitations.* Major crises, such as a strike, are usually not confined to a single facility. There will undoubtedly be a need to coordinate efforts with the union's central office, as well as other facilities, plants, and offices that are a part of the same organization. These may be across town, at the other end of the state, nationwide, or even international. The standard telephone and cellular phone make voice contact possible quickly and with a certain degree of confidentiality. But even with multiple-party options, the telephone can't compare to a mass-distributed e-mail message.

In addition to being able to "talk" to union officials at other sites, the Internet can be used to research almost any topic, including pay scales of competing companies, projected cost-of-living increases, research reports, and so on. The additional "search" tool on the Web site opens resources the size of the Library of Congress. As negotiations are in progress, updates can be received right at the bargaining table.

7. *The proof is in the pudding.* In our last negotiation between APSCUF and the SSHE, e-mail was a fabulous tool that helped promote the union's efforts. It added to the union's solidarity and kept the membership informed with official and accurate updates from the local president and state union officials. The rumor mill had little impact because of the ease in which factual information could be retrieved. APSCUF was able to delay a potential job action until that action would best serve the purposes of the union membership. SSHE's "last best offer" was virtually stagnant for most of the negotiation period.

Once a job action was authorized and a date set for it to begin, the membership was as ready as it could have been. We felt our cause was just and that we would succeed in having a contract that was truly negotiated and not simply management's last best offer.

I actually retired the evening prior to the day the strike was to begin under the assumption that I would be on a picket line the next morning rather than in a classroom. But as many other contracts have been settled, this one went to the wire, the eleventh hour so to speak.

The package the union agreed to was not unanimously accepted by the rank-and-file. It had some sections that favored management's perspective, and some that favored the union's. Love it or hate it, the contract was a truly negotiated document, and in negotiation each side has to give a little to get a little.

8. *Not an end in itself, but a means to an end.* The purpose of my essay is *not* to herald e-mail as the sole method of communication for union mem-

bers during times of crisis. It is to illustrate how effective it could be, and was, during a pending job action for APSCUF.

E-mail *enhances* a movement that already has a sound plan of action in an organization that shares at least a fundamental sense of solidarity. It will never replace an inspiring speech by a charismatic union official or the face-to-face contact that is needed to convince fellow union members of the importance in walking a picket line.

There are unions where e-mail simply isn't as effective an option as it was to APSCUF. Members of a migrant farm worker's union, for example, would have neither the facilities nor the hardware to utilize many of the suggestions made in this essay. But for those organizations that have the capability to utilize electronic mail, it is a tool of the new millennium that will advance our effectiveness as union brothers and sisters.

---

39. How the Internet Sustained a Strike

Paul Andrews

It is one thing to imagine how using the Internet might help a strike-bound local in this way or that: It is far better to be able to examine how things actually worked out, warts and all. From the case study below we can extract several pieces of advice about the role of Internet use when a strike is bitter, long, and intractable.

Careful reading of this short journalistic account sheds light on such matters as the ability of the Internet to serve as "the strike's silent partner." We learn about the reaction of nonstriking members of the customer community to an alternative Internet-based striker newspaper. We get an explanation for the notion that e-mails can help "in ways not possible even in group meetings." And, overall, we learn about how to adroitly use computer power when a strike hardens and morale comes under serious attack.

A digital Joe Hill helped carry the torch for the Seattle newspaper strike. Economies of scale. Low barriers to entry. Reduced distribution costs. Creation of community. The Internet was the strike's silent partner. It was one of the best examples anywhere yet of the Net's power to unite people in a cause.

With all the hoo-ha over e-commerce and dot-this 'n' that in recent times, the prodigious community-building powers of the Net had been all but obscured. The Seattle strike served notice that the Internet is a force for the common individual—one to be reckoned with in any organizational endeavor.

Not only did the Net make possible the popular strike newspaper, the *Seattle Union Record*, it also knit the strikers together through e-mail updates, discussion lists, and morale boosts.

Ten, then sixteen, Macintoshes. Ethernet network hubs and cables. A DSL connection. A few hundred feet of office space. And a bunch of outraged newsies looking to sustain their craft. That was all it took to help get the *Union Record* rolling. A "to" e-mail address field that grew to hundreds of names. That was all it took to help keep the strike spirit energized.

The *Union Record*'s name was an homage to a Seattle labor newspaper of the early 1900s, when newspapers were put together with state-of-the-art technology tools of their day—typewriters and hot lead. Today's versions are word processors, HTML, and Web servers. But the object was the same: producing high-quality journalism to remind readers that what counts in the process is people.

Within hours of the *Union Record*'s first Web posting at 4:00 A.M. on November 21 [2000], managing editor Chuck Taylor was besieged by hundreds of congratulatory e-mails. The community's support gave a jolt of encouragement to the fledgling effort. Readers cared! Readers appreciated the experience, insight, polish, and authority that came with original, professional journalism. Taylor was immensely gratified. "I'm astonished, given our modest beginning, that so many people responded," he wrote in a staff e-mail.

Gradually, as the strike endured and people sensed a need to communicate, the e-mails started circulating. First among close friends, then on small lists. Eventually it fell to [the Seattle] *Times* editorial writer O. Casey Corr to be Keeper of the List. Corr proved an evenhanded moderator, circulating others' missives for comment while occasionally raising an issue or two on his own.

"It just seemed natural because we were all accustomed to communicating that way from e-messaging and e-bulletin boards at *The Times*," Corr noted. When nerves frayed or spirits flagged, someone always came up with an encouraging e-mail to pass around.

The mailing list provided an instant, no-holds-barred forum for airing frustrations as well as testing membership sentiment. Strikers got to hear each other out in ways not possible even in group meetings. In the process they got to know one another better and build a communality in purpose reminiscent of the college papers where many got their start in journalism. Without the electronic maypole to rally around, the strike might have dissolved in infighting and battle fatigue.

It was all an experiment in New Journalism, recalling Tom Wolfe's content revolution of the 1960s. Back then the issue was to tell the truth through new forms of prose. The Web's mission is to tell the truth through new forms of production and distribution—although Web content, too, is taking on its own distinctive flavor.

Taylor saw the *Union Record* as an opportunity to prove that a Web newspaper had value on its own merits—not just as a derivation of a print version. "Most newspaper Web sites are an afterthought," he observed. He "wanted to turn the newspaper-Web paradigm upside-down." Taylor also wanted to show how, in the Web era, a geographically distributed newsroom could work. Most staff members filed stories from home computers and used Internet connections to e-mail them in for editing and processing.

A top Web news executive told me over breakfast recently, "Newspapers have the local franchise. The head counts, the production values, the community's support." International and national news may be "commoditized" [or turned into businesses] by the Web, he noted, but local news would always be the local newspaper's domain.

To protect the local franchise, however, will require newspapers to leverage the efficiencies of the Internet as well. That process is still being ferreted out as online advertising and subscription models evolve. But the *Union Record* proved, if there was any doubt, that an online journal can differentiate from a traditional print newspaper while maintaining and even amplifying the high standards of professional journalism.

[Note:] A full archive of the *Union Record*'s "daily miracle" is being compiled on a CD-ROM.

---

40. Picketing Cyberspace
William Puette

Given that the Internet has, as is contended below, created a "new shop floor in cyberspace," strike leaders have major new concerns. They must confront for the first time the specter of "cyberscabbing" and the possibility of self-centered members crossing the picket line to access their (company-maintained) computer, along with a host of similarly novel threats to solidarity. Contrarily, a striking local may find that the need to finally gather as many home-based e-mail addresses as possible is an overdue gain of lasting worth.

All of this, and far more, gets a helpful airing in the advice-packed essay below. Answers are offered to such questions as: How can you finesse the possibility of losing e-mail contact with your members? What might a flood of e-mail during a strike suggest about morale? How much does it matter that management is reading all of your strike e-mail? Is it possible for disloyal members to circumvent the strike electronically, and so what? Above all, what might a striking local focus on as a major cyberstep forward?

They say strikes aren't what they used to be, but more to the point, strikes can't be what they used to be in simpler times. The workaday world for more and more people has changed radically with the information technology (IT) revolution. Half of the U.S. workforce regularly used a desktop or laptop computer at work as early as 1997, and the Internet is still recasting labor-management relations in fundamental ways.

Increasingly, the Internet is creating a new shop floor in cyberspace. So, naturally, labor's rights to organize, bargain, and engage in concerted activity need new definitions. When it does become necessary for IT-based workers to strike or engage in concerted activity, the rules of engagement must take this new arena into account.

In April of 2001 The University of Hawaii's Professors Association (UHPA), the union representing the 3,000 faculty at the University of Hawaii's ten-campus system, struck the state of Hawaii for thirteen days. In an unprecedented expression of solidarity, 90 percent of the faculty went out. By all measures the strike was as effective in shutting down the university as could have been imagined.

Traditional picketing, though necessary, was not enough to make the strike effective.

During the weeks prior to the strike, an important fact was realized: Members are heavily dependent on their work-based e-mail system. Like many schools and universities, at UH all faculty and all students are provided with e-mail accounts by the university.

More and more, traditional campus-based classroom instruction is being supplemented by Internet-based "distance education." When the keyboard is a podium and the monitor is a chalkboard, the professor can theoretically be teaching entirely from home or any other off-campus location with a computer and a modem. Universities may be at the leading edge of this new-age homework, but many other work sites are moving just as deeply into cyberspace as academia.

Not all of the impacts of distance education and work-based e-mail were negative to strike participation. It is an old joke that organizing faculty is like herding cats. And yet, the flood of e-mail and list-server debates in the weeks before the strike authorization vote actually galvanized the membership in ways that had never been possible before. They could see that decisions were being made with grassroots involvement by colleagues.

The old whine of paranoia and conspiracy theories about staff domination and hidden agendas was neutralized and overpowered by strong, clear, and articulate membership voices in support of the bargaining team and strike support. The downside, however, was that this open forum of debate was completely open to the employer. Nothing was confidential; nothing, private. The university and the state administration were, unfortunately, aware of every position we took, and every argument, pro and con, was on the table, laid bare for all to see.

In the end, though, the openness of our communication was an advantage and naysayers in our ranks were either overwhelmed or discredited by the sheer volume of support from the unquestioned majority of the membership.

As we moved into the strike, however, a bigger worry about e-mail and the Internet was that the strength of the dependence our members have on this medium would make it impossible for them to completely stop their student-focused work.

Without actual data, we knew, nevertheless, that most of our members relied exclusively on their university e-mail. With this open and generally unrestricted, and therefore uninhibited, Internet access at work, the majority of our members did not bother to have personal or home-based Internet accounts. This would be roughly analogous to a situation where the union members had only office telephones and no home phones.

Our union communications had relied on the employer's systems as well. What would happen if the employer bothered to shut access down to strikers? And, even if that didn't happen, how can we communicate sensitive bargaining and strike strategy information if we need to? Worst of all, continuing to use the employers' e-mail server to communicate with our members during the strike would have required that better than half of our members would have to cross our picket lines to log on to their office computers! Furthermore, we could see that such access to their university-based e-mail would tempt them irresistibly to keep working with their students, making and accepting assignments, in essence, cyberscabbing.

Solutions: From Our "Strike Committee Instructions to Faculty"

- Do not use your university e-mail, phone line, or voice mail during the strike. We will want to communicate by e-mail with you if possible.

Tell your picket captain or faculty rep your private, non-UH e-mail address, and home and cell phone numbers.

- If you do not have a private e-mail account but can access the Internet by an off-campus computer, ask us for our instruction sheet to sign up for a free Web-based Hotmail or Yahoo e-mail address. Send an e-mail from this non-UH e-mail address with your name, home or cell phone, and your campus to strike@uhpa.org.
- A faculty member on strike DOES NOT ENTER THE CAMPUS until the strike is over. We don't teach classes, conduct research, supervise athletic or theatrical events, meet with students, etc. Likewise, all distance education and Internet-based teaching must stop completely.
- DO NOT TRY TO CIRCUMVENT THE STRIKE electronically. In this day of instant communication, it is possible to use a variety of Internet or e-mail vehicles to continue "business as usual." But such actions are not *clever*; they're disingenuous.

Because of the last-minute nature of our efforts, collecting and organizing home-based e-mail addresses for our members was such a huge task that we only managed to get about one-third of the striking faculty addresses in place by the strike date.

One major lesson of the strike was the importance of collecting, organizing, and updating our members' home e-mail addresses as a part of our normal records. In many ways, a home e-mail address is more important than a home phone number or address, and much more useful.

A huge amount of time was invested in reading and responding to our members e-mail, but it was time well spent. I give a lot of credit to our executive director and staff, not to mention the loaned staff we got from the National Education Association for the long hours they invested in the keeping up with the electronic mail. In this, our strike Web site was greatly assisted by getting common questions and answers out quickly.

Nor were we alone in cyberspace. Both the university and the governor's office set up strike pages, and the local news media regularly posted all three URLs as the Internet became part of our battle to win public support as well.

In the end, cell phones, e-mail, and Web sites worked in tandem to help us support our pickets and keep the information flowing.

XII. Promoting Organizing

What can labor do for itself? The answer is not difficult.
Labor can organize, it can unify, it can consolidate its forces.
This done, it can demand and command.
—Eugene Debs, labor leader

The decision to reserve this subject for last was not hard to make as it is the most important challenge confronting labor. Union membership dropped to a sixty-year low in 2000, "a trend labor leaders fear could worsen under the Bush administration." The percentage of American workers belonging to unions fell to 13.5 percent or 16.3 million workers in 2000, from 13.9 percent in 1999, according to a Bureau of Labor Statistics report (Ramstack 2001).

Thanks, however, to computer strength in speed and accessibility (as in labor's use of online discussion groups, e-mail, instant messaging, sign-up programs, etc.), strategic and encouraging organizing gains are being made. Union activists increasingly recognize in computer uses a new tool that, if creatively combined with face-to-face ways, just might make the critical difference: "The instantaneous communication, the anonymity, and the ability for employees to speak to each other, across the globe and without fear, are truly the new empowerment that we have today through the Internet" (Guyer 2001, 14).

Naturally, nearly every one of the handbook's forty-six chapters has some advice to share where organizing is concerned. To sample from just the first ten:

- Lelinski (Chapter 1) suggests that we can, anyone of us, learn as he did how to create our own Web site, this time for organizing purposes.
- Dassaro (Chapter 2) highlights the appeal a local's new "high tech" razzle-dazzle can have to prospective members.
- Smoot (Chapter 3) reminds us of the "high touch" uses of the Internet's "high tech" prowess, a balance in perspective indispensable in organizing campaigns.
- Lazarovici (Chapter 4) relates how an AFGE activist overcame wide dispersion of prospective members by the smart use of the Internet.
- Hart (Chapter 5) recommends consideration of PDAs.
- Bupp (Chapter 6) highlights the sort of Internet-use hazard organizers can turn to advantage, as in offering protection, and so forth.
- Friedman (Chapter 7) suggests "circuit riders" dispatched by a union might help locals with their computer-aided organizing drives.
- Zetterström (Chapter 8) recommends placing organizing PR spots on the major portals in target areas.
- Downes (Chapter 9) reminds us indirectly that our reliance as organizers on high tech is only as strong as the weakest link.
- Hertenstein (Chapter 10) identifies problems with computer uses that should be addressed lest they undermine an organizing effort.

All ten of these opening chapters and the ones that follow inspire an empowering sort of confidence that smart use of computer power is already making a valuable contribution on the organizing front. It is not just a matter of bytes replacing paper. Rather, it appears that Internet-based communications significantly "changes the way people behave and interact. The roles they play and the dynamics that occur are now, in the online world, sometimes much different than in traditional organizing" (Guyer 2001, 2).

For example, as webmaster Linda Mathews explains in Chapter 20,

> It gives us the ability to reach the unorganized worker in the comfort of his living room and away from the company's prying eyes and pressure tactics. When that person is up late at night, unable to sleep, and searching the Web in desperation for help in dealing with his crummy boss, lousy work environment, and inadequate pay, the Web gives us the ability to reach out to him. I've been witness to this ability. But a Web contact has to be followed by a personal contact, otherwise we have failed in our duties.
>
> We could learn a lot from those who have had successful campaigns

using the Web as a major support system . . . [as when] you can join the union online.

Paying attention to the Internet's tools should mean developing a checklist of organizing tips and tricks that might include the following:

1. Create a closed e-mail list for the organizing committee, along with a password-protected area for organizers only.
2. Employ pictures of members on your Web site to help prospective members identify with the drive and to boost its credibility.
3. Offer fliers that organizers can download and customize for their site.
4. Provide a printable sign-up form that can be copied and handed out.
5. Provide downloadable PDF files of your newsletter.
6. Update an extensive education section with links to relevant current studies and sites on the Internet.
7. Offer links to labor cartoons, labor-relevant movie and book reviews, community newspaper coverage of the campaign, and other areas of interest.
8. Make it possible to join the union 24/7 from home as a dues-paying voting member, using a secure Web page for credit card information: "If my seventy-seven-year-old aunt can order a book from amazon.com, than anyone with access to a computer should be able to sign up for a union online" (Guyer 2001, 13).
9. Offer an area on your Web site where members can submit their own comments ("Your Issues"), as on the site run by the current organizing effort at Intel (www.faceintel. com).

Thanks to the four chapters that follow, this short list is vastly extended and enriched: The first recounts an unexpected success in organizing, one with surprising lessons. The second urges new attention to cyberworkers as candidates for membership. The third is a case study of a frontier effort to organize cyberworkers (the Microsoft campaign). And the fourth recommends unorthodox ways well worth pondering. Taken together, the essays underline the availability in computer power of an extraordinary tool.

References

Guyer, Linda. "Real-World Experiences of Online Organizing." Unpublished paper prepared for the Unions and the Internet Conference, London, UK, May 11–12,

2001. See also an AFL-CIO Department for Professional Employees report, *The Professional and Technical Work Force: A New Frontier for Unions*. Washington, DC: AFL-CIO, 2001.

Ramstack, Tom. "Labor Leaders Hope to Stop Decline." *Washington Times*, January 24, 2001, p. A-1.

---

41. How a Former Union Organizer Accidentally Sparked a Nationwide Election Protest Movement, All via the Internet

Zack Exley

Lessons we learn accidentally, as from a serendipitous experience, are often among the most striking, memorable, and valuable, in part for being unexpected. A former union organizer shares the tale below of a wholly unexpected windfall of sorts, one that dramatically illustrates how powerful an organizing tool labor has in the Internet. Note especially the notion that the people themselves can drive much of the organizing process, and at warp speed!

As a union organizer in the 1990s, I had low expectations for how the Internet could be used in grassroots organizing. I knew that e-mail had been used in some unionization drives, but I assumed it was just a tool that allowed organizers to do old tasks in new ways. Now I know better.

Last month, almost by accident, I set in motion an organizing drive that mobilized thousands of people across the country, using the Net. One month before the [2000 national] election, on a lark, I spent about an hour putting up a Web site proposing nationwide protests if Al Gore were to win the popular vote but lose the electoral college.

Countercoup [www.countercoup.org] listed my suggested protest locations in a few big cities for the Saturday following the election and asked people to nominate spots for their own cities. E-mailing everyone in my address book drew a few hundred visits to the site and a handful of e-mails essentially saying, "Why are you wasting your time?"

The day after the election, I watched the news all morning. My fears, it seemed, had come true. I finally checked my e-mail around noon. To my astonishment, hundreds of messages had come in that morning suggesting more protest locations. People who had seen the site a month ago were now forwarding it to friends.

I began adding the new locations to the Web page. By the time I was done another two dozen e-mails had already landed in my mailbox. Like a chain reaction, word of the "nationwide prodemocracy protests" was spreading across the Internet. Everyone wanted to know who was planning the protest in their city.

I e-mailed them all back saying, "These are spontaneous protests, no one is organizing them—just show up! People will be there!" I tried to make a list of people willing to be local contacts, but it turned out to be too much to coordinate. By Thursday morning I had received more than 1,000 e-mails and the Web site had received almost 100,000 visitors. It was natural for people to be angry and want to protest after the election, but without the Internet there would have been no way for a single person to propose a day of protests, and for word of it to spread to so many people. The Internet allowed me to post the proposal where tens of millions could see it.

Before the Internet, this would have required an organization (like the Democratic party) with a huge list of potentially interested people and a phone-banking effort involving acres of rented telemarketing space, thousands of volunteers, and countless phone lines. And this was just the beginning. To get out from under the avalanche of e-mail, I used a free, Web-based service to create an Internet group to allow people to connect with each other directly. I linked the Web site to the group and sent an e-mail out telling everyone who was already involved to join. Within an hour, there were more than 100 messages posted to the message board.

Here's a typical exchange: A woman named Julie wrote asking, "Is the DC protest definitely happening? I live in Chapel Hill . . . before I drive five hours I want to know this is real." Someone responded immediately saying, "We definitely need more info regarding DC. I live here, and have heard next to nothing." At first I thought exchanges like that would bring an abrupt end to this mini-movement, which had been based on a bluff. But plenty of determined optimists posted replies that saved the day. "WE'RE COMING! And I don't care if my husband and I are the only ones on the Capitol steps!" wrote one.

By midday Friday 1,000 people had subscribed to the group, and ABC News, *Slate,* the *Boston Globe,* NPR, and a Belgian radio station all wanted to know who was in charge. I encouraged the local protest organizers to talk to the press, generating coverage in several major outlets.

Practical organizing activity on the message board reached a fever pitch on the eve of our protests. Graphic designers stayed late at their jobs making fliers, which people downloaded and used to make signs. In kitchens across the country people made signs and banners using slogans that others had posted to the message board. Employees at PR firms faxed out press releases which local activists had written and posted to the group. Using the Internet, hundreds of local organizers, who didn't even know each other, were coordinating their activities and lending each other support. The protests were set for 1:00 P.M., local times.

My friend Michael, who had been bringing me take-out for the two days that I was pinned to my computer, came with me to the Boston rally at the Statehouse. "How many people do you think will show?" I asked. "Maybe fifty," he said. "Fifty? Not a chance!" I responded. An iron law of organizing is that most of the people who say they're coming never do. Only a handful of people from each city had said they were coming; everyone else had only asked if the protests were really happening.

I predicted a turnout of ten. But when we got to the Statehouse at 1:00 P.M., there were already hundreds of people there. People were holding blown-up versions of the signs the graphic designers had made and homemade signs with the slogans that I had posted. I asked someone how they had heard about the protest. "I got an e-mail . . . somebody named Countercoup."

"Ah . . . " I said, and crept out the back of the crowd.

By the time I got home, reports had already come in from the other protests sites: New York 500; Philadelphia 200; DC 300. Two friends in Los Angeles called in to say there were a couple of thousand people out at their site. Before the demonstrations had even ended, people were uploading photos from their digital cameras and making up Web pages of their own.

A volunteer compiled it all onto a new page for the Countercoup site. [There were] accounts of protests in forty-two cities, including places like Fayetteville, Arkansas, and Asheville, North Carolina. I created new newsgroups for each city and state where organizing had taken place and asked people to continue organizing for November 18. Organizers used the message boards to divide tasks among themselves and to schedule planning meetings, where people who had been talking via e-mail met for the first time.

After the second round of protests, a few of us formed a steering committee, to which I turned over the national mailing list and the Web site. A national organization, with chapters in dozens of cities, was born. The protests had little impact on the political scene, but for many of us involved, the experience demonstrated that a fundamental change is taking place in our national political life.

It's not the Internet per se, but the emerging potential for any individual to communicate—for free and anonymously—with any other individual. Whether one is organizing a union, a revolution, or a company softball league, there's always a catch-22 involved: People are leery of acting before a consensus has been reached to act, but forming that consensus requires action, like going to a meeting.

In the case of our protests, the Internet allowed thousands of grassroots leaders to reach a consensus to act. Thousands of people talked via e-mail during their coffee breaks at work or their time between classes. They were not sacrificing hours in planning meetings, they never had to risk going to a meeting where they might be the only ones, or where they'd find that those organizing the meeting were crazy or incompetent.

This represents a radical breakthrough for grassroots organizing. As a union organizer, I dealt with the catch-22 of organizing like this: My colleagues and I would visit all the natural leaders in a workplace at their homes individually, asking each one, "If most of the natural leaders in your workplace were pro-union and agreed to come to a meeting to consider organizing, would you come?" Most said yes, because our question was conditional on everyone else coming. After having that conversation and getting the "yes" from everyone, we'd then go back and report to each one individually that everyone else had also said yes, give them the date for the meeting and they'd all show. But that process took months, even just for a small facility.

The Internet takes the place of that organizer driving from house to house and having all those individual conversations, by allowing the natural leaders to communicate with each other all and once and anonymously. Online, in those days after the election, I watched the same process I used to organize unions take place—but without an organizer. Using the Internet, people were able to drive the process themselves—and to do it at warp speed.

---

42. Look for the CyberUnion Label

Thomas James Katona

The importance of organizing is emphasized as strongly as possible in the straight-forward essay below, with answers offered to such questions as:

- *How vital is a full-time webmaster? When can a pro bono volunteer from the ranks (or from among the teenagers of members) suffice?*

- *Is there any reward from creating multiple Web sites?*
- *Why should unionists be adding their URL to their business cards?*
- *How can a site best appeal to the unorganized?*
- *What sort of information age, "new economy" types might labor try now to unionize—and how?*

Above all, note the upbeat attitude: Confidence that the job can *be done plays a big part in assuring that it does get done!*

Many years ago I remember being mesmerized by some of the commercials that used to pop up on television. One of the jingles that sticks in my mind almost thirty years after first hearing it was the famous song sung by members of the old International Ladies Garment Workers Union (ILGWU), a song that urged Americans to "Look for the union label."

Sadly, unions don't advertise on the television anymore. That may not be such a bad thing. While the cost of television advertising is extremely expensive, it can be argued that television is no longer destined to be considered the major way in which people seek and receive news and information. Or entertainment for that matter. Therefore, television advertising may be a waste of scarce resources.

The Internet will soon overtake TV as the primary electronic medium. The majority of individuals will seek news, information, and entertainment through it. The number of Americans connected to the Web increases every year. Among union members, it is estimated that over 60 percent now have Internet access in their homes. I suspect that a great number more have it at work.

If this figure and these trends are to be believed, it's time for unions to start "advertising" on this medium. It's time for unions to tell people to "look for the CyberUnion label." Such a concentrated effort could be the driving force in presenting labor's message. The labor movement needs to accomplish this in four particular different ways.

1. First, and most basically, international and local unions need to establish a presence on the Internet. Every union, from the largest international, to the smallest local needs to have an e-mail address and a Web site.

If you are a large, well-funded international union or an affluent local, why not do what many other organizations have done and hire a full-time webmaster? Many labor organizations, as well as most large corporations, have created one or more full-time positions devoted to developing and maintaining an Internet presence. Prime examples include the AFL-CIO, the UAW, and a dozen other large unions. These experts can create and maintain a state-of-the-art Web site.

If you are not so affluent, establishing a Web presence need not be a costly venture. There are still some free site-hosting services out there. Just about every group these days has someone who can post a page. If yours does not, designate someone who is willing to learn and send them to a training course. Web design is not difficult and many community colleges offer low-cost courses.

Another inexpensive solution is to hire a high school kid to design and maintain your site. I learned how to do Web pages after observing my teenagers creating them. I figured, if they can do it, I can too! An additional benefit to this approach is that you are able to educate a young person about the benefits of unions. They will, without a doubt, tell their friends about their new project and soon the friends will visit the site. Hopefully, many young people will visit, and perhaps a few will become interested in the labor movement.

2. After you create a site for your union, consider creating another one about a union-related topic. It could be a local historical event, labor poetry, or some other labor-related topic. People often "surf" the Web for entertainment, seeking out unique and interesting sites.

Here's an example: I created a Web site for a local event in labor history that was fading away into the mists of time. In less than two years, the Italian Hall Disaster Web site (www.ih1913.eg.st) had over 1,100 hits! That's close to three visits per day. I hope that the site not only helped to preserve the memory of this event, but also that it was able to lift the consciousness of at least a few of the visitors. Naturally, the site carries the union label. Make sure your sites do, too.

3. A third way in which unions need to more fully utilize this new medium is in regard to organizing. The Internet offers tremendous opportunity to generate results in recruitment of new members. Additionally, it can be used for internal organizing and mobilization of existing members.

I would strongly recommend that every union Web site have an organizing page as part of the overall site, in addition to a union label. While Web sites will never replace the traditional organizing tactic of the home visit, they can certainly augment them. After such a visit, give the individual your business card with your URL on it. Tell them to consider what you have talked about and to check your site for additional information. The page should make a variety of resources available to potential members, including a downloadable, printable sign-up card.

4. Finally, union activists need to turn to the Internet as a vast source of potential new members. This year, the AFL-CIO has set lofty goals of organizing 1 million new members. A union like OPEIU, the Office and Professional Employees International Union, should be able to help meet or exceed these goals, as it has targeted new economy jobs such as engineers, nurses, and technicians. OPEIU is also at the forefront of organizing guilds for

independent contractors and workers who cannot collectively bargain under state or federal laws.

My point is that if the labor movement is to grow, it needs to start looking at the new economy and the types of jobs it is creating. In essence, this new economy is creating two distinct types of jobs. The first is the low-end service-based job. Service Employees International Union (SEIU) has done an excellent job in organizing this type of work. Especially notable is the Justice for Janitors campaign.

But what about at the high end of the scale? How about the hundreds of thousands of jobs where people work at home, telecommute, or toil as highly skilled independent contractors? Computers in general, and the Internet in specific, have created new jobs to be organized in new ways.

Web design and the corollary tasks that accompany it are prime examples of these jobs. Webmasters work independently, posting data and information in a creative manner. In many ways their job can be seen as sort of a "cyberprinter." The difference is that many print shops are organized. How many webmasters are? Unfortunately, very few.

The HTML Writers Guild is not a labor organization at all. It provides training courses, software, and resources for its members. Nonetheless, over 125,000 webmasters have joined it! Sadly, to date, no AFL-CIO union has tried to organize this group.

In sum, labor organizations need to start utilizing cyber-resources in a very serious way. They need to use the technology to get our message across. Further, they need to use the technology to build strong internal organizations. Last but not least, they need to organize cyberworkers into new and innovative organizations that reflect labor's goals and values. Just as the ILGWU urged people to "look for the union label," today's modern labor organizations need to urge people to look for the CyberUnion label.

———

43. The WashTech/CWA Project: A Work in Progress

Danielle D. van Jaarsveld

> *We are using Microsoft's technology to organize Microsoft's workers.*
> —Marcus Courtney, WashTech/CWA organizer

If organized labor is to make fresh organizing gains in the early twenty-first century, some should come in the high-profile matter of high-tech workers—

a type notoriously hard for unions to draw into membership. Thanks, however, to some very creative efforts on the West Coast, labor has new confidence it may slowly and steadily gain even in this hard-to-reach and resistant sector of the workforce.

Note especially answers below to such questions as:

- *What motivates "new economy" workers to consider unionizing?*
- *What is permatemping, and how does it bear on organizing?*
- *How do major IT firms oppose organizing?*
- *What part are established unions playing in organizing new economy workers?*
- *How might an "electronic community" best be created among new economy workers?*

Transferable lessons from the ongoing exciting and creative West Coast organizing campaign discussed below warrant close attention from all those eager to help bring a special type of information age employee into labor's ranks.

Founded in 1998, the Washington Alliance of Technology Workers (WashTech/CWA) is a fascinating and highly instructive example of how technological tools can be used both to organize and service high-technology workers. While some of the Alliance methods may not be immediately useful to unions whose members presently have little access to computers, access across industries steadily increases. Accordingly, WashTech/CWA's campaign to represent workers at Microsoft and Amazon.com offers valuable lessons for labor's future.

As well, the existence of the Alliance has importance beyond its innovative use of technological tools. It challenges the notion that collective representation is irrelevant for high-tech workers because they allegedly have neither economic nor noneconomic reasons to organize. On the contrary, the "new economy" workers in the Alliance decided to form WashTech/CWA for "old economy reasons": low benefits coverage, low wages, and lack of respect and voice in the workplace.

Background

WashTech/CWA's main constituency at its inception consisted of Microsoft workers known as agency contractors (people with such job titles as 3D artists, accountants, content coordinators, graphic designers, programmers/

writers, technical writers, and Web developers). Microsoft referred to them as temporary workers because they were hired through temporary employment agencies. Many, however, referred to themselves as permatemps, since their assignments could last for years. In 2000 approximately 35 percent of Microsoft's high-skilled workforce (6,800 workers nationwide) were agency contractors, and roughly 5,326 of those workers were located in the Seattle area.

As the workers were assigned to Microsoft by temporary employment agencies, the agencies were considered the primary employer. The agencies were responsible for the administration of wages and benefits, which could range from health benefits to training stipends. In exchange, the agencies charged each worker a fee that was deducted from their paycheck.

Five especially stressful aspects of the relationship between Microsoft, the temporary employment agencies, and the workers—stressors that can be expected to take a comparable toll elsewhere in the labor force early in the twenty-first century—convinced some of the agency contractors to seek collective representation.

First, the temporary employment agencies angered workers by not disclosing information to them about how much the agencies were charging Microsoft for their services. Also, the agencies included noncompetition clauses in some employment agreements that discouraged a worker's mobility across agencies.

Second, agency contractors, because of permatemping, often found themselves performing many of the same functions as full-time Microsoft employees, although their compensation was quite different. The disparity in wages and benefits that existed between the agency contractors and the full-time employees was a source of considerable frustration.

Third, before Microsoft required agencies to offer workers a minimum standard of benefits, agency contractors complained about the differences in benefits packages across the agencies. Also, they could not move to the agencies that offered better benefits because of the noncompetition clauses included in their employment agreements.

Fourth, many agency contractors felt that Microsoft policies were designed to treat agency contractors like second-class citizens. They were prohibited from attending morale-building events and from shopping at the company store. They were required to wear a stigmatizing orange badge, designating them as contingent workers, rather than a blue one (full-time).

Fifth, in 1997, the Washington State Department of Labor and Industries enacted a rule that eliminated overtime for computer professionals who earned more than $27.63 per hour. The fury generated by this issue helped unite high-skilled contingent workers and highlighted the absence of a "voice" for them. Because many of these workers, such as the Microsoft agency contractors, were classified as temporary workers, WashTech/CWA could not follow a traditional collective bargaining strategy to represent them. The Alliance had to be creative in its campaign to attract membership.

Strategies

E-mail is a powerful tool for organizers, and it can be easier for organizers to get access to e-mail addresses as opposed to phone numbers. Many workers e-mailed the Department of Labor and Industries to protest the elimination of overtime. Organizers obtained e-mails and were able to create a list of contacts. The content convinced the organizers that working conditions in the high-tech industry were not satisfactory.

WashTech/CWA also uses a list server with 2,000 registered members to spread information about legislative changes affecting contingent workers, Microsoft policy changes, general industry news, and meetings to discuss concerns about the industry. The Alliance distributes its newsletter, *WashTech-News*, through its list server (washtech-news@lists.speakeasy.org).

The Alliance's Web site, www.washtech.org, receives 80,000 hits per month. This has enhanced its ability to keep the workforce informed and educated about the benefits of collective representation. The Alliance administers Web-based surveys and maintains a "digital bulletin board," an opportunity for workers to voice their opinions on topics of interest. As nonmembers have access to much on the Web site, this helps attract new members. Workers can join online via a membership form.

Typical of the information shared on the Web site is this excerpt:

> After coming together as an all-volunteer organization for 8 months, WashTech affiliated with the *Communications Workers of America (CWA)*, an organization of 600,000 other information industry workers. This alliance provides all WashTech members with valuable resources, including legal advice and connections with similar organizations nationwide.
>
> For specific workplace issues, we come together in localized groups. For broader issues, we research public policy and industry trends and work with national and government groups to make sure high-tech workers have a place at the table when decisions are made. We are democratically run and driven by the issues, creativity, and volunteer energy of our membership.

Contact us at (206) 726–8580 or e-mail us at contact@washtech.org to learn more about establishing a WashTech chapter at your company.

Controversial Move

While the use of e-mail and their Web site are an integral component of WashTech/CWA's organizing strategy, the use of the Internet also has its downside. For example, the use of the Internet facilitates the appearance of free riders. The Alliance has encountered reluctance to become dues-paying members among workers who frequently visit its Web site.

In an attempt to encourage more workers to sign up, the Alliance decided to create a members-only section. Prior to this it had gained access to agency billing rates, the amount agencies charged client firms for workers. Because this information is so valuable to agency workers, WashTech/CWA staff members thought disclosing it only to its members would encourage nonmembers to join. In fact, it seems to have stirred some backlash of resentment against this exclusivity and may not have earned many new memberships.

Cultural and Employer Problems

Reluctance to join, in part, is related to anti-union sentiment among certain high-tech workers. Many think of themselves as individualists and eschew any and all collective projects—a mind-set labor will struggle to alter for decades to come. The Alliance is fully aware of the challenge, and continues to study, test, and improve counteracting strategies.

In addition, high-tech firms exhibit significant levels of resistance to unionization, and, not surprisingly, use technological tools to thwart WashTech/CWA's efforts. Microsoft, for example, administered its own Web-based surveys to agency contractors to better understand reasons why workers would be seeking collective representation.

Summary

Many lessons can be drawn from WashTech/CWA's ongoing project. Its organizers, through their creative and custom-tailored use of computer power, have built solidarity among the members, conducted valuable research, informed both members and nonmembers, mobilized their supporters, and created an "electronic community" for a workforce more accustomed to anomic work conditions and exploited work lives. While the Alliance target is a workforce wedded to computers, its strategies instruct in how the Internet can be used to facilitate the organizing of any and all types of workers.

---

44. Plugged In, Turned On Unionism

John Klusinske

*How might labor leverage the interactive power of the Internet for new orga-
nizing gains? The essay below offers three action possibilities, three unusual
models for a labor movement more computer-savvy than ever before. Attention is called to virtual union meetings, to a local labor market intervention
plan, and to representation of workers without a contract or recognition.*

*Controversial and complex, the three reforms nevertheless deserve seri-
ous consideration lest our organizing strategies, prepared as they were in
pre-Information Age years, continue to focus on "building sandcastles where
the tide washes in and out."*

Surveys of workers always show support for unions at a significantly higher
rate than that of unionization. What sort of labor movement could take in all
who wish to belong? How might new uses of computers make *the* critical
difference?

The key is interactivity. For example, union members in a new computer-
sensitive labor movement could design and post screen savers on a union
Web site that could be downloaded during contract bargaining. This would
be the electronic equivalent of workers making their own signs for an informational picket—except that computer technology would enhance the effect
in time, space, and location.

A computer-sensitive movement has at least three major models on which
to draw. One suggests a cyberspace remedy for lousy attendance at local
union meetings. A second suggests a computer-modeling way to control wages
in a local labor market. And a third points up a computer-enabled approach
to reaching millions of unorganized workers by redefining what membership means—and how dues might be collected. All three models require pragmatic but also creative use of computer power—and all three cannot be tried
soon enough.

1. Launching the "Meeting"

The National Writers Union, a subset of the United Auto Workers, is a virtual union. It addresses setting working standards and advocacy for writers

in a very different fashion than do traditional unions. Chapters may be formed wherever members want to associate—regardless of industry or craft lines—for their mutual benefit or to more effectively support the national common interest, as in dealing with copyright questions. No meeting halls exist, and no mandatory attendance is expected at monthly meetings. Instead, there is an expectation of thoughtful participation in extensive cyberspace dialogue. When lobbying on critical items for writers, such as copyright law, there is no need to convert snail-mail–paced tradition to electronic e-mail speed; this union already functions that way.

2. Modeling the Desirable

Another much older, but still relevant model is that of the sheet metal workers in the early industrial age around the San Francisco region. A union hiring hall was run, which is nothing unusual. What was special is that the union set the rates rather than bargain them. Through the union, the members hired economists to figure out the highest rate of compensation that would not result in an influx of sheet metal workers, and thereby lower the market rate of compensation.

With powerful new computers, this consequential sort of economic modeling is made all the easier and stronger—local unions could adopt this model anywhere and in nearly any industry. Of course this model did eventually fail its previous trial because it was not expanded in response to competitive pressures. That points out that the more dynamic the model and the potential for success, the more important it becomes to continue to organize.

3. Going for Those "Others"

Central labor councils offer a third model to build on. At present, only area AFL-CIO–affiliated local unions are entitled to participation, leaving the great mass of area workers on the outside looking in. CLCs could instead directly invite in millions of workers who support unions, but do not currently have representation. Their very reduced dues could be deducted through electronic funds transfer authorizations that are as efficient as bargained dues deduction. Internet-based communications via e-mail and/or list servers could make up for geographic and bureaucratic distances and related obstacles. The opportunity here to increase labors' political effectiveness is obvious and enormous.

Representation for workers without recognition or a contract could focus on noncontract matters, at least initially. Rights under discrimination laws, the Americans with Disabilities Act, state workers compensation laws, the Occupational Health and Safety Act—all could be a starting point. Living-wage campaigns across the country can also help labor tap into diverse and sparsely connected worker pools, dealing as these campaigns do with building coalitions and following a legislative strategy.

At the point where a strategically sufficient number of workers in any employment demographic commit to upholding a union standard of compensation and working conditions, the employers of those employees would have to choose between not having enough employees or going through a CLCs Web site for employees such as www.UnionHiringHall.org. When already-in-place employees would be approached to join in to get or lock in union standards for themselves, the case for joining in would have already been made.

Of course, such a dramatic strategy would cause a major backlash of employer opposition in the media, in politics, and in the legal system *if* momentum was gained. The beauty of a flexible worker-based union operating by Web site and e-mail would be that political and consumer actions would be as easily facilitated as would union actions. Structuring UnionHiringHall.org in a fashion similar to temporary help agencies and employee stock ownership plans could provide legal shelter. It would be critical to continue to organize to eliminate wages as a basis for competition and to have the anticipation and initiative to do so effectively. In a dot com world unionism could zoom up or down much as have companies.

Summary

The only way for the labor movement to outrace the pace of electronic commerce is to be there first by having workers in union membership before hiring. Building static reactive site- and enterprise-based organizations, as with today's labor unions, and expecting them to forever deal effectively with newly virtual and transitory enterprises (the kind the economy is moving toward) is like building sandcastles where the tide washes in and out.

A union movement based on workers rather than on enterprises is the alternative. The AFL-CIO—with its computer-savvy Organizing Institute focusing on organizing first and the question of which international union second—shows the way.

Needed elements for redefining the movement and advancing a computer-sensitive approach already exist, for example, untapped support among the populace. The opportunity to go "virtual." The opportunity to use computer-modeling. And the opportunity to convert CLCs into mass-organizing instruments.

Computers are the indispensable tools to compile, analyze, and communicate ever better information and ideas more efficiently. That ability can enable the labor movement to be based directly on a relationship to workers rather than in connection with and dependent upon workers and employers. The opportunity afforded through joining worker, consumer, and citizen power should not be missed. As business increasingly tries to reshape our world through its computers, labor's best chance is to commit to doing so better and faster.

Epilogue: And Tomorrow?

Let your watchword be: Union and progress,
and until then, no surrender.
—Samuel Gompers, labor leader

Early in 2000 union activist friends, many of them former students of mine, helped by persistently asking three guiding question: "Why a handbook? Who are you to do it? And who is it for?" In the summer of 2001, on learning I had finally sent the manuscript to the publisher, they followed up by asking: "What do you think you accomplished?"

I'd like to think seven things: First, I managed to get forty-nine very busy and very knowledgeable people to share some very good tips and tricks for improving labor's use of computer power. Many have never published elsewhere, save perhaps in cyberspace, and all have always deserved the largest possible audience.

Second, I surrounded their essays with some action-oriented recommendations of my own. This enabled me to highlight the sort of cutting-edge possibilities not common to labor dialogue, and thereby challenge readers to "think outside of the box."

Third, I highlighted the transferable lessons American labor can take from nonlabor organizations and the world of labor overseas (with its 2,700 labor Web sites) (Freeman and Diamond 2001). This enabled me to dismiss the orthodoxy that says, "If it was not invented here, we are not interested." In its place I urged use of the widest possible scanning and the most creative possible adaptation of field-tested and even blue-sky ideas.

Fourth, I highlighted some exemplary labor Web sites and list servers, even while urging upgrades in the best. I suggested specific assessment criteria and, with the help of several volunteer assessors, made public the first-ever rating system and scores for AFL-CIO affiliates (see the closing essay of the volume, deliberately placed there as ballast, and also as a prod to further progress).

Fifth, I raised the possibility that computer-use impacts may be a matter of kind, rather than merely degree: Fundamental changes may be possible, some of which appear long overdue. New grants of power to an informed membership, new forms of lifelong education for eager union staffers, new techniques for invigorating union democracy, and new tools for bolstering negotiation and strike power—all these and more reach deep to help labor reinvent itself for an information age. (See, in this connection, the essay by Peter Lewis that immediately follows.)

Sixth, I packaged everything in a mood of optimism, predicated on my conviction that a critical transformation is under way and *will* be achieved. I emphasized the indispensability of imagination, the rightness of risk taking, the value of lessons garnered from setbacks, the resiliency of labor and its members, and the magical power of an empowering vision, in this case, that of the CyberUnion.

And finally, I made a case throughout for unions and locals going beyond today's best standard (the Cyber Gain model) and pressing on toward another that makes far more of computer-use possibilities (the CyberUnion model) (Shostak 1999).

Naturally, there is far more I could have attempted and far more I wish I had covered. Additional attention is owed, for example, to expanded "peoplepower" features of the AFL-CIO's Working Families e-activist Network (www.aflcio.org), especially features to promote "online activism with an off-line impact." Similarly, an innovative portal of the National Education Association expects to soon have 400 credit-earning courses taught by members in its higher education bargaining units, thereby creating both job opportunities and providing job advancement at the same time. In five years the NEA expects to be cosponsoring 4,000 courses per year with as many as 200,000 students.

And, as if these gains were not encouraging enough, a pioneering list server for union webmasters gets greater use and proves more useful all the time (contact linda@cybersolidarity.com). Attention is also being paid to the possibility of creating one's own Internet service provider, as did Hawaii's HGEA/AFSCME in 1995 (see www.hgea.org). Finally, the TAGS system (technology assisted group solutions) of the Federal Mediation and Conciliation Service, a remarkable computer-based system, is winning acclaim for helping unionists conduct shorter, more productive, problem-focused meetings (http://tags.fmcs.gov).

Time, however, grows short, and a warranted sense of urgency courses through this handbook. A leading information technology research firm keeps a list of U.S. industries ranked by the speed at which they are adopting information technology (Gower 2001). Unless and until organized labor ranks as highly as the industries with which it deals, if not higher, the well-being of working men and women will be in greater jeopardy than is good for them . . . and for other Americans as well (elites and business types included).

Thanks to their FIST orientation, CyberUnions hold out the potential to rapidly end labor's uneven and suboptimum use of computer power, and to replace it with something quite extraordinary. CyberUnions replace a narrow "putting out fires" orientation with a longer futures perspective, one that extends five and ten years beyond it. They replace shopworn communication tools (newsletters, mailings, etc.) with high-tech innovations (e-mail for all, list servers for many). They replace yesteryears' services with a broader and better range. And they replace hollow observances of union traditions with wholehearted celebrations; for example, a local's history and traditions might be "captured" in a memorable CD-ROM valued by all.

Changes like these, changes in kind rather than only in degree, should help put labor unions on a par with the very creative, powerful, and driven cybercorps rapidly coming their way. They should enable Americans to think of unions, and not just corporations, when the public thinks about successful, cutting-edge twenty-first–century organizations.

Changes like these should send the message that labor is finally and actually "with it!"—a message of import for the union's potential and actual membership, the media, the public, and the business community alike. They should empower the rank and file as never before. They should invigorate adapters, inspire the membership, favorably impress potential members, intimidate opponents, win over vote-seekers, and in 101 other valuable ways, significantly bolster labor's chances.

Accordingly, the two essays with which the handbook closes look both forward and also around: The first raises fundamental questions about the wisest core focus of organized labor and suggests it be workers per se, rather than organizations of workers. Ways are suggested for using computer power to alter and improve labor's focus. The second looks about and finds the quality of labor's Web sites impressive and encouraging. Ways are suggested for making even more of the matter.

In sum, I would like to believe this handbook will help a cadre of users move their Cyber Naught unions and locals off of the staring line. Help a cadre of users get their Cyber Drift unions and locals on course. Help a cadre of users push the envelop where their Cyber Gain unions and locals are involved, and help everyone in organized labor (and legions of outside allies) begin to give the still distant, but very attainable, CyberUnion model the field test it merits.

References

Freeman, Richard, and Wayne Diamond, as quoted in Robert Taylor, p. 3.

Gower, Timothy. "IT to the ER, Stat!" www.Economy. com, April, 2001, p. 99.

Shostak, Arthur B. *CyberUnion: Empowering Labor Through Computer Technology.* Armonk, NY: M.E. Sharpe, 1999.

Taylor, Robert. "Trade Unions: Workers Unite on the Internet," *Financial Times*, May 11, 2001.

----

45. Unions and the Web: Where to Now?

Peter Lewis

Where next? Perhaps a wise course would be back to the beginning, to labor's sound origins in the desire people have to work together on matters of mutual concern. But to make gains in this way is to first confront and best a tendency that unions everywhere have to merge, grow big, and turn distant . . . a tendency to grow away from, rather than toward the membership.

The essay below offers a bold idea for how to help labor regain its focus on the genuine needs of the rank and file, whether traditional or new economy members: "If trade unions are serious about connecting with workers, I think it is time they started developing Web presences to match the needs of their members, rather than just reflecting the structure of the institution. I'm talking Web sites based on the nature of a particular job, rather than the institution."

Readers of this handbook who grasp the strategic opportunity the Internet affords for involving workers in a new type of unionism will see in the essay a possibility worth creative and "Can do!" attention.

The Story So Far . . .

I've spent the past three years working inside the Australian trade union movement, attempting to build an online presence. I came into the scene as a journalist excited by the possibilities of this new technology to deliver new types of information. In a country where the mass media is dominated by a couple of media dynasties, it has been increasingly difficult for trade unions to have a say. The Web has given the labor movement a wonderful opportunity to reach its membership and the general public, unfiltered by commercial interests and priorities.

Through the New South Wales Labor Council—a state-based peak union body—significant advances have been made in creating a space for trade unions in cyberspace. Workers Online, a weekly online e-zine, has established itself as the most popular political Web site in the country. Union officials, activists, and members can get an overview of the issues driving the movement in any given week, providing the forum for synergies to develop across industries. The e-zine has also become an important primary news source for journalists—who not only follow stories broken on Workers Online, but report on comment and opinion mediated through the site.

But probably the most enduring impact of Workers Online has been the way it has shown union leaders that they can create an online culture for their membership—provided they have the right tools and the appropriate content. The discipline of putting a message out every week creates a demand for activity that creates its own momentum. Trade unions are learning that creating an online culture is an important part of developing a modern trade union presence.

What We Do Well

The Web has a natural fit with the labor movement because it is driven by the same concept that has always sustained us. It is a network builder. Trade unions emerged because people were motivated to work together to promote their mutual interests. For the last 100 years these networks have deepened and strengthened between working people. Through industrial campaigns, political activism, and international solidarity the ties between workers have become ingrained. Even in an era where consultants are paid huge fees to break the union, the culture continues to resonate among large numbers of working people.

The companies that rose and fell on the Internet bubble were, in essence, trying to do overnight what we had done in 100 years. They went out and raised capital on the promise of creating a network of people who would use a particular technology, application, or service. Largely, they fell because it soon became apparent that, while the new technology makes any network conceptually possible, it takes more to actually consolidate that potential into a real culture.

In contrast, the trade unions that have made the transition to cyberspace have found it fits neatly with traditional functions. Communications between officials, between delegates, activists and rank-and-file members have been enhanced by e-mail lists, Web-to-fax applications, and even Web to SMS.

Online journals like Workers Online give information in real time to members. And online forms that target political decision makers by generating multiple e-mail postings to groups of politicians provide a new political lobbying tool that makes it easy for rank-and-filers to participate in campaigns. The Web is also emerging as a potent campaigning tool; in a recent campaign for workers compensation the Web became *the* mainstream story when members of Parliament who opposed the legislation were named on the site.

So looking at the reasonably limited applications to debate, there's no denying that unions are the type of network organizations that should not only make a smooth transition to the Internet, but also will gain much from its enabling technologies.

The Curse of the Industrial Age

The big problems trade unions face in Australia (and no doubt internationally) is that they have become institutions in their own right. A recent survey of young people found that they saw trade unions as part of the power structure—sitting alongside bosses and the state as instruments of power. The irony is that the workers' structure has become so entrenched that they are now seen as "them" rather than as "us."

In Australia this has been extenuated by a policy of amalgamations through the 1990s that has resulted in a number of superunions, all struggling to forge an identity out of the myriad of smaller unions that had been previously created. In Australia, think trade unions and you think an acronym—you have the CFMEU (Construction, Forestry, Mining, and Energy Union), the CEPU (Communications, Electrical, and Plumbing Union) and ALHMWU (Australian Liquor, Hospitality, and Miscellaneous Workers Union) and, my favorite, the SDA (Shop, Distributive, and Allied Employees Association). Other unions have managed tighter identification, such as the Finance Sector Union (FSU) and the Australian Services Union (ASU), but even here the unions are often a group of disparate branches. In my state alone, each of the three separate divisions of the ASU has its own separate Web site.

What does this mean for workers? Even where trade unions have established a Web presence, the Web presence revolves around the institution, rather than the worker. Visit your average trade union Web-page and you are more likely to see a photo of the national secretary than you are to find any relevant information about your working life. Even relatively advanced Web sites tend to trumpet "union victory," "union does this," "union opposes that," rather than focus on the practical working needs of its membership.

It's the Workers, Stupid

If trade unions are serious about connecting with workers, I think it is time they started developing Web presences to match the needs of their members, rather than reflecting the structure of the institution. I'm talking Web sites based on the nature of a particular job, rather than the institution. The trade union should be the sponsor of these sites—and would be responsible for the industrial information on the site.

But I see a broader opportunity for trade unions to provide the online cultural space for groups of workers. A hotel workers Web space, for instance, would clearly have relevant information on pay rates, conditions, and health and safety issues.

But it would also have a place for members to share info on where they go after work for a drink, what training is available to move within and outside the industry, even tips on where to get their tax done. It may also include members-only chat facilities where members can unload after work—not necessarily to be used in an industrial sense—more as personal therapy. (Taxi drivers are one group that I think would take to this type of initiative.)

The first signs of this workers-over-union strategy are beginning to appear in Australia. Call Central is one attempt to provide a space for call center workers—covered by a myriad of unions that few care to join—and incorporates news, services, and career-related information. But the site is struggling because of constraints in budget to provide ongoing content. The ALHMWU has also attempted to build specialist subsites for both casino workers and childcare workers.

My organization, the Labor Council, is also endeavoring to go down this track through the establishment of an IT Workers Alliance Web site. The idea is to make the site noninstitutional. Information and space will be provided for members of existing trade unions as well as people who have never been in a union, to—over time—generate their own online culture and create their own issues. The concept is what I am advocating: Sponsor the site as a trade union, but do not constrain the space to the organization or the industrial domain.

Too Much to Gain

Of course, for this strategy to work, the old barriers of political alliances, turf wars, and power plays need to be subjugated. Membership communications are still closely guarded assets by ruling cabals, who see the sharing of this information as an invitation to challenge their leadership. But tempering these dangers may potentially lead to the creation of an environment where trade unionism again plays a central role in a worker's life by providing an online space to supplement the work they do on the ground.

We've come full circle. For most of the last century industrialism isolated people and fragmented communities. Now that same industrialism has spawned a new technology that offers some hope of a better way of existing. People may not necessarily go out to meetings that have a community benefit, but they can still collaborate to create their own forms of public participation.

By developing a Web presence and doing it smart—in a way that connects with workers on their terms, not ours—we can help speed up this process and place organized labor firmly in the center of a new activism. To do so, unions need to shed their institutional garments and hand the power to their members.

---

46. Labor Web-Site Reviews

G. Peter Shostak, Karen Chamberlain, and Arthur B. Shostak

Thanks to a lot of help from seven volunteers, organized labor has a rich resource below to study and act on. Both experienced webmasters and also union activists eager to launch their first Web site have much to learn from shared site reviews, a tool all too rare in labor circles (more on this in closing). In section 1, a brother of mine, G. Peter Shostak, shares insightful and frank thoughts about several representative sites. Although not a unionist himself, he brings a valuable objectivity, freshness, and sensitivity to the task of evaluating the sites much as a prospective member might do. (Note also that the first site he reviews is the creation of the author of Chapter 27.)

In section 2, an older returning student, Karen Chamberlain, shares her considered thoughts about sites I asked her to assess. Although not a unionist, like my brother she stands in for many nonunion adults to whom labor's Web sites must appeal.

In section 3, I share feedback from two teams of undergraduate students of mine. They volunteered in the academic year 2000–2001 to assess AFL-CIO union sites, and they used the same ten evaluative questions I posed to Peter and Karen, questions that might serve anyone as a helpful check list for labor Web sites:

1. *Was the site clear? Could you easily get around?*
2. *Was the site attractive? Did it grab you—hold your interest?*
3. *Was the material very timely, or old and stale?*
4. *Was there a chat room or some space for a member to ask or say anything?*
5. *Do you have the impression a prospective member would find the site impressive? Why or why not?*
6. *Did the graphics include women? Nonwhites? Workers of different ages?*
7. *What links exist from the site? To what other organizations (please list)?*
8. *Was there material identified as available only to members?*
9. *Was the name or e-mail address given for the webmaster?*
10. *What recommendations would you make to improve the site?*

Once again, both old-timers and newcomers alike to the world of Web development and upgrading have much to profit from the thoughts of the young collegians, a type labor must do better with in the years ahead if it is to prosper.

1. Reflections from an Onlooker

G. Peter Shostak

GMP Local 215—February 15, 2001

1. It is not at all difficult to see why GMP Local 238 of Kokomo, Indiana, won the competition for LabourStart's Best Web Site in 2000. The glass, molder, pottery union's home page (www.gmp238.org) is a veritable gold mine of current, useful information for the union member and his or her family. In addition, its links offer the member access to news, weather, sports, and events in the Kokomo area. A one-stop shop for both labor and "no labor" information.
2. Attractive and colorful, the site is easy to navigate, with most major items hyperlinked to additional information. The use of a limited pallet of color makes for a very attractive visual impression.
3. The information appears to be updated daily. What I read dealt with subjects of current and ongoing interest to members. Contract negotiations and organizing were treated as news items.
4. The only disappointment was the lack of a chat room in which mem-

bers could exchange ideas, information, and stories. I was however very pleased to read that one is under development and will be available shortly.

5. I believe a new member would immediately feel at home at this union's Web site and, further, would be made to feel positive about his/her decision to join the union given the information to be found (e.g., benefits) and the impression created by the site for this union local.

6. During my brief visit I saw no graphics representing members. The union logo does present two arms, hands, shaking. They are obviously of different color.

7. Links available take the member to the national and to other locals.

8. There were specific areas dealing with "internal matters"—negotiations and organizing efforts that were available to "members only."

9. No webmaster was identified by name. There was a link for expressing opinions and offering suggestions about the site.

10. With the addition of a chat room (coming soon), I would agree with those who rated this site so highly. It is a wonderful information resource and, no doubt, a source of tremendous pride to the local and its members.

AFT—February 17, 2001

Saturday morning—time for a leisurely visit to the American Federation of Teachers national Web site (www.aft.org). As a new teacher in the public school system of Fort Collins, Colorado, I was very impressed.

1. The visitor is greeted by a bright, colorful content-packed front page. Hyperlinks abound, making movement from the cover stories to additional material available with a click of the mouse.

2. Additional features of the site are clearly labeled and made easily accessible from the first page. Divided into "Features" and "Topics" each of these sections whet the visitor's appetite with easily understood subject identifiers. (I could have spent the rest of the morning working my way through this material.)

3. The information provided not only dealt with the "topics of the day," but also provided thorough and well-developed insights into key policy positions taken by the national. The areas dealt with are timely and of practical application for members. From news and positions of the national union on a variety of issues to "online shopping for the convenience of members," this site has it all.

4. An online chat room provides and encourages interaction between members. As a teacher, I can envision using such a facility to help me with lesson planning on particularly difficult subjects as well as soliciting the opinions of more experienced teachers in approaching issues that confront me every day I enter the classroom environment.

5. I strongly believe that new members to AFT would not only find this site impressive, but a true asset in fulfilling the challenging role of educator.

6. The graphics used on the site's multiple pages were topic specific. Human representation was not used. Instead symbols relevant to the subject area make the information more readily identifiable—dollar signs ($) for finance-related subjects, for example.

7. The links, too numerous to identify here, provide the member with easy access to a number of subject specific areas.

8. I did not notice member-only restrictions on any of the material, but I must admit to not having pursued every subject and link available. Such a visit would have consumed more time than I had available. Such exploration is certainly encouraged during one's first visit.

9. Access to the Web master is a mouse click away. No problem here in getting to the top.

10. I found this site not only informative, but exciting as well. Had time allowed, I could easily have spent a few hours during my first visit. My only recommendation, and it is one I would make to all education-related Web sites, is that more attention be given to the needs of the substitute teacher. This is a growing population of educators upon whom the system will become increasingly dependent as thousands of today's teachers prepare for retirement. I might also suggest that the population of former professionals coming to education for a second career are a rich opportunity for further organizing. Most of us are not union members.

AFSCME—February 18, 2001

I visited the site of the American Federation of State, County, and Municipal Employees (AFSCME) this morning (www.afscme.org). Perhaps due to my thirty years of working in hospitals among the sick and dying, I have always thought of pale pea-soup green in the context of nausea and rigor mortis. With that in mind I was initially turned off by the overwhelming green appearance of this otherwise wonderful national Web site.

This is the first site visited with "people graphics" and they were appropriately quite diverse in the population presented. Perhaps even more significant, this is the first site found to have an "*En Español*" link on the front page. While I am sure others must include this recognition of their Hispanic membership, this is the first I have found in my tour of sites.

This is an easily navigated, excellent information-packed resource that is bound to have tremendous appeal to the national, local, and personal interests of its membership. The material presented was important and timely. It included news of a recent contract acceptance by one local's membership and the victory of another local in gaining recognition as the bargaining agent for a public school district's teachers.

In addition, features such as a Stewards Handbook, and a Financial Standards Code, are available at the click of the mouse. Of special note was the opportunity to enter one's zip code and thereby be provided with a link for direct communication via e-mail with one's congressman. While there was no obvious chat room, there was a direct link to the webmaster, and to the national. A state-by-state list of locals is also provided to facilitate communication.

I have no doubt this site would be very attractive and impressive as a source of information by both new and long-standing members of AFSCME. The calendar with its important dates to remember will keep involved members coming back on a monthly basis.

My only recommendation regarding this site is to do away with the green and adopt a color more representative of this union's vibrant personality.

SEIU Local 715—February 26, 2001

The Service Employees International Union Web site (www.seiu.org) was strange. One is greeted with a purple on purple color scheme with flashes of yellow. Easter? Gay stuffed animals? (Some time ago the Reverend Jerry Falwell objected to the color purple as an intrusion of the gay movement into children's toys.)

Then there is the question of what is the real message of this local? Are they a part of a unified labor movement or an angry splinter local out to make their own name? The interested reader is no doubt captured by the boldly declared Vision Statement and the follow-up piece, "The Situation We Face." For the casual visitor it is a very wordy presentation not likely to capture an audience. Pictures of a diverse membership involved in union-related actions flash across the top of the screen, creating momentary interest. There are no descriptions of the pictures, so the interest level subsides as the clips repeat themselves.

The rather negative statements about the current "situation" surrounding organized labor are very provocative. This position taken by a local is problematic for me. They identify "declining real wages, assaults on health workers, increased racism, sexism and homophobia, loss of jobs to overseas" as the primary causes for the decline in strength of organized labor. A decline of 14 percent, according to this local.

They then go on to suggest this is due to labor leadership that is not always accountable or effective. Finally they note that leadership has not always reflected the diversity of the membership.

Reading between the lines, I heard that "we" (members of local 715) are the answer to these problems, although there was no strong evidence presented to demonstrate that.

On a brighter note, the site included direct access to the Chief Steward, who had a password-controlled page. I was also impressed by well-done Question and Answer presentations throughout the site. Although there was a "News" page, I was unable to get it to download. I experienced the same difficulty with a page entitled "Side Show," which opened with great music but then failed to download its images.

All in all, I found this site confusing. What are they trying to accomplish? If it is to embarrass their national and its leadership, I would say they are off to a strong start. If, however, they are a part of a national movement trying to demonstrate solidarity with the rest of organized labor, this one visitor believes a change in direction will be required.

CAW, TCA—February 27, 2001

At my brother Art's suggestion, I went to the site of the Canadian Auto Workers Union (CAW, TCA): www.caw.ca. The ambience of the cover page (created by the colors used) gives one the feeling that they are entering the lobby of a very upscale hotel. This is a class act. The visitor is immediately invited to select an English or French version of the text that follows. It's a real nice touch. (Perhaps nationals here in the United States might offer the same to their Hispanic and Asian members.)

The next feature to catch your eye is a moving line of text containing the headlines of news and feature articles contained in this edition. These serve as hyperlinks to the full stories. I was also impressed to find a number of book reviews recommending books to the membership for their reading pleasure, education, and entertainment.

The remainder of the page may not be as catchy as some other sites I have visited, but the easy-to-use specialized pull-down menus offered on a variety of subjects made it difficult to leave, without checking out what's available. *And*, once you get to the featured material included in these subject-specific areas, you're hooked. The information is presented in an informative and crisp format. The hyperlink menus include News, Newsletters, a Sisterline (a nice feature recognizing the special interests of female members), a membership profile, a photo gallery, e-mail links, and a direct link to the president of the national.

As you can tell, I was very impressed with my first virtual "trip" to Canada. I will no doubt make others. I have got to believe it will be hard to match the positive impression created by the CAW, TCA National Home Page.

2. Reflections from an Onlooker

Karen Chamberlain

The Labour Website of the Year for 2000: www.labourstart.org/lwsoty

1. *Was the site clear?* Yes, it was well organized. *Could you easily get around?* Yes, the table of contents on the left made it easy, but what was especially helpful was the Local 238 message board. *Can you maneuver?* Yes, all pages had a home button, and any link address changes automatically took you to the new site.
2. *Was the site attractive?* Yes, good color scheme. *Did it grab you— hold your interest?* Yes, because the message board mentions that it is an award-winning site, chosen from thirty-seven sites, and there was information to help the nonunion person as well as the union worker.
3. *Was the material very timely, or old and stale?* It was timely material that stated recent activities in newsletters and announcements about benefits, membership, and contracts. The union news dated from 2000 back to 1998.
4. *Was there a chat room or some space for a member to ask or say anything?* They have a labor action network for members only, and they have three ways of contacting them (e-mail, mail, or submit a form). They are launching a new chat group soon on the Kokomo connection part of the site.
5. *Do you have the impression a prospective member would find the site impressive?* Yes. *Why or why not?* Because the site claims to be an online resource center for organizing nonunion workplaces, and union issues are covered in depth for members. It has an article about the higher percentages of union pay opposed to nonunion pay in different industries from 1998. They also had a lot of focus on 401k plans and retirement benefits and recent contract negotiations. There is a grid listing working benefits.

6. *Did the graphics include women? Nonwhites? Workers of different ages?* The logo of two hands shaking seemed as though one was slightly darker than the other, indicating equality. The limited graphics also included clip art of a computer screen on the Kokomo connection, which had men and women of color, to signal equality.

7. *What links exist from the site? To what other organizations (please list)?* The Web resources page had numerous links:

    a) *Web Resources*
       - GMP (Glass, Molder, Pottery) union links
       - The Indiana Educational Conference of the GMP (This site hosts a "Web page forum" for many GMP locals in Indiana.)
       - The GMP International site
       - GMP Local 322 in Auburn, Indiana

    b) *Larry's Labor Links*—These are the favorite labor links of Larry Johnson, GMP Local 238's recording secretary and Internet guru:
       - *www.cybersolidarity.com* is a new, innovative, and well designed site committed to human rights and social justice for workers. It has many features and links—you've got to check it out.
       - *George Meany Center for Labor Studies:* education and training for union members through programs, conferences, and degree programs in labor studies.
       - *www.unionpriv.org* is a new site from the AFL-CIO, providing cost-saving buying programs and services for union members. These programs harness the purchasing power of the 13 million members of the AFL-CIO—this site contains the most comprehensive coverage of key labor issues in the United States.

    c) *LabourStart,* from the United Kingdom, gives you global labor news updated every five minutes—and much more.

    d) *Labor News*, from the publisher of the printed weekly *Labor News* in Indianapolis, is a good site for Indiana and national labor news and more.

    e) *LaborNet*, a great site by folks that support human rights and economic justice for workers.

    f) *Labor Online* is a colorful site that is dedicated to empowering unions through interactive technology.

    g) *www.gpmu.org.uk* is the award-winning Web site of the Printing, Paper, and Media Union representing 200,000 workers in the United Kingdom and Ireland.

h) *Jobs with Justice* is a national campaign for workers' rights and economic justice.

i) *Labor Link*, a gateway to resources related to organized labor, employment law, labor relations, and workplace issues.

j) *Union People Products, Inc.*, with union products (T-shirts, caps, jackets, mugs, etc.) made by union people.

8. *Was there material identified as available only to members?* Only the labor action page. Everything else was accessible.

9. *Was the name or e-mail address given for the webmaster?* I could not find any information about the webmaster.

10. *What recommendations would you make to improve the site?* The newsletter, Kokomo connection, and events page (sometimes called calendar) did not have a table of contents on the left, as the other pages did, which I would include to make the site conform to the same format. Other than that the site was quite accommodating and informative without busy graphics confusing the reader. It was a very involved site as most have become these days, which means you can easily get sidetracked on various links.

http://afge.ibelong.com/afge/html/frameslinks/gc01.html—January 12, 2001

1. *Was the site clear?* Yes. *Could you easily get around?* Yes. The table of contents on the left and the navigational bar at the bottom made this American Federation of Government Employees site negotiable. *Can you easily get around?* Yes. You do need adobe acrobat reader for some bulletins.

2. *Was the site attractive? Did it grab you—hold your interest?* Fairly attractive. It was a bit bland. A membership window flashed in and then left, very annoying.

3. *Was the material very timely, or old and stale?* Timely information regarding news releases, publications, and letters to the editor (2001 back to 1997).

4. *Was there a chat room or some space for a member to ask or say anything?* Maybe in the members-only sections; otherwise, no.

5. *Do you have the impression a prospective member would find the site impressive? Why or why not?* I would think they would be interested in the AFGE local near them, in membership benefits, and in the family fun page. The articles touch on a variety of different agendas. For example: VHA Settles With AFGE; Year 2000—Chock Full of AFGE Accomplishments; Paying Dues Not Necessary for VA

Employees to Participate in Historic Vote; AFGE Moves to Block Contracting Out; Election Directed for Reunification Vote; AFGE Fights for and Wins Annual Pay Raise for VA Nurses—AFGE News Release; AFGE Applauds House Action to Repeal Retirement Tax—AFGE News Release; National President Harnage Testifies About Needlestick Protection for VA Health Care Workers—Congressional Testimony; AFGE Tells Congress: Include Federal Workers at the FEHBP Bargaining Table—AFGE News Release; AFGE's Stance on Contracting Out.

6. *Did the graphics include women? Nonwhites? Workers of different ages?* The logo is a world with a red, yellow, and blue kind of stick figure holding it. There was a graphic with a dark woman and a light male.

7. *What links exist from the site? To what other organizations (please list)?* There is a variety of links: AFGE-related Web sites index, AFGE sites, labor sites, political sites, resource sites, news sites, and membership forms for AFGE 1187 (for federal government employees) and DC277 (for District of Columbia government employees).

8. *Was there material identified as available only to members?* Yes, on the member-only page.

9. *Was the name or e-mail address given for the webmaster?* They have a Website administrator: comments@afge.org. They also had a guest book.

10. *What recommendations would you make to improve the site?* Some of the bulletins would not load, or were slow. I would fix that.

http://afscme.ibelong.com/afscme/html/frameslinks/
gclink01.html—January 12, 2001

1. *Was the site clear?* A large task bar on the left of this American Federation of State, County, and Municipal Employees site was informative. *Could you easily get around?* Yes for the most part. *Can you maneuver?* Some of the pages only had a back button as an option.

2. *Was the site attractive? Did it grab you—hold your interest?* Soft color scheme. Nonintrusive.

3. *Was the material very timely, or old and stale?* Timely news articles (2001 back to 2000).

4. *Was there a chat room or some space for a member to ask or say anything?* Nothing indicated a chat room.

5. *Do you have the impression a prospective member would find the*

site impressive? Why or why not? Yes, because it shows diverse people, and it is also available in Spanish. Worker safety and privatization articles, links to gay rights plus women's rights. There is also a financial standards code page.

6. *Did the graphics include women? Nonwhites? Workers of different ages?* Pictures of all types of race and age groups were prevalent throughout the site, with both genders.

7. *What links exist from the site? To what other organizations (please list)?* The AFSCME Web page has listings of the locals for every state. In addition, there are many links, noted below.

> *Unions on the Web*
>> AFSCME and affiliates; Other U.S. labor unions and associations; International labor unions and associations
>
> *Bargaining Table*
>> Collective Bargaining Reporter; Statistics for Bargaining; Census Data; Public Sector Collective Bargaining Laws
>
> *Classification and Compensation*
>> Private Surveys; National Surveys; State Government
>
> *Corporate Research*
>> Companies; Nonprofit Entities
>
> *Corrections and Law Enforcement Resources*
>> AFSCME Corrections United; Corrections; Federal Agencies; Police; Prison Privatization
>
> *Diversity Resources*
>> General; African American; Hispanic American; Asian American; Native American
>
> *Employee Benefits*
>> General; Health Insurance; Pensions; Flexible Benefits; EAPs; Domestic Partner Benefits
>
> *Employee Testing*
>> Alcohol and Drug Testing
>
> *Federal Government Resources*
>> Indexes, Directories & Publications; Executive Branch; Legislative Branch
>
> *Gay and Lesbian Resources*
>> Workplace Issues; Public Employee Groups; Indexes; Organizations; Transgender Resources
>
> *Healthcare Resources*
>> First Aid; Healthcare Quality; Health Policy; Hospitals; Journals; Managed Care; Medicare; Medicine; Mental Health;

Nursing; Nursing Homes; Physicians

Labor Resources
Federal Agencies; State Agencies; Other Organizations and Publications; Labor Media

Labor Studies
Labor Studies Programs; Archives; Labor History and Culture

Legal Resources
Indexes; Laws and Codes; Labor Law; Public Sector Collective Bargaining Laws; Court Decisions

News and Reference
News, Weather, Sports; Reference; Phone Numbers, Area Codes, Zip Codes; Personal Finance; Language/Writing; Travel and Maps

Occupational Safety/Environmental Resources
General Publications and Indexes; Government Agencies; Groups and Associations; Ergonomics; Bloodborne/Infectious Diseases; Hazardous Materials; Latex Allergy; Workplace Violence; Stress; Environmental Resources

Political News and Information Sources
National News and Information; Campaign Finance; Voting and Political Participation

Privatization Resources
AFSCME Privatization Resources; Prison Privatization

Public Policy
General; Child Welfare; Economy; Education and Head Start; Health Policy; Living Wage; Welfare Reform

Redesigning Government
State and Local Government TQM Programs

Retiree Resources
Indexes; Eldercare/Nursing Homes; Federal Agencies; Legal/Financial Issues; Medicare; Organizations; Social Security; Public Employee Retirement Systems

State and Local Government Resources
Indexes and Directories; Departments of Labor; Public Employee Relations Boards; Public Employee Retirement Systems; Workers' Compensation Divisions; State/Local Government Associations

Women's Resources
General; Equal Pay; Child Care; Family and Medical Leave

Act; Sexual Discrimination and Harassment; Domestic
Violence
Workers' Compensation
General; State Workers' Compensation Divisions

8. W*as there material identified as available only to members?* Mostly
everything is available for the general public.
9. *Was the name or e-mail address given for the webmaster?* Yes:
webmaster@afscme.org There is a webmaster's corner page.
10. *What recommendations would you make to improve the site?* I
think some of the pages that do not have a home button should
be revised.

*http://aft.ibelong.com/cgi-bin/gx.cgi/AppLogic%2bFT
ContentServer?pagename=iBelong/Groups/aft/HomePage—
January 14, 2001*

1. *Was the site clear?* The American Federation of Teachers chose to
use the working families format and not have a true home page.
Could you easily get around? I hit a dead end and could not get back
to the home page when I clicked on student discipline and safety.
Had to start all over. This was a turn-off. *Can you maneuver?* All of
the informational links in the middle of the page under myaft.org
were not complicated.
2. *Was the site attractive? Did it grab you—hold your interest?* Yes,
but the articles were lengthy. The site pages were all text. The pages
loaded very quickly. Cool blue color.
3. *Was the material very timely, or old and stale?* Updated and timely
dealing with various teacher issues. The education week link was
especially informative concerning teachers and their battles with
everything from government to students.
4. *Was there a chat room or some space for a member to ask or say
anything?* No, but you could e-mail them.
5. *Do you have the impression a prospective member would find the
site impressive? Why or why not?* Yes. Some repetition of the articles, but it did have pay issues, as well as benefits. You could even
contact congress to find out how your representatives voted on key
AFT issues and let them know where you stand.
6. *Did the graphics include women? Nonwhites? Workers of different
ages?* No graphics, all text.
7. *What links exist from the site? To what other organizations (please
list)?* Many sites designed for teachers, as well as teacher locals.

8. *Was there material identified as available only to members?* No.
9. *Was the name or e-mail address given for the webmaster?* No, but you could contact the organization by mail, e-mail, or phone.
10. *What recommendations would you make to improve the site?* They could have a home page instead of using the working families page, but I don't know if that would make any difference in their site. Maybe more graphics and condensed articles with the option to read further if you so desire.

www.bmwe.ca/main.htm—January 16, 2001

1. *Was the site clear?* The Brotherhood of Maintenance of Way Employees (BMWE) home page was hard to get to from the working family page. This is a Canadian site in both English and French. *Could you easily get around?* No, there were several home pages. One was under construction. *Can you maneuver?* The different links on the site were not uniform in the layout.
2. *Was the site attractive? Did it grab you—hold your interest?* The pages that had a task bar on the bottom and top were attractive and useful. Nice color scheme. They also had a help page for newcomers to the Internet and their site.
3. *Was the material very timely, or old and stale?* News and information from 2001 back to 1996.
4. *Was there a chat room or some space for a member to ask or say anything?* No, but you could contact various departments with questions.
5. *Do you have the impression a prospective member would find the site impressive? Why or why not?* Yes, because they featured bargaining and retirement updates. They also had a nice article about the trying November 2000 U.S. election outcome. There was information on free HAZMAT training courses. It was general information and didn't seem to be directed toward any of the above.
6. *Did the graphics include women? Nonwhites? Workers of different ages?* Limited graphics of men with shovels and picks.
7. *What links exist from the site? To what other organizations (please list)?* One link page was blank. The other link page had this to offer: "This is our Links area, where you can find out information about other railroad and union related organizations on the World Wide Web. We do consider links to lodges and systems provided they contain no campaigning propaganda. Also, most of these links will take you outside the BMWE Web site, so have fun and come visit us again. Rail-

road Related Links. Safety Related Links. System & Subordinate Lodge Related Links. Union Related Links. Web Related Links."

8. *Was there material identified as available only to members?* Just the members-only page.
9. *Was the name or e-mail address given for the webmaster?* They have a Web-site administrator: webadmin@bmwe.org.
10. *What recommendations would you make to improve the site?* Just try to get to the home page from the working family site better, and fix the construction.

3. Reflections from Undergraduate Students

Arthur B. Shostak

The first team, made up of Adam O'Donnell and Megan Donahue, reported in March 2001 that fifty-five of the AFL-CIO's sixty-seven affiliates had a Web site they could locate and evaluate. (By June, after a merger, the numbers had changed to sixty-one of sixty-five, a rapid change in the right direction!)

The team used a scale of one to five, with one signifying a strong *No!* This allowed them to sort the fifty-five sites into three categories: *Disappointing* (propped up only by the barest of minimums required to hold together a Web site), *Average* (merely a high-tech, top-down "newspaper"), and *Good* (the best available). Employing these categories, the team judged 21 percent of the AFL-CIO union Web sites as *Average* (a score of three). While 13 percent of the sites scored in the *Disappointing* category (six of the fifty-five earned a score of one or two), a far greater number, thirty-seven (or 66 percent) were judged *Good* (a score of four or five). Fourteen (or 25 percent of all) actually earned a score of five!

The team was particularly disappointed that only fourteen of all fifty-five Web sites (25 percent) had some desirable form of a Members-Only section: "A 'virtual water cooler' of sorts for the members of a local and IU where ideas can be freely discussed and debated." And they considered the number of message boards and real-time functionalities "astonishingly low."

The team urged the *Good* sites to go further toward what they dubbed a community-centered model, "something the members would be proud to use as their home page." These sites would encourage the rank-and-file to "have a hand in the creation of what is available on the site . . . participate in conversation with other unionists, submit pictures from their local, and network with other members of the international union from around the country. . . . Imagine having tens of thousands of unionists checking into a Web site daily to collaborate with each other on ideas, being constantly alerted to threats to the union, and always being ready to act."

Despite the high quality of sites in the *Good* category, the team thought none of them yet worthy of the designation "community-centered Web site." To get there from here, the team made five specific recommendations.

First, *employ user feedback forms*. "It consists of static HTML code that drops responses into an e-mail location. Simple to implement, and requiring little Web maintenance, it will help the creators of the Web site keep in touch with the membership."

Second, *employ a review panel*. "A team of representatives, either as a group of volunteers, or elected by the rank-and-file, would revisit the site on a regular basis to provide feedback to the group developing the Web site and its contents. A team of this nature would help to increase awareness of the site's contents and help signify how critical the Web site is to the future of the union."

Third, *employ peer education services*. "Set up a mailing list for webmasters representing the locals so as to allow peer education on how to develop and maintain a top-notch Web site. This would help alleviate time wasted in the learning and relearning of concepts that have already been explored by other webmasters."

Fourth, *create members-only sections*. "The Web sites that are built by unions are not just information brochures for the general public but also gathering places for the rank and file. This is really the goal of a community-centered Web site."

Fifth, *work with the free software movement*. "Although the implementation of a community-centered Web site may seem like a costly investment, . . . it can be implemented for far less than one may expect. The operating system . . . is available to everyone, free of cost. . . . The GNU/Linux operating system is now distributed for free over the Internet or at a low cost from computer stores." (See Part VII in this handbook.)

In all, the student team wound up—as made clear in their oral report to my class—encouraged by progress made to date and inclined to expect even more progress in the near future (their term paper is rich with site-specific terse recommendations for each of the fifty-five sites, available on request).

Three months later, in June 2001, a team of three undergraduate students— Patrick Ehret, Daisy Lau, and Sara Lundblad—employed the same questions and five-point evaluation scheme. They concluded there had in fact been some slight progress in the sixty-one–site picture (up from fifty-five only three months before!), albeit not of a statistically significant magnitude, at least in the right direction.

This team judged as *Disappointing* only 4 percent of fifty-nine accessible AFL-CIO sites, down from 13 percent three months earlier. Three such sites were "not aesthetically pleasing, due to the vast amount of unorganized information displayed. As a result, it was difficult finding the table of contents used to navigate the material within the site. . . . Less than 10 percent did not have any attractive pictures or lacked color. . . . Five percent had links that were obsolete."

Another twelve sites, or 21 percent, were *Average*—just as three months earlier. And there were weaknesses in these sites: "About 11 percent were not frequently updated. Surprisingly, 33 percent did not have any contact information. . . . Only about 10 percent displayed officers' e-mail addresses, while about 25 percent listed mailing addresses as contact information instead of e-mail addresses."

Particularly good news from labor's perspective was a slight shift toward improved Web sites: Whereas 66 percent had been thought *Good* in March, some 75 percent earned this honor in June. Whereas 41 percent had been given a score of four in March, 47 percent were so designated in June. And while 25 percent had earned a score of five, the percentage increased to 28.

Special praise went to 15 percent of the sites that offered merchandise with the union's logo, 18 percent that offered safety lessons, 20 percent that featured photos of members engaged in community service (charity events, cancer awareness marathons, building houses in neighborhoods, scholarships for members' children, etc.), and 34 percent with a members-only feature (up from 25 percent three months earlier).

As with the earlier team, this one also had reform ideas to share (including site-specific terse recommendations available on request): "The greatest recommendation to come from our research is to develop a better, more consistent, more qualitative approach toward the evaluation of union Web sites. A better points system needs to be developed so that when Web sites are evaluated, the evaluation is not obscured by the evaluator. Sites could be evaluated more frequently by more people."

The team went beyond these recommendations to also share daring contentions, such as the notion that perhaps 72 percent (or forty-two) of the fifty-nine AFL-CIO unions whose sites they studied looked like Cyber Gain organizations. Another 14 percent appeared more like Cyber Naught operations, and the remaining 14 percent seemed caught in a Cyber Drift miasma.

As if this was not venturesome enough, the three students, basing their speculation only on a Web site and its movement over a three-month period, boldly hazarded a guess that about 30 percent (or thirteen) of the forty-two Cyber Gain unions were struggling toward CyberUnion status. If time and further research bears out this line of speculation, it will indicate a very healthy early drive to steadily upgrade labor's cyberspace world.

Next Step: Continuous Research. Plainly, though, given the subjective nature of the material above, and the very small number of assessors reporting, we have barely begun the research process. In the spirit of the fine start my seven friends provide, we need now to take the entire matter of assessment to a higher plane. For as the team of O'Donnell and Donahue point out, "If the administrators of a Web site do not receive quality or timely feedback, they will be completely in the dark as to the problems that the users feel must be addressed. One can imagine an even more difficult problem to address, wherein the users do not know how good a site can be, and therefore sit idly by thinking their electronic presence is 'sufficient.'"

Some official body, such as a unionized research firm contracted to the AFL-CIO, might start with an invitational conference and Web site devoted to clarifying the project's purpose. It must be emphatically clear from the outset that the research is to aid and abet, rather than carp or harm. (Anxiety about this sort of "outsider" measurement is commonplace in labor.)

The research firm could use the Web sites of AFL-CIO unions and related list servers (such as an excellent one for labor webmasters, cybersolidarity @yahoogroups.com, and also www.unionwebservices.com) to recruit scores of volunteers from across the country. They would be trained in the use of a rigorous measurement scheme. And their data would be regularly and systematically collected, analyzed, and widely distributed, as for example, in the form of an insert to the magazine *America@Work*.

In short order this research could advisedly be expanded to include locals, city central bodies, state federations, and all the other varieties of labor organizations with a Web presence. Provided, that is, that each organization agreed to such constructive scrutiny (a provision could allow confidential reporting back to organizations with good reasons for not yet wanting the public sharing of their ratings).

Summary

To judge with the utmost caution, the largest number of Web sites of AFL-CIO affiliates in 2000 and 2001 appear sound, strong, and steadily improving. While shortcomings are obvious, pragmatic remedies are apparent. The picture is quite encouraging. Labor should upgrade this sort of baseline research, for a powerful beam of (research) light can help show the way.

Note: The editor alone is responsible for the interpretations made in this essay.

Internet Resource Guide

Prepared by Nancy Bupp

Contents

Searching the Net

Search Engines

www.altavista.com
www.askjeeves.com
www.euroseek.com
www.excite.com
www.go.com
www.google.com
www.hotbot.com
www.lycos.com
www.nbci.com/
www.northernlight.com

Meta Search Engines

www.dogpile.com
www.highway61.com
www.mamma.com
www.metacrawler.com
www.profusion.com

Search Directories

www.looksmart.com
www.yahoo.com

Search Tips

Operators Used in Keyword Searches

"Operators" are the rules or specific instructions used in a keyword search for composing the question or query. You begin a keyword search by typing your query in the search box of the search engine's home page. To construct the query, use the appropriate operators for the selected search engine. While each search engine has its own operators, some are common to a number of search engines. The following describes three more frequently used operators.

Boolean. Employs AND, OR, NEAR, and NOT to connect the words and phrases (i.e., term) used in the query. AND requires that both terms are present somewhere within the document being sought. NEAR requires that one of the terms must be found within a specified number of words. OR requires that at least one term is present. NOT excludes a term from the query.

When using these operators, remember to capitalize them as shown above, and do not leave a space between the operator and the term that follows. *Example:* labor AND history

Plus/Minus signs. Employ the plus sign (+) before a term, with no space in between, to *retrieve* only the documents containing that term. It is similar to the Boolean "AND." Use a minus sign (-) before a term, with no space in between, to *exclude* that term from the search. It is similar to the Boolean NOT. *Example:* +labor+history

Quote marks. Use quote marks to indicate that the words within the quote marks are to be treated as an exact phrase, or reasonably close to it. It is similar to the Boolean NEAR. *Example:* "labor history"

Other Helpful Tips

Expand your search by using wildcards. By typing an asterisk (*) at the end of a keyword, you can search for the word with multiple endings. *Example:* Try wish* to find wish, wishes, wishful, wishbone, and wishy-washy.

Be specific. Use specific words as opposed to general ones. For example, a search for "Lamborghini" will return more targeted results than a search for "sports cars."

Parentheses ( ). Use to group portions of Boolean queries together for more complicated queries. For example, to find documents that contain the word "fruit" and either the word "banana" or the word "apple," enter: fruit AND (banana OR apple).

Corporate Financial Information

General Information

American manufacturers: www.thomasregistry.com

Business news from almost sixty local markets: bizjournals.bcentral.com/

CEO salaries—Find CEO and other top officials salaries.

Look at Proxy statements: people.edgar-online.com/people/

Company annual reports mailed to you, free—Maintains brief financial profiles and press releases on a limited number of companies: www. prars.com

Company information—Provides key information on over 900,000 companies with an online presence: www.companiesonline.com

Company profile and contact information—Brief summary financial data (income statements and balance sheets) and SEC filings for public companies: www.freeedgar.com

Company research: www.lycos.com/business/comp_research.html

Company Sleuth—Register to receive daily e-mail reports on up to ten U.S. public companies: companysleuth.com/

Corporate research—Broken down into U.S. public companies, U.S. private companies with state business links, and industrial sector links. Also contains links to sites in other countries for research on foreign companies: www.corporateinformation.com

Database subscription of public information on the Internet: www. knowx.com/

Dun & Bradstreet—Comprehensive global database of companies: www. dnb.com

Economic snapshots of companies, free; fee-based full reports ($2.50/report or $9.95/ monthly for unlimited use): multexinvestor.com.

Executive Paywatch (AFL-CIO)—Provides CEO salaries for most major companies listed on the stock exchange and compares fat-cat salaries to average worker wages: www.paywatch.org

Financial and ratio analysis—Comparison analysis, industry analysis: www. stockselector.com

Financial information on companies: www.quicken.com

Financial information on over 10,000 public companies: www. invest quest.com

Hoovers Online—Capsule summaries. Links to Web sites, news, company press releases, and competitors: www.hoovers.com

Links to international business, trade, country-specific sites, and economic information: libweb.uncc.edu/ref-bus/vibehome.htm

Nonprofit Companies: www.guidestar.org; www.nonprofits.org/; www. mapnp.org/library/finance/np_fnce/np_fnce.htm

Report Gallery—Find out if a public company's annual report is online: www. reportgallery.com

Researching companies on-line: home.sprintmail.com/~debflanagan/ index.html

Research public opinion on companies and competitors—Search news groups and some mailing lists for discussions about companies and their products: groups.google.com/googlegroups/deja_announcement.html

Resources and analysis: www.forbes.com

Securities and Exchange Commission (SEC), The Electronic Data Gathering, Analysis, and Retrieval system (EDGAR)—Submissions by companies and others who are required by law to file forms with the United States: www.sec.gov/cgi-bin/srch-edgar

Securities and Exchange Commission's Filings—Provides free real-time online access and full-text search to the SEC's filings EDGAR system: www.tenkwizard.com

Silicon Investor's Stock Talk—Site for reviewing public discussions on stock performance: www.techstocks.com/

Stock information—Shows the performance of the company relative to its industry. Provides basic contact information, chief officers, and brief company description. Gives the top fifty institutional shareholders and the top mutual fund holders in the company. Lead-ins to the SEC filings: www.stocksmart.com

Stock ticker symbol links to news, graphs/charts, research, reports and summaries. Good vehicle for research on Canadian companies. Registered users can customize to track their portfolios: www.wsrn.com

Ticker symbol look up sites: quote.fool.com/index.htm; quote.yahoo.com/lookup; www.secapl.com/secapl/quoteserver/ticks.html

Wall Street Research Net—One-stop shopping for company research links: www.wsrn.com/

Yahoo—Offers profile, news, stock quotes, address, phone and fax numbers, brief summary of the company's main activities, and the company's home page (if available): biz.yahoo.com/news

Management Information

American Chamber of Commerce Executives: www.acce.org

American Management Association International: www.amanet.org

American Society of Association Executives, Gateway to Associations—Comprehensive directory to Web sites of business and professional associations: www.asaenet.org/Gateway/OnlineAssocSlist.html

Associations on the Net—A collection of over 1,100 sites to professional, trade, academic, and research organizations: www.ipl.org/ref/AON/

Business information: www.businessnation.com

Business roundtable: www.brtable.org

CEO Express—Loaded with categorized links: www.ceoexpress.com/

Employee Benefit Research Institute: www.ebri.org

ESOP Association: www.the-esop-emplowner.org

International Personnel Management Association: www.ipma-hr.org

National Alliance of Business: www.nab.com

National Association of Manufacturers: www.nam.org

Outsourcing center—Provides outsourcing information resources: www.outsourcing-experts.com/

Price's List of Lists—A comprehensive clearinghouse of links to articles listing the top-ranked industries, organizations, schools, products, and people: gwis2.circ.gwu.edu/~gprice/listof.htm

Society of Human Resources Management: www.shrm.org

Technology Research Center: www.eoexchange.com/home/index.html

Tech Savvy—A powerful technical Web site that helps you identify suppliers, locate critical information, and order worldwide standards, military specifications, millions of parts, and hard to find historical data: www.techsavvy.com

U.S. Chamber of Commerce: www.uschamber.org

Industry Information

General Information

Fuld & Company—Offers links to key sites in twenty-seven industries: www.fuld.com/i3/index.html

Industry information—Comprehensive listing: www.globalsources.com/MAGAZINE/MAGFRM.HTM

Industry news—Click on "browse our news channels" for industry categories: www.headlinespot.com/subject/industry/; news.excite.com/business/industry/

Industry publications—Review the Michigan Electronic Library for a variety of segments: mel.lib.mi.us/business/BU-IPmenu.html

Industry Research Desk—Provides links to U.S. and international industry home pages in over thirty areas: www.virtualpet.com/industry/mfg/mfg.htm

Industry Week 1000—Free database to view the entire 1,000 companies or sort the list by several categories including industry, country, ranking, and financial performance measures: www.industryweek.com/iwinprint/iw1000/2001/database/iw01Enter.asp

Smaller companies—Directory site is particularly useful for finding smaller companies; listed alphabetically by industry: dir.yahoo.com/Business _and_Economy/Directories/Companies/

Yahoo! Industry News—Check industry press releases and current news: biz.yahoo.com/industry/

Aerospace

Aerospace Industries Association: www.aia-aerospace.org

American Helicopter Society: www.vtol.org

American Institute of Aeronautics and Astronautics: www.aiaa.org

Aviation Week and Space Technology: www.awgnet.com/aviation

Defence Systems Daily: defence-data.com

Defense, aerospace, and transportation information—Up-to-date information on what the world is doing to protect its nations and its peoples. News and information of the world's military actions, politics, security, and military: www.janes.com/

Defense news: www.defensenews.com

Helicopter Association International: www.rotor.com

National Aeronautics and Space Administration (NASA): www.nasa.gov

Space news: www.spacenews.com

Airline Transport Industry

Aerospace/airline industry research: www.mrweb.com/aero-tr.htm

Airline industry business and financial site: www.planebusiness.com/

Airline news: www.airlinequality.com/news/news_industry.htm

Air Transport Association of America: www.air-transport.org

Aviation and airline resources: www.aviationindustry.com/

Federal Aviation Administration: www.faa.gov

General Aviation Manufacturers Association: www.generalaviation.org

Internet's aviation magazine and news service: www.avweb.com/

National Air Transportation Association: www.nata-online.org

Office of Airline Information: www.bts.gov/programs/oai

Regional Airline Association: www.raa.org

Technology in the Airline Industry: www.ufla.org/~hsmith/airlineindustry.html

U.S. Department of Transportation, The Office of Airline Information: www.bts.gov/oai

Aluminum and Nonferrous Metals

Aluminum Association, Inc.: www.aluminum.org

Aluminum Industry Server: www.aluminum.net/

Can Manufacturers Institute: www.cancentral.com

Automotive

American International Automobile Dealers Association: www.aiada.org

American Trucking Association: www.truckline.com/

AMX-Files—History of American Motors: www.amxfiles.com

Automotive Parts and Accessories Association: www.apaa.org

International Automobile Manufacturers Association: www.aiam.org

Japan Automobile Manufacturers Association: www.japanauto.com

Brewery

Beer Institute: www.beerinstitute.org/

Beer Network: www.breworld.com/main2f.html

Distilled Spirits Council: www.discus.health.org

Modern Brewery Age: breweryage.com/Beer_Ale.htm

Construction and Erection

American Builders and Contractors: www.abcpoint.com/default.asp

American Conditioning and Refrigerating Institute: www.ari.org

American Road and Transportation Builders Association: www.artba-hq.org

American Society of Civil Engineers (ASCE): www.asce.org

Association of General Contractors of America: www.agc.org

Mechanical Contractors Association of America: www.mcaa.org

National Association of Home Builders: www.nahb.com

National Association of Plumbing, Heating, and Cooling Contractors: www.naphcc.org

National Concrete Masonry Association: www.ncma.org

Electronics

Armed Forces Communications and Electronics Association: www.afcea.org

Electronics Industry Alliance: www.eia.org

International Communications Industry Association: www.icia.org

Telecommunications Industry Association: www.tiaonline.org

U.T.C.—the telecommunications association: www.utc.org

Machine and Manufacturing

American Gear Manufacturers Association: www.agma.org

American Iron and Steel Institute: www.steel.org

Association for Manufacturing Technology (formerly National Machine Tool Builders Association): www.mfgtech.org

Gas Appliance Manufacturers Association: www.gamanet.org

Machine Dealers National Association: www.mdna.org

National Corrugated Steel Pipe Association: www.ncspa.org

National Tooling and Machining Association: www.ntma.org

Packaging Machinery Manufacturers Institute: www.packexpo.com

Paperboard Packaging Council: www.ppcnet.org

Rubber Manufacturers Association: www.rma.org

Specialty Steel Industry of North America: www.ssina.com

Valve Manufacturers Association: www.vma.org

Mining and Refining

American Gas Association: www.aga.com

American Petroleum Institute: www.api.org

Gold and Silver Institute: www.goldinstitute.com

International Magnesium Association: www.intlmag.org/

National Petroleum Council: www.npc.org

Natural Gas Supply Association: www.naturalgas.org

Railroads (see also Government)

American Association of Railroads: www.aar.org/aarhome. nsf?Open Database

Companies within the railroad industry sector: www.railsoft.com/railrd.html

Company research and business information tool for the railroad industry; subscription: www.railroadbrowser.com/

Fatigue countermeasures in the railroad industry—Current status: www.du.edu/~psherry/fatigue/

Railcar marketplace—Internet-based marketplace for railcar sales, short-term leasing, and services, specifically the secondary market for used railcars and related maintenance and customization services: www.railmatch.com/

Railroad industry: www.railusa.com/industry.shtml

Railroad industry, union home pages, U.S. Railroad Retirement Board, and other links: www.rrb.gov/rrlinks.html

Railroad industry organizations: www.railserve.com/Industry/

Railroad information online: krypton.mnsu.edu/~schumann/www/rr/news.html

Railroad jobs—View current railroad-industry–related jobs: www.railjobs.com/

Railroad links: jj.railfan.net/links-industry.html

Railroad search engine—Comprehensive: www.railsearch.com/index.html

Railroads and You—A Basic Guide to the North American Railroad Industry: www.personal.kent.edu/~bwmyers/

Railway business information—Headline news stories and many other regularly updated features for the world's railway industry: www.railgaz.co.uk/home.htm

Railway industry: www.railway-technology.com/

Webville and Hypertext Railroad Company: www.spikesys.com/webville.html

Shipbuilding and Marine Interests

American Association of Port Authorities: www.aapa-ports.org

International Maritime Organization: www.imo.org

Marine Technology Society: www.mtsociety.org/

National Shipyard Association: www.vesselalliance.com/

Shipbuilders Council of America: www.shipbuilders.org

Textiles and Apparel

American Fiber Manufacturers Association: www.fibersource.com

American Textile Manufacturers Institute: www.atmi.org

Industrial Fabrics Association International: www.ifai.com/

Transportation

American Public Transit Association: www.apta.com

Association for Transportation Law, Logistics, and Policy: www.transportlink.com/atllp

Community Transportation Association: www.cta.org/

National Industrial Transportation League: www.nitl.org

Specialized Carriers and Rigging Association: www.scranet.org

Transportation Institute: www.trans-inst.org

Wood, Pulp, and Paper

American Forest and Paper Association: www.afandpa.org

American Forests: www.amfor.org

American Paper and Forest Association: www.woodcom.com/woodcom/afpa/index.html

Forest products markets—The source for information: www.random lengths.com

Hardwood, Plywood, and Veneer Association: www.hpva.org

National Composite Panel Association (formerly the Particleboard Association): www.pbmdf.com

National Paper Trade Association: www.gonpta.com/

Society of American Foresters: www.safnet.org

U.S. Department of Argiculture, Forest Service: www.fs.fed.us/

OnLine Media

National and Regional Newspapers

Atlanta Journal-Constitution: www.accessatlanta.com/ajc/

Baltimore Sun: www.sunspot.net/

Boston Globe: www.boston.com/globe/

Buffalo News: www.buffalolive.com/

Chicago Tribune: www.chicago.tribune.com/

Christian Science Monitor: www.csmonitor.com/

Cleveland Plain-Dealer: www.cleveland.com/

Dallas Morning News: www.dallasnews.com/

Denver Post: www.denverpost.com/

Globe & Mail (Canada): www.theglobeandmail.com/

Houston Chronicle: www.chron.com/

Indianapolis Star: www.starnews.com/

Kansas City Star: www.kcstar.com/

Las Vegas Sun: www.lasvegassun.com/

Len-Net—Links you to the Web sites of every major newspaper in the United States and most magazines, TV and movies studios, reference sites, etc.: www.lni.net/cowabunga/newspapers.htm

Los Angeles Times: www.latimes.com/HOME/NEWS/NATION/

Miami Herald: www.herald.com/

Milwaukee Journal Sentinel: www.onwis.com/

Minneapolis Star-Tribune: www.startribune.com/

News Central—Links to 3,500 newspapers: www.all-links.com/newscentral/

Newslink—U.S. and non-U.S. newspapers arranged by state, type, etc.: ajr.newslink.org

New York Times: www.nytimes.com/

Ottawa Citizen (Canada): www.ottawacitizen.com/

Philadelphia Inquirer: www.phillynews.com/

Pittsburgh Post-Gazette: www.post-gazette.com/

San Diego Union-Tribune: www.uniontrib.com

San Jose Mercury News: www.sjmercury.com/

Seattle Post-Intelligencer: www.seattle-pi.com/

St. Louis Post-Dispatch: www.stlnet.com/

Toronto Star (Canada): www.thestar.com/

Washington Post: www.washingtonpost.com/

Magazines and Online News

ABC News: www.abcnews.go.com

Aviation Today: www.aviationtoday.com

Aviation Week: www.aviationnow.com/

Barrons Online—Includes the Inc. 500, America's 500 fastest growing private companies; Shows revenue, profitability, number of employees, location, industry, year founded, and home page address (if available): www.barrons.com

Business Week: www.businessweek.com/

Canada's full-text newswire service: www.newswire.ca

Canadian Broadcasting Corporation: www.cbc.ca/

CBS News: www.cbs.com

CNN On-Line: www.cnn.com/

Defense Daily: www.defensedaily.com

Dollars and Sense: www.igc.apc.org/dollars/index.html

Financial Times—Editorial analysis of financial markets, industries, and companies: www.ft.com/

Forbes—The Forbes 500 Annual Directory, the 200 Best Small Companies, and the 500 Largest Private Companies, including revenues, profits, number of employees, a brief profile, address, phone, and name and educational background of CEO: www.forbes.com/

Fortune: www.fortune.com/

Inc.: www.inc.com

Industry Week: www.iwgc.com/

In These Times: www.inthesetimes.com/

Miscellaneous links—Classified ad papers, ethnic and minority publications, religious periodicals, etc.: www.newspapers.com/

Mother Jones: www.motherjones.com/

MSNBC On-Line: www.msnbc.com/

Multinational Monitor magazine, online edition—It is archived back to 1992. The annual December issue lists the ten worst corporations of the year. Fully searchable: www.essential.org/monitor/monitor.html

The Nation: thenation.com/

National Public Radio: www.npr.org/

News Alert, Inc.—Current news classified by industry: www.newsalert.com

News Page—Can be customized by company, industry, and topic. Provides title, author, and source of recent news articles, and the first sentence of the article is free. Provides the full text of press releases free and tells the price of full text on other articles. Different levels of subscription service and stock quotes, as well as a site search engine: www.individual.com/

Newsweek: www.newsweek.com/

Online article-search service—Search for quality articles in more than 300 reputable magazines and journals: www.findarticles.com/

Public Relations Newswire: www.prnewswire.com/

Slate: slate.msn.com

Smart Money: www.smartmoney.com/

Time: time.com/time

US News and World Report: www.usnews.com/usnews/home.htm

Z Magazine: www.zmag.org

Government

General Information

Air Force Civil Engineering Support System—Provides a full array of A-76 support services: www.afcesa.af.mil/Directorate/CEO/Contracts/Outsourcing/A76/templates.htm

Bureau of Economic Analysis (BEA)—Nation's economic accountant, preparing estimates that illuminate key national, international, and regional aspects of the U.S. economy: www.bea.doc.gov/

Bureau of Labor Statistics: stats.bls.gov

Bureau of National Affairs: www.bna.com

Bureau of the Public Debt: www.publicdebt.treas.gov/bpd/bpdhome.htm

Buyers and Vendors—An online community for government buyers and vendors: www.fedmarket.com/

Equal Employment Opportunity Commission: www.eeoc.gov/

Federal Election Commission: www.fec.gov/

Federal Employees—Top stories affecting federal employees: www.federaltimes.com/

Federal Labor Relations Authority—The FLRA is an independent agency responsible for administering the labor-management relations program for 1.9 million federal employees worldwide, approximately 1.1 million of whom are exclusively represented in 2,200 bargaining units. Its mission is to promote stable and constructive labor-management relations that contribute to an efficient and effective government: flra.gov

Federal Mediation and Conciliation Service (FMCS)—Forms (including fillable forms) are available online, including Federal Sector Labor Relations Notice to Federal Mediation and Conciliation Services (Form F-53), Notice to Mediation Agencies (Form-7), Arbitrator's Report and Fee Statement (Form R-19), Request for Arbitration Panel (Form R-43), and Arbitrator's Personal Data Questionnaire (Form R-22): fmcs.gov/

Federal programs—Information about federal programs, benefits, or services: info.gov

Federal statistics—Links to statistics from more than seventy federal Web sites: www.fedstats.gov

FedWorld Information Network—Contains links to more than 100 federal government agencies: www.fedworld.gov

General Accounting Office—Investigative arm of Congress: www.gao.gov

Government Contracting/Subcontracting Directory—Excellent directory of federal prime contractors, arranged by state and occasionally by subcontractor: gopher://www.sbaonline.sba.gov/11/Government-Contracting/Subcontracting-Directory

Library of Congress: www.loc.gov

National Labor Relations Board: www.nlrb.gov

National Mediation Board: www.nmb.gov/

National Partnership for Reinventing Government: www.npr.gov/

Professional resources—Resource for professionals in the public sector: www.govcon.com/

Railroad Retirement Board: www.rrb.gov/

Social Security Online: www.ssa.gov/

Strategic Sourcing—A NAVFAC/NAVSUP joint office established to assist the Navy with OMB Circular A-76 competitions and other competitive initiatives: help.n4.hq.navy.mil/

U.S. Census Bureau: www.census.gov/

U.S. Commission on Civil Rights: www.usccr.gov/

U.S. Department of Commerce: www.doc.gov/

U.S. Department of Defense: www.defenselink.mil/

U.S. Department of Labor: www.dol.gov

U.S. Department of Transportation: www.dot.gov/

U.S. Office of Government Ethics: www.usoge.gov/

U.S. Office of Personnel Management—The federal government's Human Resources Agency: www.opm.gov/

U.S. Office of Special Counsel (OSC)—An independent federal investigative and prosecutorial agency. Basic authorities come from three federal statutes, the Civil Service Reform Act, the Whistleblower Protection Act, and the Hatch Act: www.osc.gov/index.htm

Legal and Regulatory

Court decisions—Comprehensive index source for legal information on the Internet. Provides links to all the federal and state court decision Web pages. Many are maintained by law schools, and they vary greatly in both currency and the quality of the onsite search mechanisms. Each court system must be searched separately: www.lawguru.com/caselaw.html

Environmental Protection Agency: www.epa.gov/

Findlaw—links to a broad range of legal subjects: www.findlaw.com

Incorporation—Most states require companies incorporated in those states to file annual reports. These public records contain information about officers and directors. This Web site gives contact information for the state agencies responsible for incorporation filings: www.afscme.org/wrkplace/incorp.htm

Legal research: www.romingerlegal.com/

Securities and Exchange Commission Enforcement Division Actions—Includes administrative proceedings, commission opinions, investor alerts, and releases describing civil and selected criminal proceedings filed in federal court by the SEC. Fully searchable: www.sec.gov/enforce.htm

Securities Class Action Clearinghouse: securities.stanford.edu/

Workers Compensation—A state-by-state listing that includes links to state statutes and workers' compensation forms: www. workerscompensation.com

Worldwide Legal Information Association—Provides international legal news updates and advice: www.wwlia.org/wwlia.htm

Pensions

I.A.M. National Pension Plan: www.iamnpf.org

The Pension Benefit Guaranty Corporation (PBGC): www.pbgc.gov

Pension questions and answers—Real answers to questions about specific pension and benefit plans. Also contains a Labor Library: freeerisa.com/

Political and Legislative Information

Capital Web Works—The Internet guide to the U.S. Congress: www.capweb.com

Common Cause—Citizens working to reform government ethics: common cause.org

Congressional Quarterly—The American Voter: www.cq.com

Contacting the Congress: www.visi.com/juan/congress

House and Senate bills searchable by keywords or by bill number—Current and last year's full text of legislation, all versions: thomas.loc.gov

House of Representatives: www.house.gov

Money in Politics Data: www.opensecrets.org

Politics UK—Business political donors. Site offers information organized alphabetically by company name of British corporate contributions to British political parties: users.powernet.co.uk/hack/sleaze/

Senators: www.senate.gov

U.S. Government: www.firstgov.gov

Vote Smart: Tracks the performance of over 13,000 political leaders: www.vote-smart.org

White House: www.whitehouse.gov/WH/Welcome.html

Watchdog Groups and Policy Organizations

Corporate Watch: www.corpwatch.org/

Fairness and Accuracy in Reporting (FAIR)—Monitors the mainstream press for procorporation antiworker bias: www.fair.org

National Consumers League: www.natlconsumersleague.org

Nike Campaign: www.saigon.com/~nike

Public Information Network—Details some of the negative practices of transnational corporations. Strong on environmental issues. Site is indexed both alphabetically by company name and geographically: endgame.org

National and International Labor
(see also Government, Pensions, Miscellaneous)

AFL-CIO: www.aflcio.org

AFL-CIO—Union-busting tactics; companies and other information: www.aflcio.org/unionbuster/index.htm

Air Line Pilots Association (ALPA): www.alpa.org

Air Traffic Controllers Association: atca.org

American Federation of Government Employees (AFGE): www.afge.org

American Federation of State, County, and Municipal Employees, The (AFSCME): www.afscme.org

American Federation of Teachers (AFT): www.aft.org

American Postal Workers Union: www.apwu.org

Association of Flight Attendants: www.flightattendant-afa.org/

Bakery, Confectionery, Tobacco Workers, and Grain Millers International Union, The: www.bctgm.org/

British Columbian Federation of Labor: www.bcfed.com/

Brotherhood of Maintenance of Way Employees: www.bmwe.org/

Canadian Labour Congress (CLC): www.clc-ctc.ca/eng-index.html

Communication Workers of America (CWA): www.cwa-union.org/

Democracy in the global economy: www.globalexchange.org/

Electrical Radio and Machine Workers, United (UE): www.igc.apc.org/unitedelect

Food and Commercial Workers Union, United (UFCW): www.ufcw.org

Glass, Molders, Pottery, Plastics, and Allied Workers International Union: www.gmpiu.org/

Global solidarity site—Analysis, theory, and strategy: www.antenna.nl/~waterman/

Hotel Employees and Restaurant Employees International Union (HERE): www.hereunion.org

Industrial Workers of the World: www.iww.org/

Interfaith Committee for Worker Justice: www.nicwj.org/index.html

International Association of Machinists and Aerospace Workers (IAMAW): www.goiam.org

International Brotherhood of Boilermakers, Iron Ship Builders, Blacksmiths, Forgers, and Helpers, The: www.boilermakers.org

International Brotherhood of Electrical Workers (IBEW): ibew.org

International Brotherhood of Teamsters (IBT): www.teamster.org/

International Confederation of Free Trade Unions (ICFTU): www.icftu.org/

International Labor Organization (ILO): www.ilo.org/

International Metalworkers Federation (IMF): www.imfmetal.org/imf/main/main.cfm

Laborers' International Union of North America: www.liuna.org/

Labornet—A democratic communication network for the labor movement: www.labornet.org

Labour and Society International, The—Features labor news and numerous links to trade union Web sites around the world. Also an online forum for all unionists, directory of online labor conferences and community forums: www.labourstart.org

Local unions—Find a local's Web site and hundreds of other links organized by state: www.unions.org

National Association of Letter Carriers (NALC): www.nalc.org/

National Education Association (NEA): www.nea.org

National Federation of Federal Employees (NFFE): www.nffe.org

National Postal Mail Handlers Union (NPMHU): www.npmhu.org/

National Writers Union (NWU): www.nwu.org/

Newspaper Guild: www.newsguild.org

Office and Professional Employees International Union (OPEIU): www.opeiu.org

Paper, Allied-Industrial, Chemical, and Energy Workers International Union: www.paceunion.org/

Service Employees International Union (SEIU): www.seiu.org

Sheet Metal Workers International Association (SMWIA): www.smwia.org

Transport Workers Union of America: www.twu.com/

Union Network International (UNI): The largest international grouping of individual trade unions. It is a key part of an online network dedicated to giving members a bigger global voice and to helping their unions cooperate across national frontiers: www.union-network.org/

Union of Needletrades, Industrial, and Textile Employees: www.uniteunion.org/

United Association of Labor Educators: www.uale.org

United Auto Workers (UAW): www.uaw.org

United Farm Workers: www.ufw.org/

United Mine Workers of America: www.umwa.org

United Steelworkers of America (USWA): www.uswa.org/

William W. Winpisinger Education and Technology Center: winpisinger.iamaw.org

Workers' Education Local 189—Extensive links to labor-related Web sites: www.erols.com/czarlab/index.html

Safety and Health

Airsafe: www.airsafe.com

American Association of Health Care Consultants: www.aahc.net

American Association of Health Plans: www.aahp.org

American Dental Association: www.ada.org

American Hospital Association: www.aha.org

American Industrial Hygiene Association: www.aiha.org

American Medical Association: www.ama-assn.org

American Occupational Therapy Association: www.aota.org

Duke University Occupational Medicine—Oriented to medical professionals but has excellent databases, updated listings of other great sites: gilligan.mc.duke.edu/oem/

ErgoWeb—A resource center for data, tools, other Internet links related to ergonomics: www.ergoweb.com/

Industrial Safety Equipment Association: www.safetycentral.org/isea

Material Safety Data Sheets (MSDSs)—Searchable compilations of MSDS sheets covering a large number of toxic and hazardous chemicals: www.ilpi.com/msds/index.html;hazard.com/msds/

Mine Safety Administration: www.msha.gov/

National Institute for Occupational Safety and Health (NIOSH)—Federal agency specializing in research on workplace health and safety: www.cdc.gov/niosh/homepage.html

Nuclear Regulatory Agency: www.nrc.gov

Occupational Safety and Health Administration (OSHA)—Now allows online complaint filing: www.osha.gov

OSHA statistics and data—Web site allows searching of OSHA inspection data and citations by establishment. The database goes back to 1972 and allows sorting by date of inspection, establishment name, or state. As an added bonus, the citation records reveal whether or not the establishment is unionized: www.osha.gov/oshstats/

OSHWeb—Contains links to other health and safety sites: oshweb.me.tut.fi/index.html

Society of Toxicology: www.toxicology.org

University of Virginia Office of Environmental Health and Safety: keats. admin.virginia.edu/

U.S. Chemical Safety and Hazard Investigation Board: www.chemsafety.gov/

World Health Organization (WHO): www.who.int/

Universities and Think Tanks

Cornell University School of Industrial and Labor Relations: www. ilr.cornell.edu/graphicalhome.html

Economic Policy Network—Site with links to progressive research and advocacy organizations: www.epn.org

Foreign Policy—A think tank without walls working to make the United States a more responsible global leader and partner: www.foreignpolicy-infocus.org/

Michigan State University, School of Labor and Industrial Relations: www.lir.msu.edu/

Responsible Wealth: www.responsiblewealth.org

Sources and experts—Leads to official experts in a variety of subject matter: www.ibiblio.org/slanews/internet/experts.html

United for a Fair Economy—Labor advocacy group that specializes in matters of economic justice: www.ufenet.org

University of California–Berkeley, Institute of Industrial Relations: socrates.berkeley.edu/~iir/

University of Illinois, Institute of Labor and Industrial Relations: www. ilir.uiuc.edu/

University of Michigan, Institute of Labor and Industrial Relations: www. umich.edu/~ilir/

University of Minnesota, Industrial Relations Center: www.irc.csom.umn.edu/

University of Toronto, Center for Industrial Relations: www.chass.utoronto.ca/ cir/

University of Wisconsin–Milwaukee, Masters in Human Resources and Labor Relations: www.uwm.edu:80/Dept/MHRLR/

Canadian Information (see also National and International Labor)

Alberta Federation of Labour: www.afl.org/

British Columbia Federation of Labour: www.bcfed.com/

Canadian Association of Labour Media: www.calm.ca/

Canadian business resources: www.canadaone.com/business/index.html

Canadian Center for Occupational Health and Safety (CCOHS): www.ccohs.ca

Canadian Centre for Policy Alternatives: www.policyalternatives.ca

Canadian company information: www.fin-info.com/

Canadian Council on Social Development: www.ccsd.ca/

Canadian Depository for Securities—System for electronic document analysis and retrieval. Searches Canada's electronic securities documentation filing system, equivalent to the SEC in the United States. Securities Information, Ontario: www.osc.gov.on.ca/

Canada Industry—Business information by sector. English or French: strategis.ic.gc.ca

Canada Pension Plan Home Page—Canada Pension Plan Investment Board Act: www.cpp-rpc.gc.ca/indexe.html

Canadian Human Rights Commission: www.chrc-ccdp.ca/

Canadian International Trade Tribunal—Full-text searches of decisions related to trade, dumping, subsidizing, and procurement: www.tcce.gc.ca/menu_e.htm

Canadian Labour Congress: clc-ctc.ca

Canadian Trade Index, The—Database of 25,000 Canadian manufacturers sponsored by the Alliance of Manufacturers and Exporters, Canada. Detailed descriptions of products and lists of countries to which a given company exports are provided. The database can be searched by name, product, region or export country: www.ctidirectory.com

Company and CEO compensation rankings—Top 1,000 Companies, Top 300 Private Companies, Top 50 CEOs (by compensation), Top 50 Employers, and others, with links to both public and private company profiles: www.robmagazine.com/top1000

Council of Canadians, The: www.canadians.org/

Find a person: canada411.sympatico.ca

Government of Canada: www.gc.ca

Guide to Canadian labour history resources: www.nlc-bnc.ca/6/

Guide to corporate reports: www.mmltd.com/

Human Resources Development, Canada: labour-travail.hrdc-drhc.gc.ca/

Industrial, Wood, and Allied Workers of Canada, with links to other Canadian information: iwa.ca

Labor market information—Making career sense of labor market information: workinfonet.bc.ca/lmisi/Making/Mcstoc.htm

Legal resources: www.weirfoulds.com/media/ads.htm

Legislative Assemblies of Canada: www.cs.cmu.edu/Unofficial/Canadiana/legislatures.html

Machinery and Equipment Manufactures Association—Database of approximately 100 members. Provides company addresses, phone numbers, products, and names of managers and other contacts: www.memac.org/memdir.htm

Manitoba Federation of Labour: www.mfl.mb.ca/

Marketing Magazine—For $69.50 (Canadian) per year you can obtain valuable market-share information and access an extensive archive of articles on public and private Canadian companies: www.marketingmag.ca

National Library of Canada—Information by subject: www.nlc-bnc.ca/caninfo/ep06.htm

National Pollutant Release Inventory—Environment Canada provides a database of pollutants released at every company location since 1994 (each year must be searched separately): www.ec.gc.ca/pdb/npri/index.html

New Brunswick Federation of Labour: www.intellis.net/fttnbfl/english.htm

Old Age Security and Canadian Pension Plan: www.hrdc-drhc.gc.ca/isp/common/home.shtml

Ontario Federation of Labour: www.ofl-fto.on.ca/

Pension investment and employee benefits: www.benefitscanada.com/

Provincial labor ministries—Provides links to each: labour.hrdc-drhc.gc.ca/wip/othersites/htmo-ssi

Quebec Federation of Labour: www.ftq.qc.ca/ftq.html

Quick reference to Canadian law: www.hronline.com/lib/quick.html

Securities information: www.sedar.com

Site-by-Site—A tremendous collection of Canadian links is provided: www.site-by-site.com/canada/astock.htm

Statistics Canada: www.statcan.ca/start.html

Workers Health and Safety Centre: whsc.on.ca/

Workplace management issues: www.workplace.ca/

Work Research Foundation—Created for the purpose of doing research and education in economics and industrial relations: www.interlog.com/~wrf/search.htm

Miscellaneous

General Information

Academically valuable resources—14,000 listings: lib-www.ucr.edu

Carol Simpson Cartoons: www.cartoonwork.com/

Cartoons—More Resources: www.bulbul.com/

Classified collection of links: rfe.wustl.edu

Economic information and analysis site: www.dismal.com

Electronic books—Full texts of many books in the public domain, from Shakespeare to Sir Arthur Conan Doyle to Lewis Carroll and thousands of others: www.promo.net/pg

Encyclopedia Britannica: www.britannica.com/

Find a business: www.zip2.com/; yellowpages.excite.com/bus/

Find businesses and people—Worldwide: www.worldpages.com/

Guide to Robert's Rules of Order: www.robertsrules.com

Index of online phone books—Over 350 links to yellow pages, white pages, business directories, e-mail addresses, and fax listings from over 150 countries all around the world: www.teldir.com/eng/

Internet address finder—If you're looking specifically for an Internet address rather than a home address or phone number: www.iaf.net

Internet Public Library Reference: www.ipl.org/ref/RR

Libraries—Gateway to more than 5,000 libraries around the world: libraryspot.com

People finders—Combines popular people finders such as WhoWhere, Infospace, and Anywho on one page, plus reverse searching and maps: www.theultimates.com/white/

Postal service—Provides a Canadian postal code and U.S. zip-code directory: www.westminster.ca/

Research information: www.iTools.com/research-it/

Rominger Legal's New People Finder Page—Contains interfaces to e-mail, phone, and address searches. Features advanced interfaces like reverse phone number look-ups: www.romingerlegal.com/finder.htm

Search—Direct links to the search interfaces of resources that are not easily searchable from general search tools such as Alta Vista, Hotbot, and Infoseek: gwis2.circ.gwu.edu/~gprice/direct.htm

Statistical resources—Comprehensive subjects: www.lib.umich.edu:80/libhome/Documents.center/stcomp.html

Toll-free number directory: inter800.com/

Virtual reference desk: thorplus.lib.purdue.edu/reference

WebEx—Online meeting service requires only a browser and a telephone to put together collaborative meetings over the Web: webex.com

Yellow pages—Search nationwide yellow pages: www.bigbook.com/

Zip codes: www.usps.gov/ncsc/lookups/lookup_zip+4.html

Labor-Related

"American made" Web sites: www.madeinusa.org/; www. Manufactured inUSA.com/; www.unionlabel.org/; www. howtobuyamerican.com/; www.onlyamerican.com

Buy Union Now: www.buyunionnow.com

Huck/Konopacki Labor Cartoons: www.solidarity.com/hkcartoons/

Labor Relations Institute—Union busting site: www.lrionline.com/

Northland Poster Collective, The—Sells its prolabor and other progressive posters, T-shirts, buttons, etc. through its Web site: www. northlandposter.com

Quotes—Compendium of quotes on labor subjects. A useful resource to those preparing literature, publications, speeches, and everything that has anything to do with organizing: www.igc.apc.org/laborquotes/

Union Privilege—Details union privilege benefits and provides an e-mail form for requesting further information: www.unionprivilege.org

Maps

home.nbci.com/search/map/form/0,161,home-0,00.html?st.sn.srch.0.mp

maps.excite.com/address/

maps.yahoo.com/py/maps.py

www.delorme.com/cybermaps/

www.infospace.com/info.go2net/fillc?nf=mapdir.html

www.lycos.com/roadmap.html

www.mapblast.com/mblast/index.mb

www.mapquest.com/

www.mapsonus.com/

www.savewealth.com/links/travel/maps/index.html

People

home.nbci.com/search/people/results/0,57,home-0,00.html?st. sn.srch.0.wp

home.netscape.com/netcenter/whitepages.html?cp=ntserch

in-105.infospace.com/info.go2net/index_ppl.htm

knowx.com

mesa.rrzn.uni-hannover.de/

people.yahoo.com/

tracersinfo.com/

www.hotbot.com/partners/people.asp

www.whowhere.lycos.com/

Government people: www.whowhere.lycos.com/Govt/main.html

International people finder: www.whowhere.lycos.com/wwphone/excite_world.html

Maps, people, and businesses: www.bigfoot.com/

Meta-search engine for finding e-mail addresses: www.switchboard.com

Reverse Directories

4phonenumbers.4anything.com

555-1212.com

www.anywho.com

www.reversephonedirectory.com

www.theultimates.com

www.wwwinfospace.com/info/reverse.htm

Recommended Web Sites

Prepared by Nicole L. Whittaker

Even with over 1 billion sites already available, the honor roll of relevant and worthy sources seems endless. Many scores are cited in the handbook's chapters and the Internet Resource Guide, and all are worth checking out.

A former undergraduate student of mine, Nicole L. Whittaker, volunteered in the fall and winter of 2000/2001 to prepare the eighteen Web site annotations below. (I added two more at the end to make it an even twenty.)

Both of us are keenly aware of how small and random is the list, arranged, moreover, in no particular order. But we never intended it to do more than illustrate the extraordinary array of resources that beckon. CyberUnions, relying on an army of rank-and-file volunteers (and their family members), will be endlessly on the alert for empowering sites to draw on, call attention to, dialogue and share links with, and otherwise make the most of.

1. The International Socialist Organization believes that working people should democratically control society and run it on the basis of human needs. Through several activities this group aims to "link today's fights to the struggle for socialism." Their Web site contains group background information as well as information on the issues and activities they are involved in: www.internationalsocialist.org

2. Since 1970 the Institute for Southern Studies has provided resources to those who would like to bring social and economic change to the South. It helps to develop research and publication projects related to grassroots organizing. They have a journal, *Southern Exposure,* that was started in 1973. You can receive information concerning the journal on their Web site, which

also has a catalog, links, and membership information: www. southernstudies. org

3. Organizers' Collaborative realizes the potential of the Internet and technology. They work to make computers accessible for community-based organizations fighting for social change, so that communication between groups is made easier. Their very helpful Web site includes information on how to join, as well as links and "tech tips": www.organizenow.net

4. Founded in 1985, the Rainforest Action Network works to protect rain forests and the rights of those living in and around them. The RAN holds conferences, leads boycotts, forms action groups, and circulates publications in order to bring the rain forest to the attention of the American public. It places emphasis on grassroots education and action, networking, and mobilizing citizen activists quickly. Their Web site is loaded with information and covers everything from rain forest fact sheets to a kid's corner, with much in between: www.ran.org/

5. The focus of Reform America is the youth of our country. The group reaches out to youth by helping them to develop leadership skills in hope of making changes in voting and politics. Because "leaders are born and die every day," the youth are key in keeping the spirit alive and achieving true peace. If you are interested in learning more about this organization, visit their Web site, which contains speeches, current issues, and tips on how to get your local university or high school motivated: www.reformamericainc.org

6. The Ruckus Society provides nonviolent civil-disobedience training for those interested in environmental and human rights issues. The organization hosts several "action camps" to teach these skills. Their Web site has an application. By attending a camp, the society provides you with the tools and skills to become a catalyst for change, because "actions speak louder than words": www.ruckus.org

7. The Alliance for Democracy considers itself a movement aimed to "take back our democracy from the unelected mega-corporations that have stolen it from us." It has a Web site that contains a calendar of events, related links, and a membership form. It operates mostly in local chapters, but you can contact the national office by phone (1-888-466-TAFD), by e-mail (peoplesall@aol.com), or by mail (Alliance for Democracy, 681 Main Street, Waltham MA 02451): www.afd-online.org

8. The Campaign to End the Death Penalty was organized to win support for prisoners currently on death row. The campaign holds forums throughout the year. Everyone opposing capital punishment is welcome to join in order to build a bloc of opposition that is vocal and visible. Their Web site contains contact information, fact sheets, an events calendar, and the latest edition of their newsletter, the *New Abolitionist*. Visiting the Web site is recommended to anyone interested in becoming a member or learning more about the organization: www.nodeathpenalty.org

9. The Center for Voting and Democracy is a nonpartisan, nonprofit organization that studies voting systems and their effects on voter turnout, representation, and governance. They believe voting reform could "reinvigorate American politics, decrease the impact of money in elections, promote greater participation in elections and governance and provide for majority rule, fair representation of political minorities and more inclusive representation of women and racial and ethnic minorities." Their Web site offers a large amount of information via an online library, contact information, and related links: www.fairvote.org

10. It is the belief of the Committees of Correspondence for Democracy and Socialism that they can be a catalyst for change for those who feel the brunt of oppression in America. Members of all social movements are invited to come together to create positive, constructive solutions to the problems of the United States. By visiting their Web site, you can access discussion groups, links, and publications, as well as information on their chapters and task forces: www.cofc.org

11. The Global Network Against Weapons and Nuclear Power in Space is an organization dealing with space ethics and moral issues, in particular, space law. This well-organized Web site is packed with information and articles, including reports, European news, and special sections dedicated to the moon and Mars. There is even a picture gallery! For anyone interested in joining, contact and membership information is also posted: www. space4 peace.org

12. The Peace and Freedom Party was founded in 1967. It works on a national and state level, with the help of similar groups, to build a mass-based socialist party. To learn more about the party, visit their Web site, which contains information pertaining to the party's history, leaflets, and contact information. To get a better grasp of the party's views, a list of long- and short-term goals is posted: www.peaceandfreedom.org

13. The Alliance for Sustainable Jobs and the Environment was formed by environmental and labor leaders in order to come together to make corporations accountable for their behavior. Their Web site contains the group's latest news, a mailing list, and suggestions on how to "take action." Information on their magazine is also included: www.asje.org

14. The Greens/GPUSA carries forth a vision based on "grassroots political and economic democracy, nonviolence, social justice, and ecological sustainability." It is the original Green Party organization in the United States Most Greens work in smaller groups called locals. By visiting the Greens/GPUSA Web site you can access information to contact these locals and can find various articles, publications, links, and their political platform. The Web site is large and filled with valuable information: www.greenparty.org

15. The Independent Progressive Politics Network calls upon representatives of grassroots organizations to band together to create a united voice strong enough to resist our current two-party political system. They do this by organizing summits, publishing a newsletter, working with like-minded organizations, and supporting potential candidates. By visiting their Web site, you can read about their past summits and plans for the future. The site also contains useful resources and contact information: www.ippn.org

16. The National Lawyers Guild is a human rights organization dedicated to fighting for social and economic justice both in the United States and internationally. It was founded in 1937 and has over 6,000 members, many of whom are lawyers, law students, legal workers, and jailhouse lawyers. At their Web site you can read up on the organization's history and current publications. Contact addresses and membership information are also posted: www.nlg.org

17. Quantum Leap 2000 is a small group of potential catalysts aiming to change our society. They believe it is time for humans to make a leap, emotionally and spiritually. If you are ready to make this leap, or are at least a little interested, don't hesitate to visit their Web site, to become part of the "creative minority": www.quantumleap2000.org

18. Project South is a community-based group that develops and conducts popular political and economic education and action research for organizing and liberation. They organize and develop popular educators from grassroots and scholarly backgrounds, bringing them together on the basis of equality to join in the process of understanding and transforming our soci-

ety. They aim to know what is possible and how to achieve it. Their Web site contains projects, research groups, publications, and contact information: www.projectsouth.org

19. Working Families e-Activist Network (peoplepower@aflcio.org) is *the* most vital list for unionists—bar none! To join the e-Activist Network, visit their Web site: www.aflcio.org

20. Pay special attention to *Workplace Issues Today*. Its Web site stands out above and beyond all others in offering the Web addresses of well chosen sources—daily!—to those of us trying to stay abreast of fast-breaking developments in industrial and labor relations and related matters: www.ilr.cornell.edu/library/wit/

Annotated Bibliography

> *Sit down and read. Educate yourself for the coming conflicts.*
> —Mother Jones, labor leader

With 60,000 books published annually in America in English alone, it is very hard to know where to devote scarce reading time. Hopefully, some readers will soon make use of my Web site (www.cyberunions.net) to help me highlight books there of special value to those of us eager to promote field trials of the CyberUnion model.

In the meantime, I recommend that you familiarize yourself with the following small sample of the many relevant books I have read as part of my work preparing this handbook and try to and stay abreast of fast-breaking developments where labor's use of computer power is concerned:

Baird, Robert M., et al., eds. *Cyberethics: Social and Moral Issues in the Computer Age.* Amherst, NY: Prometheus Books, 2000. An anthology of thoughtful answers to questions concerning anonymity, personal identity, privacy, ownership of intellectual property, and the impact of computers on democracy and community—all complex moral issues union activists are well advised to explore.

Burton, Terence T., and John W. Moran. *The Future-Focused Organization: Complete Organizational Alignment for Breakthrough Results.* Englewood Cliffs, NJ: Prentice Hall, 1995. A how-to guide to measuring the current state of an organization's culture, and how to move it along to a more desired state.

Clark, Paul F. *Building More Effective Unions.* Ithaca, NY: ILR Press, 2000. Unlike most such books, it actually notices labor's use of computers; like most such books, it barely does so (three pages out of 192).

Katz, Jon. *Geeks: How Two Lost Boys Rode the Internet Out of Idaho.* New York: Villard, 2000. An engaging and illuminating exploration of the world of a new cultural elite, a "techno-centered community of social discontents," to whom organized labor may increasingly look for advice and support.

Kush, Christopher. *Cybercitizen: How to Use Your Computer to Fight for ALL the Issues You Care About.* New York: St. Martin's Griffin, 2000. A practical, nonpartisan guide to the best sites for activists, including strategy tips from professionals in getting things (political) done.

Lee, Eric. *The Labour Movement and the Internet: The New Internationalism.* London: Pluto Press, 1996. The bible in this area, the first and still greatest book of its kind—an indispensable guide to the past, present, and future of labor in the information age. If you read only one such book, this should be it!

Mishel, Lawrence, Jared Bernstein, and John Schmitt, eds. *The State of Working America, 2000–2001.* Ithaca, NY: ILR Press, 2001. Prepared biennially since 1988 by the Economic Policy Institute, the volume sums up the problems and challenges facing American workers. Drawing on both original research and published sources, the authors present a wide variety of data on family incomes, taxes, wages, unemployment, wealth, and poverty—data that enable them to closely examine the impact of the economy on the living standards of the American people.

Osborne, David, and Peter Plastrik. *The Reinventor's Fieldbook: Tools for Transforming Your Government.* San Francisco: Jossey-Bass, 2000. Features real-world examples of reinvention projects, along with advice and critical insights that union activists will find of great value.

Pesce, Mark. *The Playful World: How Technology Is Transforming Our Imagination.* New York: Ballantine, 2000. A unique exploration of "the future of magic, the confusion of human intelligence with distributed intelligence, of natural forms with engineered structures, of my knowledge with yours." While seemingly way-out and esoteric, this sort of "stuff" belongs in the mental kit bag of every union activist intent on staying up with information age "chaos."

Schuler, Douglas. *New Community Networks: Wired for Change.* Reading, MA: Addison-Wesley, 1996. Offers practical how-to advice for lay people trying to develop and sustain their own community networks—material easily adapted by union activists, who might also want to pitch in and help community activists at this task.

Siegel, David. *Futurize Your Enterprise: Business Strategy in the Age of the E-Customer.* New York: John Wiley, 1999. A comprehensive strategy, predicated on unorthodox concepts for total overhaul of an organization: "90% of the problems companies have online are caused by management, not technology."

Smith, Marc A., and Peter Kollock, eds. *Communities in Cyberspace.* London: Routledge, 1999. An exceedingly academic collection of essays exploring emerging social ecologies of virtual spaces—a vital frontier for

union activists of the digerati persuasion to explore, especially as organized labor is likely soon to spend more and more time and effort there.

Wacker, Watts, and Jim Taylor. *The Visionary's Handbook: Nine Paradoxes
That Will Shape the Future of Your Business.* New York: HarperBusiness,
2000. Very helpful in defining a desirable future as a self-created serial
experience (explains how and why we should become part of our own
story, much as union activists urge).

Wayner, Peter. *Free for All: How Linux and the Free Software Movement
Undercut the High-Tech Titans.* New York: HarperBusiness, 2000. An
exceedingly well-written and revealing account of the fight to change the
ethos of computer software use, rife with implications for labor's ideological and business alignment with one side or the other.

Finally, and in a revealing way, I would cite not another book, but some
Web sites:

- The Resource Center for Cyberculture Studies (http://faculty.
washington.edu/dsilver). It maintains an annotated bibliography of
Internet studies. Particularly helpful is a section called "Book of the
Month," which offers reviews and essays by Internet scholars evaluating the recent literature in their fields.

- The Association of Internet Researchers (www.aoir.org) also has a Web
site that provides links to numerous online journals devoted to Internet
scholarship.

- Invaluable as well is a Cornell University seb site that offers a free subscription to *Workplace Issues Today* (www.ilr.cornell.edu/library/wit/),
and one that archives several listserves for social justice activists
(www.topica.com/lists).

Index

Notes on the Editor and Contributors

> *"Alone we're nothing, together we're everything—*
> *it's the whole philosophy of labor."*
> —Leon Davis, union leader

Paul Andrews, a veteran technology writer, is the author of two books, including the national bestseller *Gates*, a biography of the Microsoft cofounder, and *How the Web Was Won*, about Microsoft's Internet transformation. For twelve years he was lead technology writer for the *Seattle Times* and wrote an award-winning weekly personal-computing column, *User Friendly*. In 1994 Andrews helped create the *Times*'s Sunday Personal Technology section, which was a runner-up in the distinguished Penney-Missouri Awards in 1995. He also has written for *US News & World Report*, the *New York Times*, *Fortune*, *Barron's*, and a variety of other publications. He can be reached at paul@paulandrews.com.

Miguel Abrantes Antunes is a recent graduate from Drexel University who majored in sociology. He participates in social action involving labor activists and is currently involved with the Fair Trade Coffee movement: "One of this movement's many goals is to allow farmers in developing nations to form unions so as to increase their rights as laborers and their standard of living."

Nancy Bupp (M.A., Industrial Relations, West Virginia Graduate College, 1997) has been a member of the International Association of Machinists and Aerospace Workers for twenty-four years. She teaches at the William W. Winpisinger Education and Technology Center (the Machinists Union labor education facility) in Hollywood, Maryland. Previously Bupp worked in a chemical plant in West Virginia for seventeen years. She can be reached at nbupp@iamaw.org.

Karen Chamberlain is a recent Drexel Corporate Communications graduate and holds an Associate's Degree in Journalism and Psychology. Before returning to college, Karen was in radio and television broadcasting for ten years.

Will Collette conducts strategic research for the Building and Construction Trades Department, AFL-CIO, in Washington, DC. He has run or worked on more than a dozen corporate campaigns and teaches construction union organizers corporate campaign and research techniques as part of the Building Trades's Advanced Organizer Training and at the AFL-CIO George Meany Center. He can be reached at collette@bctd.org.

Ed Czarnecki (Ph.D., Georgetown University) formerly published *Czarnecki's Labor Education Newsletter* (users.erols.com/czarlab/) and now publishes the Web Newsletter for the United Association for Labor Education (UALE). Previously he worked as assistant director for Research and Education, International Brotherhood of Electrical Workers (IBEW) (1958–1966), Associate Professor and Director of Labor Center, University of Iowa (1966–1977), and Assistant Education Director, AFL-CIO (1977–1993). He can be reached at czarlab@erols.com.

Joseph N. Dassaro (B.A., Labor Studies, National Labor College, 2001) is a senior U.S. border patrol agent assigned to the San Diego, California, area. He became active with the union in 1995 and held a variety of positions, including union representative, chief union representative, and vice president. Currently, he is the president of Local 1613 of the National Border Patrol Council located in San Diego. Dassaro also serves in the capacity of executive assistant to the council president. He can be reached at jndassaro@home.com or at www.borderpatrol11613.org.

Stuart W. Davidson (J.D., Harvard Law School) is a partner in the law firm of Willig, Williams, and Davidson in Philadelphia. He has been engaged in the representation of labor unions and employee benefit funds for his entire career and has served as legal counsel and, in some instances, chief negotiator for many diverse labor organizations. He can be reached at sdavidson@wwdlaw.com.

Stephen Downes (M.A., Philosophy, University of Calgary) is an information architect employed by the Faculty of Extension at the University of

Alberta in Edmonton. Previously Downes was employed as a distance education and new instructional media design specialist with Assiniboine Community College in Brandon, Manitoba. He has also taught philosophy for Athabasca University. He can be reached at stephen@downes.ca or www.downes.ca.

Zack Exley was a union organizer during the 1960s with SEIU, UAW, 1199, and the AFL-CIO. His book, *Trust the People*, based on that experience, is forthcoming from Softskull Press. His online projects, including GWBush.com and CNNdn.com, have drawn international press coverage as well as legal action from George W. Bush, AOL-Time-Warner, the Federal Elections Commission, and even the Log Cabin Republicans. He can be reached at zack@gwbush.com.

Eric M. Fink (New York University School of Law, M.Sc., London School of Economics) is an associate at Willig, Williams and Davidson, where he represents labor unions and workers in collective bargaining, arbitration, and litigation. He can be reached at efink@wwdlaw.com.

Mark Friedman is the former state coordinator of Speaking for Ourselves, a consumer-run disability rights organization in Pennsylvania. During his tenure of nineteen years he vigorously applied cutting-edge nonprofit practices, an effort that culminated in the receipt of the prestigious Williams Award for Nonprofit Management Excellence of the Philadelphia Foundation. He is currently a Ph.D. candidate at the Union Institute where he is pursuing research on the use of technology to further social justice causes. He can be reached at friedman@voicenet.com.

Karin Hart is the northern California apprenticeship coordinator for the Communications Workers of America (CWA) and teaches labor studies and telecommunications at local community colleges. In the past she was a principal officer of CWA Local 9415. She can be reached at karin@union.org.za.

Edward Hertenstein is assistant professor of Labor and Industrial Relations assigned to the Labor Education Program at the University of Illinois at Urbana-Champaign. Prior to entering labor education, he spent twenty years as a newspaper press operator and served as a local union officer for seventeen years with the Graphic Communications International Union and its predecessor union. Since 1994 he has taught unionists about the Internet in the Indiana University Division of Labor Studies and the University of Illinois Labor Education Program. He can be reached at hertenst@uiuc.edu.

Rick Inclima is the director of Education and Safety for the Brotherhood of Maintenance of Way Employes (BMWE), currently headquartered in Southfield, Michigan. He began his railroad career in 1975 as a track laborer for the Penn Central Railroad in New Haven, Connecticut. Subsequently, he transferred to Amtrak, where he worked as a welder and welder foreman until taking a leave of absence in 1991 to accept an appointment with the BMWE.

Donna Jablonski (B.A., Labor Studies, National Labor College, 2001) is deputy director of Public Affairs for Publications, Web, and Broadcast at the AFL-CIO. She began her career as a newspaper reporter in southwest Florida and subsequently served as Publications Director at the nonprofit Children's Defense Fund for twelve years.

Larry Johnson has been recording secretary for Local 238 of the Glass, Molder, Pottery International Union (GMP) in Kokomo, Indiana, since 1980. He is in charge of the Local 238 Web site, as well as the GMP Organizing Web site. He also works on organizing campaigns for the GMP International Union and is on the Indiana University Labor Advisory Board for North Central Indiana. Johnson has received organizing training at the George Meany Center and is working on a degree in labor studies at Indiana University. He can be reached at joingmp@workingfamilies.com, www.gmp238.org, and www.gmporganizing.org.

Deborah Joseph (Schmidle) (M.L.S., Syracuse University) was the outreach services librarian at the Martin P. Catherwood Library at Cornell University from 1997 to 2001. She designed and taught Internet research training workshops for labor union members in various cities throughout the northeast. In 1998 she presented a paper on Internet training for unionists at the International Labour Organization in Geneva, Switzerland. Joseph is cochair of the American Library Association's joint ALA/AFL-CIO committee on Library Service to Labor Groups, coeditor of a special issue of *Library Trends* that deals with the partnership between labor and libraries, and is a member of the Capitol District Labor/Religion Coalition. She can be reached at schmidle@albany.edu.

Thomas James Katona is the organizer and webmaster for the Office and Professional Employees International Union (OPEIU) Local 512 in Michigan. He holds a Master's Degree in Labor Relations and is a graduate of the AFL-CIO Organizing Institute. Katona is also a member of the National Writers Union (NWU, United Auto Workers) Local 1981, and the International Workers of the World (IWW). He can be reached at tkatona@ portup.com, and his local's zine is at http://www.geocities.com/local512.

John Klusinske (B.A., Antioch University/George Meany Center) is a contract administrator for the Clerical-Technical Union of Michigan State University and for CTU-2 at the Michigan State University, Detroit College of Law. He is completing a Masters Degree in Labor and Industrial Relations at Michigan State University. He can be reached at klusins1@msu.edu.

Robert Kolb (B.S., Criminal Justice and Sociology, University of Illinois at Chicago) has been a union sheet-metal worker since 1984. Previously, he was a member of the United Food and Commercial Workers International Union (UFCW). Robert administers all of his own Internet exposure and builds his own computers and servers. He believes technology will be necessary to fend off anti-union forces and maintain labor's growth.

Charles H. Laskonis is a rank-and-file member in good standing of the International Brotherhood of Electrical Workers (IBEW), Local 364, where he is also recording secretary, a member of the Web site committee, and of the press committee. He is also a delegate from his local to his Central Labor Council. In addition, Laskonis is a member of Chicago's independent rank-and-file labor public access cable television production group, Labor Beat. He can be reached at laz346@ibew.workingfamilies.com.

Laureen Lazarovici is an assistant editor of *America@Work*, the AFL-CIO's monthly magazine. She has been an American Political Science Association fellow in the offices of Senator Paul Wellstone (D-Minnesota) and Representative Jane Harman (D-California). Before coming to Washington, DC, she wrote for the *Los Angeles Weekly*.

Eric Lee, the founder of LabourStart, is the information and communications technology (ICT) Coordinator for Labour and Society International, based in London. He is the author of *The Labour Movement and the Internet: The New Internationalism* (Pluto Press, 1996). He can be reached at ericlee@labourstart.org.

Steven J. Lelinski (National Labor College, 2001) is a police officer in a metropolitan area in the Midwest. His union is one of the few police unions in that region that is affiliated with the AFL-CIO. After several years as a steward at his work location, he was elected as chief steward. In 1999 he was elected to the union's executive board, where he holds a position of trustee.

He can be reached at lelinski@prodigy.net or at his Web site, www.lelin ski.com.

Peter Lewis is a journalist who worked in mainstream media and politics before joining the labor movement. He edits Workers Online (www.workers.labor.net.au), Australia's most popular political Web site, and is a vigorous advocate for trade unions to place more resources into Web development.

Bob Marino began his career with the New York State AFL-CIO in 1993 as the workplace education coordinator and is presently the technology director. He initiated his union career in 1981 as an inside wireman apprentice working for International Brotherhood of Electrical Workers (IBEW) Local 166, Schenectady, New York (which recently merged to become 236). He can be reached at bmarino@mysaflcio.org.

Linda Mathews is in her third term as president of the International Brotherhood of Electrical Workers (IBEW) Local 1613 and has more than eight years of experience in operating labor Web sites. She is the Web wizard of four sites—cybersolidarity.com, ibew1613.org, ibew11th.org, and www.home.earthlink.net/~solidarity. She also maintains the Webmasters Community for Labor and Human Rights Activists (see www.cybersolidarity. com). Mathews can be reached at linda@cybersolidarity.com.

Brian Mitchell (B.S., Labor Studies, Antioch University/George Meany Center, 1995) has been an International Rep for the United Auto Workers (UAW) for sixteen years. He teaches labor history in the plumbers apprentice programs and collective bargaining and labor history for the UAW at regional summer schools. He is a Journeyman Millwright and has been employed at General Motors since 1975. He can be reached at brimitch@motion.net.

Cheryl Mitchell was General Motors foundry system's first female skilled tradesman (person) and carries a Journeyman's (person's) card. Through the GM-UAW tuition assistance program she completed a Ph.D. (ABD in Technology Education) from the University of Illinois. She can be reached at carfardust@aol.com.

Peggy Myrie has worked for General Motors for twenty-two years and has been a Journeyman Tinsmith member of UAW Local 652, Lansing, Michigan, for seventeen years. With the changing mode of operation and subcontracting within General Motors, her job may be eliminated. An Educational

Opportunity Program (EOP) enabled Myrie to complete three semesters at George Meany Labor College and obtain a degree in Labor Studies. She can be reached at pegbob@la4u.net.

Kat Nagel is a freelance technical writer and owner of MasterWork Consulting Services and can be contacted at members.aol.com/mwrk in Rochester, New York.

Matt Noyes is the education coordinator for the Association for Union Democracy, an independent, prolabor organization that champions the cause of union democracy and provides education, legal counseling, and organizing advice to union members in North America. Matt is also a lecturer at the Queens College Worker Education Extension Center, and the webmaster for www.uniondemocracy.org. He is a member of the NWU, UAW Local 1981. He can be reached at and@igc.org.

Mindy Pines is a technology resource teacher at Lakeshore Alternative Elementary School, San Francisco Unified School District, and communications representative and webmaster for United Educators of San Francisco. The site at www.uesf.org is the winner of the Best Web site Communications Award for 2000 by the California Federation of Teachers, AFT, AFL-CIO. She can be reached at slinkster1@earthlink.net.

William Puette is the director of the Center for Labor Education and Research (CLEAR) at the University of Hawaii, West Oahu, and serves on the board of directors of the faculty union. The chair of the union's grievance committee, he was the chair of the ad hoc 2001 strike preparation committee and strike coordinator, responsible for erecting and maintaining over fifty picket lines. He is a self-taught webmaster and has set up and maintained the union's "Strike Pages." He can be reached though the CLEAR Home Page (www.uhwo.hawaii.edu/clear) or puette@hawaii.edu.

Bill Ringle is "America's Internet Business Coach." He works with business leaders who want to make better decisions about using technology. Ringle is a popular conference presenter, panelist, and facilitator. He personalizes the content for each event audience and knows how to make complex technical ideas understandable, meaningful, and engaging. Visit www.BillRingle.com for access to free articles, coaching advice, and useful tips.

T Santora (B.A., Union Leadership and Administration, National Labor College) is President Emeritus of Pride At Work, the lesbian, gay, bisexual, and transgender constituency group of the AFL-CIO. Santora has been an activist member of the Communcations Workers of America for twenty-five years. He is currently working as a lobbyist for the union in Washington, DC, and can be reached at tsantora@cwa-union.org.

Matt Seng is the principal for Seng Design, located on the Web at www.sengdesign.com. Clients include *Health Magazine*; Council Oak Press; Department of Music, University of California, Davis; and the San Francisco-based theater company Crowded Fire. Along with Web design, Seng Design is also a print design firm, specializing in posters, marketing campaigns, book jackets, and logos. He can be reached at matt@sengdesign.com.

Arthur B. Shostak is professor of Sociology at Drexel University in Philadelphia, Pennsylvania, and adjunct sociologist on the faculty of the National Labor Relations College at the AFL-CIO George Meany Center for Labor Studies in Silver Springs, Maryland. He can be reached at shostaka@drexel.edu, and at cyberunions.net.

G. Peter Shostak (M.A., Hospital Administration, University of Minnesota Graduate School of Public Health, 1969) is a retired hospital administrator and part-time public school teacher. He spent thirty years in Health Services Administration. He is a Life Diplomat in the American College of Health Care Executives and has served as a clinical professor of Public Administration at the University of Southern California and a clinical preceptor for the University of Minnesota, Northwestern University, and the University of Ohio. He can be reached at gps818@msn.com.

Lawrence R. Smoot, Jr. (B.A., Labor Studies, National Labor College) currently works for Communication Workers of America (CWA), is a member of the Office and Professional Employees International Union (OPEIU) Local 2, and is now copresident of the Baltimore-Washington Pride At Work Chapter. He has been an active union member for the past eight years. He can be reached at lsmoot@cwa-union.org.

Sam Stark is a trustee with the southeast Michigan unit of the NWU, UAW Local 1981. He is also the founder and coordinator of SEM-NWU's annual Worker Writer Festival. Most recently he chaired a virtual committee of busy activists who drafted a set of bylaws and a mission statement over the Internet for the newly formed Jobs with Justice chapter in Detroit. He can be reached at sdsklh@yahoo.com.

Danielle D. van Jaarsveld is a Ph.D. student in the Collective Bargaining Department at the New York State School of Industrial and Labor Relations at Cornell University. She received an M.S. from Cornell University where she wrote about the WashTech/CWA campaign at Microsoft for her master's thesis. She can be reached at ddv1@cornell.edu.

Brandon Weber has been a computer consultant and trainer with local and international unions, in addition to labor press organizations in the Midwest, for over ten years. He is coeditor of UAW Local 889's *White Collar News*. He works for Union Built PC. He can be reached at brandinius@aol.com and brandon@unionbuiltpc.com.

Nicole L. Whittaker is a student at Drexel University who has studied sociology with Professor Arthur B. Shostak and has assisted on Shostak's research projects.

Mike Wisniewski is a twenty-nine–year member, past vice president, and currently the secretary of Local 590 AFSCME (American Federation of State, County and Municipal Employees), affiliated with District Council 47 AFSCME in Philadelphia. In addition to being the webmaster of www.dc47afscme, he is also webmaster for www.comeylaborstudies.org, the site of the Comey Institute for Industrial Relations at St. Joseph's University in Philadelphia.

Steve Zeltzer is a member of the International Union of Operating Engineers Local 39 in San Francisco. He also founded the Labor Video Project in 1983, which has produced the longest running labor cable show in the United States, as well as labor video documentaries. It is programmed in San Francisco, Sacramento, Philadelphia, and Kalamazoo. He helped found LaborNet (www.labornet.org), the Union Producers and Programmers Network in 1989, and LaborTech in 1990. In addition to his labor communication work he helped establish LaborFest (www.laborfest.net), an annual labor cultural arts and international working-class film and video festival in San Francisco. It is held every July to commemorate the 1934 San Francisco General Strike. He can be reached at lvpsf@labornet.org.

Gunnar Zetterström has worked thirty-eight years with computers for many different companies. His educational background includes university studies in mathematics, numerical analysis, and operations analysis. Today, he is a Systems Architect and Project Leader at Förenings Sparbanken AB, one of Sweden's major bank concerns. He is a member of the board of the FSU-S, the Financial Sector Union of Sweden (some 34,000 members), chairman of the board for the FSU Union Local Branch for the

IT-department at Förenings Sparbanken (some 500 members), and FSU-S board representative on the board of "Datafolket," a special branch of the union focusing on the IT professionals (some 2,500 members). He can be reached at gunnar.zetterstrom@gro.pp.se.

Anthony W. Zumpetta is a professor in the Department of Anthropology and Sociology at West Chester University, West Chester, Pennsylvania. Prior to joining the academic community in 1988, he worked in Pennsylvania's Department of Corrections in an upper-level management position at one of the state's major institutions. He specializes in teaching courses related to criminology, deviance, and delinquency. Dr. Zumpetta has been a member of APSCUF (Association of Pennsylvania State College and University Faculties) since joining the university and has worked on various union committees. He can be reached at azumpetta@wcupa.edu.

Books by the Editor

CyberUnion: Empowering Labor Through Computer Technology. Armonk, NY: M.E. Sharpe, 1999. A thoroughgoing discussion of the first book to discuss the impact of computerization on the labor movement here and abroad. Offers a typology of three current union models (Cyber Naught, Cyber Drift, Cyber Gain) and outlines a distant and vastly improved model (CyberUnion) for labor's consideration.

Impacts of Changing Employment: If the Good Jobs Go Away. Thousand Oaks, CA: Sage, 1996. An edited collection of fourteen original essays exploring the potential of massive job loss and alternative public policy options before and after such an event.

Private Sociology: Unsparing Reflections, Uncommon Gains. Dix Hills, NY: General Hall, 1996. An edited collection of twenty-three first-person studies of "that which we hesitate to tell," the first such book of its kind in American sociology. Essays cover such topics as childhood sexual victimization, the loss by murder of one's brother, the experience of having one's research stolen, the experience of dying in the aftermath of a medical mistake, the challenge of growing up a minority member, and so on.

For Labor's Sake: Gains and Pains as Told by 28 Creative Inside Reformers. Lanham, MD: University Press of America, 1995. An edited collection of twenty-eight first-person accounts by grassroots activists of ongoing efforts to renew the labor movement.

Guidelines from Gomberg: No-Nonsense Advice for Labor-Management Relations. Philadelphia: Chapel, 1992. An edited collection of six timely essays by an internationally renowned professor of industrial and labor relations, William Gomberg, complete with commentary.

Robust Unionism: Innovations in the Labor Movement. Ithaca, NY: ILR Press, 1991. A scholarly monograph that explores and assesses the state of risk taking and planned change in and by organized labor in this country.

The Air Controllers' Controversy. Coauthored with Dave Skocik. New York: Human Sciences, 1986. An analysis of the 1981 strike of Professional Air Traffic Controllers Organization (PATCO), the firing of 11,400 strikers, and the lessons in this historic event for modern labor-management relations.

Men and Abortion: Lessons, Losses, and Love. Coauthored with Gary McLouth and Lynn Seng. New York: Praeger, 1984. A scholarly exploration of the meaning of the abortion experience for 1,000 men located in the waiting rooms of thirty clinics in eighteen states.

Blue-Collar Stress. Reading, MA: Addison-Wesley, 1980. A scholarly monograph that focuses on work problems and reform possibilities where male manual workers are concerned.

Our Sociological Eye: Personal Essays on Society and Culture. Sherman Oaks, CA: Alfred, 1977. An introductory text and reader. Combines basic concept discussions with illustrative first-person reflexive essays from twenty-four contributors.

Modern Social Reforms: Solving Today's Social Problems. New York: Macmillan, 1974. A scholarly monograph that explores overseas and frontier remedies for long-standing social dilemmas such as alleviating poverty, delivering optimum healthcare, improving educational institutions, and many others.

Privilege in America: An End to Inequality? Coprepared with Jon and Sally Bould Von Til. Englewood Cliffs, NJ: Prentice-Hall, Spectrum Series, 1974. A scholarly monograph on various aspects of social stratification and social egalitarianism. Includes three chapters by Arthur Shostak on the New Populism, the New Socialism, and the Ethnic Revival.

Putting Sociology to Work: Case Studies in the Application of Sociology to Modern Social Problems. New York: David McKay, 1974. An edited collection of twenty-six original essays exploring off-campus uses of sociology in contemporary social reform projects.

Sociology and Student Life. New York: David McKay, 1972. An edited collection of thirty-two reprinted essays that help illuminate both modern campus issues and the basic concepts of academic sociology.

Blue-Collar Life. New York: Random House, 1968. A scholarly monograph analyzing hundreds of scattered research reports and proposing original reforms for pressing blue-collar problems.

Sociology in Action: Case Studies in Social Problems and Directed Social Change. Homewood, IL: Dorsey Press, 1966. An edited collection of thirty-eight first-person accounts of applied projects (twenty-three original essays).

New Perspectives on Poverty. Coedited with William Gomberg. Englewood Cliffs, NJ: Prentice Hall, 1965. An edited collection of twenty essays (six originals) exploring promising reforms for key aspects of poverty.

Blue-Collar World: Studies of the American Worker. Coedited with William Gomberg. Englewood Cliffs, NJ: Prentice Hall, 1964. An edited collection of sixty-two essays (fifty-five originals) about blue-collar realities.

America's Forgotten Labor Organization: The Role of the Single-Firm Independent Union in American Industry. Princeton, NJ: Industrial Relations Section, 1962. A scholarly monograph drawing on Shostak's 1961 Ph.D. thesis research into unaffiliated so-called "company unions."

Milton Keynes UK
Ingram Content Group UK Ltd.
UKHW031141141024
449569UK00024B/1168